Language, Religion, and Ethnic Assertiveness

Language, Religion, and Ethnic Assertiveness

The Growth of Sinhalese Nationalism in Sri Lanka

K. N. O. Dharmadasa

Ann Arbor

THE UNIVERSITY OF MICHIGAN PRESS

Published in the United States of America by
The University of Michigan Press
Manufactured in the United States of America

1995 1994 1993 1992 4 3 2 1

Library of Congress Cataloging-in-Publication Data

Dharmadāsa, Kē. En. Ō., 1938–
Language, religion, and ethnic assertiveness : the growth of Sinhalese nationalism in Sri Lanka / by K.N.O. Dharmadasa.
p. cm.
Abstract of thesis (Ph.D.)—Monash University, 1979
Includes bibliographical references and index.
ISBN 0-472-10288-5 (alk. paper)
1. Sri Lanka—Politics and government. 2. Sinhalese (Sri Lankan people)—Ethnic identity. 3. Sinhalese language—Political aspects. 4. Buddhism and politics—Sri Lanka. 5. Ethnic relations—Sri Lanka. I. Title.
DS489.7.D52 1993
305.8′0095493—dc20 92-31734
CIP

Acknowledgments

This is a substantially revised version of a dissertation entitled "The Rise of Sinhalese Language Nationalism: A Study in the Sociology of Language" for which I was awarded a Ph.D. by Monash University in 1979. I was supported by a scholarship from Monash University during my stay there from 1977 to 1979. My supervisor was the late Professor John T. Platt, whose guidance was the mainstay in the formative stages of this work. My examiners were Professor Joshua A. Fishman and the late Professor M. W. Sugathapala de Silva, whose reports, according to the practice at Monash, were made available to me. I am most grateful to them for their very useful comments. Subsequently, the dissertation in its original form was read by the late Professor W. J. F. La Brooy, Dr. Kitsiri Malalgoda, and Dr. Michael Roberts, who made many valuable suggestions for revision. Professor Sirima Kiribamune and Professor John Holt read some parts of it, and their criticisms were most useful.

I very much appreciate the assistance I received from the librarians and staffs of the libraries of the University of Peradeniya, Monash University, the Colombo Museum, and the Sri Lanka Department of National Archives. My special thanks are due to the late Ven. Kalukondayawe Prajnasekera Maha Nayaka Thero, who placed at my disposal his magnificent collection of Sinhala journals (which was later donated to the Colombo Museum Library).

The typescript of the final draft was prepared at the International Centre for Ethnic Studies (ICES), Kandy, Sri Lanka, with which I have had the pleasure of being associated as a consultant on a number of projects. I would like to place on record my special gratitude to Professor K. M. de Silva, executive director of the ICES, who very kindly placed its resources at my disposal for the revision of the original version into this final form. The text also benefited greatly from the care and many long hours he devoted to reading and criticizing it. Neither he nor the others who read the text and made comments are responsible for any errors that may remain.

Bernadine Perera and Sepali Liyanamanna converted the original typescript, which bore all the untidy marks of correction, into a clear and readable text for submission to the publisher. I am very grateful to them for the skill they displayed in this work and for their exemplary patience. My wife and my two daughters provided for me the comfort of a home where I could peacefully engage in academic activity, and I am dedicating this work to them.

Dedicated with fondness

to

Sumangalika,

Dinithi Sevanji, and Lahiru Chaturika

Contents

Transliteration and Pronunciation of Sinhala Words

In transliterating Sinhala (and Pali and Sanskrit) words I have followed the standard practice in transliterating Indian languages. The vowel sounds *a, ä, e, i, o,* and *u* are those found in the pronunciation of b*u*n, b*a*t, B*e*n, b*i*t, s*o*d, and b*u*ll, respectively. A short dash over a vowel denotes a long vowel as in *ā* (sounding like the long vowel in English b*a*rd). The Sanskrit vowel *r* is pronounced as in American cu*r*.

Of the consonants *c* is pronounced as the first sound in English *ch*urch and *ñ* as in Spanish *mañana* (i.e., *ny*). The letters *t* and *d* are pronounced dentally, partway to English sounds spelled with *th* (as in *th*in and *th*en), and *ṭ* and *ḍ* are retroflex. There is a historical distinction between "dental" *n* and *l* as against retroflex *ṇ* and *ḷ*, which is not reflected in pronunciation. The *ś* is considered a "palatal" letter and *ṣ* a "cerebral" letter. But both are pronounced palatally, similar to the sibilant in English "*sh*ow." The letter *h* after a consonant denotes aspiration. The letter *n̆* or *m̆* before a consonant (found only in four instances: *n̆g, n̆d, n̆ḍ,* or *m̆b*) denotes the nasalization of that consonant. The *ṃ* denotes a pure nasal, the letter *v* denotes a sound in between English *v* and *w,* and in final position it is pronounced as a semivowel.

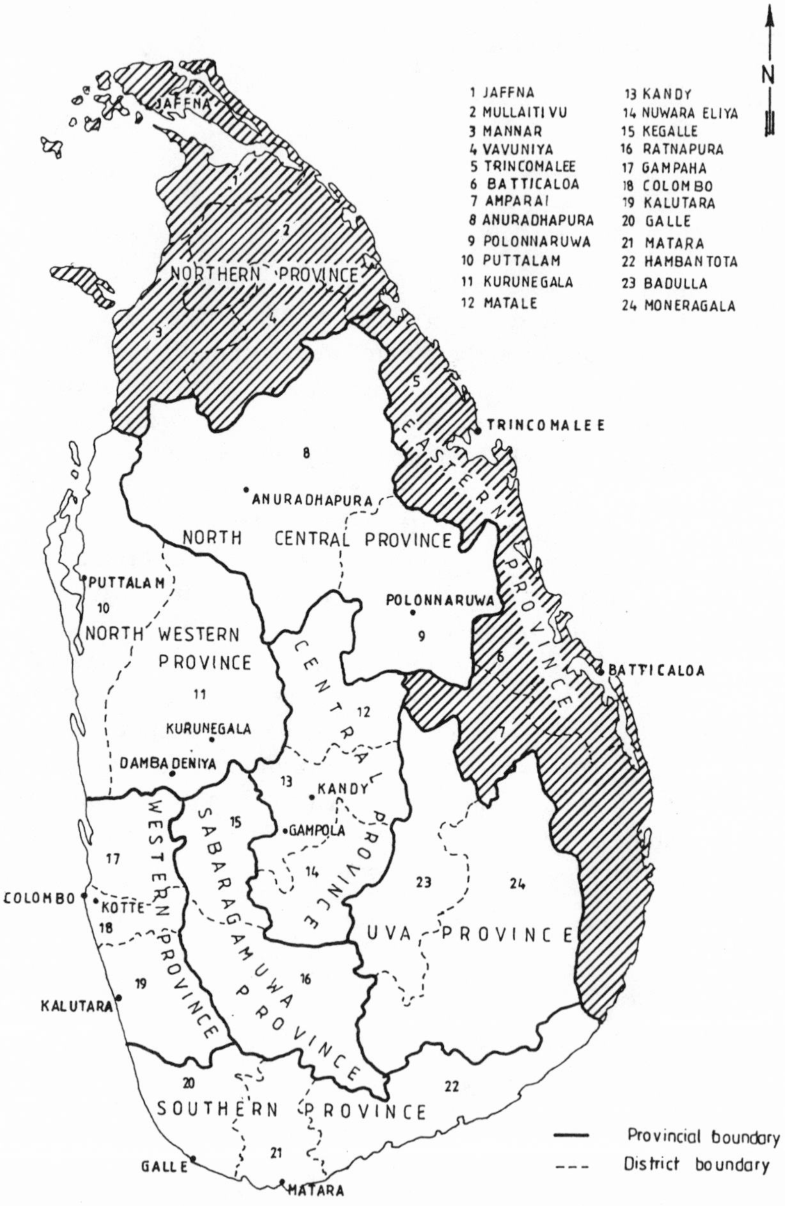

Provinces and Districts of Sri Lanka, 1981. The shaded area indicates the envisaged Tamil state (Eelam).

Introduction

The island republic of Sri Lanka has been, for the last three decades, the scene of an escalating ethnic conflict between the majority Sinhalese (74 percent of the population) and the Sri Lankan Tamils, who form the largest minority (12.6 percent).[1] The present conflict originated in the mid-1950s over the selection of a national official language after the country became independent of the British empire. As befitting the hopes and aspirations of the newly independent state, English, the language of the colonial administration (1815–1948), had to be replaced by an indigenous language or languages. In this connection there were two opposing propositions: "Sinhala Only" and "Parity of Status for Sinhala and Tamil."

The question of the official language was a key issue in the general election of 1956. The Sinhala only proposition was to win the day, and legislation was soon enacted making the Sinhala language "the one official language" of Sri Lanka. This period saw the high-water mark of popular feeling toward the Sinhala language and may be typified as the triumph of Sinhala language nationalism. As a political phenomenon, language nationalism was a novelty in mid-twentieth-century Sri Lanka.[2] But situations in which language becomes a symbol of group cohesiveness and self-assertion are not uncommon in world history.[3] In Sri Lanka "all the major political parties were baffled" by its dramatic eruption in the mid-1950s.[4] Perhaps the occasion and the manner in which it emerged were unexpected. A consideration of the developments during the previous decades indicates a gradual buildup of conditions so that by the 1950s there was a readiness to respond to political mobilization in the cause of language.

Language is generally not considered "a conscious factor in the

---

1. In addition there are 5.5 percent Indian Tamils, 7 percent Moors, 0.3 percent Malays, 0.3 percent Eurasians and Burghers, and 0.2 percent "others," among whom are, most notably, the aborigines of the island called the Veddas (Department of Census and Statistics, Sri Lanka, *Report of the Census of 1981*).

2. K. M. de Silva 1986:162.

3. See Fishman 1972a.

4. K. M. de Silva 1986:162.

primordial world."[5] But advanced ideological extensions of primordial ethnicity are characterized by "heightened and integrated behaviour towards language."[6] Thus, it is of interest to consider how an unideologized facet of primordial in-group consciousness is transformed into an overt instrument of group solidarity and self-assertion.

Sinhala, the subject of the present study, is an Indo-European language confined to the island of Sri Lanka. Its speakers number about twelve million today. We know that a significant feature of the Indian linguistic area is the dominance of the Indo-European group of languages. And as could be expected, the origin of the Sinhala language and the ethnic group is traced to an immigration from the Indian subcontinent. A peculiar feature of the geographical position of Sinhala is that a wide belt of Dravidian languages separates it from the other Indo-European languages that are in north India. Linguistically, this has contributed to the development of Sinhala as a distinct individual language. A special feature of its individuality is the influence of Tamil, the nearest Dravidian language, which, in addition to the nearly three million of its speakers in Sri Lanka, has about sixty million speakers in Tamil Nadu, which lies about twenty miles away on the opposite side of the narrow sea dividing the island from the Indian subcontinent.

A more pertinent aspect, especially in the context of the ethnic conflict in the island today, is the strong sense of national identity among the Sinhalese wherein language and religion (Buddhism) play pivotal roles. The term *Sinhalese-Buddhist,* although it came into parlance in the early twentieth century, reflects an ethnic cum religious identity, the origin of which can be traced to very early times. The intensity with which the Sinhalese identity is expressed in modern times appears to be the outcome of over two millennia of mainly conflictual contact with Dravidian neighbors, particularly the Tamils.[7] Considering the diminutive size of the Sinhalese community, confined as it was to the island of Sri Lanka, compared to the more expansive habitation of the Tamils in South India, this protracted conflict would have involved a tremendous physical and ideological effort. Ethnic self-assertion, using language and religion as means as well as criteria, may be considered a crucial ingredient of that ideological equipment.

5. Fishman 1965.

6. Fishman 1972a:149.

7. History records invasions beginning in the third century B.C. See K. M. de Silva 1986:11–16.

In exploring the ideological and behavioral features of modern Sinhalese nationalism many scholars today seek to identify and criticize recent reconstructions, particularly by activists such as Anagarika Dharmapala who were inspired by nineteenth-century European scholars. These reconstructions, it is alleged, held a simplistic view of the past, identifying the Sinhalese and the Tamils as two homogenous groups permanently opposed to each other. They are also criticized for having an ahistorical view of the past, which failed to recognize variations in time and space and other complexities. It is also alleged that the reconstructionist views ignored comparative evidence from other societies, thus endowing the Sinhalese with a unique history.[8] Such critical observations on modern Sinhalese nationalism, it appears to me, while having the very positive virtue of exposing overzealous exaggerations, also have a serious drawback, namely they overlook some special features of the Sinhalese case. The most notable of these, as I see it, is the existence of a long-standing literary tradition.

In view of this long-standing literary tradition we should say that the Sinhalese have a considerably "full" past.[9] A realistic appraisal of the origin and growth of modern Sinhalese nationalism cannot be achieved without a thorough knowledge of this literary tradition of the community—a tradition starting with a substantial corpus of inscriptions dating from about the third century B.C.[10] and a sizable corpus of literary works, in Pali as well as Sinhala, the extant specimens of which date from the early centuries of the Christian era. We know that only some of these documents are of direct importance for the understanding of historical and ideological facts. But as a whole, they represent a special phenomenon that cannot be overlooked by a student of history or ideology—that is, an inordinate and almost continuous concern for maintaining records of events. The most significant feature of this tradition, for our purpose, is the literary genre known as *vaṃśa* (lineage or history), and the Sinhalese can claim a special place in the South and Southeast Asian region as the earliest people to keep such historical records. Whereas the earliest *vaṃśa* in the Sri Lankan tradition had appeared by about A.D. fourth or fifth century, no comparable work appeared anywhere in the Indian subcontinent till about the twelfth

---

8. For these views, see Gunawardana 1979; Nissan and Stirrat 1987:4–8; Wilson 1988:28.

9. For "full" and "empty," see A. D. Smith 1986:177–78.

10. L. S. Perera 1959:66–72; Paranavitana 1970; 1983.

century.[11] To digress here, we need to keep in mind that the island people are credited with one of the most significant literary acts in the history of Buddhism—the writing down of the corpus of the Buddha's teachings in the first century B.C., which had been brought down in the oral tradition for about four centuries.

Of the *vaṃśa* literature the *Mahāvaṃsa* stands out as a unique chronicle. Initially written about the sixth century, it was updated three times—in the twelfth century, the fourteenth century, and, finally, in the eighteenth century, thus producing a continuous historical record. Our attention should focus here first on the antecedents of the *Mahāvaṃsa*, the *Dīpavaṃsa*, written one or two centuries previously, and the now extinct *Sīhalaṭṭhakathā Mahāvaṃsa;* and second on the very ideology that prompted the production of these works and the decision to "update" them from time to time. These phenomena indicate an exceptional awareness of and a highly consistent behavior toward the past. The motivation for this behavior has been differently conjectured. One interpretation sees it as religious—the attempt of the Theravadins to affirm the authenticity of their doctrine.[12] Another sees in it a concern of the Sinhalese to preserve their cultural identity in the face of constant threats from south India.[13] In my view the motivation would have been largely religious. But ethnic and dynastic considerations also would have played a part.

We know that the existence of written records helps as well as inhibits the manipulation of historical information. It is more the latter than the former. In the case of the nationalist activist, for example, he or she must work within the constraints of a generally well-defined factual framework. In the present study my aim has been to draw attention to the existence of such a framework in the growth of modern Sinhalese nationalism.

---

11. Kiribamune 1978:125.

12. Kiribamune 1979:99.

13. Guruge 1989:89–92. The manner in which this explanation is given seems to raise a doubt about whether modern concepts are being transported to the past.

Chapter 1

Sinhalese National Consciousness: Early Nineteenth-Century Manifestations

> One thing is certain, no foreign foe be it English, Dutch, French or Kaffir, will conquer Lanka. Through the protection of the four gods, the Guardians of its Religion, and the Merits of the King, for five thousand years no foe will continue to reside here.
>
> —From a dispatch of the Kandyan Court to the British Governor in Colombo (1811)

The Kandyan kingdom, the last phase of the Sinhalese polity, for over three centuries withstood all attempts by three European powers to bring it under control.[1] For a people sustaining a long period of military resistance requires equipping themselves with armaments as well as with ideological resources. In the case of the Sinhalese, placed as they were on an island so close to a peninsular landmass, resisting invaders had been a frequent feature of their communal existence. For over two millennia they were accustomed, in times of adversity, to drawing strength from certain features of the ethnocommunal tradition. When their kingdom faced a most exacting period in the early nineteenth century, the peculiarities of the political situation in Kandy at the time seems to have forced some of those incipient ideological factors to surface once again.

1. This, according to a modern historian, is "a triumphant record of resistance to the foreigner, which forms a contrast to the record in many parts of the world where imperial rule was established with great economy of effort" (K. M. de Silva 1973e:249).

The Subjugation of the Last Sinhalese Kingdom and the Kandyan Convention

The British, who had replaced the Dutch as masters of the maritime regions in 1796, were able in 1815 to bring the kingdom of Kandy in the central highlands under their control, thus establishing their suzerainty over the whole island. In the context of the European presence on the island beginning in the sixteenth century, this was a notable achievement. The Portuguese, who had arrived in 1505, being the first European power to gain a foothold in the island, controlled much of the littoral from about the mid sixteenth century to 1658, when they were ousted by the Dutch, who in turn were replaced by the British.

Throughout this period a Sinhalese kingdom controlled most of the interior and parts of the coast. With its capital in Kandy, this was the last Sinhalese kingdom in a history of over two millennia. The first British expedition to set out to conquer Kandy—in 1803—was as much of a disaster as Portuguese and Dutch invasions had been in the past. The second time, however, the British were better prepared. Equally significant was the fact that there was internal dissension in Kandy; a group of powerful ministers hostile to the king were prepared to support the British against him and, indeed, gave active support in that enterprise. The king was captured on 18 February 1815, and twelve days later the kingdom was formally ceded to the British at a convention in Kandy. The Kandyan Convention, the treaty of cession, was signed by Sir Robert Brownrigg, the governor on behalf of the British, and by nine principal chieftains on behalf of the Kandyans.[2]

The Kandyan Convention provides an index to certain salient features of the ideological tradition of the Sinhalese people. These ideological themes, which had found expression in literary works and in popular folklore and which endured as a bedrock of opinion, had the potential of surfacing and controlling the actions of people in times of difficulty and crisis. They were to be salient, time and again, in the years ahead. The Kandyan Convention, we need to remember, was a document drawn up by the British in consultation with the chieftains who had risen in "rebellion" against their king, and it can even be described as an attempt to justify the treasonable act of handing over the kingdom

2. The following quotations are from a photocopy of the original published in Nanawimala 1946:x–xii. It is in both Sinhala and English languages. The cession was declared on the second, but the actual signing took place on the tenth of March.

to foreign hands. Obviously, there was a pressing need to persuade those who were not happy about the cession.

With regard to Buddhism in particular, the British saw a great urgency to "quiet all uneasiness" regarding the fear of losing its traditional privileges.[3] In this endeavor existing ideological resources had to be utilized. Arguments to convince the unconvinced had to be based on solid ideological foundations. Thus, in the Kandyan Convention three features of the Sinhalese ideological tradition stand out: ethnicity, religion, and an identification of the two with the historical legacy of the geographical entity that is the island of Sri Lanka.

The Ethnic Factor

In the Kandyan Convention a noteworthy emphasis is placed on the ethnic disparity that existed between the ruling family and its subjects in the Kandyan kingdom during its last phase. The deposed ruler is referred to as *demala rajjuruvo* (the Tamil king), and, to register unequivocally in the minds of the Sinhalese people the peculiar political situation that existed and its potentialities, it is proclaimed that:

> All claim and title of the Tamil race to govern the land of the Sinhalese people is abolished and extinguished.[4]

King Sri Vikrama Rajasinghe (1798–1815), referred to as *demala rajjuruvo* in the convention, belonged to a line of kings known as the Nayakkars, originally Telegu-speaking Hindus from south India. In the convention they were referred to as the *demala vargaya* (Tamil race).

Undoubtedly, the British were intent on fully exploiting the ethnic disparity between the Kandyans and their ruler. Loyalty to the king was strong, however, because in the eyes of the Kandyans he was their "Supreme Majesty of the *Kṣatriyavaṃsa*" (royal lineage), which they believed had existed continuously from the day the Sinhalese dynasty was founded by Prince Vijaya in the sixth century B.C.[5] But there lin-

3. These are the words of Governor Brownrigg, who negotiated the cession.

4. Clause 2. My translation. For the word *demala* in the Sinhala version, the English version used the word *Malabar,* which was the contemporary conceptualization based on geographical criteria. But the concept as it would have appeared to the Sinhalese people with its ethnic connotations is better represented by the word *Tamil.*

5. The Nayakkar rulers claimed succession from the ancient royal line of the Sinha-

gered in Kandyan circles, especially among some sections of the aristocracy and the *sangha*, a latent aversion to the "alien" dynasty, which no doubt facilitated the task of the British.

The Nayakkar dynasty's succession to the throne of Kandy occurred with Sri Vijaya Rajasinghe (1739–47), who was the brother-in-law of the last of the ethnically Sinhalese kings, Sri Viraparakrama Narendrasinghe (1707–39). Sri Vijaya ascended the throne ostensibly because Narendrasinghe had no other heir of "pure *kṣatriya* lineage" to succeed him.[6] The "alien" dynasty continued thereafter, up to the end of the Kandyan kingdom, with the reigns of Kirti Sri Rajasinghe (1747–82), Rajadhi Rajasinghe (1782–98), and, finally, Sri Vikrama Rajasinghe (1798–15).

The history of Nayakkar rule reveals that on several occasions the "alienness" of the ruler became the focus of attention. But on the whole the new dynasty was accepted by the people because of the eagerness of all Nayakkar rulers to play the role that was traditionally expected of a Sinhalese king. They became zealous patrons of Buddhism, Sinhala literature, and the arts.[7] Yet as ethnic and religious memories die hard, especially in a literate culture, several incidents occurred in which the latent cleavage between the Nayakkars and their subjects came to the fore. Conspiracies arose from among the ranks of the elite, who were aware of historical precedents and in whose minds the alienness of the dynasty was a lingering memory.

An account in the historical poem the *Mandārampura Puvata*, written about two decades after the accession of Sri Vijaya, describes the circumstances under which the crown was handed over to a "foreign nation" (*para däya*).

---

lese. See, for example, the Asgiriya Alut Vihara Inscription (1800) of Sri Vikrama Rajasinghe and the author's statement at the end of *Srī Saddharmāvavāda Sangrahaya* by Tibbotuvave Buddharaksita (1773), an edificatory compendium written during the time of the second Nayakkar ruler, Kirti Sri Rajasinghe. (Dhammananda 1969:39–42; and Amaramoli 1956:583, respectively.)

6. For details about this succession, see Devaraja 1972:76–77.

7. The most lavish patrons of the religious and literary revival in eighteenth-century Kandy were Sri Vijaya, Kirti Sri, and Rajadhi. Among them, too, Kirthi Sri stands out. He was responsible for facilitating the reestablishment of the Higher Ordination with the help of the Siamese *bhikkhus*, and almost all the important Buddhist shrines in the Kandyan kingdom were renovated by him. Rajadhi was not only a patron of literary activity but also an accomplished poet, composing *Asadisa Dā Kava*. Finally, even Sri Vikrama made several additions to the temples in Kandy. See Devaraja 1972:127–28; and Vacissara 1960.

> [King Narendrasinghe] as he had neither son nor daughter to succeed to the royal splendour, acting in accordance with the wishes of the monk [Saranankara] and the ministers, [decided on] the brother of the queen who is descended from the pure royal line of Madura and who was supreme in virtue, [and] taking that *vaḍiga* prince's right hand [the king] placed it on the hand of the monk Saranankara (telling him) "teach him the [Buddhist] doctrine and the arts and get him to protect well the *sāsana* and the kingdom in future."[8]

At the death of Narendrasinghe, Saranankara faithfully carried out his wish.

> [Saranankara] presented to the ministers with his own hands that famous prince who was decked in all the [royal] ornaments [and] appraising him of all the duties of kingship and the traditional rights of the ministers handed over Lanka [to him] and the great ministers received with due honour the kind words of the monk who desired the good of Lanka and they *who had never* [before] *handed over the Sinhala crown to a foreign nation* thought of placing [it], for the first time, on his [Sri Vijaya's] head.[9]

The crucial factor in the choice of Sri Vijaya, who belonged to a so-called foreign nation, was the sponsorship he received from Saranankara, the most revered and influential of the *bhikkhus* of the day. As tradition demanded, no one but a *kṣatriya* from both father's and mother's side could be king. Sri Vijaya was seen to have that qualification; and he had received the traditional training incumbent on a Sinhalese ruler-to-be.[10]

It would appear that the *Mandārampura Puvata* is anxious to justify the choice of a "foreigner" to ascend the throne of Kandy. In this connection we learn from other sources that at the death of Narendrasinghe there was a group of ministers who espoused the cause of

8. Lankananda 1958, vv. 510 and 511. I am providing a free translation of the meaning in the two verses, since a line-by-line translation would lead to awkward expressions. This policy will be followed in all translations in this book. This part of the work (compiled in three parts at three successive stages) was written sometime during 1753 and 1760. See Lankananda's introduction (ix). The term *vadiga* is an appellation of the Nayakkars which later took a pejorative connotation.

9. Lankananda 1958, vv. 521, 522; emphasis added.

10. Devaraja 1972:76.

another prince named Unambuve Bandara, who was a Sinhalese ethnic, being a son of Narendrasinghe by a non-*kṣatriya* Sinhalese lady. But Unambuve's claim could not be pressed because he was not fully qualified as a *kṣatriya*.[11] On ascending the throne Sri Vijaya not only strove hard to play the role traditionally expected of a Kandyan monarch but, by a policy of reconciliation, also won over the faction that sponsored Unambuve.[12]

It should be noted that the Nayakkar presence in the Kandyan court had been resented and had even provoked a revolt during the reign of Narendrasinghe himself. The king had married two Nayakkar consorts, and evidently each of these marriages was followed by the influx to Kandy of a large number of *vaḍiga* kinsmen. Their exclusivism, "heathenism," and the fact that they seemed to form a power bloc above the native aristocracy would have provided considerable provocation. The crisis came to a head when Narendrasinghe appointed a "*vaḍiga* Tamil" (*demalaku vaḍiga*) to the important administrative post of Maha Gabada Nilame (chief of the king's stores). A serious revolt ensued in protest against this violation of tradition, and the foreigner was killed. The king crushed the revolt ruthlessly, having enlisted the support of the Dutch.[13] After the king's anger had subsided, the senior ministers took counsel with him and, according to the *Mandārampura Puvata* (479), told him that

> for all the time of the existence of the island of Lanka we have not even heard, except on this occasion, of foreign people (*para dana*) having obtained ministerial position.

It would appear that this uprising of 1732 had the desired effect. For never again, not even when a Nayakkar sat on the throne, do we hear of an administrative appointment being given to a Nayakkar, at least not in the higher ranks of the service.[14]

The subsequent reign of Sri Vijaya, which lasted eight years, was peaceful. But the next Nayakkar king, Kirti Sri, had to face two rebel-

11. Devaraja 1972:76. Such children were called *bhinna matuka*, born of a mother of unequal rank. See Devaraja 1972:35–36.

12. Devaraja 1972:77.

13. Lankananda, ed., 1958, v. 469. According to it, about two thousand men of rank were executed, and several villages were burnt to the ground (see v. 472). Also see Devaraja 1972:72.

14. Devaraja 1972:74.

lions. The first occurred in 1749, barely two years after his accession; in it all the Sinhalese ministers united against the perceived arrogance of Nayakkar kinsmen, especially the king's father, Narenappa. The king was forced to concede, and Narenappa was advised not to meddle in the affairs of government.[15] The other rebellion, in 1760, appears to have been a more serious conspiracy. The principal Buddhist dignitaries Saranankara, now elevated to the position of Sangha Raja (the supreme head of the monkhood) and the deputy Sangha Raja Tibbotuvave, the head of Malvatte Viharaya (one of the two principal monastaries in Kandy), along with some leading ministers, were found to be involved in it. The religioethnic motivation for the conspiracy is clearly evident in the following account given in the *Śāsanāvatīrṇa Varṇanāva*, a history of Buddhism written toward the mid-nineteenth century:

> The Sangharaja and other leading monks, having failed in the attempt to preach and persuade the king to give up his heretical practice of anointing himself, with ash, declared "we cannot sustain the Sasana in co-operation with this heretical Tamil (*mityādritṣṭi demala*)," and the monks of Malvatte temple and the chieftains taking counsel decided "let us appoint some other worthy person as our king. . . . "[16]

Anointing consecrated ash on the forehead, breast, and arms is a practice common to Saivite Hindus, and Kirti Sri, a Hindu by birth and early upbringing, did not give up some of these Hindu practices even after assuming the role of Sinhalese-Buddhist monarch. Hence the *sangha* were led to doubt the sincerity of his professed Buddhist beliefs. The use of the epithet *mityādriṣṭi demala* ("heretical Tamil") reveals that the ethnic disparity, with its strong historical associations, was a further factor in their mistrust of the king.

The conspirators against the king could not decide at first who should be "the other worthy person." They first considered Pattiye Bandara, a Sinhalese, but dropped him because he did not have *kṣatriya* qualifications. The caste factor as well as jealousies within the ranks of

15. We do not have many details about this incident. See Devaraja 1972:96–97.

16. Godakumbura, ed., 1956:22–25. It was written about ninety years after the incident, and its reliability has been doubted by Gunawardana 1979:25. I have argued elsewhere why it can be considered reliable (Dharmadasa 1989).

the Kandyan aristocracy would have prevented an aristocrat from being sponsored as king. In the absence of a suitable Sinhalese the conspirators turned to the Siamese *bhikkhus* who had arrived in Kandy a few years earlier to help revive the Higher Ordination. A Siamese prince was brought to Kandy, disguised as a *bhikkhu*, with the intention that he could replace the "heretical Tamil." Apparently, this exotic foreigner, who was a Buddhist *kṣatriya*, seemed preferable to a non-*kṣatriya* Sinhalese, and the incumbent heretical Tamil, with a horde of parasitic relations.[17]

The conspiracy was discovered, however, in time. Although the plotters were severely punished, the king also reformed his religious ways.[18] What is of interest for the present discussion is the upsurge of anti-Nayakkar feeling based on religious and ethnic criteria. Such "treasonable" feelings which could not be expressed overtly earlier came out openly and with a vengeance at the fall of the Nayakkar monarchy.

The two literary works *Kiraḷa Sandēśaya* (The Message of the Lapwing)[19] and *Vaḍiga Haṭana* (The Tale of the Vadigas),[20] both written immediately after the fall of Sri Vikrama Rajasinghe (i.e., between 1815 and 1818), set forth the sentiments against the Tamil heretics quite lucidly. In the *Kiraḷa Sandēśaya* reference is made to

> heretical and thieving Tamil hordes (*kudiṭu nisasara demaḷa käla*) who were destroying the most immaculate *sāsana* which was destined to flourish for five thousand years. . . . (v. 189)

And the *Vaḍiga Haṭana* speaks of Sri Vikrama, who,

> not satisfied with eating up this Tri Sinhala, killed people and grabbing their wealth gave it over to wicked Tamils (*säḍi demaḷu*). (v. 177)

Reference is also made to:

> Tamils who like hordes of Mara [god of death] were destroying the most immaculate *sāsana* of our Lord Buddha. (v. 112)

---

17. For details, see Dharmadasa 1989.
18. For details, see Dharmadasa 1989.
19. Godakumbura 1961.
20. M. E. Fernando n.d.

Why these religious and ethnic factors assumed such salience can only be understood in the context of a strand in the complex braiding of the Sinhalese ideological tradition, which viewed the Tamil-Hindus as a perennial threat. It needs to be emphasized, however, that such an ethnoreligious antagonism was not an ever-present factor and that it manifested itself only in some crisis situations.

Sinhalese historiography, chiefly the work of the *bhikkhus* and dating from about the fourth century A.D., records that the Sinhalese kingdom, first established in the northern plains of the island in the 6th century B.C. by a prince named Vijaya who came from north India, subsequently became a frequent target for invasions from neighboring south India. In fact, until the thirteenth century, when invasions from Kalinga in Orissa and Sri Vijaya in Malaya took place, the only foreigners to have invaded the Sinhalese kingdom were the south Indians. They were indeed a powerful factor in molding the political destiny of the island. Thus, it was to a large extent due to their devastations that in the eleventh century Anuradhapaura, the first capital of the Sinhalese kingdom, was abandoned in favor of Polonnaruva, situated further to the southeast. Later, in the thirteenth century, after a long period of sociopolitical instability—culminating in an invasion by Magha of Kalinga with an army identified in the Sinhalese chronicles as *damiḷa*—the Sinhalese kings found it more congenial to abandon the area altogether and move to the southwest.[21]

The manner in which Magha's invasion is depicted in the *Mahāvaṃsa,* the main historical chronicle of the Sinhalese,[22] eloquently expresses a common assessment of the reverses suffered:

> They [Magha's army] tore from the people their garments, their ornaments and the like, corrupted the good morals of the family which had been observed for ages . . . destroyed many houses and tied up oxen and other cattle which they made their own property. . . . They wrecked image houses, destroyed many *cētiyas,* ravaged the *vihāras,* and maltreated the lay brethren. They flogged the children, tormented the five groups of the comrades of the Buddhist order, made the people carry burdens and forced them

21. There were other factors as well. See Indrapala 1971. The *Pujavaliya* of the thirteenth century calls Magha's army *damila* (Dhammananda [Walane] 1916:690). But the invaders came from different kingdoms in south India such as Cola, Pandya, and Pallava. Etymologically, *damila* means "Dravidian."

22. For details about this chronicle and its name, see n. 55.

> to do heavy labour. Many books known and famous, they tore from their cord and strewed them hither and thither. The beautiful and vast *cētiyas* like to Ruwanweli Cetiya and others which embodied as it were the glory of former pious kings, they destroyed by overthrowing them and allowing, alas, many of the body relics, their life as it were, to disappear. Thus the *damiḷa* warriors, in imitation of Mara, destroyed, in the evil of their nature, the laity and the Buddhist Order. (*Mahāvaṃsa*, pt. 2, chap. 1, vv. 58–73)

Although Magha's invasion is not depicted in similar terms in some other historical sources,[23] it is clear that his reign (1215–36) and his subsequent activities in the north of the island led to far-reaching political consequences. During the next two centuries, with the "drift to the southwest," the Sinhalese gradually abandoned the northern plains, hitherto the main center of their civilization, and settled in the southwestern and central regions. The Tamils, who had been coming to the island as peaceful settlers, and in times of war as soldiers, established themselves in the north. Others settled in the south and southwest and were integrated into the Sinhalese society.[24] Thus, the main Tamil settlements, which were concentrated in the northernmost region of the island, close to south India, retained their ethnocultural identity. Magha, having been ousted from Polonnaruva by the Sinhalese, had founded a kingdom in the north, which subsequently became the Tamil kingdom of Jaffna. The Jaffna kingdom, although it generally acknowledged the suzerainty of the Sinhalese kingdom in the south, sometimes proved to be a powerful military rival to the latter.[25] While there were periods of peace characterized by cultural and religious assimilation, inevitably, during periods of conflict and stress, there was an upsurge of historical antagonism between the two communities.

The belief that the ancient Sinhalese civilization in the northern plains collapsed and its heartland came to be abandoned because of the

23. The *Nikaya Sangrahaya* (fourteenth century) and the *Saddharmaratnakara* (fifteenth century) refer to him without animosity. See Nicholas and Paranavitana 1961:245.

24. Roberts 1982:21–34.

25. For its origin, see Nicholas and Paranavitana 1961:286; Indrapala 1966. The Jaffna kingdom for the most part of its four-century existence was confined to the Jaffna peninsula. For its subsequent history—during which it became powerful enough to challenge the Sinhalese kingdoms—its subjugation by the latter in the fifteenth century, and its final fall with the capture by the Portuguese in early seventeenth century, see C. R. de Silva 1987:91–93.

devastations of the south Indians has persisted, and the tradition of viewing the south Indians, under the blanket term *damiḷa* or *demaḷa*, as enemies of the Sinhalese people has continued down the ages. This theme is found in the writings of the literati represented by works such as the *Mahāvaṃsa*, the *Thūpavaṃsa*, and the *Pūjāvaliya* and in the popular tradition of folktales, poems, and folklore in general.[26]

The Religious Factor

In the Sinhalese ideological tradition religion per se seems to have played a much more important role than ethnicity. Hence even foreigners, if they were Buddhist by religion or became Buddhists, could lay claim to the throne–which explains the choice of the Nayakkars in 1739 and the sponsorship received by the Siamese prince in 1760. The Convention of 1815, while guaranteeing "to all classes of people the safety of their persons and property with their civil rights and immunities, according to the laws, institutions and customs established and in force among them" (clause 4) made special provision in a separate clause (clause 5) to the effect that

> the religion of Boodhoo [*sic*] professed by the chiefs and inhabitants of these provinces is declared inviolable, and its Rites, Ministers and Places of Worship are to be maintained and protected.

Also, soon after the British administration of the Kandyan provinces began, Sir John D'Oyly, the principal British official in Kandy, publicly declared:

> We have not come to this country to destroy the Religion of Buddha and the Gods, which have prevailed from ancient time in the country, but to protect and promote it.[27]

The fact that the British were compelled by force of circumstances to grant these concessions to Buddhism is borne out by the explanation

26. For details, see Bechert 1974; and Roberts 1979. Gunawardana (1979) presents a different view on the growth of Sinhalese identity, but his interpretations are often not supported by the Sinhalese sources. For details, see Dharmadasa 1989.

27. Codrington 1920: entry for 8 April 1815.

regarding the matter sent by Governor Robert Brownrigg to his superiors in London. Conceding the fact that the language employed in the clause referring to Buddhism was "more emphatical than would have been my choice," he revealed that:

> in truth our secure possession of the country hinged upon this point. . . . I found it necessary to quiet all uneasiness respecting it, by an article of guarantee couched in the most unqualified terms.[28]

This statement is indicative of the great urgency with which the guarantee was sought. Henry Marshall, a contemporary observer, noted:

> It was rumored at the time that the alleged treaty was drawn up with sufficient care not to infringe certain prejudices of the chiefs. Perhaps the preservation of the religion of Boodhoo [*sic*] was considered of the highest importance. . . . [29]

Even in their hour of "treason" the chiefs were mindful of obtaining the strongest possible guarantees concerning their religion. D'Oyly records that, prior to signing the convention on 10 March 1815, the most senior *bhikkhus* in Kandy, the chief high prelates of the Malvatta and Asgiriya monasteries, had an audience with the governor, who assured them that "they will receive under the British government full protection and security." The Nayaka Theros, on their part, declared:

> Since the time of Wijaya [*sic*] the Religion of Buddha has been aided and supported in this island by the sovereigns who have successively reigned. . . . [30]

Behind the deep concern of the Kandyans with regard to the future of their religion there stretches a long tradition of association between the state and Buddhism in Sri Lanka. From its very introduction to the island in the third century B.C. Buddhism came to be inextricably linked with the affairs of state. This development, which at first seems peculiar to a religion whose teachings pointed to self-realization and attainment

28. Quoted in K. M. de Silva 1965:64–65.
29. Marshall 1969:122–23.
30. Codrington 1920:321.

of release (*Nirvāṇa*) from the cycle of birth and death, seems to have taken place primarily because of the circumstances in which Buddhism was introduced. The Indian emperor Asoka, who was instrumental in sending the first Buddhist missionaries to the island, had given the lead in state-religion relations, and in Sri Lanka the first converts were the king and the royal family.[31] The Buddhist connection eventually became a factor taken for granted. It was at one stage claimed that a king puts on "the sacred crown in order to look after the Buddhist religion" and that none but *bōdhisattvas* (Buddhas to be) would become kings of Lanka.[32] The importance assigned to Buddhism in the affairs of state is best summed up in the following statement attributed to king Dutthagamini (161–137 B.C.) while engaged in the task of liberating the kingdom from a south Indian usurper:

> Not for the joy of sovereignty is this toil of mine; my striving has ever been to establish to doctrine of the Sambuddha. (*Mahāvaṃsa*, pt. 1, chap. 25, v. 17)

The king was the principal lay devotee (*upāsaka*) of the Buddhist dispensation (*sāsana*). He was expected to patronize the *sangha* (the order of monks) by providing them with the four requisites (*sivpasaya*): food, clothing, shelter, and medicine. A king who liberally patronized the monasteries by building new shrines and dwelling places for the monkhood and by granting them rich endowments, received lavish praise in the writings of *bhikkhu* historiographers. This, in fact, appears to be the major concern of the Sri Lankan chronicles.

The *sangha*, for their part, were expected to be the custodians of learning and scholarship in addition to being religious virtuosi. *Pirivenas*, the *bhikkhu* institutions of learning, were attached to Buddhist monasteries for lay and ecclesiastical pupils to receive traditional education. In addition to teaching the *sangha* literati attached to these institutions produced literary works and scholarly treatises. These works, as the history of Sinhalese literature shows, were not confined to religious subject matter. Sometimes the writings of these *bhikkhu* authors would encompass material of secular taste and interest, a point that demonstrates the wide and varied scope of their scholarship. The fact that the *sangha* were traditionally entrusted with some parts of the

31. Rahula 1966:6–9, 48–51.
32. From a tenth-century inscription (*Epigraphia Zeylanica* 1: 234).

education of the royal family is indicative of the range of their scholarly competence as well as of the tremendous influence they wielded over the Sinhalese polity.[33] In a situation where the political, religious, and educational institutions were interdependent, scholarly activity, literature, and other arts flourished when there was political stability and ample patronage forthcoming from the king and other powerful personalities. This is most cogently articulated by an anonymous poet who wrote the *Sasadāvata* in the twelfth century:

> Poetry is the creation of intellect. For this tranquillity of mind is necessary. Essential preconditions for that are, prosperity of the land, and a powerful king with virtuous ministers.[34]

In Sinhalese historical tradition several regnal periods are identified as times in which these factors were fully realized. Prominent among them were the reigns of Kassapa V (914–23) at Anuradhapura, Parakramabahu II (1235–70) at Dambadeniya, and Parakramabahu VI (1412–67) at Kotte. About sixty years before its cession to the British there was a period of literary and artistic efflorescence in the kingdom of Kandy. *Bhikkhu* Velivita Saranankara (1698–1778) spearheaded a religious and literary revival, and in this task he received generous support from royalty, especially the Nayakkar rulers, who in sheer anxiety to compensate for their marginal status in Sinhalese society were the most lavish patrons of the revival. In this Kirti Sri Rajasinghe (1747–82) stands out. His brother and successor, Rajadhi Rajasinghe (1782–98) was not only a patron of the arts but also an accomplished poet himself, having received his education under *bhikkhu* Moratota Dhammakkanda, who later became head of the Malvatte Viharaya.[35] Although the troubled political climate during the reign of the last king of Kandy, Sri Vikrama Rajasinghe (1798–1815), did not permit the revival to proceed with the same vigor in the Kandyan areas, the movement had by then spread to the southern region, which was at that time under British rule. Here it was carried on under the leadership of several *bhikkhus* who had the support of some chieftains of the area.[36]

The Kandyan ministers who contrived to cede their kingdom to the

33. Devaraja 1972:132.

34. Cumaratungu 2843 B.E., v. 10.

35. Hewawasam 1968:201–11; Devaraja 1972:132.

36. See chapter 2.

British in 1815 no doubt believed, and in fact were made to believe by the firm guarantees of the British, that their cherished institutions, customs, and traditional arrangements with regard to religion, language, and literary activity, among other things, would continue as yore. But as they were to realize soon enough, this was not to be.[37]

The Conceptual Permeation of Geography with Ethnicity and Religion

Possessive feelings about the geographical setting in which the national community emerged as a distinct identity and attained maturity are a central feature of nationalist ideologies. A salient aspect of the Sinhalese ideological tradition, however, is its long-established and explicitly stated identification of the island with one ethnic group and one religious community—Sinhalese and Buddhist—which were considered constituent elements of a single identity.[38] The fact that Sri Lanka is an island made the identification easy and conceptually feasible—a basis of delimitation had been provided by nature, as it were.

The Kandyan Convention refers to the Kandyan kingdom as *Sinhalé,* meaning "the territory of the Sinhalese people." This specific name is a legacy from the time when the Sinhalese kingdom was considered as encompassing the whole island. There is strong literary evidence to show that the Sinhalese and Buddhist identifications of the island date back at least to the fourth century A.D. The historical chronicle the *Dīpavaṃśa* (the chronicle of the island), assigned to the fourth century or early fifth century A.D., refers to the fact that the island was known as *Sīhala* "on account of the lion," the mythical progenitor of the community. Hence we find the name *Sīhaḷadvīpa* (the island of the Sinhalas) being used in the *Samantapāsādikā,* a Pali work compiled in the early fifth century by *bhikkhu* Buddhaghosa, a visitor from India. In the same vein the Chinese *bhikkhu* Fa-Hian, who also stayed on the island for about two years in the fifth century, refers to it as "the country of the lions." It is of particular interest that the derivations of the word *Sīhaḷa* (which is Pali and whose Sinhalese form is *Sinhaḷa*) had gained wide currency abroad, being used in south Indian inscriptions and literary works of the first or the second centuries A.D., in the fourth century Allahabad Inscription of Samudragupta in north India, and in

37. For details, see chapter 2.

38. See Obeysekere 1975:234.

some Chinese literary works of the second and third centuries.[39] *Bhikkhu* Buddhaghosa, who arrived on the island in the early fifth century to translate the Buddhist commentaries, which were in Sinhalese, into Pali, the language of the Buddhist canon, not only refers to the island as "*Sīhaḷadvīpa*" but also speaks of the Sinhalese language (*Sīhaḷabhāsā*) as "a delightful language."[40]

An eighth-century graffito at Sigiriya refers to the island as *Heḷa Div* (*Sinhaḷadvīpa*).[41] And we have other evidence that strongly supports the view that by the late Anuradhapura period the conceptual ramifications of the Sinhalese identity were quite clear—at least in the minds of the literati. Thus, the *Dhampiā Aṭuvā Gāṭapadaya,* an exegetical work of the tenth century, after paraphrasing the Pali phrase *dīpa bhāsāya* ("in the island language") as *heḷu basin* ("in the Sinhala language"), explains the derivation of the latter term thus:

> How do [we] obtain [the term] "from the *heḷu* language?" [That is,] from the fact that the island people are *heḷu.* From where do [we get the word] *helese?* King Sinhabahu having killed a lion was named "Siihaḷa" . . . since prince Vijaya was his son he [too] was called "Siihaḷa." The others since [they] were his (Vijaya's) followers [they too] came to be called "Siihaḷa."[42]

Here we see that, by the tenth century, in the national perception the dynasty, the people, the language, and the land all have been identified as *heḷa* (Sinhala).[43]

The ingredients of group consciousness mentioned above were kept alive principally because the Sinhalese people had a literate culture starting from about the third century B.C.[44] Linguistic research has revealed that the processes of individual development whereby Sinhala emerged as an independent language distinct from Sanskrit and

---

39. For these references, see M. H. P. Silva 1966:app. 1; Gunawardana 1979:4; Dharmadasa 1989.

40. See Jayawickrama 1962:xx. For references to *Sīnhaladvīpa* in Buddhaghosa's writings, see Adikaram 1953:app. 1B, xxv.

41. Paranavitana 1956, 2:179. Pali *Sinhaḷadvīpa* becomes *heḷa div* in Sinhala. For the derivation of Hela, see n. 42.

42. Hettiaratchi 1974:6. For the legend of the lion, see Kiribamune 1979. (The derivation of the word Eḷu is as follows: Sinhaḷa > Siihaḷa > Heḷa > Heḷu > Eḷu).

43. In making these statements I am conscious of the fact that I am rejecting the conclusions of Gunawardana (1979). For details, see Dharmadasa 1989.

44. Wijayaratne 1956:iv; Paranavitana 1970:xxii.

other Indian languages seem to have started as early as the third century B.C., reaching fruition during the period from about the fourth to the eighth century A.D.[45] Obviously, it was in that context that Buddhaghosa called Sinhala "a delightful language." As pointed out by Heinz Bechert,

> The Sinhalese were almost the only South Asian people not to pass over from Prakrit to Sanskrit as the language of epigraphical records in the early medieval period. Retaining the use of the local language, an expression of a conservative attitude, was at the same time the cause of an important innovation, viz. the formation of the Sinhalese literary language, an act of self-assurance of the Sinhalese nation as well.[46]

The independent development of the Sinhala language seems to have coincided with similar trends in other aspects of culture: architecture, sculpture, painting, and technology.[47] As could be expected, continental models influenced the island civilization from time to time. It is clear that a Sinhalese cultural identity, as distinct from that of any part of the subcontinent, and indeed having unique features that distinguish it from the pan-Indian cultural world, had emerged by the late Anuradhapura period.[48]

Centers of learning were attached to the Buddhist temples, and the *bhikkhus* were the literary specialists who produced most of the literature and disseminated literacy and knowledge. More significant, they were the community's historians. In their hands the political ideology of the unity between the Sinhalese ethnic group, the Buddhist religion, and the island of Lanka was kept alive by a series of historical chronicles

45. Jayatilaka 1933:ix. For the individual features found in the earliest Sinhala records, see Norman 1978:30–31.

46. Bechert 1978:6.

47. Paranavitana 1971:6; Rowland 1958:84; Zimmer 1961:170, 366–67; Murphy 1957:184; Bandaranayake 1984:xv.

48. The Anuradhapura period is circa fifth century B.C. to the eleventh century A.D. Apart from the persistence of Buddhism, which disappeared from India before the end of the fifteenth century, Bechert (1978) mentions three special features of Sinhalese culture: differences in language; differences in the popular deities; and the absence of a *Rāmāyana* tradition. Also compare: "We have as a factor of great consequence for us historically, Sri Lanka's separation from that land mass, its distinct evolution from the societies of the subcontinent. Sri Lanka's distinct character and structure as an island civilization stands in contradistinction to its close relationship with the south Asian mainland" (Bandaranayake 1978:81).

(*vaṃśa*) which recorded the stories of diverse objects of veneration: the Buddha's corporeal relics (*sārīrika dhātu*); articles he used, such as his alms bowl (*pāribhōgika dhātu*); and the ficus tree under which he attained enlightenment (*Bōdhi*), a branch of the original being planted in Anuradhapura in the third century B.C.

There is a distinct historical consciousness that recognizes the unique role of the island people in the preservation of the Buddha's doctrine. The successive authors of the *vaṃśa* histories have expressed and maintained this historical consciousness continuously. Apart from the *Dīpavaṃśa* (fourth and fifth centuries), and the first part of the *Mahāvaṃśa* (sixth century), which we have with us today, there were two other chronicles, now extinct, dealing with the general history of the island, the *Sīhalaṭṭhakathā Mahāvaṃśa* and the *Uttara Vihāra Vaṃśa*, both of which appear to have been compiled sometime during the period from the third century B.C. to the fourth century A.D. We also know about other extinct works such as the *Daḷadā Vaṃśa* (History of the Tooth Relic), the *Kēsadhātu Vaṃśa* (History of the Hair Relic), a *Thūpa Vaṃśa* (History of the Stupa), and a *Mahā Bōdhi Vaṃśa* (History of the Great Bodhi Tree), all written in the early Sinhala language.[49] Of this corpus of *vaṃśa* literature the following works are extant today: a Pali *Dāṭhā Vaṃśa* (History of the Tooth Relic) of the twelfth century, a Sinhala *Daḷadā Sirita* (Story of the Tooth Relic) of the fourteenth century, a Pali *Thūpa Vaṃśa* of the twelfth century, a Sinhala *Thūpa Vaṃśa* of the thirteenth century, a Pali *Mahā Bōdhi Vaṃśa* of about the seventh or eighth century, a Sinhala *Mahā Bōdhi Vaṃśa* of the fourteenth century, a Sinhala *Cūla Bōdhi Vaṃśa* (History of the Lesser Bodhi Trees) of the sixteenth century, and a Pali *Ḷaláṭa Dhātu Vaṃśa* (History of the Forehead Relic) of the sixteenth century. The underlying theme of the *vaṃśa* literature is the identification of the island as the repository of Buddhism—the *Dhammadvīpa*.

This historical vision is found in other edificatory works as well. A prominent example is the *Pūjāvaliya*, written by *bhikkhu* Mayurapada in the thirteenth century, a long treatise justifying the epithet *arahaṃ* (worthy of offerings) to the Buddha. In chapter 33, describing the advent of four Buddhas to the island of Lanka, the author states:

> Since it is definite that the right branches of the Bodhi trees, the precious doctrine and the dispensations of innumerable Buddhas

49. See Godakumbura 1955:105–26; Sannasgala 1961:39, 49, 50; Kiribamune 1979.

will be established here, this island of Lanka decidedly belongs to the Buddhas. It is like a treasury filled by the Triple Gem. Therefore the sojourn of wrong-believers in this island of Lanka will indeed not be permanent just as the sojourn of *yakkhas* of yore here was not permanent. If a king of false-belief were to rule here by force the fact that this dynasty will not take root is due to the special powers of the Buddhas themselves. Since this island of Lanka befits only the kings with the true belief it is indeed certain that only their family line will remain here.[50]

The association of the island with Buddhism is thus unequivocally stated. The "false-believers" in this context are principally the Tamil Hindus. Several pages later, in chapter 34, while describing the material offerings provided by various "meritorious kings, the lords of Sinhala" (*sinhalādhipati pinvat rajun*), *bhikkhu* Mayurapada describes how the island had been offered to the Buddha five times, each for seven days.[51]

The fact that the Sinhalese ethnic group was exclusively confined to the island would have led to the formulation of the *Sinhaladvīpa* concept. We notice, however, that ethnicity was usually not promoted alone. It was part of the more important Buddhist identity. Beginning with the *Dīpavaṃśa* and *Mahāvaṃśa,* we see the idea that "the island of Lanka belongs to the Buddhas," the *Dhammadvīpa* concept, being the basis of all historical thinking. The *Dīpavaṃśa* states that the Buddha, having foreseen Lanka as the place where his doctrine would shine in glory, hallowed the island by three visits (three being a magical number that confers legitimacy) and urged Sakka, the King of the Gods, to watch over the island in future. The *Mahāvaṃśa,* narrating the events more dramatically, reports how the Buddha, lying on his deathbed, told Sakra:

Vijaya, the son of king Sinhabahu, is come to Lanka from the country of Lala, together with seven hundred followers. In Lanka, Oh

50. According to Buddhist belief, there were many Buddhas before the advent of Siddhartha Gautama, the Buddha of the present age, and there will be many more in the future. The *yakkhas* were malevolent supernatural beings who were expelled by the present Buddha when he visited the island prior to the establishment of the Sinhalese kingdom, which later became the repository of Buddhism. For details, see Kiribamune 1979. The quotation is from W. Dhammananda 1916:656–57.

51. W. Dhammananda 1916:679.

lord of gods, will my religion be established, therefore carefully protect him with his followers and Lanka. (chap. 7, vv. 3 and 4)

Thus, the identification of the interests of the ethnic group with the land is given a "holy" mandate as it were—bearing close similarity to the "chosen people" concept of the Jews in connection with Israel.[52] Obviously, the crystallization of this self-estimation, a holy destiny not assigned to the Sinhalese by the Buddhist tradition in any other country, occurred under the perennial pressure on the Sinhalese-Buddhist polity from the Tamil-Hindu societies in south India.

The *vaṃśa* literature mentioned above, especially the *Dīpavaṃśa* and the *Mahāvaṃśa,* with their emphasis on political history, display a historical consciousness unique in South Asia. Although a sense of history is evident in the epics and the *Purāṇas* of India, which took their final form in the early centuries of the Christian era, we find no historical chronicle similar to the *Dīpavaṃśa* and the *Mahāvaṃśa* in any part of India until the Kashmiri chronicle, the *Rājataranginī,* appeared in the twelfth century.[53] Significantly, the tradition of compiling historiographical works by the Sinhalese seems to be linked to the emergence of a literate culture, and the earliest "historical" compendium, given the appellation *Sīhalaṭṭhakathā Mahāvaṃśa,* seems to have been written sometime during the period from the first century B.C. to the first century A.D.[54] From the numerous inscriptions of the following period we learn that literary activity expanded rapidly, and the Buddhist monasteries would have played a central part in this process. The fact that the *vaṃśa* literature was by and large a product of the *sangha* explains their religious bias. The historical tradition that embodied the *Sinhaladvīpa* and *Dhammadvīpa* concepts was kept alive by successive writers, usually *bhikkhus,* until the end of the Sinhalese kingdom.

The *Mahāvaṃśa* was the *vaṃśa* par excellence, and a striking feature of the literary tradition of the Sinhalese is the way which this chronicle was updated from time to time, thus maintaining a continuous historical narration until late eighteenth century. The first part of the *Mahāvaṃśa,* written by *bhikkhu* Mahanama, ended with the reign of Mahasen (274–301). It was continued from that date until the reign of Parakramabahu I (1153–86) by a contemporary, *bhikkhu* Dharmakirti. About two

52. Malalgoda 1970:431.

53. Kiribamune 1978:125.

54. Adikaram 1953:87; Kiribamune 1978:129–30.

centuries later an unknown writer brought the chronicle up to date, narrating events to the end of the reign of Parakramabahu IV (ca. 1325). Finally, during the reign of Kirti Sri Rajasinghe (1747–82) *bhikkhu* Tibbotuvave Buddharakshita updated the chronicle for the last time during Sinhalese monarchy.[55]

The resurgence of the Sinhalese-Buddhist ideology during the last decades of the Kandyan kingdom had as its backdrop the cultural revival that took place during the mid eighteenth century.[56] The preceding period – the sixteenth and seventeenth centuries – was characterized by a low ebb in learning and literary activity and is considered a "dark age" in Sinhalese scholarship. A decline had set in after a period of political stability, economic prosperity, and cultural activity during the reign of Parakramabahu VI (1411–66). Conditions worsened with the political unrest following the advent of the Portuguese in 1505. The *sāsana* declined and with it the system of scholarship.

A revival in these spheres came in the eighteenth century after a long and sustained effort by Saranankara and a small group of associates such as Tibbotuvave. Saranankara and Tibbotuvave would have been quite conversant with the historical tradition of the community. They themselves revived the *Pūjāvaliya* tradition of edificatory works in writing *Śrī Saddharma Sārārtha Sangrahaya*[57] and *Śrī Saddharmāvavāda Sangrahaya*.[58] Tibbotuvave would have been singularly alive to the tradition as the scholar who updated the *Mahāvaṃśa*. Saranankara, apart from being mentor to the group of revivalists, was for his part the author of nine books reviving old genres, and one of them was a Sinhala paraphrase of the Pali *Mahā Bōdhi Vaṃśaya*[59] (the Chronicle of the Bodhi Tree). Considering the revivalist zeal of these *bhikkhus*, their complicity in the conspiracy of 1760 appears as no surprise. Coming to the last days of the Kandyan kingdom, we are reminded of the fact that Väligala Kavisundara, the author of *Vaḍiga Haṭana*, which contained very strong anti-Nayakkar feelings, was a pupil of Tibbotuvave.[60]

---

55. In treating the *Mahāvaṃsa* as a continuous chronicle, updated from time to time, I am following Rahula (1966:xxii n. 1), thereby not identifying a separate chronicle called the *Cūlavaṃsa*, as done by W. Geiger, who translated all parts of the chronicle into English (see Geiger 1950: Intro.). I believe Rahula's view is the more accurate of the two, reflecting as it does the traditional attitude of the ancient chroniclers.

56. For details, see Vacissara 1964: chaps. 17, 19; Devaraja 1972: chap. 6.

57. By Saranankara. See Godakumbura 1955:66–69; Sannasgala 1961:396–98.

58. By Tibbotuvave. See Godakumbura 1955:69–71; Sannasgala 1961:420–21.

59. Vacissara 1964:242–43.

60. Sannasgala 1961:530.

The historical tradition maintained by the scholars and based on the *vihāra* had received considerable symbolic elaboration during a long period of literary history. Thus, at least among the ranks of the literati the Sinhalese ethnic consciousness was no longer "the primordial and unconscious ethnicity" usually found in nonliterate societies.[61] It was a "proto-nationalism" with a long-standing historical consciousness.[62]

61. As pointed out by Fishman (1973), "unconscious and primordial ethnicity" has to be transformed into "conscious nationalism" by conceptual elaboration.

62. K. M. de Silva (1973e) suggests this term, while Roberts (1979) calls it "traditional patriotism-cum-nationalism."

Chapter 2

The Triumph of English and the Emergence of Sinhala Language Loyalty

> Numbers among the Sinhalese proficient in Greek or Latin, and English, are unable to read a common Sinhalese manuscript . . . or read the Bible in their mother tongue.
>
> —James D'Alwis, *Memoirs*

The Kandyans were hopeful that the Sinhalese traditions governing the relationship between the state and religion would be maintained by the British, as had been solemnly agreed to by the latter in 1815. But this was not to be. Under a government manned by administrators, who believed in the superiority of their own culture and the need to bring the light of "civilization" to the "natives" whom they governed, the traditional system was soon being undermined probably by neglect more than design. The Kandyans realized very soon that a legal guarantee by the British was no substitute for a Kandyan rule if the age-old system was to be perpetuated. The rebellion that broke out two years after they ceded their kingdom to the British was the result of this realization.[1] This attempt to restore the status quo ante was, however, ruthlessly put down, and the opportunity was taken to reduce the powers of the Sinhalese chiefs drastically and to change "slightly" the guarantees on Buddhism. Nevertheless, the British were cautioned by political expediency not to adopt any overt policy of undermining the traditional religious and educational systems.[2] What happened in practice, however, as the years passed, contributed to such an effect.

1. For details, see P. E. Pieris 1950.
2. K. M. de Silva 1965:65.

The Progress of English Education

The British expected to gain the support of groups and individuals in Sinhalese society who, naturally enough, considered it in their interest to collaborate with the new rulers. As Frederick North, the first British governor on the island (1798–1805) put it, it was opportune to create a class of people "connected with England by education."[3] This practical need was augmented by the "British conscience," which sought to improve the condition of the natives in the colonies. Thus, a British missionary, Robert Percival, in his *Account of the Island of Ceylon* in 1803, "hoped that more attention will be paid to their cultivation and improvement by our countrymen than their former masters, the Dutch and the Portuguese."[4]

In this policy of creating a class of natives connected with England by education the Anglican missionaries who accompanied the empire builders became willing accomplices. Thus, James Cordiner, the first resident Anglican padre, was appointed the principal of schools, and, more specifically, the seminary at Wolfendal, the principal educational institution in the territories captured from the Dutch, was placed under his direct charge. The education envisaged there was in essence a Christian one. Percival's observation in this regard may be taken to reflect the general attitude of the rulers:

> A zealous effort on the part of our government to introduce our learning and religion among the natives is the surest means of improving and consolidating our empire in the island.[5]

Thus, some native youth belonging to elite families were given a preliminary English education in the island and sent thereafter to England for higher education and to be trained as clergymen. They were to return as parish priests to be in charge of the religious and educational activities of the provinces.[6] This arrangement was to lead to a complete control of the new educational system by the Christian clergy.

The government, having neither a separate secular policy with re-

3. Quoted in Jayaweera 1971.
4. Percival 1972:220.
5. Percival 1972:227–28.
6. R. Pieris 1964:435.

gard to education nor an administrative machinery for an educational system, was content to leave educational affairs to the enterprise of the missionaries.[7] In addition to the Anglican establishment, which from the time of Cordiner had been placed in charge of the schools inherited from the Dutch, several other missionary organizations began their activities on the island during the early nineteenth century—the London Mission Society in 1804, the Baptist Mission in 1812, the Wesleyan Methodist Mission in 1814, the American Mission in 1816, and the Church Missionary Society in 1818. Education figured prominently in the missionary endeavor. In the new schools, as distinct from the traditional Buddhist seats of learning, Christian control was most marked. They were considered as "little seminaries of Sion . . . where we teach them to pray as we teach them to read."[8]

The missionaries—most of whom were Protestants—seem to have believed that the best method of conversion was by imparting the divine message in the vernacular. Nevertheless, there was at the same time recognition of the need to disseminate the English language, both as a medium of administration as well as the fountainhead of Western civilization. As Governor Sir Edward Barnes put it: "Instruction in the English language should be promoted and encouraged as much as possible, when the people would be enabled to come more directly at the evidence of Christianity."[9] Thus, as a via media as it were, most of the early schools in the new educational system were bilingual. Some private schools did provide an education solely in the English medium, but the students there were few in number and were from privileged strata of society. The traditional Sinhalese institutions of learning in the Buddhist monasteries were outside the new educational system and kept dwindling in number, due to lack of patronage and support.[10]

Until 1832 educational activity under British rule was on the whole a continuation of the system that prevailed under the Portuguese and the Dutch. As in contemporary Britain, there was no clear-cut state policy with regard to education in the colonies, and it was left largely to the initiative of the missionaries.[11] Subsequently, a definite govern-

7. K. M. de Silva 1973c:66.

8. Robert Newstead, a missionary, writing in 1818. Quoted in Gooneratne 1968:6.

9. Gooneratne 1968:6.

10. Ames 1967:19.

11. See Das Gupta 1970:41.

ment policy emerged from the recommendations of the Colebrooke-Cameron Commission.[12] Most of their proposals on education were adopted and implemented. Cameron himself argued that

> the peculiar circumstances of Ceylon both physical and moral seem to point it out to the British government as the fittest spot in our Eastern Dominions in which to plant the seeds of European civilization whence we may not unreasonably hope that it will hereafter spread over the whole of those vast territories. (152)

In coming to this conclusion the commissioners were no doubt influenced by the progress so far made by Christianity and the English language. They viewed with approbation "the disposition already evinced by the natives to cultivate European attainments" (71). Furthermore, they thought of the advantages of having "a competent class of candidates for general employment in the public service who would . . . be capable of holding responsible situations upon reduced salaries" (215). We have seen that similar sentiments had been expressed earlier by individual administrators such as North and others such as Percival. Until 1832, however, these views were not formulated coherently enough to serve as sure guidelines of governmental policy.

The most prominent theme in the commission's recommendations regarding education was the emphasis on English as the medium of instruction. The education provided by "the native priesthood in their temples and colleges" was unhesitatingly dismissed as one that "scarcely merits any notice" (73). They regretted that "the English missionaries have not generally appreciated the importance of diffusing a knowledge of the English language through the medium of their schools," and, not surprisingly, it was with great satisfaction that they viewed the activities of the American missionaries in the north of the island, who were

> fully impressed with the importance of rendering the English language the general medium of instruction and the inestimable value of this acquirement in itself to the people. (73)

12. This was the Commission of Eastern Inquiry, whose members were W. M. G. Colbrooke and C. H. Cameron. See Mendis 1956. The following quotations are from this report.

Recommending that government employment be made open to natives "who would qualify themselves for holding some of the higher appointments," the commissioners set about delineating ways and means by which the natives would be given "opportunities of instruction." The English language was to be diffused as widely as possible, and government educational policy was to be concentrated on it. Competence in English was made a condition of employment of teachers in government schools. In order to better utilize scarce resources the missionaries were to be allowed a monopoly in educational activity in areas where they already had English schools. This was to be done by closing down the government schools in those areas. As a goal and a model, as it were, a higher educational institution teaching in English was to be established in Colombo, in charge of a professor recruited from England. The practice of sending students to England for education was to be abandoned, and local facilities were to be improved. Furthermore, to underline governmental responsibility with regard to education, a Schools Commission was to be set up which could decide on policies and see that they were implemented.

Endorsing the Colebrooke-Cameron Commission's recommendations, the secretary of state for the colonies wrote in 1833 to the governor in Colombo:

> The dissemination of the English language is an object which I cannot but esteem of the greatest importance, as a medium of instruction and as a bond of union with this country.[13]

Following upon the adoption of the recommendations of this commission, the educational policy of the government came to be concentrated on opening and maintaining English schools. Eleven English elementary schools were opened in 1835, and in 1837 they were increased to thirty-five. Directions given to the Schools Commission (created in 1834) refer time and again to the need for promoting English education. There were, indeed, instances when appeals for the opening of vernacular schools were refused. Thus, by 1839 only five government vernacular schools remained.[14] Although a powerful section of the Christian clergy, who had come to dominate the Schools Commission

13. Quoted in Jayaweera 1971:156.

14. Jayaweera 1971:156.

from its inception, believed in education in the vernacular as a prelude to education in English,[15] the Colonial Office emphatically stated that:

> It would be unnecessary for the government to direct its attention to devote funds available for education to instruction in the native languages . . . the preferable plan would be to encourage an acquirement of the English language by conveying instruction in that language to the scholars, both male and female, in all schools conducted by the government.[16]

In addition to the provincial English schools the government set up three "superior" English schools, one in Colombo and the others in the major towns of Kandy and Galle. The model institution for English education envisaged by the Colebrooke Report was established in Colombo in 1836.[17] These superior institutions were joined later by several missionary schools.[18] All these had as their objective the creation of a class of natives proficient in the English language who had also imbibed Western culture. The acquisition of English was encouraged as "a means of civilization."[19] Apparently, Christian faith was considered a major ingredient of this "civilization"—the prime requirement for upward social mobility. Thus, the disposition among the natives, observed earlier by Colebrooke, "to cultivate European attainments," became stronger after 1832. As Governor Sir Colin Campbell reported to the Colonial Office in the mid-1840s:

> Every day the natives of all classes are assimilating more and more European habits and views, and in some cases becoming more qualified to mix in society with Europeans.[20]

---

15. The most prominent figure in this respect was Rev. D. J. Gogerly, who received the active support of Governor Stewert Mackenzie (1837–41). See K. M. de Silva 1965.

16. Quoted in Jayaweera 1971:157.

17. This was the Colombo Academy, at first a private institution under Rev. J. Marsh. The government took it over, and in 1881 it was renamed Royal College. It became one of the most elitist schools in the island, a position maintained up to this day.

18. Thus, St. Thomas' College, Colombo (1851), and the Trinity College, Kandy (1872), by the Anglicans; Jaffna Central College (1870) and Wesley College, Colombo (1874), by the Methodists; St. John's College, Panadura (1891), by the Church Missionary Society; and St. Joseph College, Colombo (1891), by the Catholics, to cite a few.

19. Governor Sir Stewert Mackenzie. Quoted in K. M. de Silva 1965:153.

20. Quoted in R. Pieris 1964:483.

The commanding position of English in this milieu stemmed from its use as the language of administration and the courts of law. Thus, one Englishman observed in 1857 that the minor branches of the civil service were staffed by fluent speakers of English and that the courts of law were filled with "proctors and pleaders who would bear . . . comparison with the Bar of England."[21] Also there emerged in the 1830s a local English press that, although originally established by Englishmen, was soon attracting Sri Lankans in large numbers. Furthermore, English seems to have been favored as the language of the church by the new native elite.[22]

Concomitant with these advances of the English language and other features of European culture, the vernacular language and other fields of "Oriental" study came to be neglected. Thus, as early as 1837, George Turnour, who translated the Pali historical chronicle the *Mahāvaṃśa,* into English, commented regretfully that the Sinhalese upper class was rapidly losing touch with its language and culture:

> Their education, as regards the acquisition of their native language, was formerly seldom persevered in beyond the attainment of a grammatical knowledge of Singhalese: – the ancient history of their country and the mysteries of the religion of their ancestors, rarely engaged their serious attention. Their principal study was the English language pursued in order that they might qualify themselves for those official appointments, which were the objects of their ambition.[23]

The neglect of the vernacular languages was such that the Rev. D. J. Gogerley, a Wesleyan missionary, had to provide an English translation of an anti-Buddhist pamphlet, which he originally wrote in Sinhalese in 1849, for

> knowing that the majority of the young Singhalese who study Occidental literatures systematically neglect their own language, I fear the Singhalese edition will not be easily understood by them.[24]

21. George Barrow, in 1857. Quoted in Gooneratne 1968:17.
22. Gooneratne 1968:9ff.
23. Turnour, 1837:v.
24. Quoted in Gooneratne 1968:16.

This was so because, as two contemporary observers noted, "their mother tongue has been despised by those who have acquired a smattering of English."[25] There was little or no encouragement for the study of the vernacular in the schools. "Sinhalese composition," observed those writers, "has greatly been neglected hitherto in educational institutions in Ceylon."[26] Even many vernacular schools began introducing English into the curriculum and became "Anglo-vernacular" schools.[27] The curriculum arrangement in the different types of schools, the prestige factor, and, above all, the pragmatic value as far as socioeconomic advancement was concerned all tended to encourage the study of English and hence to downgrade vernacular education. The result was a situation where "many who have made some progress in English [were] unable to write their own language."[28]

The Position of the Vernacular

We have seen how, during the days of the independent kingdom of the Sinhalese, the cultivation of the arts, including literary and scholarly activity, had been sustained by the patronage of the royalty, ministers, and other powerful personalities in the realm. We have also seen how the *sangha* were, so to speak, the custodians of learning and literary activity. Thus, the well-being of the Buddhist dispensation was another vital prerequisite for the continuity of these arts.

Those preconditions inevitably ceased to exist during the early part of the nineteenth century. Indeed, the situation under British rule created conditions that were adverse to the continuance of the traditional institutions and the culture that was sustained by them.

The primary source of patronage on which the Buddhist dispensation and the literary and other arts depended was removed with the end of Sinhalese kingship. The situation was aggravated with the curtailment of the power and wealth of the Kandyan aristocracy after the rebellion of 1818. Furthermore, with the passing of the old order, the *sangha* lost its preeminent status in society. British administrators often expressed unconcealed disdain of Buddhism and proceeded to pro-

25. Murdoch and Nicholson 1868:v.
26. Murdoch and Nicholson 1868:49.
27. Wickramaratne 1973:177.
28. Murdoch and Nicholson 1868:49.

mote the interests of their own faith.[29] Also the educational and administrative policies of the government, where the English language was placed in a preeminent position, contributed in effect to the neglect of the vernacular languages. Finally, the social prestige attached to the adoption of "European attainments," including Christianity, seems to have made the traditional cultural pursuits and activities of little value and importance.

The tradition of literary and scholarly activity, which had undergone a revival in the mid eighteenth century, was sustained by its momentum during the early nineteenth century.[30] The *bhikkhus,* in spite of heavy odds against them, continued with their scholarly and literary pursuits and played the role of educators in their *pansala* schools. Thus, John Davy, an Englishman who toured the Kandyan provinces immediately after their cession in 1815, noted that:

> Reading and writing are far from uncommon acquirements and are about as general as in England amongst the male part of the population to whom they are generally confined.[31]

Again the archdeacon of Colombo, replying to a questionnaire sent by Colebrooke in 1829, stated that, "Heathens are taught to read and write Singhalese much better by the Buddhist priests."[32] British records indicate that in 1828 there existed ninety-four *pansala* schools in the island.[33]

The revival in learning and literary activity initiated in Kandy in the mid eighteenth century spread to the coastal areas, particularly the south, then under the control of the Dutch and later the British. Although the momentum of the movement subsided somewhat in Kandy during the last stages of its kingship, the scholars of the south continued to follow their vacation with diligence, as attested to in the works of Pattayame Lekama (the poems *Kav Mini Koňḍola, Viyōvaga*

29. Although the British, unlike the Portuguese and the Dutch before them, had no "state policy" for the promotion of Christianity, the activities of many an official in his personal capacity contributed much to the same effect in the early nineteenth century. See K. M. de Silva 1965:24ff.

30. Hewawasam 1968.

31. Davy 1969:76.

32. Quoted in Sumatipala 1968:9.

33. Ames 1967: table 1.

Ratna Mālaya, and *Ratavatī Katāva*); Katuwane Dissanayaka (the poems *Kav Mini Maldama* and *Makaradhvajaya*); *bhikkhu* Saliele Maniratana (the poems *Kav Mutu Hara, Prātihārya Satakaya,* and *Amārasaya*); *bhikkhu* Kirama Dhammananda (the poems *Siyabas Maldama, Kānchana Dēvi Katāva, Nandiya Velaňda Vata,* and *Vibat Maldama); bhikkhu* Karatota Dhammarama (author of the poem *Bārasa Kāvyaya* and consulted by the philologist Rasmusk Rask in his visit to the island in 1821); *bhikkhu* Miripenne Dhammaratana (author of a large number of short poems such as "Ava Duk," "Lansimeta," and "Surapanaya";[34] and Thomis Muhandiram (the poem *Gangārōhana Varnanāva*). The maintenance of a high standard of scholarship in Pali and Buddhist scriptures by the *bhikkhus* is also demonstrated by the several debates among them in the mid nineteenth century about the authenticity of some ecclesiastical procedures.[35]

This vigorous literary and scholarly activity was made possible largely because of the patronage extended by several aristocratic families in the south. Many among them had received education under the traditional system and were themselves scholars of considerable merit, including Maha Mudaliyar Don David Jayatilaka Abeysiriwardene Ilangakkon, who was the patron of Pattayame,[36] and Abayaratne Ekanayake Muhandiram, who patronized Saliele.[37] There were others such as Mudaliyar David De Saram,[38] Mudaliyar Don Abraham De Saram,[39] and Thomis Samarasekara Dissanayaka Muhandiram,[40] who themselves were accomplished scholars.

It needs to be mentioned, however, that this scholarly activity was confined to a small elite. The poets and men of letters mentioned above wrote and discussed literature and related subjects within a small circle of learned men.[41] Sadly, it was a group whose numbers were declining rapidly and whose literary activity was, for all its creativity, becoming ossified by a pedantic adherence to traditional literary norms. This elite

34. See Hewawasam 1968:433–49.

35. See chapter 4.

36. Hewawasam 1968:53.

37. Hewawasam 1968:166.

38. Author of the poem *Mahā Kanha Jātakaya.*

39. Author of several short Sinhala poems. See D'Alwis 1852:247.

40. Author of the poem *Gangārōhana Varnanāva.*

41. For example, *Gangārōhana Varnanāva* was sent to a learned *mudaliyar* in Galle and by him to *bhikkhu* Mihiripenne for comment. See Hewawasam 1968:314–16, 111, 115.

was dwindling also because the enlightened aristocracy, which was, in the generation mentioned above, the product of the old educational system, was soon to undergo a drastic change in its cultural orientations.

Intent on creating a loyal class of English educated natives, the British found a natural and convenient source in the low-country aristocracy. Frederick North, the first British governor, indicated his interest in creating a loyalist element "connected with England by education" from among the "respectable individuals" of "the principal native families in the country,"[42] a line of policy that his immediate successors continued. That missionary educational policy fitted in neatly with this requirement is evident in the instructions of the Anglican bishop of Calcutta to his subordinates in Sri Lanka that students in the mission schools were to be drawn "from among the best families in the island."[43] Indeed, the expectations of the rulers found a positive response from among sections of the aristocracy. Because of their long-standing contact with foreigners, the aristocratic families in the coastal areas were particularly amenable to the new situation. No doubt, they hardly needed to be reminded of the advantages of doing so. Few among the native population were better equipped than those groups to take advantage of the educational opportunities provided. Thus, it was observed that the children of the native headmen—especially the *mudaliyars*—comprised the largest group, other than the Burghers, in the English schools of the day.[44] Their children not only learned the English language but were also encouraged to emulate the life-style of their colonial masters. Thus, their "English education comprehended all that relates to social life," and many of these students were boarded with English families for this purpose.[45] As early as 1830, a missionary writer rejoiced to see an "enlightened" generation of *mudaliyars* growing up. "The education they have got and are getting," he observed, "is of that kind, that whatever may be cast into it, there is little fear of *Buddhism* ever being allowed to take root in it."[46]

The process of acculturation proceeded steadily from the early nineteenth century. Soon a new generation of low-country aristocracy

42. Jayaweera 1971:153.
43. A dispatch of 1819. Quoted in Gooneratne 1968:15.
44. Wickramaratne 1973:179.
45. A missionary dispatch of 1830. From Wickramaratne 1973:179.
46. Letter of a missionary, 1830. From Gooneratne 1968:10.

emerged, having imbibed "European attainments" and with little or no concern for the indigenous culture. In this way the last source of traditional sustenance of vernacular literary and scholarly pursuits dried up.

Here was a situation, as observed by one of the more sensitive and discerning natives, in which the Sinhala language was considered, by the average English-educated native, as "a necessary evil for the purpose of maintaining intercourse with his countrymen."[47] This observer was James D'Alwis (1823–78), himself a product of the new educational system. He noticed that this unfortunate tendency grew stronger as time passed—"each generation following the *habits* and feelings of that which preceded it" and growing "more and more neglectful" of Sinhalese. A powerful factor was reinforcing the propensity:

> these habits and feelings in respect to their own language acquiring greater strength in their course, from the increased facilities afforded to them by the government in the study of the English.[48]

This educational system, it appeared to him, was so designed as to engineer a language shift. "It is generally understood," he said, "that with a view to make English the sole language of the natives, the course of education now imparted to them is exclusively English." Such a plan, he wanted to point out, "is productive of far greater injury than real good."[49]

James D'Alwis was himself the scion of an aristocratic family,[50] a Christian, and he had received the best English education available in the island. But a deep impression created in him by a realization of his own inadequacy as an heir to a rich cultural tradition led him to express feelings to strong language loyalty. He had been oblivious to the attractions and values of that tradition because of an education "replete with more mischief than benefit."[51] Most of the rulers, the European expatri-

47. D'Alwis, Introduction to the translation of *Sidat Sangarava* 1852:CCXLIX. Hereafter this work will be referred to as *SS*.

48. *SS*:CCXLIX.

49. *SS*:CCL.

50. James's father was *mudaliyar* Don Abraham D'Alwis (d.1838), who stood sixth in the rank among the native headmen in the British administration. His father's brother Andiris was "Mudaliyar of the Governor's Gate" and chief interpreter of the Supreme Court. Both Abraham and Andiris had received English adduction under the missionaries. For details, see D'Alwis, 1939:14–15. Hereafter this work will be referred to as *Memoirs*.

51. *SS*:CCXLIX.

ates, treated that tradition with indifference, if not disparagement. Hence he was convinced of the need to "make a struggle for our language."[52]

The Making of a Language Loyalist

Members of James D'Alwis's family were already in the service of the British government and were Christian by religion. Needless to say, children of the family were given an English education.[53] Sinhala, however, was not entirely neglected, especially by the female members of the family. Thus, D'Alwis received his first lessons in Sinhala from his mother and "occasionally" from an ex-*bhikkhu*. Yet this Sinhala education did not go beyond the primary stage.[54] Thereafter the study of Sinhala was abandoned altogether, and D'Alwis concentrated on English until his graduation from the high school in the Colombo Academy.

D'Alwis thereafter secured the position of an interpreter at the district court in Colombo. His first attempt to perform his duty ended in a dismal failure, and this incident was to dramatically alter his outlook and open up a completely new area of interest in his career:

> I rose on my legs to convey to a party what the judge had to say. I could scarcely utter three words before I felt my inability to proceed. Mr. Dias prompted me, but the help thus proffered only added to my wild confusion. My tongue was tied, my head was in a whirl, and I sat down amidst the laughter of that class of men who generally take a pleasure in the failings of their fellow creatures.[55]

D'Alwis would have taken up the job of an interpreter with the complacency of one who took it for granted that he "knew" Sinhala, although he had not studied it as an academic subject. But he was shocked into the realization that he was wrong. He had to admit to him-

52. *SS*:CCLXI.

53. D'Alwis mentions several English schools he attended: the private tutory of George Dupy; the Colombo Government Seminary; the academy opposite the Kacceri; Mr. Van Twest's school in Pettah; the school of F. de Livera, the late district judge of Colombo; the school of S. W. Dias, the Sinhalese colonial chaplain; and the public Seminary of Rev. Joseph Marsh (*Memoirs*:20–21).

54. Not beyond *Vyāsakāra* (*Memoirs*:16), a Sanskrit text usually read in the second or third standards in Sinhala schools of the day.

55. *Memoirs*:65.

self that he "was utterly ignorant of legal terms" and, furthermore, "not sufficiently acquainted with Sinhalese so as to convey by it, even that with which [he] had some acquaintance." Like many others who had gone into English education, his

> book learning in Sinhalese . . . was such that . . . [it] had not extended beyond *Vyasakara,* and it . . . was a fact . . . [that he] could not translate three lines of the easiest book from English into Sinhalese.[56]

Personally, it was a critical moment in his life. "My failure was for my good," he later stated, "for I became sensible of my deficiencies." He resolved hence "to abandon all ideas, at least for a time, of becoming an interpreter, and devote my earnest attention to the study of the Singhalese language."[57]

The incident in the court may be categorized as one where the bilingual D'Alwis was made to feel "chagrin or regret for losing ties with his native group."[58] The English-educated class to which he belonged had been quite complacent with their lot. "Placed under the mild and benignant sway of England," they had "found the desirability, if not the necessity, of acquiring English."[59] The loss of contact with indigenous traditions had not at all been a matter of concern. Indeed, if, due to the force of circumstances, any contact with the tradition became necessary, it was considered "a necessary evil."[60] But D'Alwis, dramatically brought to the realization of the gravity of losing his cultural patrimony, proceeded eagerly to renew ties with his cultural inheritance. His marginality vis-à-vis the mainstream of the Sinhalese-Buddhist culture, of which he was made more and more aware as his study of Sinhala classics proceeded, activated a search for personal identity, thus intensifying his commitment to the traditions of his community.[61] Like many a

56. *Memoirs*:65.

57. *Memoirs*:65.

58. For this problem faced by bilinguals, see Lambert 1967:101.

59. *SS*:CCXLVII.

60. *SS*:CCXLIX.

61. As Fishman (1972c:17) has pointed out, the early nationalist leaders in many communities "stemmed from other backgrounds than the people whom they sought to organize. Others had long lived or been educated abroad, or in exile, and were marginally ethnic in their personal lives," and "part of the emotional and intellectual intensity of their work is interpretable as a search for personal identity and for a usable personal past."

nationalist in similar circumstances, he proceeded to forge "sentimental and behavioral links" with the traditions of his community.[62]

In this enterprise, however, D'Alwis was very much a lone figure among the English-educated Sinhalese in mid-nineteenth-century Sri Lanka. Perhaps the other English-educated Sinhalese were the more "realistic" found in such situations, seeking to better their lot by associating with the dominant group, in this case the British masters. The sight of these "betrayals" would have caused a resentment within D'Alwis. He noted that "even the most favoured of the natives devote but little attention to the study of their own language."[63] He was a more "steadfast" member of the Sinhalese community, the one being dominated, the one whose language, among other things, was threatened with extinction—a profound sense of loss which stimulated a feeling of intense language loyalty.[64]

It is evident that there was another factor at work in this process, a sense of grievance against the British rulers which spurred him to take a nationalist stance. English education had opened up government employment and other white-collar careers for the natives, and, in addition, they had been eagerly acquiring "European attainments." But however far they went and however much they succeeded in these spheres, they were not accepted as equals by their rulers. British exclusivism, which had been apparent from the beginning of their sojourn in the island,[65] had not changed, notwithstanding the utilitarian principles enunciated by the Colebrooke commissioners in 1832.

Governor Campbell reported to London in 1844 that:

> every day the natives of all classes are assmilating more and more European habits and views, and in some cases becoming more qualified to mix in society with Europeans—but at present an almost impassable barrier is drawn which cuts off a clerk from promotion to any high office.[66]

62. For similar situations elsewhere, see Fishman 1972c:44.

63. *SS*:CCLIX.

64. Cf. Weinreich's generalization that "the sight of such betrayals invariably causes resentment among the more steadfast members of the dominated group, a resentment which brings with it unswerving language loyalty" (1964:101).

65. Thus, Percival observed in 1803: "From the naturally distant and haughty temper of our countrymen and their unacquaintance with the native language, they never dream of associating with Cingalese or receiving them into their parties" (1972:220).

66. Quoted in R. Pieris 1964:440.

This impassable barrier, as far as government employment was concerned, was to continue for a long time to come.[67] Closely connected with the barrier in job opportunities was a social barrier, which was perhaps most painful for the English educated natives. D'Alwis notes in his *Memoirs:*

> Those who live in Ceylon need not be told of the great antipathy, not to say hate which the *white* man has to the black. That the former, especially the Saxon race, when brought in contact with the latter, in the colonies has ever been found to "establish certain social barriers between himself and his dark skinned brothers" is a truism which none will attempt to gainsay. The Englishman is the greatest caste-proud man out of England. The cant of Exeter Hall—"we are brethren"—has no influence out of England.[68]

English education, among other things, had opened up new vistas of political and social thinking for the natives. Expectations, however, ended in frustration when it came to relationships with the governing race, who, ironically enough, had been instrumental in creating those expectations in the native mind.[69] In spite of all his achievements in education, wealth, or the acquirement of European attainments, a native had to face symbolic slights at the hands of Englishmen. As for D'Alwis, such slights would have appeared all the more painful when seen in the light of the history of the Sinhalese nation. Was it not a fact that the Sinhalese themselves were a cultured people with a long-standing civilization? D'Alwis's study of the history of his people made a deep impression on him concerning the greatness of its achievements. Almost certainly, the slights encountered in the present magnified the glories of the past as much as the impressions of past greatness made the present all the more painful. This was indeed a situation that contributed to the upsurge of "cultural nationalism."[70]

---

67. See Warnapala 1971:62.

68. *Memoirs:*12.

69. Cf. the idea that colonialism "produces the intellectuals and yet, by its very existence, it frustrates them and hence arouses their opposition" (Kautsky 1962).

70. Cf. the statement that "cultural nationalism appears in its purest form when people are subjected to a foreign rule. In this even 'national thought' prefers to busy itself with the culture building activities of the people and tries to keep the national consciousness alive by recollections of vanished glory and past greatness which has already become legend and a slavish present makes the people doubly sensitive to the injustices suffered" (Rocker 1937:213).

Once the rich cultural heritage he was heir to—and which had existed unknown to him because of the formal and informal education he had received—was revealed to him with dramatic suddenness and to his great embarrassment, D'Alwis perhaps became doubly sensitive to the injustices suffered by his community. As far as the mid nineteenth century was concerned, his community was in the throes of a rapid and volatile social transformation. No doubt, D'Alwis, perceptive observer as he was, felt the impact of this cultural crisis more acutely than many of his contemporaries.

The early decades of the nineteenth century witnessed a drastic transformation of the island's economic and social structure along with the great political and educational changes. The processes of modernization were set afoot not only in the maritime regions but also in the Kandyan areas where European influences had so far not penetrated. "Cash crops," primarily coffee at the early stages (to be joined later in the century by tea and rubber), came to be introduced as major factors in the economy.[71] Roads were being constructed for military as well as commercial purposes, so that by 1831 a good part of the island was accessible from Colombo by road. British capital flowed into the Kandyan areas, where coffee plantations were being opened up in the late 1830s and early 1840s at a speed that invited the epithet "coffee-mania" (coined by historian Sir James Emerson Tennent). Enterprising men from the maritime regions rushed in to exploit the opportunities available in the territories being "developed." Facets of modernization appeared in the interior with the blessings and the problems of the new civilization.[72]

Thus, the modernization of nineteenth-century Sri Lanka was taking place under historically unfavorable conditions for a large segment of the population, particularly the Kandyan peasantry. For political disturbances such as the conspiracies and the attempts at rebellion in 1820, 1823, 1834, and 1842,[73] the dislocation of the traditional religion due to the severance of the government's connection with Buddhism,[74] and

71. Roberts and Wickramaratne 1973:92ff.

72. Major Thomas Skinner, who had served in the island for nearly fifty years in the early nineteenth century, stated that the influx of money and other aspects of the new civilization brought about "temptations to and examples of intemperance and vice of every kind . . . the most profligate of low-country Singhalese flocked from the maritime provinces into the interior and spread far and wide their contaminating influences over a previously sober, orderly, honest race" (1974:136–37).

73. Mills 1933:165–66.

74. K. M. de Silva 1965:chap. 2, chap. 3.

the erosion of traditional authority networks[75] occurred simultaneously with the economic transformation.

The old order was in the process of disintegration, while a new one had not yet fully crystallized in its place, a classic situation of anomie.[76] Contemporary observers noted that there was a growth in intemperance, crime, and lawlessness.[77] With these negative conditions lurking in the background, the attempt by the government to impose some new taxes precipitated a series of riots in 1848.[78]

It was a time in which the old political, social, and economic institutions were being replaced or were in the process of disintegration; at the same time the traditional culture, which had been sustained by them, was in decline. The Buddhist institutions of learning were bereft of patronage, and traditional scholarship was on the wane. In the new educational system, where the Christian missions had so much influence, a central feature, the English language, was making great headway. Governmental policy was as biased toward Evangelicalism and the promotion of English education as it was also overtly hostile to the interests of Buddhism and the cultivation of Sinhala and other Oriental studies. In this way traditional Sinhalese culture, which had been a viable concern only a few decades previously, now appeared to be inevitably doomed.

Reactions to these developments came in the form of nativistic ideologies. At the level of the unsophisticated masses there was magical nativism in the form of millennialistic aspirations in which was manifest the hope that the old order would dramatically return triumphant.[79] On the other hand, there was a rational nativism among the more sophisticated sections of the people. Thus, during the latter half of the nineteenth century the *bhikkhus* were to launch a counteroffensive against Christian expansionism.[80] But to D'Alwis, a native who

75. See R. Pieris 1951–52.

76. Gunasinghe 1972:94–95.

77. Skinner observed, "I have known districts of the population which, some years ago, not one in a hundred could be induced to taste spirits, where drunkenness now prevails to such an extent that villagers have been known to pawn their crops upon the ground to tavern keepers for arrack. . . . Robberies and blood-shed became familiar to the Kandyan, in districts where a few years before any amount of property would have been perfectly safe in the open air" (1974:137).

78. This was the last attempt to overthrow the British power in the island by violence. For details, see K. M. de Silva 1965.

79. Malalgoda 1970.

80. See chapter 4.

had acquired European attainments and thus belonged to a new and special stratum of the native population, the Sinhala language appeared to be a particular element of traditional culture which deserved his absolute commitment. He adopted it as a cause and proceeded to "make a struggle" for its preservation.[81]

81. Cf. the statement: "What really happens in all nativistic movements is that certain current or remembered elements of culture are selected for emphasis and given symbolic value" (Linton 1943).

Chapter 3

The Sinhala Language as a Nationalist Cause

> It is utterly impossible to uproot and exterminate the Sinhalese as a language. It may be neglected, its classical authors destroyed, and its books lost; but the language itself will continue in some shape or the other.
>
> —James D'Alwis, Introduction to the *Sidat Saṅgarāva,* 1852

When one looks at the continuity of the Sinhalese group identity down through the ages it becomes evident that language has never been emphasized as a group-defining criterion.[1] This appears to be the case with any primordial group sentiment before it is transformed into self-conscious modern nationalism. But as we saw in chapter 1, the Sinhalese identity had received symbolic elaboration in certain aspects during historical times. With regard to language, no doubt it would have been a major boundary-defining device for the Sinhala people throughout their history, particularly in marking off the principal alien and antagonist—the south Indian invader.[2] Yet in the expression of the Sinhalese identity through time and change the most prominent ingredient has been the Buddhist religion.[3] Indeed, the major thrust of

1. Whatever references there are to language take the route from ethnicity to language and not vice versa. See, for example, the citation from the *Dhampiā Aṭuvā Gāṭapadaya* given in chapter 1 and the following passage from the twelfth-century exegetical work *Dharmapradīpikāva:* "At the place where mention is made of the Sinhala language, what can 'Sinhala language' mean? As it is said: 'Since king Sinhabahu took the Sinha (lion) captive, he was (called) Sinhala, and his descendants were (thence also called) Sinhala; so (therefore) the name Sinhala is derived from the circumstance of the lion being taken by Sinhabahu . . . " (*SS:*XXV).

2. The south Indians were the almost exclusive threat to the Sinhalese kingdoms before the advent of the Europeans starting from early sixteenth century.

3. Obeysekera 1975:232.

Sinhalese nationalism under British rule was Buddhistic in content.[4] D'Alwis, however, considered language as the most vital aspect of the Sinhalese identity. His unswerving loyalty to the Sinhala language is the pervading factor found in his introduction to the translation of the *Sidat Sañgarāva.*

No doubt his choice of language was most influenced by his personal predicament. D'Alwis was born into a Christian family and, during his educational career, was made more steadfast in his religious convictions. He remained a devout Christian to the end of his life. Yet Buddhism had been so much intertwined with other aspects of national identity that, as a scholar, he could not ignore its importance in the national tradition. Thus, while speaking of the Sinhala language as "the national language" of the Sinhalese people, he was also prepared to acknowledge Buddhism as their "national religion."[5] It needs to be noted that he was writing at a time when the Christian missionaries were zealously engaged in an endeavor to pull down "this stronghold of Satan."[6] Hence the ambivalence of D'Alwis's nationalist stance. While upholding his national heritage, he had at the same time to affirm his devotion to Christianity.[7]

If the fact that he was a Christian prevented D'Alwis from upholding the validity of Buddhism, there was another personal factor that made him see language as the crucial ingredient of the Sinhalese identity. As already noted, he had received largely an English education and had been oblivious to his cultural heritage until an incident in adult life forced him to study the Sinhala language. This contact with the linguistic heritage of the group was the path through which he discovered his lost cultural patrimony. Hence the importance language attained in his scale of values. Indeed, it may be said that language thus assumed an ideologized status in the process of D'Alwis's search for a personal identity.[8]

Apart from D'Alwis's personal predicament, social propensities of

4. This was manifest in the Buddhist revival during the last decades of the nineteenth century. Its beginnings were seen about a decade after D'Alwis's publication of the *Sidat Sañgarāva.* See chapter 4.

5. *SS*:XVIII.

6. Rev. Daniel John Gogerly (1792–1862). Quoted in Gooneratne 1968:90.

7. Note, e.g., the remark that "it behoves everyone who feels assured that the religion of the Bible will in process of time become the universal faith of the Ceylonese, to have the scriptures translated into correct, idiomatic Sinhalese" (*SS*:XXXIV); and also the mention of the usefulness of the study of Sinhala to the missionary "in exposing the monstrous wickedness and artful sophistry of Buddhism" (*SS*:CCLII).

8. Cf. "The leaders of the nationalist movements . . . tend to be marginal in their

his milieu too perhaps did call forth a more widely encompassing group symbol than Buddhism. This would have arisen from the peculiar situation in which the Sinhalese ethnic group was placed in the early nineteenth century. After a long period of political division in which the people of the "low" country lived under European administration while those in the Kandyan areas were ruled by indigenous kings, the establishment of British rule over the whole island in 1815 found the Sinhalese people placed under a single government. The situation contributed greatly to the growth of group consciousness, a feeling of camaraderie, between those of the low country and those of the Kandyan provinces. Thus, we find, for example, D'Alwis, a low-country Sinhalese, taking up the cause of the Kandyan peasantry in the dedication of his translation of the *Sidat Sañgarāva* to Governor Sir George Anderson.[9] Referring to the state trials after the rebellion of 1848, D'Alwis pointed to the gulf that existed between the rulers and the ruled in these remote areas. Such a sentiment, particularly in the mind of a nationalist thinker such as D'Alwis, was no doubt actuated by the "threat" posed by the encroachments of the new civilization on the traditional order.

As we have seen, the nativistic reaction at the mass level was millennialistic, while at the level of the more sophisticated strata of the population two different "rational" reactions appeared. There was first an expression of strong language loyalty, cogently set forth in D'Alwis's introduction to his translation of the *Sidat Sañgarāva*. This was followed several years later by a modernistic Buddhist revival, deliberately designed to confront new circumstances. The one predated the other. The translator of the *Sidat Sañgarāva* was the more socially mobilized. Indeed, the social mobilization of the Christians was anterior to that of the Buddhists. It took much more time for the protagonists of Buddhism to organize themselves for self-preservation. Thus, D'Alwis, devout Christian that he was, made the most obvious choice when he picked up language as the most salient criterion of group identity and the most cohesive of group ties.

Those who sought to protect the Sinhalese identity in this period of its rapid decline had available to them a rich variety of symbols from which a choice could be made. In such situations, apart from the social forces that determine the choice, the decision also depends on the predicament of the agents of symbolization, who attach different

nationality, perhaps inspired by secret doubts of their nationality" (Hugh Trevor Roper, quoted in Fishman 1972c:17).

9. *SS*:VI.

values to different symbols. The leaders of the millennialistic movements chose perhaps the more concrete and obvious manifestations of the status quo ante: the kingship, the aristocracy, and the like. In the later decades of the nineteenth century the *bhikkhus* who spearheaded a religious revival naturally upheld Buddhism as the symbol par excellence. D'Alwis, however, chose language.

The Urgency for the Emphasis on the Vernacular

It was mentioned earlier that a rebellion broke out against the British administration in 1848. When a Committee of Inquiry of the British House of Commons investigated the causes of the rebellion, a principal factor that emerged was the communication gap that existed between the native populace and the British officials. Major Thomas Skinner, who had been in service in the island since 1817 and who had intimate knowledge of the interior, pointed out in a memorandum that

> want of intercourse with, knowledge of, and sympathy in, the people kept many of the European functionaries so completely in the dark as regards their social condition.[10]

Philip Anstruther, the colonial secretary of the island from 1830 to 1845, commenting on the cause of this lack of communication, declared that

> there is a complete curtain drawn in Ceylon between the government and the governed; no person concerned with government understands the language [of the people].[11]

Since the days of Governor Thomas Maitland, (1805–12), there was a provision in the recruitment and promotion procedures with regard to the higher officials in the island's administrative service which required them to obtain a knowledge of the vernacular languages. But this was never strictly observed. Indeed, many officials appeared to be unaware that such a provision existed. The administrators at the time were heavily involved in the newly opened plantation ventures. By the late 1840s the coffee mania was at its height, and "the Governor and the Council, the militia and the judges and the clergy and one half the civil

10. Skinner 1974:140.
11. Kannangara 1966:162.

servants penetrated the hills" as pioneer coffee planters.[12] Apart from the administrative officials, the missionaries, who had perhaps greater opportunities to obtain an intimate knowledge of the natives, were as enthusiastic in their attempts at spreading European attainments—which they probably expected would go together with the conversion to Christianity. Perhaps their judgment was correct so far as certain specific sections of the population were concerned. But in the larger countryside the bulk of the population, who were Buddhist in religion and who knew no other language than Sinhala, were harboring grievances of one type or another about which the rulers were unaware. The reason was obviously the nonchalance of the administrators toward the views and sentiments of the population over whom they ruled. These views were impossible for them to understand because the officials did not know the people's language. It was a fact that between 1833 and 1848 only two civil servants had passed the vernacular language requirement.[13] Hence D'Alwis was justified in posing the question:

> How often, indeed, does an ignorance of the native character, the habits and feelings of the people (*all of which spring as it were from their language*) induce Europeans to act in a manner hostile to the general interests of the island?[14]

That D'Alwis believed language to be the essence of the Sinhalese identity is clear. He was conversant with the writings of Wilhelm von Humboldt, and the extract quoted above is strongly reminiscent of von Humboldt's dictum: "their speech is their spirit and their spirit is their speech. One cannot express too strongly the identity of the two."[15] Thus, we note D'Alwis's strong conviction that a knowledge of the native language is a sine qua non for administrators if they really wished to obtain an insight into the mind of the people whom they ruled.

The official neglect of duty in this regard came into focus during the state trials after the disturbances of 1848. D'Alwis mentions in his dedication of the book to the governor that, during the proceedings in one of the state prosecutions in 1848, it was elicited in evidence that there were, in this comparatively small island, many natives who had

12. Tennent, the outgoing colonial secretary in 1848. Quoted in Hulugalle 1963:69.

13. Toussaint 1935:11.

14. *SS*:VI; emphasis added.

15. Quoted in Rocker 1937:228. For D'Alwis's references to Humboldt, see *SS*:XLVIII.

never seen an English person (*SS:*VI). This itself was evidently a source of grievance for the governed. Yet there was another matter, one of much deeper concern, and D'Alwis addressed it in the form of a question:

> But how much greater must be the vexation and annoyance to thousands to know, that the majority of whom they *do* see, and with whom they hold official intercourse, do not understand the Singhalese, and cannot correctly interpret the language of their complaints or the expression of their grievances? (*SS:* VI)

This was the basis of D'Alwis's assertion that a knowledge of the vernacular would be "advantageous" to those who govern while being "beneficial" to those being governed. Those who govern, he believed, should have a deep understanding of,

> the constitution of the native society in this island, the habits and feelings of the Singhalese, their wants and grievances, their domestic and social relations, their traditions and customs, and their all-embracing religion. (*SS:*VI)

But the fact of the matter was that the ingredients "which constitute their national character" were "very imperfectly known." The focal point of his argument was that this national character could "be understood but little without a competent knowledge of the medium through which they are perpetuated," that medium being "the *Singhalese* or *Elu* language" (*SS:*V).

From the point of view of the governed it was of paramount importance that those who governed them should understand "Singhalese" and thus "correctly interpret" their "complaints" and their "grievances." From the point of those who governed, on the other hand, it was crucial that they should be able to convey properly their sentiments to the "natives." Unless this was accomplished, D'Alwis stated, the natives "can hardly fail of being misgoverned; their habits and feelings but little understood and their wants altogether unknown" (*SS:*CCLII).

It appeared to D'Alwis that the obvious indifference of the colonial administrators toward the Sinhala language was due to its ignorance of the true nature of the language and the greatness of the literature written in it. Far worse, he found, was the fact that "erroneous representations" about the language had been made by "Europeans ignorant of our language and unqualified to pronounce an opinion thereon." This had led others to look down upon it as "a language undeserving of encouragement or study."[16] D'Alwis took upon himself the task of remedying the situation. The translation of the *Sidat Sañgarāva,* a work of the thirteenth century, recognized by a European himself as "the only acknowledged Grammar of the language" and "a book of the highest authority,"[17] was the result. He prefaced it with a lengthy introduction intended to convince his readers of the greatness of the Sinhala language and its literary heritage.

In the introduction to the translation of the *Sidat Sañgarāva,* running to two hundred eighty-six pages, D'Alwis examined the origin of the Sinhala language, the different styles of Sinhala prose writings, and the rules of Sinhala prosody. But the larger part of it was devoted to a study of the history of the language, tracing it in combination with "the Civil history of the Island."[18] In the final part of this history D'Alwis examined the state of the Sinhala language of his day, where he included a critical analysis of the various books in English for the study of Sinhala available at the time.

Apart from being an attempt at introducing the Sinhala language and its classical literature to Europeans and also to those natives who, because of their English education, had lost touch with their own cultural heritage,[19] the introduction to the translation of the *Sidat Sañgarāva* was an expression of strong language loyalty. It was a typical marshaling of both "encouraging and pessimistic facts" in an attempt to plot the position of the language in the prevailing order of things.[20] The resilience that the language had demonstrated through the trials and tribulations of over two thousand years was in itself commendable and encouraging. Its decline in his own time, however, and the fact that

16. D'Alwis 1863:78.

17. Rev. S. Lambrick. Quoted by D'Alwis in *SS:*LXXXVII.

18. Here D'Alwis sought the authority of Sir William Jones: "The civil and the literary history of nearly every part of the world are so much allied together, that one cannot be used, nor can the same be proved or illustrated, without the other" (*SS:*CXXXVIII).

19. D'Alwis was disturbed by this neglect of "the national language" and at the end of his introduction states that one of his aims was the "awakening" of "a spirit of inquiry in the minds of my countrymen" (*SS:*CCLXXXV).

20. As usual in expressions of language loyalty. See Hesbacher and Fishman 1965:145.

it was no longer seriously studied by the upper classes and had even become a badge of social inferiority were causes for deep regret.[21]

In addition to its significance as an instrument in understanding the native mentality—"a key to the heart of the native" (*SS*:LII)—the Sinhala language is upheld in the introduction as being valuable in itself, as a language of great antiquity and the vehicle of a long-standing culture. In tracing the history of the Sinhala language and literature D'Alwis perceived in it indications of the remarkable achievements of Sinhalese civilization in days gone by. It was indeed an illustration of the cultural load the language carried. Having laid before his readers the "greatness" of the language and its literature, and evidence as to the magnificient achievements of the Sinhalese people, D'Alwis was ready to pose the question:

> Is it then right or just, that *the national language of the Singhalese* should be neglected and discouraged? (*SS*:CCLI; emphasis added)

Here in the hands of D'Alwis the Sinhala language assumes a special status, much more than a communicatory medium or a mere "given" in a primordial world, and something extraneous to the intellectual confines of traditional Sinhalese scholarship, not to mention the conceptual world of the Sinhalese masses. To a much greater extent than any previous writer D'Alwis was felicitous about the rights of the Sinhalese people. Nor indeed did any previous writer champion the cause of the Sinhala language as he did in the introduction to the translation of the *Sidat Sañgarāva*. Language had become for him a cause—it was "our" language (*SS*:CCLXII), the "national language" (*SS*:X), worthy of making "a struggle for" (*SS*:CCLXII). D'Alwis was undoubtedly the first Sinhala language nationalist of British Sri Lanka.

Aspects of the Language Loyalty of James D'Alwis

It is with James D'Alwis that one notices the first "focused and conscious behaviour" on behalf of the Sinhala language.[22] He found himself placed in the unique position of being conscious of the community's linguistic heritage—which was in need of ideologization—as well

21. "The most favoured of the natives devote but little attention to the study of their own language" (*SS*:CCLIX).

22. For this characteristic of language loyalty, see Fishman 1972b:140.

as being cast in the role of espousing its cause for the purpose of preventing a language shift. With elaborate and cogent argument he produced what may be termed the charter of Sinhala language nationalism. It is a point worth noting that almost all later ideological positions in the cause of the Sinhala language find their precedents in his pioneering work.

The language loyalty of D'Alwis found expression in several ways. He was emphatic about the antiquity of the Sinhala language and the need for preserving the "purity" of the language. Again he wished to emphasize the fact that the Sinhala language had a great literary heritage. And at the same time he rose to a defense of the Sinhala language against critics who had leveled certain "charges" about "defects" in the language.

Being anxious to promote the study of Sinhala and to develop its potentialities in the modern context D'Alwis devised a formula for its maintenance, reinforcement, and enrichment. It is of interest to note that in D'Alwis's historical survey of the Sinhala language and literature is found the first modern focus on the role of the Tamil people in the political and cultural history of the Sinhalese people. This particular concern was to be a major theme in the Sinhalese nationalist thinking in the twentieth century.

The Antiquity of the Sinhala Language

D'Alwis believed that Sinhala was one of the oldest languages in Asia. He was emphatic in rejecting the notion that Sinhala was "a dialect of Sanskrit." His belief was that both Sinhala and Sanskrit were "offsprings of one common parent" (*SS:*XXXVIII). In order to establish this view he marshaled an array of arguments, some of them being: that while Sanskrit has three genders Sinhala has only two;[23] that verbs in Sanskrit are conjugated for person, number, and gender, a feature not found in Sinhala;[24] and that the *sandhi* rules are different in the two languages.[25]

23. Here D'Alwis had misconstrued a statement in the *Sidat Sañgarāva*. It is clearly evident in the inscriptions and the extant literary works of the period prior to the *SS* that a three-term gender system (masculine, feminine, and neuter) was used in Sinhala just as in Sanskrit. See Wijayaratne 1956:35–36.

24. This is not true with regard to literary Sinhala, which was the primary concern of D'Alwis. It has been discussed in Dharmadasa 1967:chap. 4.

25. Here too D'Alwis has misconstrued a statement in the *SS*. Linguists today be-

It is clear that the raising of the status of Sinhala from that of a "daughter" to a "sister" of that language with a "wonderful structure; more perfect than Greek, more copious than Latin, and more exquisitely refined than either," which was the Sanskrit,[26] was a feat of intense language loyalty. Indeed, D'Alwis's great admiration of the Sinhala language led him to view it as a language of great antiquity. "The utter absence of all traces of *the Singhalese* in India," he argued, "proves it to have been a very ancient one" (*SS*:XLVII). The crux of his argument was, that the time in which it was in use in the mainland was too far off for it to have left any traces of it in the present. In further support of his argument he adduced the fact of "the existence in it of many characteristics common to all *primitive* languages."[27] In viewing the origins of the Sinhala language in a period of great antiquity he was obviously attempting to establish for it a respectability that, he evidently believed, age could confer.

The belief that the Sinhala language was derived "from the same source whence the Sanskrit . . . and the Pali have been derived" (*SS*:XXI) had other implications. If the original inhabitants of the island had Sinhala as their language before the "invasion" of the "Singha conquerors" (*SS*:XVIII) (i.e., Vijaya and his group in the sixth century B.C.) the language would have a longer history than ascribed to it on the authority of the *Mahāvaṃśa*. Thus, viewing language as an index to civilization, D'Alwis saw in the work he was translating, and in the language embodied in it, a mirror image of the very ancient civilization of the Sinhalese people:

> Considering its [the *Sidat Saňgarāva*'s] antiquity and the comprehensiveness of its rules, which present the rudiments of a correct and well defined Oriental language, bearing close resemblance to Sanskrit, Greek, Pali and Latin, we obtain indubitable evidence of the early greatness, and the civilization of the Singhalese. (*SS*:CCLXXX)

---

lieve that the author of *SS* was describing the "poetic *sandhi*" rather than *sandhi* in general. See M. W. S. de Silva 1970.

26. This is an extract from the famous statement of Sir William Jones, which D'Alwis also quotes in *SS*:XLIV.

27. *SS*:XLVII. *Primitive* here means "original." For the concept reminiscent of Fichte's ideas on the "Ursprache," D'Alwis is probably indebted to Humboldt, Bopp, and Adam Smith. See *SS*:XLVIII.

D'Alwis uses several criteria in defining the past greatness of his ethnic group: the antiquity of the *Sidat Sañgarāva;* the fact that the grammar embodied in it is "correct and well defined"; and that Sinhala has an affinity with other better-known "languages of civilization"—Sanskrit, Greek, Pali, and Latin. Furthermore, as a sequel to these theories, he suggested the possibility of the advent of the Sinhalese settlement in the island being "coeval with their [the Indo-Aryans'] occupation of India."[28] Here we find the language loyalist going further and further into antiquity to view his beloved language as being hallowed by immemorial age and connected with a glorious civilization.

The Concern with the "Purity" of the Language

Assuming the language of the "Sinha conquerors" led by Vijaya to be either Pali or Sanskrit, D'Alwis identified the original language of the land (before Vijaya's arrival) to be "pure Sinhala or *Elu.* Supposing that the *Pali* was the language of the conqueror," he says,

> it is not a little startling to find, that the chief ingredient in the constitution of the Singhalese language as we now find it, is the *Sanskrit,* and not *Pali.* (*SS:*XXIII)

He then takes up Sanskrit and says that the possibility of early Sinhala being "a dialect of Sanskrit" also has to be ruled out because

> the further in point of time we go back in search of the Singhalese, *the purer the language is,* without that amalgamation with the Sanskrit we perceive at the present day. (*SS:*XXIII)

The "pure" Sinhala referred to here is the exclusively Sinhala form, devoid of any borrowings from Sanskrit and Pali. D'Alwis continued his argument thus:

> Our theory establishes the fact that the natives of Ceylon whom Vijaya conquered had a language of their own; the language of the

28. *SS:*XII. D'Alwis's belief that Sinhala belongs to the oldest stratum of Indo-Aryan has been disproved by later research that has shown "unmistakable evidence" that early Sinhala was a "Middle Indian dialect descended from Sanskrit" (Wijayaratne 1956:2).

> Singhalese [i.e., those original inhabitants] from its radical difference from that of the conquering nation, proves, on the other hand, the correctness of our hypothesis—that the language now denominated the *Singhalese* was the language of the aborigines. (*SS*:XXVI)

Thus, according to D'Alwis, subsequent to this "conquest" an admixture occurred of Pali and Sanskrit with the original Sinhala. He saw this coming about in the following way:

> The Singhalese language, which is the *Elu, perhaps much neglected at the invasion of this island by the Singha race,* has been since enriched by accessions from the invaluable treasures of Pali and Sanskrit literature. (*SS*:XXIV; emphasis added)

Here we get a glimpse of D'Alwis's partiality for the pure Sinhala language, and his solicitude for it makes him see in the sixth century B.C. a situation for concern to the language loyalist. It appears as if D'Alwis projected into the past an anxiety he had in his own time. It was this pure Sinhala that he found embodied in the thirteenth-century grammar the *Sidat Sañgarāva.* Finding its language *"in that purity which now no longer exists,"*[29] he observed,

> Being a grammar of the Singhalese language . . . . the writer has very properly avoided an *Elu-Sanskrit* style.[30]

D'Alwis has not specified whether he believed the sixth century B.C. linguistic form to have continued unchanged for nineteen centuries until it was codified in the *Sidat Sañgarāva.* Yet his attitude to language change was that

> whatever change a language may undergo from time to time owing to a diversity of circumstances, the principal rules by which that language is spoken or written cannot altogether be changed. (*SS*:CCLXIV)

29. *SS*:XXVI; emphasis added.

30. *SS*:CLXXX. The Elu-Sanskrit style is the one with an admixture of "pure Sinhala" with Sanskrit, which became popular with Sinhala writers later.

In his view language change was a process precipitated by the adversities faced by the speech community. He described in glowing terms the manner in which the language and the literature of the Sinhalese thrived under their own kings. At the same time he demonstrated how these national cultural pursuits faced severe setbacks from time to time due to foreign invasions. It was his argument that

> in all countries which are subject to the government of foreigners the native tongue must and will almost imperceptibly continue to undergo change. This is the case in Ceylon. (*SS*:CCLXIII)

Evidently, his belief was that, if the Sinhalese people had continued under the rule of their own kings, the language would have continued essentially unchanged. In his own time, however, the Sinhala language community was living under a foreign power. He noted "the ill-effects of this political revolution upon the literature of the Singhalese" (*SS*:CCXXXV). Connected with this was the fact that there was an "uncertain, incorrect and vulgar use of the language" (*SS*:CCLXIV) in his own day. Deeply committed as he was to the pure Sinhala form embodied in the *Sidat Saṅgarāva,* it was disturbing to D'Alwis to view the violations of "authenticity" that were found in the usage of his time.[31]

He found that "in the maritime provinces, and in the principal towns, the Singhalese is now no longer *spoken* in its original purity." This was evident in the fact that

> the greater portion of the rising generation [is] . . . incapable of carrying on a conversation for any length of time without introducing Portuguese, Dutch, English and even Tamil terms. (*SS*:CCLIX)

Having quoted several such oft-heard expressions, D'Alwis apologized for doing so, saying that he was only

> anxious to bring the matter prominently before our native readers, with a view to the discouragement of so pernicious a practice. (*SS*:CCLX)

31. For the importance of "authenticity" in nationalistic language planning, see Fishman 1972c:66.

Here was thus a matter for deep concern for the language loyalist in D'Alwis. To have lost the community's political independence was bad enough, but to a nationalist what was worse was to see one's linguistic heritage increasingly contaminated with foreign accretions and thus losing its identity. Quoting a paragraph from the Mihintale slab inscription, which he (wrongly) attributed to the third century A.D., he is eager to uphold it as

> a specimen of that pure *Elu,* or Singhalese for which we in vain look at the present day.[32]

If he believed that pure Sinhala was the language of the earliest inhabitants of the island, and also if his conviction was that this same language was embodied "in that original purity" in the *Sidat Saňgarāva,* it follows that for D'Alwis this form was a tangible and unique link with his community's past—a past that spoke of a glorious civilization, whose memory was perhaps all the more vivid in a period of national deprivation.

Having been encoded in the *Sidat Saňgarāva,* this language had survived in its pristine purity, and it was undoubtedly one of the most vital aspects of his cultural inheritance. Therefore, whether in the present or in the past, whatever be the element that appeared to be instrumental in causing its "debasement," whether it be Portuguese, Dutch, English, or Tamil or even Pali and Sanskrit, the "fall" from that "original purity" was distressing to the language loyalist. Thus, at one point in the past D'Alwis found

> the original purity and simplicity of the Sinhala language . . . abandoned for a form of composition characterized by considerable accessions of foreign terms, by the introduction of an *Elu-Sanskrit* style. (*SS:*CLXXXVII)

His resentment of such "debasements" was unmistakable when he referred to how at another stage, "an Elu-Sanskrit style was adopted, as if *our forefathers . . . were ashamed of their mother-tongue*" (*SS:*CLXIV; emphasis added).

If he believed that the subjection "to the government of foreigners"

32. *SS:*XXIII. It has been revealed by epigraphical and linguistic research later that this inscription was written in the tenth century. See *Epigraphia Zeylanica,* 1:75–113.

led to changes in the language and hence saw the Sinhala spoken in the maritime provinces in his own day as highly contaminated by foreign accretions, it would follow logically that the language used in areas where foreign rule did not extend until recently would have retained a comparative degree of purity. This indeed was what D'Alwis saw in the Sinhalese in the areas that had remained under Sinhalese monarchy until the early years of the nineteenth century:

> In the Kandyan country, there are traces still left of *the original purity* of the Singhalese language. (*SS:*CCLX; emphasis added)

Similarly, in the Southern province, where the European influence did not penetrate as much as in the Western province, he found that "the language is used (comparatively speaking) correctly" (*SS:*CCLX).

Viewing foreign domination as the catalyst in linguistic change, D'Alwis saw around him "an uncertain, incorrect and vulgar use" of the Sinhala language (*SS:*CCLXIV). It was this "vulgarization" of the language at a time when the whole of the Sinhalese ethnic group was living under foreign domination which engaged his attention. The Western province, where he saw the propensity to language contamination very highly marked, had been under the control of foreign powers for well over three hundred years. Until 1815 there was the independent kingdom of Kandy, where the possibility for the Sinhala language and literature to continue and develop in the best form of the tradition remained. But even in that region he saw the beginnings of the erosion of language purity at the time he was writing.[33]

In tracing the history of the Sinhala language he saw the pure form of the language (as embodied in the *Sidat Sañgarāva*) maintained by the Sinhalese literati, mainly by the *bhikkhus,* through a system of pupilary succession, despite the political vicissitudes that were a feature of the long history of the Sinhalese kingdom. But at the time he was writing literary activity of that caliber no longer existed. Sinhala as a subject of study was neglected, and, unlike in the days of the Sinhalese kings, there were no "rewards for genius, and those privileges and immunities attached to the study of . . . the Sinhala language" (*SS:*CCXLIX). Noticing the vulgarization of the language occurring in such circumstances, D'Alwis was no doubt led to the conclusion that foreign domination was the cause for this "change." Perhaps his concern for

33. See *SS:*XXXV.

maintaining the purity of the Sinhala language was based on a fear similar to that of Herder: "when a community loses its independence its language also will coalesce with that of the conquerors."[34]

The Greatness of the Literary Heritage

D'Alwis was writing at a time when the cultural heritage of the Sinhalese people appeared to be rapidly eroding, due on the one hand to the decline of traditional learning and on the other to the advancement of European culture. He was battling for preserving what he deemed the most crucial element of that heritage: the classical literature embodied in the Sinhala language.

In his introduction to the *Sidat Saṅgarāva* he not only traced the history of the Sinhala language but also quoted extensively from Sinhala classics, sometimes in translation. The express purpose of providing these quotations was to demonstrate their literary merits and "redeem [them] from undeserved detractions of ignorant criticism" (*SS:*LXIV). To his great chagrin he found that a great deal of "ignorant" criticism had been made by Europeans, and he ventured to state:

> Much of the lukewarmness manifested by people in the study of the Singhalese critically, has arisen, in a great measure, from adopting the views of Europeans, ignorant of our language, and unqualified to pronounce an opinion thereon.[35]

At school D'Alwis had received the conventional English grammar school education of the day. Thus, when he graduated from the Colombo Academy, the highest seat of English learning on the island, he had obtained a sound knowledge of English as well as Latin and Greek literatures. But once he encountered the classical literature of his own language during his nationalist phase he was convinced that the Sinhala literary works "do not deserve to be disparagingly spoken of by Europeans" (*SS:*LXXXVIII). Answering those who denigrated Sinhala prose as "insipid" and Sinhala poetry as "turgid, bombastic and extravagantly metaphorical" and who said that both consisted of "verbal quibbles, excessive and sustained alliteration" and "quaint and ca-

34. Quoted in Hays 1931:226.
35. D'Alwis 1863:78.

pricious comparisons," he pointed out that such criticism was "founded upon *ex-parte* evidence." Indeed, the development of his argument reminds us that he was, after all, a lawyer by profession. He said that "those who condemn the Eastern writers, do so with reference to their own particular language, their feelings and their institutions." And his rejoinder was posed in the form of a question:

> Why test the excellence or inferiority of one language in point of rhetorical elegance, by the excellence or inferiority of another? (*SS*:LXXIX)

Because, in his opinion, quite remarkable for the time in which he was writing,

> to do so is to assume a superiority in the one which is not conceded by the other.[36]

His quotations from the Sinhala classics were intended to prove that Sinhala would not "concede the superiority" of another language in the field of literary achievements. He found in some creations of Sinhala poets "*a fascination which words cannot describe.*" In one composition, for example, he found "the writer's thoughts, brilliant and original, sparkle as we go along his elegant and flowing rhymes," whereby "both ear and mind are at once satisfied."[37] Of one Sinhala classic, the poem *Kāvyasēkara* of the fifteenth century, he made the point that

> no Singhalese scholar reads it, much less hears its name . . . without mingled feelings of esteem and veneration, [because] its style is [so] elaborate and energetic; and its versification correct, smooth and elegant. (*SS*:CXC)

D'Alwis was not unaware of the fact that these views were often matters of individual judgment. "In prose and in poetry," he declared, "nothing is more to be desired than clearness and elegance of expression," and his argument following upon this was that

36. *SS*:LXXIX. D'Alwis here displays a feeling for what Sapir (1949:22) called the "universality" of language. It is a remarkable insight in an age predating modern linguistics and its assertion that "all languages are equally good and adequate" (Haugen 1971).

37. *SS*:CXCII; emphasis added.

> what that clearness and elegance are, in reference to any particular language can be decided by *none but those intimately acquainted with* the genius of that language. (*SS:*LXX; emphasis added)

Hence D'Alwis was willing to concede that perhaps it was difficult for a European, particularly an educated man, to appreciate the worth of these Sinhala literary works because he would have been "accustomed from his infancy to the peculiar expressions of his language, the numbers of his poetry, and the national and religious feelings which they convey (all of which dispose his ear and bias his judgment to give preference to his own language)" (*SS:*LXXX).

As for these European critics, he wished to point out that

> whatever may be said of their superior powers of intellect . . . [they] can never appreciate those beauties of native style which one thoroughly acquainted with the native idiom, the genius of the language, and the religion of the Singhalese, finds in *Elu* works. (*SS:*LXXVIII)

He concluded his argument thus:

> Bearing in mind that the comparisons here instituted, is with reference to the idiom of expression, the genius of the language, the habits of nationality and the peculiarities of the religion of each class of writers; the Singhalese scholar, equally with the English, finds in the writings of his country's poets, the unsurpassed sublimity of a Milton, the flowing gracefulness of a Pope, and the sparkling wit of a Goldsmith. (*SS:*LXXX)

Only a superbly competent bilingual such as D'Alwis could have envisaged such a relativist approach to the evaluation of the two literatures concerned. As for his own ethnic group, he was the first scholar to have achieved an equally intimate knowledge of Oriental and Occidental literatures. The very concepts he used were novel and extraneous as far as the intellectual vistas of his community were concerned. No doubt this facility emerged from his unique personality, a blend of Western intellectual training and a fervent loyalty to his native language and literature. The beauty he saw in many a classical Sinhala work was indeed the cause as well as symptom of his nationalist sentiments.

The Defense of Language

Indeed, some European critics had gone as far as to find defects in the Sinhala language itself. One Dr. Mac Vicar, for example, had argued that the sounds "æ" and "ææ" in Sinhala were those "heard in the bleating of sheep" and hence "ugly" and "melancholy." He had therefore expressed the hope that these sounds would "vanish" from the language when the people "rise in taste and intellect."[38] No doubt this remark was extremely offensive to the language loyalist in D'Alwis. "These vowel sounds," he pointed out, "are as much necessary part of our language as 'a' and 'aa.' " This is because "hardly can a dozen lines be written in Singhalese without introducing the sounds 'æ' and 'ææ.' " As for the unpleasantness of the sounds, which seemed to have offended Mac Vicar's taste, D'Alwis reminded him that "the ordinary short 'æ' and long 'ææ' are frequently met within the English without producing either a 'lengthened' (prolated) or a 'melancholy' sound, e.g., 'æ' in '*a*nd,' '*ca*t'; and 'ææ' in '*a*nt,' '*ma*n,' '*sta*nd' etc." To crown his argument, as it were, D'Alwis remarked that

> to suppose . . . that "æ" and "ææ" in the Singhalese will ere long vanish, is no more probable, than to suppose that their equivalent sounds in the English, will, in process of time, be similarly lost. (*SS*:LX)

Thus, D'Alwis wished those European critics to look carefully at their own languages before they made adverse judgments about Sinhala. Bilingual as he was, he would have been particularly sensitive to judgments that appeared to be founded on ethnocentrism. Were those Europeans motivated by feelings of superiority when they made such pronouncements on Sinhala? D'Alwis seems to have been convinced that this was so.[39] Hence his endeavor to refute such assumptions and

38. Quoted in *SS*:LIX. The reference is to the vowel sound (in such instances as *cat*) represented by *ä* in the present study.

39. Thus, he has mentioned in his unpublished *Sinhalese History* that if a native scholar were to point out a mistake of European scholars "they were soon roused to anger: and feeling indignant at the reflection on what they consider their superior position

establish the point that Sinhala is not a language "which should be spoken of disparagingly" (*SS*:LXXVII).

In defending Sinhala against "ignorant criticism," D'Alwis often resorted to comparing it with English. His intention here was to demonstrate that in certain areas of language activity the Sinhala speaker was at an advantage over the English speaker. It should be mentioned, however, that the point was made with remarkable restraint. Thus, for example, speaking of Sinhala prosody, he says:

> *Quantity, feet* and *pauses* are necessarily constituent parts of all verse; and one great advantage which the Singhalese poses over the Western nations, is the existence in the language of the former, of symbols of long and short sounds indubitably expressed, without reference to usage (very often an uncertain arbiter) for the ascertainment of their quantity. (*SS*:CXVIII)

D'Alwis is not making any claim of "superiority" for his own language here. It is perhaps remarkable for a language loyalist to be so moderate—and that too at an age when the "curse of Babel" induced many a scholar to glorify his own language while disparaging others. Also it needs to be mentioned that D'Alwis never asserted his language to be "more expressive," for example, or "more logical," as found commonly in expressions of language loyalty.[40]

D'Alwis's Formula for Language Maintenance, Reinforcement, and Enrichment

Obviously, the fact that all was not well with the Sinhala language of his time was the motivating factor behind D'Alwis's deep concern for it. It was receding in social function—English taking priority in administrative and educational activities—and had fallen in social esteem. The decline of traditional institutions of learning and the gradual wane in Sinhalese literary activity meant that strict adherence to grammatical norms, as studied and preserved by the literati, was no longer assured. Furthermore, with the domination of the English language seemingly unchallenged in his day, little or no assistance appeared forthcoming

and intelligence . . . (attempt) to carry their political domination to literature and give law in regard to language as the French once did in Europe." Quoted in Gooneratne 1968: 150–51.

40. See, for example, the citations found in Hesbacher and Fishman 1965.

for the cultivation or promotion of Sinhala. This was the essential background to D'Alwis's struggle for the maintenance, reinforcement, and enrichment of Sinhala. In this endeavor we see his concern for the authentic national heritage, which he attempted to preserve while conceding that a certain amount of modernization was also necessary.

The Concern for Authenticity

One of the major linguistic concerns of D'Alwis, as reflected in his translation of the *Sidat Saṅgarāva,* was stemming the tide of vulgarisms and "innovations unwarranted by use" which he noted in contemporary Sinhala. The former he attributed to "the misapplication of terms by the vulgar" (*SS:*CCLXIV), and the latter he regarded as the result of works by Europeans who produced translations and compiled Sinhala grammars introducing a "foreign (English) idiom," leading to "innovations" that were "totally inconsistent with the existing usage of the Singhalese" (*SS:*CCLXX).

In connection with the latter there were first the Bible translations undertaken as part of Evangelical activity. The first Bible translation into Sinhala in British times was by William Tolfry, the Old Testament in 1819 and the New Testament in 1823. This was considered by another group of missionaries as containing "so many words derived from the Sanskrit and Pali languages . . . and so many inflections of words different from those in common use so as to render them difficult to be understood."[41] The critics therefore proceeded to compile a revision—which was in effect a rendering into colloquial Sinhala. A controversy then ensued over which version should be the standard one, and at the time D'Alwis was writing it had not yet been resolved. He found both versions not "correct as they may or ought to be." Being the Christian as well as the language loyalist he was, D'Alwis fervently hoped that "this Book of books . . . prove to the Singhalese scholar what the English version is to the English—the best standard in the language" (*SS:*LXXXIV). Being a purist in language matters, he was particularly concerned with the flaws in the second version, the rendering into colloquial Sinhala. In his opinion this project was undertaken on the "mistaken notion that a more correct and dignified phraseology would render the translation *unintelligible*" (*SS:*CCLVI), leading to the adoption of a "vulgar and ungrammatical style." Taking into account the "authority," religious as well as linguistic, this work would come to as-

41. Balding 1922:132.

sume, he found, "such a style, especially in the Bible . . . calculated to impoverish the Singhalese as a language" (*SS:*LXXXV).

Then there were the so-called Sinhalese grammars produced by Europeans, "deriving their authority from the uncertain, incorrect and vulgar use of the language of the present day." The grammars D'Alwis had in mind here were, Rev. C. Chater's *A Grammar of the Singhalese Language* (1815) and Rev. S. Lambrick's *A Grammar of the Singhalese Language, As It Is Now* (1834).[42] As noted above, D'Alwis had a strong aversion to deviations from the classical norm, and the accretions from foreign languages he found in the colloquial language of his day were extremely unpalatable to him. The Europeans who compiled Sinhala grammars, however, appeared far too insistent upon their partiality to the colloquial language. Thus, D'Alwis was deeply disturbed to find one of them complaining that the *Sidat Sañgarāva* was "but little calculated to assist in acquiring the colloquial dialect."[43]

In his strongly puristic attitude to language D'Alwis was provoked to retort that

> a grammar . . . instead of being *little calculated,* is altogether unnecessary, if our object is merely to acquire a colloquial knowledge of a language. (*SS:*CCLXIII)

In his opinion there was the norm—"the national use of the Singhalese"—which was codified in the *Sidat Sañgarāva,* and the colloquial speech was a product of ignorance, "the misapplication of terms by the vulgar." Thus, viewing colloquial usage as containing haphazard deviations from the classical norm, D'Alwis considered it as being "never uniform in its use." From this standpoint he expressed the doubt as to whether it could "ever continue to be of any authority or weight." Besides, defending as he was the usage cultivated in learned circles, he believed as a general rule that "in all countries languages are used incorrectly by the vulgar and correctly by the educated." Following upon this, he posed the question: "shall a grammar be composed according to the standard of the vulgar . . . or according to the standard of the learned?" It is an adoption of the former policy which he saw

42. *SS:*CCLXIV. Incidentally, the Rev. Samuel Lambrick was the main figure behind the "colloquial" version of the Sinhala Bible mentioned above.

43. *SS:*CCLXIV. This was the Rev. James Chater in the introduction to his *Grammar of the Cingalese Language* (1815).

in the neglect of the *Sidat Sañgarāva* and working "for the attainment of a colloquial dialect." This, according to the logic of his argument, was "to reduce the learned to the level of the ignorant." Indeed, it was diametrically opposed to the policy he preferred to adopt. "This is unjust," he declared,

> since to raise the ignorant to the level of the learned is not only easier, but more desirable. *Easier,* because in the words of Dr. Kenrick "the ignorant understand the learned better than the learned the ignorant"—and more *desirable,* because the whole of the standard works in the Singhalese language will, in that case, be easily accessible to the nation. (*SS:*CCLXIII–IV)

Here we note the nationalistic aim of D'Alwis's formula for language maintenance and reinforcement. Little wonder that he was unable to see eye to eye with those European scholars who compiled grammars of the Sinhala language. Indeed, he held very strong opinions about the language policy adopted by those foreign grammarians:

> Those Europeans who now compile Singhalese grammars deriving their authority from the uncertain, incorrect and vulgar use of the language of the present day, and coining new expressions, terminations and words, according to the accidents of Grammar which they find in their own language (a language as different in idiom, construction etc. from the Singhalese, as any two things can possibly be) are, we feel convinced, *committing a grievous injury on our language.* (*SS:*CCLXIV; emphasis added)

Concerned as he was about the preservation of his language in its pure form, D'Alwis was apprehensive about the consequences were such a language policy and "the colloquial dialect" allowed to proceed untrammeled in their course of so-called vulgarization:

> Such a language . . . as that which is denominated *"the colloquial dialect,"* unless the same be redeemed by a strict attention to the national use of the Singhalese, will be altogether set apart for something like what which is now springing up in the West Indies called *Talkeetalkee.* (*SS:*CCLXV)

Evidently, he shared the current attitude of scorn toward Pidgins and Creoles and perhaps shuddered at the possibility of Sinhala, with such a magnificient history behind it, ending up in such a "vulgar" state. He cast a disapproving eye on Lambrick's grammar:

> As a first work it should never be placed in the student's hands; for in that case he will have to unlearn a great deal before he can acquire a competent knowledge of Singhalese. (*SS:*CCLVI)

Also he complained that Lambrick "used his best endeavours to Anglicise [the Singhalese words and phrases] . . . attending but little to the genius of the language."[44]

Having internalized a glorious picture of the history of his national language, the possibility of its ending up as an "uncouth jargon" disturbed D'Alwis. Hence his insistence on the preservation of its pure form—that which embodied, in his words, "the genius of the language." Seeking to "redeem" the current vulgar usage by disseminating a knowledge of the "correct" national usage, his firm belief appears to have been that, for language behavior to be "in consonance with the genius of a language, and its original purity, every ancient grammar is . . . of great utility" (*SS:*CCLXIV).

In the *Sidat Sañgarāva* he found the code par excellence for his endeavor. Therein was the means not only "to guard against errors to which a vulgar use of the Sinhalese leads Europeans" but also to arrive at his linguistic summum bonum—the acquisition of "a good classical style" (*SS:*CCLXVII).

Thus, we note that D'Alwis's formula for language maintenance and reinforcement was primarily a policy of inexorable authentification. It is on the basis of the past cultural greatness of the Sinhalese people that he constructed his language program. Identifying language as the most crucial factor in the national culture, he advocated the revival of the classical language norms, the rationale being that by these means the cultural greatness of the past might be resuscitated.[45]

44. *SS:*CCLVI.

45. Cf. "Nationalism is uniqueness oriented. . . . this uniqueness, it is claimed, was, in the past, responsible for glorious attainments. If it can be recaptured in all of its authenticity, then, it is predicted, surely greatness will once again be achieved and, this time, permanently retained" (Fishman 1971b).

The Necessities of Modernization

D'Alwis's enterprise in language maintenance, reinforcement, and enrichment was, however, not entirely a matter of idealizing the past. Coupled with his zest for authentification through elimination of foreign accretions was an equally enthusiastic program for modernization. Thus, while eulogizing the achievements of classical Sinhala writers, he observed with regret how, with the loss of political independence, a decline in standards had set in, a major symptom of which was the "slavish imitation . . . of both the style and modes of thought of the writers of the previous age." He was wary of the "mental debasement" that would follow and expressed fears about the possibility that "we would in process of time have nothing new" (*SS:*CCXXXV–VI). With his knowledge of the literatures of the West he was in the advantageous position of deriving new inspirations for the development of Sinhalese literature. Indeed, by this time there was a prime need for such a breakthrough.[46]

Thus, with a view, as it were, to opening new literary vistas for his "people who . . . [were] servile imitators of their ancestors," he proceeded to produce literary compositions in Sinhala wherein were combined "Eastern mythology and poetic thought" and "English thoughts."[47] Works in this vein included translations of Cowper's "I Am the Monarch of All I Survey";[48] Goldsmith's "When Lovely Woman Stoops to Folly";[49] and the original poems "A Trip to Matura"—the idea for which he conceived while reading Goldsmith's "The Traveller"[50]—"The Races of 1853," and "The Races of 1854," which described events at the Colombo racecourse.[51]

Furthermore, while exhorting his compatriots not to neglect the study of their national language, he campaigned for the provision of better educational facilities for Sinhalese studies in the educational system. Thus, as the representative of the Sinhalese people in the Legisla-

46. Cf. "By the nineteenth century we find literature languishing for want of inspiration and stimulation, for, the old Sanskrit sources had been tapped dry" (Sarathchandra 1973:343).

47. D'Alwis 1863:11.

48. D'Alwis 1863:19.

49. D'Alwis 1863:23.

50. D'Alwis 1863:49.

51. D'Alwis 1863:2–11.

tive Council,[52] he frequently advocated with great eloquence the cause of Sinhala education.

Two areas that engaged his attention were the provision of secondary school facilities in vernacular schools and the preparation of a good set of school textbooks in Sinhala.[53] His complaint about secondary education was that "absolutely nothing . . . was being done in vernacular schools, either directly under the government or receiving aid from it."[54] This along with the fact that the Sinhala textbooks used in schools were compiled by Europeans aroused a deep concern in D'Alwis the nationalist. In consultation with Sinhalese scholars he found these textbooks defective in information—they ignored certain letters of the alphabet—and disregarding traditional rules of grammar and idiom, besides being alien in content. Moreover, one of the most serious drawbacks he observed in them was that no one who used them to study the Sinhala language could have received the necessary training to "read our classics even by rote." Added to this was the fact that there was at the time no "indigenous modern literature, reflecting the current ideas . . . written by Sinhalese authors for Sinhalese readers."[55]

All these factors appeared to D'Alwis to undermine the intellectual life of his community. Thus, he found the products of this unsatisfactory system of education "leaving school every year, absolutely without the means of continuing what was but begun at school, and shut out from all the usual avenues of mental culture."[56] A commission appointed during the governorship of Sir Hercules Robinson (1865–72) to inquire into the matter of the school textbooks brought no satisfactory results. In D'Alwis's opinion this was because the ideas of the European

52. The legislative council was instituted on the recommendations of the Colebrooke Commission (1832) in order to advise the governor. It consisted of an "official" majority and a nominated, "unofficial" minority. The latter were selected to represent the European, Burgher, Sinhalese, and Tamil communities. Although popular representation did not mean much at this stage, the creation of the legislative council was the first significant step in representative government, and Sri Lanka was the first "nonwhite" colony to have such an institution. (For details, see K. M. de Silva 1973.) D'Alwis was appointed as the Sinhala representative in 1864 and again in 1875.

53. *Memoirs*:133–34. This was in 1876.

54. Here D'Alwis quotes from *The Report of the Director of Public Instruction for 1875* (*Memoirs*:134). Furthermore, the vernacular schools had a limited curriculum when compared with the English medium schools. See Jayasuriya 1976:201.

55. *Memoirs*:134.

56. *Memoirs*:134.

chairman were "diametrically opposed to those of the Sinhalese commissioners," who comprised the rest of the commission, and the former

> exhibited much impatience at the views of the native members . . . *on a matter in which the natives alone were the best judges.* (*Memoirs*:135; emphasis added)

Hence D'Alwis asked the government to appoint a commission with "three or four sensible men" to inquire into the problem and recommend "a practical scheme" for its solution.[57]

A corollary to the lack of higher educational facilities in the vernacular schools was the complete disregard of Sinhala in the English schools.[58] D'Alwis was "grieved to record" that

> there are numbers among the Sinhalese, who, whilst they are proficient in Greek, Latin and English, are unable to read a common Sinhalese manuscript.[59]

D'Alwis was making a strong plea to his fellow Sinhalese to remedy this anomaly. He often discussed the matter with his compatriots and found many agreeing with him. He believed that more attention should be paid to the study of Sinhalese in the early stage of a child's studies and that it was best to do this when the child is young (*Memoirs*:17).

He knew that under existing circumstances the study of English was essential. The scheme he proposed was: primary education in Sinhala from the age of four to six and thereafter and attendance at a "school teaching both Sinhalese and English." He conceded, however, the possibility of another scheme. Thus, after primary education,

> should [a student] give preference to the study of English, as I have done, let him by all means do so . . . [but] when he leaves his

57. The school textbook controversy was to continue, however, for some time to come. See chapter 5.

58. Thus, for example, the lower school of the Colombo Academy included English Grammar, Arithmetic, Geography, Algebra, and Drawing, while the high school syllabus had those classes plus Euclid, Latin, and Greek (*Memoirs*:32–33).

59. *Memoirs*:17. Here D'Alwis was most probably speaking about a certain category of people, probably not a very large number. As mentioned elsewhere, he says that there were no more than fifty people in the island who could write to English newspapers.

> Alma Mater let him not lose a single moment to acquire a thorough knowledge of Sinhalese. (*Memoirs*:17)

It should be noted in this connection that, by acquiring a proficiency in Sinhala, he meant not simply the ability to read and write it "*but to understand all our classical writers and to imitate the style of composition suitable for different subjects*" (*Memoirs*:18; emphasis added).

It is of special significance that D'Alwis did not advocate the use of Sinhala as the exclusive medium of education. He knew the value of studying English for socioeconomic mobility and for the wider processes of modernization. His endeavor was to save the Sinhala language from neglect, to ensure its maintenance in education, and thus in social life to preserve the cultural identity of the group by preserving the language.

Conservation of the Cultural Heritage

In this arduous and often lonely struggle for the survival and resuscitation of Sinhala D'Alwis often wondered whether the official neglect of the language was based on the idea he found expressed in some quarters that "the Sinhalese language . . . [was] on the wane and destined to die."[60] In his passionate rebuttal of this idea we note the unmistakable imprint of the language loyalist:

> Nothing could be more far from the fact . . . all who had studied the subject agreed that in no case did a language like the Sinhalese which had existed for upwards of 2500 years and which was so rich as to render easy the treatment by its means any abstruse subject, die out. . . . This fact was proved by history. (*Memoirs*:138)

Obviously, it was this strong conviction, which had taken root during D'Alwis's studies on the history of the language, that motivated his design for the cultivation of the classical literary heritage. Also he had noticed how some of the more enlightened among the Europeans expressed their concern about the neglect of these cultural treasures by the English-educated natives.[61] Furthermore, he knew that those par-

60. D'Alwis is referring to a comment in *The Report of the Director of Public Instruction for 1875* (141).

61. See, for example, the quotation from George Turnour in chapter 2, which

ticular Europeans held some of the extant literary and historical works of the Sinhalese in the highest estimation.[62] Presumably, these expressions of approbation by Europeans also influenced the formation of D'Alwis's "rational nativism," one aspect of which was the promotion of the study of the community's classical literature. His nationalist sentiments found an echo in the proposals of those enlightened Europeans that this cultural heritage should be protected and saved from ultimate destruction.

It was again during the governorship of Sir Hercules Robinson that the first steps were taken to establish a public library of Oriental literature. D'Alwis, as one of those connected with the project, produced *A Descriptive Catalogue of Sanskrit, Pali and Sinhalese literary works in Ceylon.*[63] The editing and translation of classical works, which he began from the early stage of his literary career, was also part of the endeavor to save this national cultural heritage from oblivion. He evidently believed that the editing and translation of the *Sidat Saṅgarāva* would prove to be the basis for the preservation and cultivation of the classical idiom. One of the major advantages he saw in its study was that

> the whole of the standard works in the Singhalese language will, in that case, be *easily accessible to the nation.* (*SS*:CCLXIV; emphasis added)

He also edited and published *Kaccayana's Grammar of the Pali Language* in 1863 and the Sinhala classic the *Attanagalu Vaṃsaya* (14th c.) in 1866.[64] The latter he called "a historical novel," wherein were delineated "the institutions, usages, arts and sciences which prevailed . . . among the Sinhalese in ancient times."[65] Similarly, by urging the government to proceed with the project of the Oriental library by col-

D'Alwis himself reproduced along with the following statement of the English missionary Rev. D. J. Gogerly: "It was a fact also, that educated Singhalese, in giving attention to English learning and literature, had entirely overlooked their own" (*SS*:CCXLVIII).

62. He notices, for example, how after Turnour's publication of the *Mahāvaṃsa* translation it was pronounced by "high authority" as the "most valuable historical record we possess in relation to ancient India"; and how Rev. John Murdoch in a letter to the government said that "it has already been proved that the historical literature of the Singhalese is the most valuable in the East" (D'Alwis 1870:XII).

63. It was to consist of three volumes. The first came out of the Government Press in 1870, and the second was partly in print when D'Alwis died in 1878.

64. All these were printed at the Government Press, Colombo.

65. D'Alwis 1870:25.

lecting manuscripts from the obscure corners of the island where they lay hidden, sometimes unknown even by those who were in charge of them, D'Alwis was mindful of the *manifold and lasting advantages which will accrue thereby to the Singhalese nation.*[66]

Thus, the nationalistic goals of D'Alwis's endeavors for language maintenance, reinforcement, and enrichment are quite clear. It was an endeavor strongly partial to authentification and the preservation of the classical heritage. The modernization he sought to accomplish was with regard to the content of literature, while the language form he steadfastly upheld remained the classical idiom. He never lost sight of this commitment to the classical heritage, even when he was working under trying circumstances.

It is significant that, while fighting the cause of his own language, D'Alwis was equally intent on the retention of English, evidently as a pragmatically indispensable instrument. What he advocated appears to have been the preservation of Sinhala as a symbol of group identity and integrity while conceding to English the primacy of place as the medium of higher administration and modern knowledge.

Focus on the Role of the Tamils in the History of the Sinhalese

James D'Alwis was one of the first Sinhalese to compile a history of his ethnic group in modern times, and evidently it was his work that received the greatest attention among such historical studies.[67] He was also the first Sinhalese historian to view the community's history from the point of view of its cultural achievements, primarily those connected with language. Writing, as he was, at a time when the literary

66. D'Alwis 1870:XXI; emphasis added.

67. Here I am referring to the historical discussion in the introduction to *SS*. Before it there were four Sinhalese histories written in the nineteenth century: *Sulurājāvaliya* (comp. 1818–21; MS. until 1959); *Narēndracaritāvalōkana Pradīpikāva* (1834, MS); and two printed works, *Heladiv Rajaniya* by John Pereira, a Christian school teacher (Wesleyan Mission Press, 1853), and *Sinhala Rājāvaliya,* by a missionary writer (Kandy 1853). Although the last two would have reached a larger audience than the two manuscripts, the greater impact on nationalist thinking would have been D'Alwis's work. Because the Sinhalese political leadership were English educated (see chap. 6), it would have been consulted more extensively than the others. Furthermore, because of its nationalist bias, unlike the works of Pereira and the missionary, it would have had a greater appeal. We must also remember that there is a separate "Sinhalese History" by D'Alwis which is still in manuscript form. See Gooneratne 1968:150.

and scholarly activity in Sinhala was in decline and when all other cultural pursuits of the community had also lost their former élan and vibrancy, with the Sinhalese people living in subjugation to a foreign power, a study of the community's independent and glorious past would likely have been for him a painful experience. Many a nationalist under similar circumstances had tended to give a new interpretation to the history of the community, emphasizing certain aspects and underplaying certain others, by a process of selective rememberings and forgettings. The hand of D'Alwis, the nationalist historian, in manipulating the raw materials of the past is clearly evident in the manner in which he depicted the role of the Tamil people in the history of the Sinhalese.

For the Tamil kingdoms in south India, their close neighbor, the Sinhalese kingdom on the island of Lanka, was through the ages a very convenient target for adventure, imperial expansion, and plunder. There were instances too, although not as frequent, when the Sinhalese found opportunity for similar exploits in south India.[68] Concurrently with these antagonisms, there would have been some merging of "ideas, interest and genes,"[69] for at certain times there were peaceful relations as well. Constant migration and settlement by the numerically larger group, the south Indians, to the northernmost point of the island resulted in the establishment of an independent Tamil kingdom by the thirteenth century. Subsequently, it had sporadic conflicts with the Sinhalese kingdoms, located in the south. But, like the other small principalities, which arose from time to time, it also generally accepted the overlordship of the principal Sinhalese kingdom in the island. With the advent of the Western powers since the early sixteenth century both ethnic groups were faced with a similar predicament. The Jaffna kingdom fell to the Portuguese in 1619, and the Sinhalese kingdom was to struggle for nearly two centuries more until falling into British hands in 1815. By the time D'Alwis was writing his history the Tamils along with the Sinhalese were subjects of the British empire, and both communities were undergoing similar cultural deprivation. As such, there was no indication of any cause for interethnic conflict or competition between them.

In describing the fortunes of the Sinhalese-Buddhist kingdom, Sinhalese historiography has traditionally viewed south India as a

68. See Nicholas and Paranavitana 1961:143, 227–36.

69. Green 1965:552.

perennial source of destruction and disruption. It appears as if there existed in some sections of the communal consciousness a magnified portrayal of the dire vicissitudes through which the community had passed.[70] But whenever the stability of its sociopolitical system had been disturbed the restoration of the polity had been accomplished and links with the national tradition reestablished. This was undoubtedly satisfying to the community's self-image as one that was uniquely destined to survive, since it had a specific sacred mission to fulfill. Indeed, the depiction of destruction by foreign agency followed invariably by indigenous restoration appears to be a major focus in Sinhalese historiography.[71] D'Alwis's historical survey was based essentially on traditional works. Hence it was perhaps inevitable that they dictated a particular attitude to, and interpretation of, past events. Yet D'Alwis sometimes displays a remarkable independence in utilizing these historical sources. He ventures, for example, to give a new interpretation to the *Mahāvaṃśa* account of the arrival of the Sinhalese on the island. Obviously, this interpretation is more satisfying to the nationalist ego.[72] In that context his attitude toward the south Indian impact on Sinhalese history does not appear to be a product of mere chance. It is more likely that it was founded on deliberate choice.

It was perhaps inevitable that the Sinhalese historians of the past adopted in general a defensive attitude toward the south Indians. In their world south India always appeared to be a potential threat to their ethnoreligious polity. But circumstances had changed by the time D'Alwis was writing—the sword of Damocles from south India was no longer quite so menacing. Yet D'Alwis, who, on occasion, chose to deviate from the historical tradition and put forward his own interpretation of events, decided in this instance not only to derive his attitude to the south Indians from the traditional Sinhalese sources but also to charge it with a highly emotive form. This feeling most likely emanated from his intense language loyalty. In his historical survey the magnification of the devastations by south Indians was to perform a specific function: that is, to bolster the historically satisfying image of the Sinhala language.

D'Alwis often dwelt on the glorious past of the Sinhalese people

70. See chapter 1.

71. For details see Dharmadasa 1979:104, 107.

72. See *SS*:XI–XXVI.

and their great achievements in civilization, as in the following quotation from his translation of the *Sidat Sañgarāva:*

> To their literature and variety of other polite Arts and Sciences . . . must be assigned a proud position in the history of the world. (*SS:*CLXII)

He would highlight those cultural achievements of the past by reminding his readers that the continuity and steady development of the civilization were periodically interrupted by foreign invasions. It is as if the hope is projected into the past that but for such periodical devastations the community's history would have been even more glorious. Also this conviction no doubt provided a convenient excuse for any shortcoming that might be perceived in what the community had achieved.

Thus, not long after the establishment of the Sinhalese kingdom, D'Alwis found that "the Malabars who inhabited the frontiers of the Island soon became the bane of Ceylon!"[73] Again he sees "the march of improvement" of the Sinhalese civilization arrested by their invasion (*SS:*CXLV). And at another instance "the growing prosperity of the island . . . [to] suffer" in their hands (*SS:*CLXVIII). Moreover, he speaks of "the cruel tyranny of Malabar despotism" which led to several successive waves of destruction (*SS:*CLXIII). Apart from such emotion laden imagery in reference to the south Indians, D'Alwis views them as possessing a willful motive for destruction:

> Whenever they were successful in usurping the throne, and for however short a time, they demolished our institutions, extinguished our literature and attempted to uproot the religion of the land. (*SS:*CLXVI)

This statement is indicative of a familiar theme found in the perception of the Sinhalese about the history of their literature. That is, that the larger part of the literary and scholarly creations of their forebears became extinct in the course of time and that the major cause of this loss was the destruction caused by south Indian invaders. Thus, D'Alwis says,

73. *SS:*CLXVI. In the English writings of the period the word *Malabar* is used to designate the south Indians in general and also the Tamil people in Sri Lanka.

> for whilst the scriptures of the Singhalese were destroyed, the south Indian foreigners failed not to extinguish their literary records. *Few indeed are the works that escaped the fury of the Malabars.* (*SS:*CLXVIII; emphasis added)

Because he was a language loyalist, D'Alwis perceived in one of those periods of intense national deprivation the possibility of "the Singhalese language itself . . . being nearly sacrificed to their [the south Indians] animosity" (*SS:*CCLXVIII; emphasis added).

The immense destruction that, according to the records, was caused by the south Indians conversely highlights the tenacity for survival displayed by the national culture. Is it not a cause for elation for the language loyalist to find his beloved language possessed of such powers of resiliency as to have survived so many dire vicissitudes? Thus, toward the end of his historical survey D'Alwis declares,

> *We have already seen how utterly impossible it is to uproot and exterminate the Singhalese as a language.* It may be neglected–its classical authors destroyed–and its books lost; but *the language itself will continue in some shape or other.* (*SS:*CCLI; emphasis added)

It is as if to arrive at this triumphant conclusion that the destruction caused by that "bane of Ceylon" (*SS:*CLXVI) is portrayed so vividly. The demonizing of the opponent becomes a device for underscoring the group's capacity for survival. And, we must remember, for D'Alwis the particular focus of attention is the successful survival of the language.

In D'Alwis's belief the Sinhala language had not only managed to outlive those intense trials and tribulations for over two thousand five hundred years but also at the same time it had succeeded in retaining its essential characteristics. Thus, he finds it

> not a little remarkable . . . that between the oldest Singhalese writings found on slabs and rocks at Mihihtala and the modern Singhalese there is (comparatively speaking) far less difference than between the first specimens of ancient English given by Dr. Johnson in his history of the English language, and the modern writings of a Brougham or a Macaulay.[74]

74. *SS:*XXIV. D'Alwis is quite emphatic on this point. Also compare: "the difference

Evidently, D'Alwis was using the *literary Sinhala* of his own day for the comparison.[75] From the present it was the nearest and the most tangible link with the community's glorious past. Is it not highly significant that this link was found in language, in particular in the form he was ardently espousing in the face of vulgarisms and "unwarrantable innovations"?

It was possible therefore that, in order to glorify the resiliency of his language, D'Alwis was magnifying its struggles for survival under trying circumstances, particularly during the invasions from south India. We notice here that, in portraying the south Indians as the cause of periodic arrest and destruction of Sinhalese civilization, D'Alwis was, no doubt inadvertently, putting the edge on Sinhalese ideological weaponry for a retrospective hatred toward the Tamils in modern times.

Although there is no evidence of an interethnic conflict between the Sinhalese and the Tamils resident on the island at the time D'Alwis was writing, the *potential* for such a conflict was always there. In the main it existed in the collective memory of the Sinhalese people. In vividly portraying the destructive role played by the south Indians in the history of the Sinhalese, D'Alwis was, unintentionally, reviving an age-old antagonism. His major concern was no doubt the promotion of nationalistic sentiments in the minds of the Sinhalese. Very likely, the negative implications of the device he was using were not apparent to him. There is no indication about whether he was aware of the effect his exercise might have in regard to interethnic relations between the Sinhalese and the Tamils in his day or in the future. The Tamils resident on the island were the descendants of those ancient enemies. The identification of one with the other perhaps did not need much stretching of the imagination. Such an identification existed perhaps in certain quarters.[76] But by and large only the cultural differences between the two communities would have been visible at that time.

---

between the ancient and modern Singhalese presents no peculiarity of grammatical forms" (*SS*:XXIX).

75. For by this time the diglossic situation in Sinhala had been in existence for over a century and there was a marked difference between the colloquial and literary forms of the language. See M. W. S. de Silva 1967; Dharmadasa 1967.

76. As often happens in recent Sinhala writings. See, for example, Seelaratana 1955 and Nandarama and Samarasinghe 1967.

Nationalistic ideologies thrive on the availability of antagonists.[77] Perhaps such a need becomes more urgent when the group finds itself in circumstances of subservience while being superior in self-conception – and thus in a position of relative deprivation. For D'Alwis, fighting the cause of his culture under the aegis of British rule, the contemporary antagonist could not possibly be a target of direct attack. Hence antagonists of the past, "the Malabars," assumed the position of convenient whipping boys. Although in this he was not possibly promoting an attitude of hostility toward people of Tamil ethnicity in general, the bitterness of the past thus codified for the first time in the modern era, and most convincingly and "rationally" for that matter, was evidently to be a stepping-stone for future antagonisms.

D'Alwis's Place in the Development of Sinhalese Language Nationalism

With D'Alwis we find the first attempt in recent times to launch a so-called rational struggle in the defense of Sinhalese culture. Under subjugation to a foreign power in the nineteenth century the group's self-assertive struggles and aspirations had so far been for the restoration of the traditional sociopolitical system.[78] As the century progressed, the traditional order was being eroded rapidly in the face of the processes of modernization, and the old symbols of group assertion and identity would have concomitantly diminished in appeal. This would have been especially so for the newly emergent class of English-educated Sinhalese. The fact that this new stratum of the Sinhalese community was not single-minded in its new cultural orientation was dramatically displayed for the first time in the career of James D'Alwis.

Whatever be the rewards of the new education and however sweet were the fruits of European attainments, the presence of a long-standing "Great Tradition," albeit in a state of decline, was not a factor that could be ignored, and situations were to arise when its potency would become apparent. The inevitable contradictions and anomalies of a society in transition made D'Alwis look for a source of personal and

77. Cf. "Sociologically a nationality is a conflict group" (Louis Wirth quoted in Fishman 1972c:22), which in political terms can be "identifying oppressors and cultivating a sense of grievance against them" (Brass 1974:44).

78. Thus, the major rebellions of 1818 and 1848 were aimed at restoring the Sinhalese monarchy. Available evidence on the minor plots and conspiracies during the early nineteenth century indicate the same motive.

group identity. Because the traditional sociopolitical structures were no longer meaningful, D'Alwis found a substitute for them in a compelling form, in a facet of the community's culture, in the Sinhala language. Thus, in the career of James D'Alwis we find epitomized a transition from tradition to modernity. Perhaps for D'Alwis it appeared that language was the most overarching and least divisive of all facets of Sinhalese culture. Hence we find the initial ideological formulation of modern Sinhalese cultural nationalism taking the form of a language nationalism.

D'Alwis's search for a compelling source of identity was facilitated by the existence of a religio-ethnicist Great Tradition. In the course of the history of the community it had crystallized, as it were, into a bedrock of opinion, and it appeared to rise to the surface dramatically in situations of collective danger.[79] While drawing sustenance from this tradition, D'Alwis gave it a peculiar twist, especially to suit his primary and overriding interest in language. In the formulation of this vision of the relationship between language and literature on the one hand and national identity on the other, D'Alwis was no doubt influenced by European scholarship. We should note in particular that his translation of the *Sidat Saṅgarāva* predated the publication of Max Müller's celebrated works by about a decade. But he was conversant with the writings of earlier European scholars such as William Jones, Wilhelm von Humboldt, Franz Bopp, and Adam Smith.[80] Thus, his vision of Sinhalese national identity may be considered a synthesis between indigenous tradition and Western thought.

In reacting to what appeared to him as an impending language shift D'Alwis turned to various activities of language loyalty. His own researches into Sinhalese history and studies of classical Sinhala language and literature were in the nature of an elegant superstructure built on the solid foundation of his education on Western lines. Through a process of harmonizing the superstructure with the foundation he was able to transform an exclusively Sinhalese ideology into a coherent and convincing form. Although the corpus of the ideology he was thus able to produce did not generate an immediate and dramatic response because of the circumstances of his day, it was evidently to

79. See chapter 1. For details about such occurrences up to 1815, see Dharmadasa 1979:109–21.

80. Gunawardena (1979) is wrong in attributing this influence to Max Müller. For details see Dharmadasa 1989.

be a source of inspiration, consciously or unconsciously, in the future. One finds many of the features of his varied language loyalty endeavors appearing and reappearing in the future course of Sinhala language nationalism.

Inspired as he was by the view of the traditional historians who saw the island of Lanka as *Sinhaladvīpa*—"the island of the Sinhala people"—D'Alwis was apparently oblivious to the changes in the island's ethnic composition which had taken place since the days of ancient Sinhalese historiography. The Tamils, who had usually been the almost exclusive agents of disruption of the Sinhalese polities through the ages, had now come to be a permanent feature of the island's population. For the Sinhalese people, however, a conceptual adjustment of the fait accompli was evidently not an easy task. The historical concept of *Sinhaladvīpa* was always reinforced by the reality of the geographical phenomenon, and, ironically enough, the political circumstances of administrative unity under the British in the nineteenth century appeared to stimulate the revival of the age-old concept. In the case of an English-educated individual such as James D'Alwis the projection of Sinhalese nationalism to an all-island focus would have been actuated also by his awareness of European nationalist and liberal thinking—the Sinhalese ethnic group having not only historical claims but also comprising the preponderant majority of the island's population.[81] In this way it is with D'Alwis that we find the first modern reassertion of the *Sinhaladvīpa* concept.[82] It was to be, either influenced by his thinking or propounded individually by others, one of the key features of Sinhala language nationalism.

As far as the development of Sinhala language nationalism is concerned, D'Alwis appears to be its first "spokesman," or "prophet," who formulated, in relation to the myths of the past and dreams of the future, a coherent ideological format with regard to the Sinhala language.

---

81. Due to the importation of south Indian labor for work on the plantations, beginning from the 1840s, the Tamil element of the island population nearly doubled by the end of the century, making it 26.7 percent by 1901 (Panditaratne and Selvanayagam 1973). Before this development, however, the Sinhalese would have comprised about 90 percent of the population. Obviously, by the time D'Alwis was writing the introduction to the *SS* (1851) the implications of south Indian migration were not yet apparent. But this was to be a political issue later (see chap. 2).

82. There are indications that by the time D'Alwis was writing the idea of a "Ceylonese" community comprising all ethnic strands was beginning to form and was being eagerly espoused by the Burghers associated with the newspaper *Young Ceylon* from 1850 to 1852 (Candidus 1853).

It is with him that we find the first focused and conscious behavior on behalf of the Sinhala language. He was the first to display overt behavioral manifestations of calculated language loyalty such as *consciousness* of mother tongue; *knowledge* of its synchronic variants, of its history, and its literature; and *the perception of language as a component of "groupness."*[83]

D'Alwis's endeavor may be categorized as a nativistic reaction in the face of a perceived "threat" to the traditional culture. The focus of his interest, as noted above, was the Sinhala language. Although chronologically language thus came to be upheld first as the most vital aspect of Sinhalese culture, there was no immediate follow-up and no escalation of a movement with mass participation. In a sociohistorical sense D'Alwis may be considered more a "cultural leader" than an "organizational leader."[84] He perceived the "dangers" faced by his own ethnocultural aggregate and prescribed remedies for them while presenting a coherent and cogent group ideology, but he did not proceed further in organizing a movement of group effort.[85] Yet a nativistic endeavor, with a different focus, along with a large degree of popular mobilization and participation, was to emerge subsequently. This time it was in connection with the Buddhist religion, socially a more compelling symbol of group identity than the Sinhala language and one that D'Alwis overlooked, evidently because of his personal position as a Christian. Historically, the enthusiasm generated by the later movement overshadowed D'Alwis's endeavors. Yet this Buddhist phase of Sinhala cultural nationalism was to have its own particular impact on the language affairs of the community.

---

83. For these characteristics of language loyalty, see Fishman 1972a:145.

84. For the distinction between these two types, see Fishman and Nahirny 1966. D'Alwis's role in the larger arena of Sinhala language nationalism may be defined in several ways: He may be considered as belonging to the "struggle generation" (after Passin 1968), or he can be called a "transitional" (after Lerner 1964:75) or "a proto-elite" (after Fishman 1972c:15).

85. His career as lawyer, member of the Legislative Council, and secretary of the short-lived organization Ceylon League (1864) seems to have touched upon only the English educated layer, especially in Colombo, of the larger Sri Lankan society. Even his public lectures, which were in English, were addressed to this social category. (See Gooneratne 1968:169). In his constant communication, however, with the Sinhala literati, including *bhikkhus,* as is evident in the introductions to his books, we find a wider social contact by which his ideas were passed on to a larger audience.

Chapter 4

The Nineteenth-Century Buddhist Revival

> This Sinhalese race will for certain be eradicated from the face of the earth the day it leaves the Buddhist fold.
> —From the play *Dutugemunu* by John de Silva, 1909

Although conditions under British rule were far from conducive, the continuity of the tradition of scholarship among the Sinhalese remained unbroken during the early nineteenth century, mostly within the confines of their monasteries (*pansalas*). These scholarly activities may have been of little or no significance to the foreign rulers—and to most of the town-dwelling "Europeanized" Sinhalese. But the fact that the tradition of scholarship retained a good deal of its former vigor was evinced on two occasions during the period: namely, the ecclesiastical controversies among the *sangha* and the literary debate known as the "Sav Sat Dam" controversy.

The Buddhist Ecclesiastical Controversies

There were two major ecclesiastical controversies during this period among the Buddhist *sangha*. The issue was the authenticity of the practices relating to certain ecclesiastical rituals. The controversies were the "Sīmā Sankara" (1831 onward) and "Adhikamāsa" (1851 onward). The letters and pamphlets through which the controversies were carried out displayed "a high degree of familiarity with scriptures and the vast corpus of exegetical literature."[1] This internal competition and rivalry did nothing to weaken the Buddhists and in no way threatened to lead to a disintegration of the Buddhist community, either among the laypeople or among the *sangha*. The restructuring of the *sangha*, of which

1. Malalgoda 1973:191; for the two controversies, see 131 and 151.

the controversies were the cause as well as the symptom, and the renewed interest in Buddhist literature they inspired, constituted an internal consolidation—truly a Buddhist "reformation"—and this was to be of crucial significance in the sociocultural developments in Sinhalese society during the second half of the nineteenth century.

By 1864 several new "fraternities" of *bhikkhus* had arisen within the Buddhist dispensation. In addition to the original "Siamese" fraternity, with its headquarters in Kandy, there were four "Amarapura" fraternities of Burmese inspiration which sprang up in the low country: *Mūlavaṃsa, Saddhammavaṃsa, Dharmarakṣitavaṃsa,* and *Kalyāṇavaṃsa.* In addition, a splinter group of the Siamese fraternity appeared in the low country, the *Kalyāṇi Sāmagrī Sangha Sabhā,* and, finally, there arose the fraternity called *Ramaññavaṃsa,* of Arakan inspiration, which was critical of all the fraternities then in existence and which claimed adherence to pristine Buddhist practices and principles.[2] One crucial factor in the emergence of the new fraternities was the upward mobility of the castes that were considered "low" in the traditional social hierarchy. Added to this was a spirit of inquiry, an attempt to search for and adhere to what could be considered as authentic in precept and practice. The new fraternities, significantly, all came up in the low country, in the south and southwestern seaboard, which had been exposed to European contact for over three centuries. These were also the regions in which the impact of modernization was being felt most intensely.

A salient feature of this Europeanization and modernization was the spread of Christianity. Christians were continuing to make great advances in the educational sphere, and, partly as a result of that and partly because of official preference, they were getting the major share of the newly created career opportunities. And Christianity, as the religion of the rulers, was enjoying great prestige. These factors, disadvantageous as they were to the Buddhists, seem to have made a strong impression in the minds of the *bhikkhus* who formed the new fraternities, which, significantly, were rising in those very areas where Christianity was making great advances.[3] Unlike the *sangha* in earlier times, who were insulated by state sanctioned patronage, the *bhikkhus* were now faced with a struggle for survival. Arising out of these conditions was a spirit of militancy in the new generation of *bhikkhus,* which was

2. For the rise of these fraternities, see Malalgoda 1976.

3. For an account of these developments, see Malalgoda 1973; and K. M. de Silva 1981:339–41.

in marked contrast to the traditional image of the *bhikkhu* as an ascetic and recluse underscored by the eighteenth-century revival in Kandy.[4] This change in the *sangha,* which came about in the low country, was a crucial feature of the Buddhist resurgence that occurred during the second half of the nineteenth century.

The Sav Sat Dam Controversy

The Sav Sat Dam was, unlike the controversies mentioned above, a literary controversy. It arose in the aftermath of the publication of James D'Alwis's *Sidat Sañgarāva* translation in 1852. In that volume D'Alwis had made adverse comments about the opinion of a late scholar-*bhikkhu* on a point of prosody found in the phrase "sav sat dam" from the poem *Gangārōhaṇa Varṇanāva* written during the early nineteenth century. This posthumous criticism of the scholar provoked his pupils to defense, and a controversy ensued. The Sav Sat Dam controversy is considered a landmark in the development of modern Sinhalese literature.[5] The controversy was in Sinhala and was carried out through letters published in the recently established Sinhalese periodicals. Thus, unlike the previous ecclesiastical controversies, which had been confined to the *sangha,* the Sav Sat Dam controversy took place before a wider public. One may say that in it many scholars, particularly the *bhikkhus,* got an opportunity to come into the national arena. As D'Alwis, a contemporary, observed, the controversy

> awakened a spirit of inquiry previously unknown in Ceylon; and aroused the dormant powers of a number of native scholars . . . who had been content to remain buried in the obscurity and seclusion of their village *pansalas.*[6]

This was the first in a series of controversies in which the Sinhalese literary elite of the day, the *bhikkhus* and their lay pupils, displayed their erudition in the classical literatures of Sinhala, Pali, and Sanskrit. The early controversies, namely the Buddhist ecclesiastical and the Sav Sat Dam, had the effect of not only sharpening the polemical skills of the *bhikkhus,* who were their main participants, but also of awakening in

4. This is the image the Saranankara revival sought to project. See Vacissara 1964.
5. See Sarathchandra 1950:44; and D'Alwis 1863:IX.
6. D'Alwis 1863:IX.

their minds a new enthusiasm for their religious and literary heritage. The close study of the scriptural literature which the *Sīmāsankara* and the *Adhikamāsa* engendered was of special significance when viewed from the perspective of the subsequent confrontation with the Christian missionaries.

These controversies had the additional benefit of giving the *bhikkhus* a training in public debate. While the *Sīmasankara* had been conducted "privately," that is, by exchange of letters between the parties concerned, the Sav Sat Dam was a public controversy carried out in periodicals. Apart from valuable experience in the tactics of public debate, the participants in the controversies also gained a practical knowledge in the use of language in the give-and-take of polemics. The controversies also necessitated a thorough study of Pali scriptures and Sinhala classics.

Fortified in their self-confidence in this way, the *bhikkhus* were only too eager to take up their defense of Buddhism against Christianity when the need arose during the late nineteenth century. Confronted by religious adversity, there was a transformation in the character of the *bhikkhu,* a transformation that was to have long-term effects on the sociopolitical life of the community.[7] Eschewing his traditional role as religious preceptor and custodian of learning, the *bhikkhu* now emerged as a mobilizational leader spearheading a counteroffensive against the inroads of Christianity in particular and Western civilization in general. The activism of the *bhikkhus* in these spheres generated an unprecedented mass enthusiasm, first and foremost about Buddhism, which subsequently came to be channeled into a concern about various other aspects of indigenous culture. In this way the latter half of the nineteenth century saw a religious and cultural revival in Sinhala society. The revivalist ideologies affected, among other things, the language affairs of the community.

The Buddhist-Christian Controversies, 1864–73

While the Kandyan Convention of 1815 contained a clause declaring that Buddhism was "inviolable," the British government undertaking to "maintain" and "protect" its institutions,[8] subsequent developments

7. Political activism among the *bhikkhus,* which became very prominent during the mid twentieth century, may be traced to this transformation. For the "political *bhikkhus,*" see D. E. Smith, 1966: pt. 4; and Phadnis 1976: chap. 6.

8. See chapter 1.

proved that there was no matching the expectations of the Buddhists with the fiats of colonial administration. Apart from the more obvious discriminations found in the employment sphere and in matters of legal registration,[9] the missionary advances, particularly in educational activity, would have appeared to the Buddhists as antithetical to the spirit of the undertakings of 1815. Furthermore, in 1847, due to Evangelical pressure, the government severed the de jure connections with Buddhism which had been guaranteed to the Kandyans under clause 5 of the Kandyan Convention. In the perception of the missionaries this would have been the coup de grace against Buddhism—"the withdrawal of the only stay that would much longer have retarded its decay."[10] This belief, no doubt, was reinforced by the passivity and inactivity of the Buddhists during the early decades of the century. Having been conditioned for centuries by a religion whose basic tenents spoke of tolerance,[11] the Buddhists appeared to the missionaries as "slumbering in their security."[12] Engaged in their holy endeavor, the missionaries were exasperated to find "it almost impossible to move them even to wrath."[13] Whatever interpretation the missionaries preferred to give to the early Buddhist response to the new religion seems to have been nonantagonistic. This is epitomized in the statement of a *bhikkhu* to a missionary:

> The English people worshipped Jesus Christ and the Sinhalese people worshipped the Buddha . . . they were both good religions.[14]

9. From Dutch times the legally valid registration of birth, marriage, and death was in the hands of Christian clergy. It was only in 1868, due to agitation by Buddhists, that civil registration was introduced. For a list of legal and administrative restrictions placed on non-Christians during Dutch administration see K. W. Goonewardene 1989:8–9. Although there was a change of policy under the British, it appears to have taken a long time to make a definite impact.

10. Tennent, quoted in K. M. de Silva 1965:106. Tennent was colonial secretary of the colony from 1847 to 1850.

11. Here canonical Buddhism may find a contrast, for example, with Islam: "the Buddhist faith professes an abiding belief in tolerance and although its followers may not always obey its precepts, this spirit does help to condition the population" (Von Der Mehden 1963:187). Christian missionaries were often baffled by the religious tolerance they encountered in Sri Lanka in the eighteenth and early nineteenth centuries. See K. W. Goonewardane 1989; and Malalgoda 1973.

12. Rev. E. Daniel in 1942. Quoted in K. M. de Silva 1973:187.

13. Rev. R. S. Hardy in 1850. Quoted in Malalgoda 1973:194.

14. As recorded by Rev. James Selkirk in 1844. Quoted in Malalgoda 1973:194.

With the passage of time, however, the Buddhist attitude underwent a transformation. From about the 1840s, in fact, there were sporadic signs of a different response. The "rebellion" of 1848 itself had some religious undertones. In the Kandyan areas that were the center of insurrectionary activity, there was an undercurrent of discontent, most manifest among the traditional elite, the *bhikkhus* and the aristocracy, about the abrogation of the guarantees on religion given by the Convention of 1815.[15]

Although seemingly unaffected by the rebellion, certain areas in the maritime regions too evinced, at the same time and for that matter even earlier, a positive resistance to missionary activity. There was a series of antimissionary incidents in the Kalutara-Panadura-Moratuwa area, immediately south of Colombo, and these, according to the impression of the missionaries, were organized by the *bhikkhus.*[16] Again in 1849 the opposition to the attempt to build a church in Etul Kotte, also in the vicinity of Colombo, was so strong that the missionaries reported the proposition as having "roused the Buddhist party to far greater activity than we have ever seen in them before."[17]

Thus, it appears that by the 1840s the response to Christianity was taking an actively antagonistic form in the maritime region. Undoubtedly, this development was connected with the processes of modernization. The people in the western and southern seaboard, exposed as they had been to European influence for several centuries, were in the throes of adjustment to the new economic order introduced by the British. Unlike the more conservative Kandyans in the interior, the low-country Sinhalese were getting steadily involved in the new economic structure, as traders, transport contractors, and even owners of plantations, thus exploring avenues of upward mobility which these economic opportunities gave them. This was especially true of three caste groups in the area, namely the *Karāva, Salāgama,* and *Durāva.* Indeed, the emergence of the new Buddhist fraternities was itself largely an outcome of the social upthrust of these castes, which were considered "low" on the traditional hierarchy.[18] A flexibility available in the Sinha-

---

15. For example, a Kandyan chief is reported as having asked Governor Torrington (1847–50): "What good have we gained by British rule if you violate our treaties—not only cease to protect our religion, but on the contrary endeavour to destroy it?" Quoted in K. M. de Silva 1965:107. Also see K. M. de Silva 1973f:191.

16. Report of Rev. W. H. A. Dickson in 1948. Quoted in K. M. de Silva 1973f: 197.

17. Letter of Rev. J. F. Haslam. Quoted in K. M. de Silva 1973f:198.

18. See Ryan 1953. For the origin of these groups, see Roberts 1982: 21–34. For details about the caste aspect of the new fraternities, see Malalgoda 1976:87ff.

lese caste system, in contrast to that of India, for example, facilitated these developments. As if carrying over their assertive role in the economic and social activities to the sphere of interreligious relations, the Buddhists in the western and southern seaboard seem to have assumed an aggressive stance toward Christianity. Even the *bhikkhus* recruited from these areas apparently carried over the militancy and drive characteristic of these emergent social groups into their new role as defenders of the traditional religion.

The fact that the *sangha* in the maritime regions were adjusting themselves to the new situation was apparent even among the more traditional elements among them. Thus, a breakaway group of low-country *bhikkhus* belonging to the Siamese sect proceeded in the 1860s to set up its own headquarters in Kelaniya near Colombo. Apparently, this incident had more to it than mere disputation over ritual procedure, which was the ostensible reason for the breakaway. It was an assertion of the fact that the hub of sociocultural activity had shifted from Kandy to Colombo.[19] Also the fact that the scholar-*bhikkhus* themselves had come to recognize the need to be active in the "center" rather than be confined to the "periphery" was clearly demonstrated in 1842 when *bhikkhu* Walane Siddhartha (1811–68), who belonged to the Siamese sect and who had received his education at Ratnapura in the interior, established at Ratmalana, a southern suburb of Colombo, an institute of Oriental learning, the first of its kind in an urban area.[20] This institution attracted students from many parts of the island and proved to be the precursor to similar institutions in the Colombo region as well as in many other parts of the island.[21] Again in 1862 Walane provided the leadership to some of the leading Buddhist laymen of the time in establishing the first Sinhala newspaper of the Buddhists, the *Lak Miṇi Pahana*.[22]

These developments were indicative of a more positive role from the Buddhists in response to the predicament in which they were placed under British rule. At this stage, however, they had little or

19. Malalgoda 1976:20. The headquarters of the Siamese sect, confined to the highest (*Govigama*) caste, was in Kandy.

20. Walane's birthplace was near Weligama in the southern seaboard, and he would have had firsthand knowledge of the advances of Christianity. Also it needs mention that he was the leader of the breakaway group of the Siamese fraternity mentioned earlier.

21. See the list of his pupils given by Dharmabandhu 1973:100–102.

22. Among the laymen were Batuwantudawe and Kogglala, two ex-*bhikkhus*, and leading participants in the Sav Sat Dam controversy. For details, see *Satya Samuccaya* (15 July 1908), 39–40.

nothing in the way of an organizational apparatus with which to sustain an effective movement. Sporadic though the above instances might appear, they demonstrate that the Buddhists, in particular the *bhikkhus,* were making a multifaceted attempt to face the new situation, which was difficult and disturbing.

The loss of power and hence status for Buddhism had been a feature of colonial rule even under the Portuguese and the Dutch. Under those circumstances, however, the Buddhists in the areas ruled by the Christians could look up to the Sinhalese kingdom in Kandy as the source of ethnocultural authenticity where the traditional religion continued securely. There were, of course, in the maritime regions as elsewhere, the so-called government Christians, the Buddhists who adopted Christianity in order to obtain social or economic privileges from the government but practiced their traditional religion in the privacy of their homes. This modus vivendi, no doubt, was under constant pressure. But with the whole island coming under a Christian power the foundations of the traditional religion no longer appeared secure. Not only had Buddhism lost its preeminence as a religious system in the sociopolitical milieu to Christianity, but it also appeared in the process to have lost its "magical" potency. The assumption that:

> One thing is certain, no foreign foe be it English, Dutch, French or Kaffir will conquer Lanka. Through the protection of the four gods, the Guardians of its Religion and the Merits of the King, for five thousand years no foe will continue to reside here,[23]

had been decisively invalidated. What the Sinhalese Buddhists "had believed in was broken and re-structured on a new level of openness and uncertainty."[24] Or in other words, there was an acute distortion of the Sinhala cultural gestalt. The *bhikkhus,* as the custodians of the Sinhalese Great Tradition, would have found their perception of the place of Buddhism in the universe, which had remained undisturbed from time immemorial, suddenly and dramatically faced with a menacing challenge.

Traditionally, the Sinhalese gestalt comprised the supremacy of the Buddhist faith in magical as well as in rational terms. The Buddhist

23. From an 1812 dispatch of the Kandyan court. Quoted in Malalgoda 1970:433.

24. I have borrowed this phrase from Schwartz (1976), describing a similar situation elsewhere.

doctrine (*dhamma*) was the manifestation of "the correct vision" (*sammādiṭṭhi*) as against "false vision" (*miccādiṭṭhi*). The triumph of Buddhism, be it in intellectual deliberations or in the pursuit of personal or social goals and aspirations, was regarded as inevitable and absolute. The survival of the Sinhalese polity, which was considered the repository of the Buddhist doctrine in its pristine purity, despite the vicissitudes it confronted in several centuries of existence, was considered the most unmistakable proof of the magical potency of Buddhism. Hence the confident assertions by the Kandyan court that the kingdom would survive, uttered even when its collapse was so imminent.

As for the rational validity of Buddhism, there was in the canonical tradition a series of test situations in which this was established in no uncertain terms. First, there were the Buddha's own triumphant confrontations with polemicists professing different belief systems, ranging from nihilism to preordained fatalism. Second, there were instances of *bhikkhus* who, after the demise of the Buddha, carried on this tradition—for example, the Indian *bhikkhu* Nagasena who confronted the Greco-Bactrian philosopher king Milinda and converted him after a lengthy debate.[25] The subject matter of these various debates comprise a significant theme in classical Sinhalese literature. The twelfth-century prose work *Amāvatura*, for example, was a compendium summarizing material from canonical sources to portray the Buddha as "the charioteer-who-brings-under-control-untamed-personalities" (*purisadammasārathī*). Also the voluminous material of the debate between Nagasena and Milinda, originally in Pali and used frequently by Sinhalese writers in their edificatory compendia was finally translated into Sinhala during the eighteenth-century revival in Kandy.[26]

Christian missionaries who were active in the island during the nineteenth century were probably unaware of or insensitive to the latent strength of the Buddhist tradition, and they would not have seen the potential that lay behind the new developments among the *sangha*. Evidently, the faith of the missionaries in the magical and rational validity of their own faith matched, if not exceeded, that of the Buddhists in theirs.

Having the advantage originally of exclusive access to the printed

25. See Rhys-Davids 1890–94.

26. By *bhikkhu* Hinatikumbure Sumangala. The book contains two hundred sixty questions by Milinda and answers to them by Nagasena. Significantly, in the late nineteenth century Sinhala *Milinda Praśnaya* was edited and published by the leading figure in the Buddhist revival, *bhikkhu* Migettuwatte Gunananda.

word in religious activity,[27] the missionaries in about 1830 began a consistent program of journalistic propaganda in the vernacular. "It is by means of the press," stated the Rev. D. J. Gogerly, the manager of the Wesleyan Mission Press, "that our principal attacks must be made upon this wretched system."[28] In addition to scriptural material they published several Sinhala periodicals, the first of their kind in the language, whose subject matter was almost exclusively Christian. Of these publications the ones that characterized the missionary drive at its most aggressive were the tracts and pamphlets exhorting people to discard Buddhism and embrace Christianity.[29] Among these writings the one that led to the most far-reaching consequences was a book by the Rev. Gogerly himself entitled *Kristiāni Prajñapti* (The Evidence and Doctrine of Christianity) first published in 1849, reprinted in 1853 and 1856, and revised and enlarged in 1861 with a lengthy introduction whose subtitle was "Proofs That Buddhism Is Not a True Religion."[30] In this work we find a notable departure from the Christian literature that had appeared so far. In place of appeals to emotion *Kristiāni Prajñapti* purported to appeal to "evidences" and "proofs" claiming the superiority of Christianity on an intellectual plane. Furthermore, this book was a challenge, which came to be repeated over and over again in other tracts and missionary preachings, to the Buddhists to try if they could to disprove the "facts" presented therein. This was a challenge the *bhikkhus* were only too eager to accept. Here was an opportunity to repair and readjust the disturbed traditional gestalt. To guide them in their endeavor there was the beacon light of age-old confrontations and inevitable triumphs. What the Buddha and *bhikkhu* Nagasena did could be repeated. By triumphing over "the false vision" on rational premises, the magical validity of "the correct vision" would be automatically reasserted. Indeed, the two triumphs could be envisioned as coterminous. Hence the readiness of the *bhikkhus* to take up the challenge of the missionaries.

27. The Colombo Auxiliary Bible Society acquired the old Dutch press, the first of its kind in the island, in 1812; this was followed by the establishment of the Wesleyan Press in 1815, the Church Missionary Society Press in Kotte in 1823, and the Baptist Mission Press Kandy in 1841. Until the 1860s the Buddhists had no press for themselves.

28. Cited in Gooneratne 1968:90–91.

29. According to Murdoch and Nicholson, who prepared a catalog of these works, a total of 1,500,000 copies had been circulated during the period 1849–61 (Murdoch and Nicholson 1868:IV).

30. Malalgoda 1973:190.

For their part the *bhikkhus* who had been engaged in "internal" controversies were able thereby not only to sharpen their polemical skills but also to gain some experience in public activism in a modernizing milieu. There was another crucial factor in the alacrity of the *bhikkhus* to take up the missionary challenge. As a result of recent developments in Sinhalese society, a new type of *bhikkhu* was emerging, particularly in the low-country, who was rather more propagandist than ascetic, more public activist than religious recluse.

The figure who epitomized this transformation was *bhikkhu* Migettuwatte Gunananda (1823–90). Born in a village in the southern littoral in a family of the Salāgama caste, one of the newly assertive social groups whose upward mobility was markedly visible by the eighteenth century, he received his primary education under *bhikkhus* as well as missionaries. Later he came to Colombo, where he continued his education, gaining some proficiency in English. Eventually, he joined the Buddhist order. His mentor was his own uncle, *bhikkhu* Sinigama Dhirakkhanda of the Amarapura Saddhammavamsa fraternity, who had established a temple in Kotahena in Colombo. How these background factors contributed to mold the character of Migettuwatte is both interesting and significant. As a *bhikkhu,* too, Migettuwatte displayed the initiative and drive characteristic of the upwardly mobile social group from which he came. He was confronted with Christianity in his childhood, and no doubt with the stronger pull of the Buddhist family background he developed a detached and critical attitude toward Christianity from those early years. Again the English education he had received was to stand him in good stead in his future career, when he was to use this skill to full advantage to examine Christian scripture as well as to consult criticisms of it by European rationalists.[31] Soon after his ordination he came to live in the Kotahena temple of his uncle, *bhikkhu* Sinigama, and it appears that certain humiliations suffered by him while living in this urban milieu, where Christianity was not only triumphant but also domineering, made a deep impression on the young *bhikkhu.*[32]

31. He was to translate and publish excerpts from these European sources. One such source was *Isis Unveiled* by the Theosophist Madame Blavatsky. Another favorite source of his was the critique of Christianity by Bishop Colenso (Malalgoda 1976:62–79).

32. For example, the incident cited in one of his biographies—how a heap of cow dung was deposited in his alms bowl. See excerpts from *Srī Gunānanda Carita Kāvyaya,* in Pannasekara 1965, 1:232.

A forceful personality with an innate oratorical talent,[33] Migettuwatte was to become in time "the most brilliant polemic orator of the island, the terror of the missionaries."[34] He was by no means the first of his *bhikkhu* contemporaries to rise up in opposition to the Christian dominance of public life. No other, however, seemed to match his vigor and resourcefulness. Migettuwatte may thus be considered the leading figure in the Buddhist revivalist movement during the latter half of the nineteenth century.[35] Indeed, it was largely due to his efforts that a "movement" with an organizational structure, modern tactics, and popular participation came into being to meet the Christian challenge. With him the Buddhist reaction against the advancing forces took a systematic and determined form. He organized societies, established a printing press, wrote pamphlets and tracts, toured the island disseminating his message, and, above all, confronted the missionaries face to face in publicly staged debates. The most striking aspect of Migettuwatte's activities was the modernism of his approach. His tactics for combating Christianity were deliberately modeled on missionary methods and devices. The first society he founded, indeed the first modern association among the Sinhala Buddhists, was the Sarvagña Sāsanābhivrddhidāyaka Dharma Samāgama (1862), identified in English as the "Society for the Propagation of Buddhism." This was obviously influenced by the "Society for the Propagation of the Gospel" founded by the missionaries in 1840.[36]

Again, meeting the missionaries on their own grounds, Migettuwatte established a printing press and brought forth voluminous literature, mostly from his own pen, defending Buddhism and attacking Christianity. Adopting the practice of itinerant preaching, popularized by the missionaries, he toured the island disseminating his message of resistance to Christianity.[37] All in all one sees in his career

33. According to John Capper, a contemporary British journalist, Migettuwatte was a "consummate master in public harranguing" (Malalgoda 1973:197).

34. In the words of the American theosophist Col. Henry Steel Olcott (Jayawardene 1972).

35. Others were Walane, Hikkaduwe, and Bulathgama.

36. Malalgoda 1973:192. Two other societies founded by Migettuwatte were the Bodhiraja Samitiya (against the cutting down of Bo trees, which were objects of Buddhist worship, for road building and other "modern" purposes) and Abhyagiri Caityopakara Samitiya (against the plan of the government to excavate a Buddhist shrine in Anuradhapura to ascertain the wealth enshrined therein). See Dhammawamsa 1971.

37. His diary is said to contain reference to over four thousand sermons thus delivered. See Siladhara 1920:23.

a striking example of "antagonistic acculturation."[38] The zeal and the doggedness with which he seems to have pursued his propagandist task bears a closer resemblance to the psychology and performance of the Christian missionary than to those of the traditional Buddhist *bhikkhu*. His career epitomized the emergence of the modern socially active Buddhist monk, the precursor of the "political *bhikkhus*" of the twentieth century.

At the same time we need to remember the pioneering work of *bhikkhu* Walane in establishing a new center of Oriental learning. Another pioneer, working first on lines similar to Migettuwatte and later following in the footsteps of his teacher Walane, was the *bhikkhu* Hikkaduwe Sumangala (1827–1911). Hikkaduwe too was born in a village on the southern littoral and entered the Buddhist order at an early age. Receiving an early education in Sinhala and Pali from the *bhikkhu* Pannamgoda Jetthuttara, a leading scholar of the time, he also learned English from a layman in Galle. To further his Oriental studies he arrived at Walane's institution near Colombo and became one of his most brilliant pupils. Going back to his temple in Hikkaduwa, he joined the *bhikkhu* Bulathgama and a small group of Buddhist activists in the southern town of Galle, who were setting up a printing press called Lankōpakāra ("succor of Lanka") to combat Christian literary warfare. With his intellectual skills and literary talents he soon became the chief spokesman of the group, and a number of Buddhist polemical works written by Hikkaduwe were published by the Lankōpakāra Press.

Another early literary combatant of missionary propaganda was the ex-*bhikkhu* Batuwantudawe (1819–92). Also born in a southern village near Galle and ordained as a *bhikkhu*, he too received higher Oriental education under Walane at Ratmalana and, being senior to Hikkaduwe, was for some time teacher to the latter. Although ill health compelled him to disrobe, he remained steadfast as a Buddhist and was the author of *Kristiāni Prajñapti Khanḍanaya* (The Tearing Asunder of *Kristiani Prajñapti*), of the earliest replies to Gogerly's *Kristiani Prajñapti*.[39] Batuwantudawe, along with his teacher Walane and some other Buddhist laymen, was among those who launched the first Sinhala newspaper of the Buddhists, the *Lak Miṇi Pahana*, in 1862.

38. "The adoption of new methods to support existing ends" (Devereaux and Loeb 1943:143).

39. Its publication was delayed because the Buddhists had no press of their own at the time. See Buddhadatta 1950:177–80.

There were several other *bhikkhus* engaged in similar activity in promoting Buddhist interests. One of these was Bulathgama Sumana (d. 1891), more an organizer than writer or polemicist. Born in the interior but migrating to the seaside town of Galle in the south and residing in a temple there, Bulathgama was one of the earliest to realize the need for the establishment of a printing press to combat missionary propaganda. His steadfastness of purpose and organizational skill were amply displayed in the manner in which he financed the Lankōpakāra Press in Galle in 1862. He collected funds not only from people in Galle and its environs but also from rich landowners in remote parts of the island. Finding these donations inadequate, he finally appealed for support, and got it, from the king of Siam, with whom he had been acquainted while studying in that country.[40] Furthermore, Bulathgama was able to obtain the collaboration of *bhikkhus* of all fraternities in this enterprise of establishing a Buddhist press, thus giving the project the substance as well as the appearance of a united Buddhist effort.[41]

Bulathgama's organizational skill was again displayed in the way in which he marshaled the Buddhist forces in confronting the missionaries at a public debate in Baddegama, near Galle, in February 1865. Among the fifty *bhikkhus* who gathered there on Bulathgama's request were all the leading scholar *bhikkhus* of every fraternity. Furthermore, shattering the belief of the missionaries that the Buddhist populace was indifferent about their religion, there were about two thousand Buddhist laymen who had come to support the *bhikkhus*.[42] This mobilization of Buddhist resources was unprecedented, and it had a decisive effect on the missonary mind. Thus, the Rev. George Parsons, chief of the missionary station where the debate took place, reported:

> Never before in Ceylon was there such a marshalling of the enemy against Christianity. The one aim of the fifty priests and their two thousand followers who assembled there on February 8th, was not to defend Buddhism but to overthrow Christianity.[43]

40. Pannasekara 1965, 1:101–4.

41. Although he belonged to one of the Amarapura fraternities, Bulathgama's role was that of coordinator between different fraternities since he commanded the respect and confidence of all. See Malalgoda 1976.

42. The Christian side, on the other hand, amounted to no more than sixty or seventy, including the clergymen. See Malalgoda 1973:156.

43. Balding 1922:119–20.

Apart from the show of strength, the impact made by the Buddhist side intellectually was no doubt due to the talents of Bulathgama's collaborators. His ability, however, in having organized and led the Buddhist party, including laymen, must not be underestimated.

It might be said that with the Baddegama controversy the missionaries had an inkling of the shape of the Buddhist counteroffensive that was to follow. The Baddegama controversy was followed by other similar public debates: at Waragoda near Colombo in August 1865, at Udanwita in the Four Korales in February 1866, and at Gampola near Kandy in January 1871. The most dramatic confrontation between Christian preachers and Buddhist *bhikkhus* took place in April 1873 at Panadura, a small town immediately south of Colombo. Here Migettuwatte, the "consumate master in public haranguing," faced two Sinhala Christian preachers, David de Silva and F. S. Sirimanne, in a two-day, publicly staged debate and impressed the crowd of nearly ten thousand who were present that the Buddhist party had achieved a resounding victory over the Christians:

> Scarcely had the last words of the above lecture [of Migettuwatte] been uttered, when cries of "sadhu sadhu" [uttered by Buddhists in religious fervor] ascended from the thousands who were present. Endeavours were made by the handful of police (who were present) to keep order, but nothing induced them to cease their vociferous cries until at the request of the learned High Priest of Adam's Peak [Hikkaduwe] the priest Migettuwatte again rose, and with a wave of hand, beckoned the men to be quiet, when all was still.[44]

The Panadura debate was the last major polemical confrontation between the Buddhists and the Christians.[45] Leaving aside the religious disputations in these debates, they demonstrated beyond doubt the strength the traditional religion was able to mobilize. Clearly, the missionaries had underestimated the potential that lay dormant, awaiting suitable times and effective agents of mobilization to be roused into full vigor and vibrancy.

The missionaries indeed underestimated the intellectual capacities

44. John Capper in 1873. Quoted in Malalgoda 1973:197.

45. The pamphlet warfare was to continue. See Pannasekara 1965: vol. 1. Also, in

of the *bhikkhus* and also their ability to inspire the Buddhist populace. Thus, the Rev. Robert Spence Hardy had noted about twenty years before the Panadura controversy that the

> countenance of the [Buddhist] priests in Ceylon are frequently less intelligent than those of the common people; indeed there is often an appearance about them of great vacancy, amounting almost to imbecility.[46]

As far as the enthusiasm they could have generated goes, the opinion was equally low. "In no part of the island that I have visited," commented Hardy, "do the [Buddhist] priests as a body appear to be respected by the people."[47] Furthermore, to European and Christian eyes the Sinhalese appeared as singularly indifferent to their traditional religion. Thus, Tennent had written in 1850:

> No national system of religion, no prevailing superstition that has ever fallen under my observation presents so dull a level, and is so pre-eminently deficient in popular influence, as Buddhism among the Sinhalese. The fervid earnestness of Christianity, even in its most degenerate forms, the fanatical enthusiasm of Islam, the proud exclusiveness of Brahma(nism) and even the zealous warmth of other Northern faiths, are all emotions utterly foreign and unknown to the followers of Buddhism in Ceylon.[48]

The possibility is there that these remarks on the *sangha* and the Buddhist populace at large were the result of prejudice or lack of insight into the real conditions of the Sinhalese society. If, indeed, these observations were accurate, however, events during the second half of the century proved that there had been a drastic change in the situation. A missionary who was present at the Panadura debate in August 1873 noted:

1899, there was another public debate at Urugodawatta, a suburb of Colombo, where the chief Buddhist spokesman was *bhikkhu* Jananananda, a pupil of Migettuwatte.

46. Quoted in Malalgoda 1973:197.

47. Quoted in Malagoda 1973:198.

48. Tennent 1850:229.

> It was one of the most remarkable things I have ever witnessed. It proved in a striking manner the strong interest, the deep anxiety which exists among the masses of the people about their religion.[49]

At Panadura the *bhikkhus* had not only displayed most effectively their intellectual and polemical skills but also proved beyond doubt their ability to inspire and mobilize the Buddhist populace in confronting the advances of Christianity. And the polemical activism of the *bhikkhus* proved to be the beginnings of a religiocultural revival.

Religion as a Mobilizational Resource

For the first time since the surge of Westernization began in the early nineteenth century a mass rebuttal from the indigenous culture was in the offing. It was noted previously how about twenty years earlier an individual, James D'Alwis, experiencing personally the stresses and strains of a cultural conflict, made a strenuous effort to conserve the traditional culture against the inroads of Westernization. His writings contained a comprehensive and cogent exposition and an ardent and resolute defense of one aspect of the indigenous tradition–the Sinhala language. The fervent language loyalty of D'Alwis, however, did not receive a wide response that would inspire a popular movement. The reason for this, apart from the fact that he was writing mostly in English and thus had a limited readership, was that language was not a forceful enough factor for mass mobilization at that time.

Religion, on the other hand, proved to be a more potent force in converting primordial bonds into instruments of conscious group defensive activity, in transforming "outward form and ordinance" to an "affair of the heart."[50] The masses were made to feel a deep "anxiety" about their religion. This was an unprecedented concern about a facet of primordial ethnicity which had apparently been taken for granted so far. It was no longer possible for Buddhists to be "slumbering in their security." It was as if, between the passing of the old order and the emergence of the new, a facet of the old order was salvaged and given a new and crucial significance. Indeed, the Buddhist religion was now

49. Quoted in Jayawardene 1972:45.
50. I borrow this phrase from Knox 1950:12.

becoming a badge of exclusive identity.[51] As characteristic of a period of transition where traditional behaviors and thought processes were still strong, the religion could truly have acted as a potent factor in igniting mass response. It was perhaps the most tangible symbol of traditional ethnicity that the "transitionals" could have grasped in their search for an identity.

As noted, the region in which the Buddhist revival originated and existed in its most potent form was the low country, in particular the coastal urban areas in the southern and southwestern parts of the island. This was the area most strongly experiencing the processes of modernization under the impact of Western civilization. In addition to the rapidly expanding city of Colombo other coastal towns were attracting populations in search of new economic ventures.[52] In these urbanizing milieus with new avenues of socioeconomic mobility and novel forms of social contact and intercourse, traditional institutions, behaviors, and thought processes were being drastically undermined. In this situation, highly disruptive of the traditional worldview with its old roles and relationships, there would have been an acute need for a sense of belonging, a base of identity upon which to place one's feet.

Revivalism as an Affirmation of Identity

The advances of Christianity formed another aspect of the disruptive impact of Western civilization. The manner in which the displacement of Buddhism from its preeminent status in society resulted in the distortion of the traditional gestalt and nativistic responses from the *sangha*, has been discussed. Apart from that, the very appearance of Christianity in Sinhalese society seems to have been, by itself, "disruptive" in another sense. It was disruptive of the traditional form of Sinhalese identity.[53] This in itself created the need for an adjustive reaction.

Prior to the advent of Christianity an integral feature of the Sinha-

51. Earlier, under the expediency of becoming "government Christians," the Buddhists found no difficulty in claiming to be Buddhist and Christian at one and the same time. Thus, when Lambrick, a missionary, once asked a Sinhalese what his religion was "the answer was 'Buddha's.' 'So then you are not a Christian?' 'Oh yes, to be sure I am; I am a Christian, and of the Reformed Dutch religion too!.' " Mentioned in Tennent 1850:313n.1.

52. Amunugama 1975:290–91.

53. The Sinhalese population was confined to the island of Sri Lanka, and all Sinhalese were generally Buddhists. We have evidence of extremely rare cases of Sinhalese Hindus who were usually progenies of Sinhalese-Indian mixed marriages.

lese identity was the adherence to the Buddhist religion. Being Sinhalese generally meant being Buddhist as well. Once some of the Sinhalese embraced Christianity this age-old form of Sinhalese identity became invalid. Every Sinhalese was no longer ipso facto a Buddhist. Those who continued to remain Buddhist were the bearers of the authentic form of the Sinhalese identity. Being Christian was considered an aberration. The *bhikkhus,* as the bearers of the Great Tradition, would have felt a strong need to lay stress upon this authentic national identity. Hence the "identity affirmation" endeavors that characterize the Buddhist revival.[54]

Evidently, so far as numbers were concerned, Christianity was by no means displacing Buddhism.[55] The concern, however, seems to have been aroused mainly by the "appearance" of the superiority of Christianity, the feeling reinforced by the loss of prestige suffered by Buddhism. Undoubtedly, concrete cases of discrimination exacerbated the anxiety. The *bhikkhus,* as a group, were the segment of the Sinhalese population who appear to have felt this anxiety most intensely. Being scholars, they were aware of the situation in the past, and, futhermore, they were the section of the population to experience most heavily the loss of status under the new dispensation. With their advantageous position as preceptors they could fan up enthusiasm and build a sense of popular concern about the old religion. This enthusiasm, however, was not aimed at spiritual ends so much (i.e., to make the people more pious) as at social-spatial ends (i.e., to reassert the lost status of Buddhism).[56] The *bhikkhus* thus manipulated an older role, which was at the time lying dormant, to generate a new sentiment over a primordial bond. The means adopted by them were modern, modeled as they were on the tactics of the adversaries, the Christian missionaries.

The Theosophist Involvement and the Borrowing of Further European Tactics

At the Panadura controversy of 1873 one saw, among other things, the capacity of the *bhikkhus* to mobilize mass participation in a group en-

54. Obeysekere 1975:255.

55. According to the census of 1881, out of a total population of 2,759,738 there were 1,698,570 Buddhists as compared to 267,977 Christians (J. Ferguson 1887:244–66). While the Buddhists were mainly Sinhalese, the total number of Christians included other races as well.

56. Saram 1977:314.

deavor. As we have seen earlier, the mass enthusiasm for Buddhism was the result both of the need for identity affirmation and the eagerness, especially of the *bhikkhus,* to adapt themselves to the new situation.

These tendencies received a strong stimulus after 1880, with the involvement of some Westerners in the island's Buddhist activities. Henry Steele Olcott (1832–1907), an American lawyer, read about the Panadura debate in an English publication.[57] Himself a critic of Christianity and an admirer of Eastern philosophy, a founder of the Theosophical Society in New York,[58] Olcott entered into communication with Migettuwatte and his associates. As a result of the link thus established, Olcott decided to visit Sri Lanka and arrived in the island in 1880 with the cofounder of the Theosophical Society, Helena Petrovna Blavatsky.

The subsequent involvement of these "first white champions" of the Buddhist religion was to have an electrifying effect on the revivalist movement, which was already gathering momentum. Olcott noted:

> The people could not do enough for us. . . . We were the first white champions of their religion, speaking of its excellence from the platforms, in the face of the missionaries, its enemies and slanderers. It was that which thrilled their nerves and filled their affectionate hearts to bursting. I may seem to use strong language. But in reality it falls far short of facts.[59]

As a contemporary observer noted, the strong stimulus provided by Olcott's arrival made the Buddhists feel "a second awakening . . . since the Panadura Controversy."[60]

Apart from heightening the enthusiasm of the Buddhists Olcott provided the Buddhist movement with further experience in organiza-

---

57. That was *Buddhism and Christianity in Discussion Face to Face; or, an Oral Debate between Rev. Miggettuwastte and Dev. D. Silva held at Panthura, Ceylon,* by Patrick Peebles (Battle Creek, Mich., 1873).

58. In 1875. Later the headquarters were shifted to Adayar in south India. The society's doctrines were an admixture of Hinduism, Buddhism, and nineteenth-century European spiritualism, occultism, and humanitarianism. Subsequently, it became an attempt to bolster the confidence and dignity of Eastern religions. See M. Singer 1972:29.

59. Olcott's diary. Quoted in Jayawardene 1972:48.

60. Dharmapala 1965:700. By about 1900, however, Dharamapala became a critic of theosophism, accusing it of going against Buddhist orthodoxy.

tion and group activity on European lines.[61] Addressing the Buddhists, he declared,

> If you ask me how we should organize our forces I point you to your great enemy, Christianity, and bid you look at their large and wealthy Bible, Tract, Sunday School, and Missionary societies, the tremendous agencies they support to keep alive and spread their religion.[62]

This was probably the clarion call for a rejuvenated Buddhism to forge ahead in earnest. Olcott himself founded the Buddhist Theosophical Society (BTS) in Colombo in 1880. In it were mobilized the newly emergent bourgeoisie eagerly looking for channels of self-assertion. Branches of the BTS were founded in Galle, Matara, Bentota, and Welitara in the southern coast and in Kandy in the interior. Other similar organizations soon followed suit.

Again in imitation of Christian institutions, Young Men's Buddhist Associations (YMBA) were established in various parts of the island.[63] Olcott published a "Buddhist Catechism" in 1881, again imitating a Christian model.[64] By this time the *bhikkhu* Migettuwatte had published *Buddha Ädahilla,* which was an attempt to provide Buddhists of his day with ritual procedures as befitting the urban circumstances.[65] In 1880 Olcott and other Buddhist activists launched a movement to have Vesak full-moon day, the birthday of the Buddha, declared a public holiday.[66] Again a committee consisting of Migettuwatte, Hik-

61. Other Europeans followed Olcott and became involved in Buddhist activities. Thus, C. W. Leadbeater, Fritz Kunz, F. L. Woodward, and Maseus Higgins became principals of Buddhist schools, and J. Bowes Daly acted for some time as the manager of the BTS schools. As noted earlier, the imitation of European tactics had already started when Olcott arrived.

62. Quoted in Malalgoda 1974:161.

63. The Colombo YMBA was founded in 1898, and others followed in the principal towns. A conference of All Ceylon YMBA's was held in Colombo in 1919. See Piyasena 1972:2.

64. The popularity of this work may be gauged from the fact that by 1884 about fourteen thousand copies had been sold. See editorial of *Sarasavi Sañdaräsa* (*Sa. Sa.*), 21 March 1884.

65. As Malalgoda observes, this work (comp. in the 1880s) has an "utterly untraditional title," being an imitation of Christian models. Malalgoda 1972:162.

66. This demand was made through the BTS newspaper *Sarasavi Sañdaräsa* as early as 1880. See its editorial on 3 April 1880. But it was granted only in 1885.

kaduwe, and several laymen designed a Buddhist flag, which was adopted in 1885.[67] Olcott's initiative was a key factor behind the inauguration of the Buddhist Theosophical Society's paper, *Sarasavi Sañdaräsa* (in December 1880), which subsequently claimed to be "the mouthpiece of two millions of Buddhists in Ceylon."[68]

A Buddhist Lay Educational System

Olcott's greatest contribution to the Buddhist revival was in the organization of an effective counter to the missionary educational system. Although the *bhikkhus* had been carrying on their traditional function of imparting rudiments of literacy in the temples, the missionaries held undisputed sway over the new educational system until the Buddhist Theosophical Society earnestly began to establish its own Buddhist schools in the 1880s. Prior to this some low-country *bhikkhus,* again adjusting themselves to the new situation, had pioneered the establishment of "modern" Buddhist schools. These attempts, however, were sporadic, and they were not organized on a national scale, as Olcott's was to be.[69] It was Olcott, applying his experience in modern organizational activity, who was able to mobilize the bubbling enthusiasm he found among the Buddhists at his advent on the island for the establishment of a firm foundation for a modern Buddhist educational system.

Others followed Olcott's example, and by the early years of the twentieth century the Buddhists were able to establish an effective rival to the Christian school system. Thus, in 1900 there were 142 Buddhist Theosophical Society schools compared to 1,117 Christian missionary schools. By 1910 the BTS schools nearly doubled, rising to 225, while another 217 "private" schools, mostly managed by Buddhists, had been established as against 1,371 Christian mission schools.[70] Although the Christians still maintained their lead, the sharp increase in the number of Buddhist schools in addition to indicating a burst of Buddhist activism seems to have disturbed the missionary mind. Thus, the European head of a missionary station near Colombo wrote in 1904:

67. Sumatipala 1970:79.

68. Bevan 1907:318.

69. Two *bhikkhus,* Dodanduwe Piyaratana, who established a school in Dodanduwa near Galle in 1868, and Koratota Sobhita, who established schools in Handapangoda and Homagama near Colombo in the 1870s, are two such pioneers. See Malalgoda 1976:158, 235.

70. Sumatipala 1968:48.

> Christianity cannot be said to be in a thriving condition here, converts are few, and the best of them seem glad to get away to other parts. Thus there are 538 Christians against 653 in 1901, whilst there are 324 children less in schools.[71]

Beginnings of Buddhist Pressure Group Activity

The establishment of schools and other self-assertive activities by the Buddhists was facilitated by the financial support of the newly emergent groups of Sinhalese entrepreneurs. Entering into the world of the new economic structure from traditional village life, this emergent bourgeoisie seems to have brought along with it its devotion to Buddhism, to refurbish it with a new symbolic value under the changed circumstances. In the cosmopolitan urban milieu Buddhism became this emerging group's badge of identity as well as the cause for social activism.

Olcott again may be considered the agent in this transformation. He came to Asia when it still had the characteristics of a feudal society and many parts of the region were in the hands of colonial powers. With his liberal experience in the United States and his legal acumen he seems to have taught the Buddhists in Sri Lanka their first lessons in the assertion of majority rights.[72] An early occasion for this were the Kotahena riots of 1883 in which a noisy but peaceful Buddhist procession was attacked by a group of Roman Catholics; one person was killed and several others were injured. Olcott, who at the time was in India, returned to the island immediately and formed the Buddhist Defence Committee (BDC) in Colombo, whose membership included the Buddhist businessmen of Colombo and the principal towns.[73] Having thus mobilized the Buddhist activists in the island, he set forth for London to present the Buddhist case for redress of grievances before the Colonial Office. Although little was achieved by this mission, the lesson in organized protest learned by the Buddhists in particular and the Sinhalese in general was to go a long way. In this connection the forma-

71. Balding 1922:125.

72. Once more the origins of such thinking can be traced to pre-Olcott days. Thus, when *bhikkhu* Walane and some other Buddhists inaugurated the first Buddhist newspaper, they were briefed about "popular rights" by the Burgher lawyers C. A. Lorenz, Frederick Nell, and Louis Nell. See the editorial in *Lak Miṇi Pahana* (*LMP*), 11 September 1862.

73. K. M. de Silva 1973d:202. For details about the riot, see Rogers 1987:176–80.

tion of the Buddhist Defence Committee is of special significance. In its role as the defender of Buddhist rights vis-à-vis the government and private employers it was the precursor of more vigorous organizations in later times.[74]

With the financial backing provided by the Buddhist entrepreneurs there was a burst of Buddhist self-assertive activity during the last decades of the nineteenth century. In their eagerness to affirm their Sinhala-Buddhist identity, these rich Buddhists embarked on ambitious projects of ostentatious Buddhist activity. Most notable among them were the projects for the restoration of Buddhist ruins in ancient centers of Sinhalese civilization and the construction of new Buddhist edifices in urban milieus. As for the restoration of Buddhist ruins, two of the massive projects undertaken were the restoration of Ruvanveli Dagaba at Anuradhapura, begun sometime in the 1870s, and the restoration of Tissamaharama Dagaba at Magama, begun a few years later.[75] Indeed, in an era of intense revivalist activity the desire to see these edifices in their pristine condition would have been a symbolic journey into the past. The societies for the "development" of these Buddhist shrines received the lavish patronage of Buddhist entrepreneurs.[76]

If the restoration work at historical sites was satisfying to the nostalgia for past glories, the construction of new Buddhist edifices in urban milieus was an emphatic assertion of group rights in the modern context. Among the achievements of many newly rich businessmen was their participation in the construction of new temples in Colombo and its environs.[77] With these activities the newly emergent entrepreneurs—individually as well as through associations—were gradually

---

74. The aim of the BDS was to "get the government to do what the Buddhists want," and the Buddhists were asked to report to it any discriminatory acts by government officers or private employers (see *Sa.Sa.*, 7 March 1884). The later organizations were the Bauddha Maha Sammelanaya (the All Ceylon Buddhist Congress), Eksath Bhikku Peramuna, and Bauddha Jatika Balavegaya. For details, see D. E. Smith 1966a, b; and Wilson 1966.

75. Both edifices date from about the second century B.C. and stand over three hundred feet covering areas of over ten acres of solid brick masonery. The latter project was completed in 1914 and the former in 1940.

76. For example, the benefactions of Colombo businessmen such as N. S. Fernando, W. E. Bastian, and Carolis Hewawitarana to the restoration works at Anuradhapura and Magama. Fernando and Bastian also constructed two massive rest houses at Anuradhapura providing free accommodation to pilgrims.

77. Some notable examples are, the Wijewardena family building the new Kelaniya temple, the Pedris family building the Isipathanaramaya in Colombo, and the Dias family the Rankot Viharaya in Panadura.

replacing the erstwhile patronage base of Buddhism and Sinhalese cultural activity, which was being rapidly eroded by the Europeanization of old aristocratic families.

The Pirivenas *as Centers of Revivalism*

The availability of the above-mentioned economic resources also facilitated the rise of Buddhist monastic colleges as modern centers of educational and cultural activity. Thus, under the patronage of some Buddhist businessmen who formed themselves into an association called the Vidyādhāra Sabhāva, a Buddhist institution of learning named Vidyōdaya Pirivena was established in 1873 at Maligakanda in Colombo. A sister institution with a similar patronage base was established two years later at Peliyagoda, on the northern outskirts of Colombo, and this was named Vidyālankāra Pirivena. The word *pirivena* was the term by which such institutions were known during the days of the Sinhalese kings, and, as *bhikkhu* Hikkaduwe Sumangala, the founder of Vidyōdaya, saw it, these were the "university colleges of the Buddhist priesthood."[78] Both Hikkaduwe and Ratmalane (the founder of Vidyālankāra) were pupils of *bhikkhu* Walane Siddhartha, whose pioneering activities in molding a modern Buddhist response have been noted. It is as if these two able pupils expanded those activities to a more systematic fruition. Soon they were followed by others, mainly their own pupils, in other parts of the island: Vidyabhāṣa Mandira in Welitara (1884), Gunaratana Mudalinda Pirivena in Matara (1890), Sadānanda Pirivena of Doranegoda (1896), Saddharmākara Pirivena of Pinwatta (1900), Srī Saddharmōdaya Pirivena of Godawila (1901), and Sikkhākara Pirivena of Welitara (1902), to mention a few. By 1917 there were sixty-two well-established *pirivenas* in different parts of the island,[79] most of which, as might be expected, were in the southern and western coastal areas.

The founding of these *pirivenas* marked a widespread revival of Oriental learning through a vigorous interest in the classical literature of Sinhala, Pali, and Sanskrit. Utilizing the newly established printing presses, scholars enthusiastically engaged themselves in projects of editing and printing classical works in these languages, which were so far available only in manuscript form. The thirteenth-century Sinhala

78. Sumangala 1907:292.
79. *Annual Report of the Director of Education* 1917:4.

grammar *Sidat Sangarāva* was one of the earliest to be so printed, and it was the classical Sinhala text that received the greatest attention by the revivalist scholars.[80] The *Siyabas Lakara,* a tenth-century work on Sinhalese rhetoric, was edited by H. Jayatilaka in 1862. The *bhikkhu* Ratmalane Dhammaloka with his brilliant pupil Ratmalane Dhammarama (1853–1918) edited the twelfth-century exegetical work *Dharmapradīpikāva* in 1886. Again H. Jayatilaka edited the twelfth-century compendium of Buddhist stories, the *Amāvatura,* in parts during 1884–86. Hendrick de Saram published a glossary of the same work in 1886. The twelfth-century eulogy of the Buddha, the *Butsaraṇa,* was edited by *bhikkhu* Mulleriyave Vipulasara in 1894. The *Muvadev Dā Vata,* a twelfth-century poem, was edited by Pundit Weragama Punchi Bandara, one of the earliest and most distinguished pupils of Vidyōdaya, in 1880. Another Sinhala poem of the twelfth century, the *Sasa Dā Vata,* was edited by *bhikkhu* Aturuwelle Dhammapala in 1901. In 1899 *bhikkhu* Madugalle Siddartha, another alumnus of Vidyōdaya, edited the thirteenth-century Sinhala *mahākavya* (epic poem) the *Kav Siḷu Miṇa.* The ex-*bhikkhu* Pundit M. Dharmaratna edited the voluminous Buddhist exegetical work, the *Visuddhi Mārga Sannaya* of the thirteenth century in 1889, and so on. This vigorous interest in classical literature was occurring contemporaneously with the forging of another link with the community's past: the excavation of ancient sites of Sinhalese civilization by archaeologists and epigraphists.

The Inspiration from the Ethnoreligious Past

Goaded by accusations by European scholars that the British administration of the island had done hardly anything to collect and preserve the valuable antiquities found there,[81] the government began by the late 1860s to take an interest in this area. Indeed, there was a marked change in government policy, and a more positive view of Buddhism and Sinhalese culture had emerged during the 1870s and 1880s. First, the task of preparing a catalog of Sanskrit, Pali, and Sinhala literary works found on the island was entrusted to James D'Alwis.[82] Subsequently, beginning in 1871, archaeological and epigraphical work con-

80. The significance of this is discussed in chap. 5.

81. For example, see the article from the *Saturday Review* of 28 July 1866, reproduced in D'Alwis 1870:IX.

82. See D'Alwis 1870; 1878.

nected with the ancient capitals Anuradhapura (fifth c. B.C.–eleventh c. A.D.) and Polonnaruva (eleventh c.–thirteenth c.), and other centers of early settlement such as Magama in the south, were taken up. Two European scholars, P. Goldschmidt and E. Müller, were entrusted with the epigraphical studies.[83] After several years of preliminary work in archaeological discovery the government established in 1890 the Archaeological Survey of Ceylon with H. C. P. Bell of the civil service as the first commissioner, and with this began the systematic excavation and preservation of ancient sites. Connected with this was the repair of ancient irrigation works, the man-made reservoirs and their canal systems, as part of the government's agricultural policy, particularly under the governorships of Sir Henry Ward (1855–60), Sir William Henry Gregory (1872–77), and Sir Arthur Gordon (1883–90).

With the bringing into light of the achievements of the ancient Sinhalese in architecture and engineering the visibility of past greatness was to intensify the desire for identity affirmation in the present. Furthermore, the contrast between the glory of the past and the contemporary "degradation" goaded several activists to persistent agitation. The most notable among them were David Hewavitarana (1864–1933), who assumed the name Anagarika Dharmapala, and David de Silva (1876–1913), who assumed the name Valisinha Harischandra. Dharmapala first and Harischandra following him adopted ascetic life-styles while remaining laymen. This novel role was to facilitate their singular mission of Sinhalese and Buddhist agitational activity. Both were prolific writers, and both toured the island speaking of the community's glorious cultural heritage and exhorting their compatriots to discard European habits and to adopt authentic Sinhalese and Buddhist ways and customs. In "A Message to the Young Men of Ceylon" in 1922 Dharmapala stated:

> No nation in the world has had a more brilliant history than ourselves. . . . The Sinhalese have for nearly a hundred years followed the path of stagnation. . . . We are blindly following the white man who has come here to demoralize us for his own gain . . . Avoid alcohol, avoid beef, and go back to the traditions of our successful forefathers who immortalized themselves

83. Their pioneering work *The Ancient Inscriptions of Ceylon* was published in 1881. This was followed by *Epigraphia Zeylanica,* the first volume edited by D. M. de Z. Wickremasinghe in 1904, with subsequent volumes edited by him and others.

> by their wonderful architectural achievements, whose vestiges we see today at Anuradhapura, Polonnaruva, and admired by those who see them.[84]

In his fascination with the ruins at Anuradhapura Harischandra declared:

> The longest a man can live is a hundred years. But the great *dāgabas*, the great tanks, and the stone monuments with beautiful carvings will remain for thousands of years. As long as they survive, the valour and the halo of fame of the Sinhalese race will for certain remain widespread.[85]

It should be noted that English-educated revivalist leaders such as Dharmapala and Harischandra would have been influenced by writings of nineteenth-century European scholars who admired the cultural achievements of Oriental people.[86] At the same time, however, we cannot underestimate the inspiration they received from the indigenous tradition, which was being mined and refined by Sinhalese scholars from about the 1840s.

The study of classical works of Sinhalese literature found further and sustained application with the establishment of the *pirivena* seats of learning. Having formal and informal links with the parent institutions in Colombo and with each other, the provincial *pirivenas* could function as disseminating centers of revivalism. By the early years of the twentieth century revivalism gained further momentum with the growth of modern social mobilization.

---

84. Dharmapala 1965:501.
85. Harischandra 1912:Intro.
86. See Wickramaratne 1984:149–50, 163–66, 207–8.

Chapter 5

Revivalism, Social Mobilization, and the Sinhala Language

> The only race which has maintained noble principles down its generations is the Aryan race. The only language with fully articulated sounds and complete letters is the Aryan language. . . . The Sinhala language developed with the Aryan Sanskrit and Pali languages as its origin. The only way in which one can know about the ancient Sinhalese who had noble qualities is through the Sinhala language.
>
> —Anagarika Dharmapala, *Sinhala Bauddhaya,* 2 March 1912

The Buddhist revival was primarily a reaction against Christian dominance and expansion. In contrast to the early nineteenth century, when the Buddhists appeared passive and inactive and unprepared to adjust themselves to the new situation, Buddhist activism by the turn of the century evinced great enthusiasm and vitality. This development was largely due to the availability and adoption of new avenues and instruments of social mobilization. Significantly, revivalist ideology had an impact on the Sinhala language as well.

New Forms of Social Mobilization

For Dharmapala, Harischandra, and other Buddhist activists extensive propagandist activity was possible because they were able to gain effective mastery of the newly introduced forms of mass media. The second half of the nineteenth century saw the growth of the Sinhalese periodical, the novel, and the theater as a consequence of rapid socioeconomic change.

The most marked feature of this change was the growth of vernacular literacy following the government's change of policy with regard to education—vernacular literacy taking priority over the spread of English. Consequently, there was a rise in the numbers literate in the vernacular. The percentage was 26.4 percent in 1911.[1] Along with the growth of literacy a middle and "working" class was growing up, consequent upon the new occupational opportunities, and urban centers were in the process of steady growth. For this urban populace there was the need for reading and entertainment to fill their leisure hours. Thus, a vernacular-educated literary clientele was rapidly emerging, especially in urban milieus, and to meet those recreational needs the Sinhalese periodical, novel, and theater arose during the second half of the nineteenth century.

Another feature seen in connection with the urban population of nineteenth-century Sri Lanka was the emergence of voluntary associations. Urbanization, as it occurred, seems to have fostered the growth of such associations, especially those with religious and ethnic aspirations. When populations from the tradition dominated countryside were thrown into the urban situation, with its multiethnic, multireligious, and multicaste social composition, the need to "belong" and to be related to something supraindividual was provided by these voluntary associations—*samāgam,* as they were called. For the new urbanites, whose ties with the traditional background were still intact, associations with (Buddhist) religious and (Sinhalese) ethnic aspirations were the natural choice.[2]

The founding of newspapers and periodicals on the one hand and the emergence of voluntary associations on the other coincided with the religiocultural revival. Indeed, the rapid and extensive growth in both these spheres was undoubtedly due to this co-incidence. Journalists, novelists, and dramatists were whipping up popular awareness and concern for various aspects of the communal identity. Similarly, revivalist activists were avidly recruiting members for (Buddhist) religious and (Sinhalese) ethnic defensive and assertive organizations. The low country, especially the southwestern and southern littoral, was the center of this mobilizational activity, which spread consequently to other regions of the island.

This social mobilization through new channels of mass contact is one of the most noteworthy features in the growth of modern Sinhalese

1. Denham 1912:401.

2. See Jayawardene 1972:11; and Roberts 1974. For a similar situation in modernizing Malaysia, see Roff 1967:178.

nationalism. For it was with this process that awareness of the community's past became a matter of deep concern at a mass level, and the populace became mobilized and responsive to suggestions from opinion leaders for group action in the cause of communal interest.

Newspapers and Periodicals as Instruments of Social Mobilization

The Christian missionaries had inaugurated the Sinhalese periodical, using it as an organ of proselytism. Thus, beginning with *Masika Täägga* (1832), eight Christian periodicals were to appear until in 1854 *Yatalaba* was inaugurated with a Buddhist as its editor.[3] The latter was, however, a scholarly journal and received the collaboration of Sinhalese-Christian scholars such as James D'Alwis. In any case *Yatalaba* was a short-lived venture, which lasted only about a year. Sinhalese periodical literature entered its most vigorous phase with the escalation of the Buddhist-Christian rivalry in the 1860s. The number of Buddhist journals rose sharply, to be countered by an equally vigorous journalistic activity by the Christians. Thus, between 1860 and 1870 the Buddhists inaugurated ten periodicals, while the Christians came up with thirteen in addition to those which were still being published.[4] As revivalist activity among the Buddhists gathered further momentum, the Buddhists outdistanced the Christians in journalistic activity. Thus, during the period from 1888 to 1900 the Buddhists published nineteen journals, seeking to "suppress the insults made to Buddhism by false-believers," as against only nine by the Christians.[5]

It should be noted that, as the revival progressed, the purely religious motivation in journalistic efforts abated, especially among the Buddhists, and more and more journals with other interests, again of a revivalist nature, came to be inaugurated. Thus, during the same period, from 1888 to 1900 there were twelve new journals intended for the publication of material of Oriental literature and five others devoted to matters concerning the "welfare of the Sinhalese people." At the same time there were three journals devoted to *āyurvēda* (traditional

3. For details, see Pannasekera 1965, 1:45–55. The editor of *Yatalaba* was Batuwantudawe, the senior-most pupil of *bhikkhu* Walane.

4. Based on information from Pannasekera 1965, vol. 1.

5. Based on information from Pannasekera 1966, vol. 2.

medicine) and astrology and another three in the Pali language, which was the language of Buddhist scripture, and these contained material on Buddhism as well as Pali philology.[6]

The avowedly propagandist Buddhist journals mentioned earlier as well as the other categories of journals that appeared subsequently were almost all edited and managed by the Buddhists, often *bhikkhus* or ex-*bhikkhus,* either alumni of or scholars closely connected with the newly emergent Buddhist seats of learning. In this way the genre of the periodical, which was introduced into Sinhala by the modernizing agency of Christianity, in time came to be dominated by the Buddhists. Of particular significance in this development was the fact that these Buddhist journalists were opinion leaders acting under revivalist exigencies.

Apart from the use of journals for religious purposes there was, from the early days of Sinhalese journalism, a growing concern with the historical heritage of the community. Indeed, it was due to the interest in classical Sinhalese literature by an early journal, *Śāstrālankāraya* (1853), edited by John Pereira, a Christian schoolteacher, that the Sav Sat Dam controversy received a platform.[7] Pereira was also the author of a history of the island entitled *Heladiv Rajaniya* (the monarchial law of the island of the Sinhalese), published in 1853. It was compiled from material collected from Pali chronicles and the classical Sinhalese literary works, and Pereira stated that in writing it his aim was the edification of

> the Sinhalese people, especially those in the maritime regions, who from childhood had been more partial to learning other people's language than their own, [and who had come] to know more about other countries and their customs and traditions than their own. . . .[8]

Later in the hands of Buddhist journalists the vision of the community's history assumed more glorious proportions. The periodical *Yatalaba* (1854), the first of its kind to be edited by a Buddhist, carried in its inaugural number a long description of the literary and scholarly heritage of the Sinhalese people. The first newspaper of the Buddhists,

6. Based on information from Pannasekera 1966, vol. 2.
7. See "Sav Sat Dam controversy" in chapter 4.
8. Pereira 1853:V.

Lak Miṇi Pahana (1862), in one of its early editorials protested against the notion of "some ignorant people" that the Sinhalese became civilized only after the Europeans arrived on the island. It proceeded to state that evidence in historical sources, the extant literature, and the ruins in places such as Anuradhapura pointed to a glorious civilization that existed in the past.[9]

In its third issue the *Lak Miṇi Pahana* carried an editorial on the Sinhala language. This editorial, probably from the pen of one of the paper's founder-scholars, contains one of the earliest expressions of language loyalty presented to the Sinhala reading public.[10] Pointing out that the Sinhala language had a "fine" (*kadima*) grammar and that various arts (*śāstra*) such as prosody, lexicography, and rhetoric have been treated in it, the editor preferred to quote the authority of a foreign scholar rather than "praise our own language ourselves," so that the beauty (*visiturukama*) of this language will become apparent. Thus, he quoted the Indian writer *bhikkhu* Buddhaghosa (fifth century), the translator-compiler of the authoritative Pali commentaries on Buddhist scriptures, who had called Sinhala "the beautiful language" (*manōraman bhāsan*). "However," added the editor, "the Sinhalese people in Lanka today do not take pains to study it well, being more keen to study other languages." The reference here was obviously to the English language. This practice of "developing other [languages] while our own is left [neglected]," according to him, was quite unlike what happens in the case of other peoples. Hence the policy of *Lak Miṇi Pahana*, it was stated, would be to publish various Sinhala compositions, old and new, so that "the beauty of this language and the fine sentiments expressed in it will be known and a love for its study be fostered."[11]

This concern for the community's cultural heritage shown by the first Buddhist newspaper was an early indication of the material that was to fill the pages of Sinhalese journals in the years to come. Thus, as the religiocultural revival entered its most vigorous phase after about 1880, there appeared stronger assertions of Sinhalese-Buddhist identity, and the past came to be invoked for the purpose of upholding the greatness of the Sinhalese people.

The *Lak Miṇi Kirula* (1881), another early Sinhala newspaper, whose policies appear to have been directed by *bhikkhu* Migettuwatte,

9. *LMP*, 1 June 1864.
10. The language loyalty of James D'Alwis was expressed in English. See chapter 3.
11. *LMP*, 17 October 1862.

carried in its second issue the first part of a serialized history of Lanka. It was claimed therein that Lanka "was a powerful kingdom even prior to the advent of Vijaya." Thus, the mythical ruler Ravana was referred to as having ruled the island in about 2837 B.C. with the assistance of a council of ten.[12] Here again is the nationalistic attempt to see the island's history as extending to the remote past and to impute to it even certain features found in modern societies: a need, as in the case of James D'Alwis, "for the conviction of cultural equivalence."[13]

The *Lankōpakāraya*, yet another Buddhist newspaper, pointed out in its first editorial that,

> although Lanka is a small country it was shining brightly during the time of our monarchs because of the all-round welfare of the people achieved in the spheres of various arts and the Buddhist religion.[14]

Mentioning that there was subsequent national decline due to invasions by "certain uncivilized races from south India," it exhorted the Sinhalese to strive with determination to bring themselves up to "the earlier noble stature."

The *Lankōpakāraya* in a later editorial castigated those Sinhalese "who had studied a little English" and "after that proceeded to disparage Sinhalese customs as well as their own language." These English-educated Sinhalese were blamed not only for getting into "the European habit of consuming liquor" but also for pretending not to be able to speak Sinhala with the excuse that "the English words were very fine and delicate and when one had got used to them one is unable to pronounce the rough words of Sinhala." The fact that these "Europeanized Sinhalese" preferred to cut off their traditionally long-grown hair (*koṇḍe*) was another cause of indictment. Exhorting the Sinhalese people to be proud of their customs and traditions, the editorial pointed to the example of "the late Hon. James D'Alwis," who, "in order to demonstrate to the Sinhalese people the desire they should have to retain their own customs, and to let it be known to others who do not know him that he was a person of the Sinhalese race, wore on his

12. *LMK*, 1 June 1881.

13. I borrow this phrase from Levenson (1959:150), who observes a similar phenomenon in modernizing China.

14. Issue dated 1 October 1881. This publication from Galle was probably guided by *bhikkhu* Bulathgama.

head the curved and straight combs even when he was acting as District Judge."[15] Here we note that Westernization was resented not only for ethical reasons but for the mere reason that it was foreign and it led to the abandonment of traditional practices such as the wearing of long hair and ornamental combs.[16]

It is with the *Sarasavi Sañdaräsa* (1880), the organ of the Buddhist Theosophical Society, which during its early years functioned under the mentorship of *bhikkhu* Hikkaduve, that one notes the most persistent and vociferous enunciation of the Sinhalese-Buddhist identity. Not only was there "an emphasis on indigenous authenticity on the basis of internal socio-cultural integration and simultaneous divergence from foreign ways,"[17] but definite strategies were also being proposed for its affirmation in the modern context.

Laying emphasis on indigenous authenticity, the *Sarasavi Sañdaräsa* carried on a campaign against foreign dress and (in particular Christian) names. "The people of Lanka quickly change their dress," it observed in an article,

> when the Dutch, the Tamils, the Malays and the English arrived in the island we began at each instance to dress like them. . . . Hence it is difficult to tell today what the original dress of the Sinhalese was.[18]

A similar loss of authenticity and national individuality was found in the practice of "abandoning the personal names which have been prevalent among the Buddhists from ancient times and adopting Christian names in their place."[19] For the Buddhists, the newspaper wanted to point out, the adoption of Christian names "has no logic or reason behind it," for most of these were the names of Christian saints.[20] Also

---

15. The editorial of 15 June 1882. The practice of wearing these ornamental combs on top of the head, after tying the long-grown hair into a knot at the back of the head, was a widely prevalent practice among low-country Sinhalese in the nineteenth and early twentieth centuries.

16. Incidentally, at a later stage of authentification, the use of combs was pointed out as an alien custom, and the Sinhalese were exhorted by activists like Anagarika Dharmapala to drop the practice.

17. I borrow this phrase characterizing similar efforts elsewhere from Fishman 1972c:30.

18. *Sa.Sa.*, 18 April 1884.

19. *Sa.Sa.*, 15 May 1885.

20. *Sa.Sa.*, 22 May 1885.

it reported how when Sinhalese Buddhists write to foreigners interested in Buddhism, signing their letters with Christian names, "they [those foreigners] are not only suspicious but treat us with contempt."[21] All these indicate a deep anxiety about the loss of distinct and authentic communal identity, which, it was believed, carried with it an inherent mark of greatness, arising from the background of a notable historical heritage. Hence publishing a compendium of "Aryan Sinhalese Names," the *Sarasavi Sañdaräsa* office urged its readers and through them the wider public to adopt these and abandon foreign names in order to "continue untramelled the Aryan-Sinhalese race."[22]

Another revivalist endeavor in the cause of national tradition was the campaign in support of *āyurvēda,* the science of indigenous medicine.[23] *Āyurvēda* was another aspect of the indigenous culture which in the modernizing urban milieu was struggling for serious recognition. A great impetus to its revival was the fact that the leading promoters of *āyurvēda* were persons heavily involved in other revivalist activities as well. Thus, Don Phillip de Silva Epa Appuhamy (1820–91), a patron of the religious and educational activities of *bhikkhus* Walane and Hikkaduwe and one of the leading figures among the Buddhist elite in nineteenth-century Colombo, published the *Sārārtha Pradīpikāva* (1863), one of the earliest Sinhala journals with a scholarly interest. Its pages were devoted to material on Buddhism, astrology, *āyurvēda,* and Sinhala literature. Epa Appuhamy, although best known as an astrologer, was the author of several treatises on *āyurvēda* and the promoter of a venture establishing an *āyurvēda* college in Colombo.[24] Again *bhikkhu* Hikkaduwe as editor of the *Samaya Sangrahaya* (1873)—another early journal devoted to scholarly material—published articles on *āyurvēda* and astrology. Furthermore, an integral part of the teaching program in the two prime seats of Oriental learning, Vidyōdaya and Vidyālankāra, was the study of *āyurvēdic* and astrological texts, two traditional "sciences" considered to be complementary. The *Sarasavi Sañdaräsa* supporting these attempts at promoting *āyurvēda,* urged lovers of that

---

21. *Sa.Sa.,* 15 May 1885.

22. See the introduction to *Ārya Sinhala Nampota,* comp. by C. P. Wijayaratna, the chief clerk of the *Sarasavi Sañdaräsa* office, Colombo, 1889.

23. Āyurvēda too is an Indian legacy. For a similar situation in modernizing India, see Leslie 1973.

24. For the founding of the Ayurveda College, see *Sa.Sa.,* 11 January 1884. Its first principal was Don Harmanis Kaviratna, a pupil of *bhikkhu* Walane.

science to assert their rights in the modern context. It was pointed out that the government was not paying salaries to Sinhala *vedavaru* (physicians), who "are curing the diseases of the Sinhalese people."[25] Again, suggesting a way in which *āyurvēda* may be modernized to suit current circumstances, it exhorted the *vedavaru* to organize a pharmaceutical drug production company that would prepare medicine for instant use.[26]

Later other journals joined in the defense of *āyurvēda* when the government refused to recognize the work of *āyurvēdic* physicians in matters concerning the registration of births and deaths. During a vociferous campaign by the Sinhala journals a staff writer of the *Dinakara Prakāśaya* noted that "all the inhabitants of Lanka indicated their total displeasure" against the government's regulations in this connection.[27] Similarly, *Satya Samuccaya,* functioning under the guidance of *bhikkhu* Ratmalane, the principal of Vidyālankāra, wrote in an editorial that "the people of this island of Lanka have more faith in their traditional system of medicine which has existed there for 2434 years."[28] Consequently, in December 1891 a society for the promotion of *āyurvēda* was inaugurated in Colombo under the patronage of *bhikkhus* Hikkaduwe and Ratmalane, the principals of Vidyōdaya and Vidyālankāra.[29]

In this way aspects of the indigenous culture, "threatened" by competitive arrivals from Europe, came to be cherished and "protected." As regards *āyurvēda,* we see in the formation of an association and the modernization of teaching and drug manufacture "the adoption of new means to support existing ends."[30] In some instances the upholding of what was traditional and indigenous was a "regressive" strategy. Thus, for example, it was maintained that the introduction of kerosene and the railway were detrimental to indigenous interests—

---

25. Editorial of 11 April 1884.

26. As the traditional method involved a slow and long-drawn process. See the editorial of 11 January 1884. Indeed, such a company was formed later at Kalutara, as noted in a news item in *Satya Samuccaya* (*Sat. Sam.*), 15 October 1890.

27. *Dinakara Prakāśaya* (*DP*), 14 October 1891.

28. *Sat. Sam.*, 31 October 1891.

29. See the report in *DP* of 9 December 1891. An earlier venture had languished due to lack of interest. The editors of *Dinakara Prakāśaya* and *Sarasavi Sańdaräsa* were among the promoters of the new venture.

30. Devereaux and Loeb (1943) have observed this as a feature of "antagonistic acculturation."

the former affecting the coconut oil industry and the latter the livelihood of the carters.[31]

It needs to be mentioned, however, that the upholding of traditional ends was not the sole concern of the Sinhala journals. Indeed, from the early days of Sinhalese-Buddhist journalism a consciousness of the uses of journalism as a modern device to be used in liberalist exercises was evident. Thus, the first newspaper of the Buddhists, the *Lak Miṇi Pahana,* in its inaugural editorial referred to the newspapers as the "Fourth Estate" in the government of a country.[32] Also it stated that the role of the newspaper is to "point out fearlessly any defect of the government while protecting the beneficial laws promulgated by it."

Such liberalist sentiments no doubt came to be intensified after the advent of the Theosophists who brought into the Buddhist movement their European experience in organized sociopolitical activity.[33] Also with the spread of English education, many Buddhists with a knowledge of English were entering the field of Sinhalese journalism, and by the turn of the century there was a notable expansion of its liberalist vistas.

Thus, *Lak Miṇi Pahana* in 1901, now edited by ex-*bhikkhu* M. Dhammaratana, carried a long editorial on the "Sinhala Newspapers and the Government," boldly asserting the rights and privileges of "Sinhala newspaper editors who were disseminating knowledge among the common people." The occasion for this editorial was the coronation celebrations at the Governor's Pavillion, to which all the editors of English newspapers were invited but not the editors of Sinhala newspapers. The *Lak Miṇi Pahana* pointed out that of the three million inhabitants of the island the readers of English newspapers were less than 1 percent and that it was the Sinhala newspapers that helped in running the government by disseminating information among the masses. The reason why this was not acknowledged was seen in the fact that "there was no one of real Sinhalese blood, having an understanding of Sinhalese ways and customs, among those in authority."[34]

31. See "Lankāvē Vävili saha Dänaṭa Lankāvaṭa Pämina Tibena Vipatti," in *Lankōpakāraya,* 15 July 1882. For similar "regressive" strategies in modernizing Bengal, see Sarkar 1973:54.

32. Editorial of 11 September 1862. For the possible source of this concept, see n. 72 of chap. 4.

33. See "Beginnings of Buddhist Pressure Group Activity," in chapter 4.

34. *LMP,* 27 April 1901. Here the reference is not only to the white masters and their native subordinates but also to the Sinhalese representatives in the Legislative Council.

Finally, it was pointed out that "if the Sinhala newspaper editors got united and wrote on any particular issue they would be able to easily influence the views of the common people of Lanka." That an Oriental scholar such as Dharmaratna was expressing such sentiments is indicative of the modernizing effects of mass media participation.[35]

Anagaraika Dharmapala, one of the most outstanding champions of the Sinhalese-Buddhist identity, had the advantage of an English education and paid special attention to make his compatriots aware of nationalist movements in other parts of the world. Thus, in exhorting the Sinhalese to develop their industries and other economic activities so that they could be self-reliant, he often pointed to the example of modernizing Japan. For him Japan seems to have held a special fascination as an Asian Buddhist country that had, through its own efforts, come to match the achievements of European nations in the field of technology. Describing the "awakening" (*prabōdhaya*) in Japan, China, India, and Korea, he urged the Sinhalese to follow the example of these other Asian nations.[36]

The Russo-Japanese War of 1905, which saw the triumph of Japan, stirred the imagination of many Asians then under the domination of Western powers.[37] The editor of the *Lak Miṇi Pahana* used this occasion to point out the moral superiority of the Asians. Contrasting the magnanimity of the Japanese soldiers with the cruelty and barbarism of the Russians, he exhorted the Sinhalese to follow their own noble customs, which they had inherited from their forebears.[38]

Inspiration was also sought from other nationalist struggles elsewhere about which the ordinary person would be hardly familiar. Dharmapala, for example, wrote about Ireland and how for genera-

---

It needs mention here that, as early as 1864, James D'Alwis, as the Sinhalese representative in the Legislative Council, had urged the government to acknowledge the role of the Sinhala newspapers as they reflected the thoughts and sentiments of the native population (D'Alwis 1939:103–4).

35. Pundit M. Dharmaratna, as he himself acknowledged, had no knowledge of English. See Pannasekera 1966:67.

36. See his articles in *Sinhala Bauddhaya* (*SB*) on 7 May 1906; 15 September 1906; 11 November 1911; and 20 April 1912. Having visited Japan several times, he even sent some of his followers there to be trained in modern industries.

37. Note the reaction as summarized by the European Theosophist Annie Besant, who was active in India and Sri Lanka at the time: "What? an Eastern nation facing a Western in a field of battle? The white people were then not resistless? They had been met and overthrown by a coloured race, by men like themselves. A thrill of hope ran through Asia." Quoted in Fishman 1972c:33.

38. *LMP*, 1 November 1905.

tions the Irish nationalists relentlessly carried on the Home Rule movement. He urged the Sinhalese to follow their example.[39] In another article, titled "Home Rule for Ceylon," this idea was further elaborated.[40] Again writing on the Chinese rebellion of 1911 and the nationalist agitation in Bengal, he urged the Sinhalese to give up following European practices and to build up patriotism and self-reliance, as other nations were doing under similar circumstances.[41]

The Novel and the Theater as Instruments of Social Mobilization

The function of disseminating the revivalist ethic performed by the newspapers and the periodicals came to be taken up even more effectively by two newly emerging genres, the novel and the theater. Although narrative art had been utilized even by classical Sinhala writers in their edificatory works,[42] the novel as a literary form was introduced only during the latter half of the nineteenth century. Again it was the Christian missionaries who introduced the novel to the Sinhalese reader, using it as a device of religious propaganda.[43] As for the theater, while there existed in the folk tradition several forms of dramatic entertainment, a more sophisticated art of theater to suit the taste of urban audiences began only in the late nineteenth century under the influence of visiting European and Indian theater groups.[44] Prior to this, however, Christian missionaries had attempted to utilize the folk dramatic tradition for proselytizing purposes.[45] As *nūrti,* the foreign inspired operatic theatrical form, caught the imagination of the urban populace, the revivalist propagandists stepped in, transforming the new genre into one of their instruments, first on a modest note, as an agent of economic nationalism,[46] and subsequently on a larger scale, as

39. *SB,* 26 August 1911. Sometimes European Theosophists brought firsthand experience from foreign nationalist movements—for example, J. Bowes Daly from Ireland, who became the manager of BTS schools in Sri Lanka.

40. *SB,* 9 September 1911.

41. *SB,* 11 November 1911.

42. Most notably, e.g., the *Amāvatura* and the *Butsaraṇa* of the twelfth century and *Saddharmaratnāvaliya* of the thirteenth century. See M. Wickremasinghe 1949:67, 81, 93.

43. Rajakaruna 1972:1–55.

44. Hapuarachchi 1981:150–56.

45. E. Pieris 1942:16.

46. That is, to prevent foreign theater companies taking money away. See Hapuarachchi 1981:151.

an instrument of Sinhalese-Buddhist propagandism, concentrating particularly on the glory of the national past. Similarly, with the Buddhists gaining ascendency in the field of journalism the art of fiction came to be utilized as an agent of anti-Christian and pro-Buddhist propaganda, which contained messages about the past glory of the community and exhortations for self-assertion in contemporary circumstances. Three figures who epitomize these developments are C. Don Bastian (1852–1921), dramatist and journalist; Piyadasa Sirisena (1875–1946), journalist and novelist; and John de Silva (1857–1922), dramatist.

Bastian, whose full name was Calutantrige Don Bastian Jayaweera Bandara, was born in Pettah, a lower-middle-class residential area in nineteenth-century Colombo. Having had the opportunity of studying under several erudite *bhikkhus* such as Hikkaduwe Sumangala, the young Bastian became a Buddhist social worker organizing a voluntary association named Gñānābhivruddhi ("development of wisdom") Samāgama and a free night school named Punyasaṃvarī ("meritorious discipline") in Pettah in 1872. Several years later Bastian became a pioneer in the establishment of Sunday Buddhist schools. He was also a keen temperance worker. Furthermore, he was one of the most prominent journalists of the time and brought out the first Sinhala daily newspaper, *Dinapatā Pravurti,* in 1895. Writing and producing *Rolīnā* (1877), based on an English story, Bastian became the pioneer of Sinhala *nurti* theater, and followed up that work with ten other productions.[47] His *Sinhabā* (1888) was the first *nurti* based on a theme from Sinhalese history (this distinction was taken up on a large scale later by John de Silva and other dramatists).

Piyadasa Sirisena, born as Pedrick Silva at Induruwa, a coastal village in the Southern Province, received primary education under *bhikkhus* and subsequently came under the influence of Anagarika Dharmapala. He changed his European name and migrated to Colombo to become a journalist, editing a periodical named *Sinhala Jātiya* (The Sinhalese Nation) in 1903. In 1904 he serialized the novel *Jayatissa saha Rosalin* in a newspaper. This novel, which criticized Western culture and upheld the virtues of the traditional Sinhalese-

47. They were: *Romlin* (1884), *Rōmeō saha Juliet* (1884), *Frankloe saha Ingerley* (1884), *Proetius saha Valentine* (1884), *Leonine saha Emaline* (1885), *Sinhabā* (1888), *Sudāsa saha Sālini* (1888), *Sīla hevat Kapaṭi Bāna* (1898), *Swarnatilakā* (1898), and *Dinatara Nāḍagama* (1912). Most of these were based on European stories, but Bastian placed emphasis on the moral of the story.

Buddhist culture, became immensely popular, and Sirisena was to write over twenty novels in the same vein, coming to be acknowledged as the foremost Sinhala novelist in the early twentieth century. In the introduction to one of his later novels Sirisena claimed that: "From all our books over a hundred thousand copies have been sold. None of these works contain empty prattle. Although they may be counted as 'new fictional stories,' we have never written a book which does not direct the human mind towards the noble and righteous [Buddhist] doctrine."[48] The revivalist propaganda of Sirisena was, from the point of view of the Sinhalese Buddhists, an urgent need of the times, and this explains the immense popularity of his works.

Makalandavage John de Silva, born in Kotte near Colombo, was able to obtain instructions in Sinhala from Pundit Batuwantudawe while studying in an English medium school. He first became a schoolteacher then studied law and became a lawyer. But his greater inclination was toward the theater. Following Bastian's example, he initially adapted foreign stories as Sinhalese plays, but later, again taking the cue from Bastian, he began dramatizing events from Sinhalese history and became the foremost dramatist on the island during the early twentieth century. In his own words his aim was

> to propagate once again the Sinhalese music that has gone into abeyance; to depict the ancient customs dress, ornaments etc.; to censure the evil habits among our people today; to re-create the national awareness that has been of yore; and to foster a love for the Sinhala language among the younger generation who now find it distasteful.[49]

John de Silva and Piyadasa Sirisena had much in common. Through the heroes in his novels, who were often made to deliver long discourses, Sirisena castigated Christianity, the consumption of liquor, and the eating of meat and ridiculed Western dress and other European customs, while at the same time upholding the Buddhist religion and traditional Sinhalese customs, beliefs, and values.[50] John de Silva,

48. *Sucaritādarśaya* (The Ideal Character), 1926. Some of his other novels were *Apaṭa Vecca Dē* (What Has Befallen Us), 1909; *Mahā Viyavula* (The Great Turmoil), 1909; and *Dingiri Māṇikā*, 1918. For a full list, see K. D. P. Wickramasinghe 1965:433–99.

49. Introduction to the play *Srī Vikrama Rājasinghe*, 1906. Some of his other historical plays were: *Siri Sangabō*, 1903; *Valagambā*, 1907; *Dutugämunu*, 1910; *Mahānama*, 1913; *Alakēśvara*, 1913; *Dēvānampiyatissa*, 1914; *Vessantara*, 1916; *Vihāra Maha Dēvi*, 1916; *Parangi Haṭane*, 1917; and *Käppeṭipola*, 1917. The last was based on the Kandyan rebellion of 1818.

50. Sarachchandra 1950:92.

writing and producing plays centered on themes drawn from Buddhist literature and Sinhalese history, extolled the virtues of the past, contrasting them with the "degradation" of the present and exhorting his audience to follow the examples of their forebears.[51] Sirisena and de Silva seem to have exerted a seminal influence on all literary activity during the early decades of the twentieth century.[52]

The clientele of this revivalist artistic activity was the rapidly swelling urban population, which was literate in the vernacular and in need of entertainment to fill its leisure hours. Newcomers to the urban milieu, as they were, and still retaining deep roots in the village and its traditions, they were pursuing avenues of identity affirmation. The belletristic activity with revivalist messages was indeed the product of this demand, while at the same time it was a force for its intensification.

The Sinhalese-Buddhist propagandists were thus utilizing modern communicational weaponry derived from their antagonists, the Christian Europeans. When the traditional communicational networks were becoming outmoded or inoperative in the face of the advances of a modern economy and new forms of sociopolitical structure, the emergent protagonists of the Sinhalese-Buddhist identity quickly gained control of the new systems of mass communication and turned them into effective channels of revivalist propaganda. The newly literate and urbanizing sections of the populace, the middle classes, expanding under modernizing conditions, were being mobilized through the new communicational networks.

The type of response this mobilizational activity evoked may be gauged not only from the manner in which the revivalist propaganda was growing in volume and intensity but also in the social behavior of the populace—who, as if to put the revivalist ethic into practice, were avidly grouping themselves into *samāgam*, voluntary associations of diverse sorts.

Voluntary Associations as Avenues of Social Mobilization

As with the periodical literature mentioned earlier, the practice of forming voluntary associations was originally another strategy of the Buddhists in their attempts at "antagonistic acculturation." Hence when the early associations, called *samāgam*, began appearing during the

51. Amunugama 1975:302–3.
52. Sarachchandra 1950; Dharmadasa 1974:165–68.

latter half of the nineteenth century the motivation remained religious or semireligious for a long time. Thus, beginning with the Śarvagña Śāsanābhivruddhi Dāyaka Dharma Samāgama inaugurated by *bhikkhu* Migettuwatte in 1862, there arose a large number of *samāgamas* whose aims were to "protect" and "develop" Buddhism. Most of them were located in Colombo. Among the *samāgamas* active in Colombo during the heyday of revivalism were: the Dharmarakkhita (Protecting the [Buddhist] Doctrine) Samāgama and the Dharmōdaya (Upliftment of the [Buddhist] Doctrine) Samāgama, both of Slave Island; the Dharmōpakārī (Support of the [Buddhist] Doctrine) Samāgama and the Sāsanōpakārī (Support of the Buddhist Dispensation) Samāgama, both of Maradana; the Sudharmōdaya (Upliftment of the Good Doctrine) Samāgama of Panchikawatta; and the Bauddhādhāra (Succor to the Buddhists) Samāgama of Grandpass.[53] Most of these associations followed their precursor in publishing polemical journals against Christianity. Similarly, the Colombo Young Men's Buddhist Association, in distinct imitation of a Christian institution, was established in 1898. Here it needs to be mentioned that, while the earlier *samāgam* were evidently associations of the vernacular-educated strata of society, the YMBA was largely an association of English-educated Buddhists.[54]

At the same time there were several other *samāgam* in Colombo which had broader aspirations: Buddhist work, literary discussion, and social welfare activities, among others. The most powerful among them, of course, was the Bauddha Paramavigñānārtha Samāgama (Buddhist Theosophical Society) founded by Olcott in 1880 and among whose membership were almost all the leading Buddhist businessmen in the city. The BTS, thus stronger financially than most Buddhist organizations and having the benefit of the vision and the organizational skill of Western activists, was able to launch an ambitious project of establishing a network of Buddhist schools on the island. An offshoot of this organization was the Bauddhārakṣaka Samāgama, the Buddhist Defence Committee, inaugurated again under the auspices of Olcott in 1884 to assume a novel role as the defender of Buddhist rights, especially in dealing with the government.

Other associations in Colombo with more literary interests were

---

53. Information from the newspapers *Lak Miṇi Kirula* (*LMK*) and *Sarasavi Sañdaräsa* (*Sa.Sa.*) during the 1880s and 1890s.

54. The personalities involved indicate the distinction. The Colombo YMBA was inaugurated by a group of twenty headed by C. S. Dissanayaka, a convert back from Christianity. See Piyasena 1972:2.

the Gñānābhivruddhi ("fostering of knowledge") Samāgama and Gñānaprabōdha ("awakening of knowledge") Samāgama, which appear to have been very active in the 1890s.[55] Evidently, many of these associations carried on some form of social welfare activity in the localities in which they existed. Although such adjustments to the modern age are noticeable, the basis of the formation of these associations remained highly traditional. Indeed, the raison d'être of their formation was primarily nativistic, the "defence" and "promotion" of Buddhism and, although not overtly stated, Sinhalese ethnicity: The *samāgam* among the Sinhalese were both the product and the engine of the religiocultural revival. There was a leaning upon traditional ethnoreligious collective feeling to attain mass involvement and participation.

As the waves of revivalism began spreading from the center in Colombo and its environs to the outlying areas, social mobilizational activity in the form of journalism as well as *samāgam* formation was seen appearing in various parts of the island. Market towns and service centers, such as Panadura, Ratgama, Kosgoda, Galle, and Matara along the southern littoral and Kandy, Kegalle, Nuwara Eliya, Hatton, and Matale in the interior, appear to have become focal points for the formation of voluntary associations and also sometimes for the publication of periodicals or newspapers. Thus, mention is made, among others, of the Dharmakāmi Bauddha ("the lovers of the Buddhist doctrine") Samāgama of Panadura, the Amadyapāna ("temperance") Samāgama of Ratgama, the Sudharmayuktika Amadyapāna ("temperance according to the good doctrine") Samāgama of Kosgoda, the Ārya Dharmādhāra ("support of the noble virtues") Samāgama of Kosgoda, the Ārya Dharmādhāra Samāgama of Matara, and Sammādiṭṭhikāmi ("lovers of the correct vision") Samāgama of Matale.[56] As for provincial journalistic activity, a paper named *Lankōpakāraya* was launched in 1881 at Galle; Kandy supported another paper *Sat Siḷumina* in 1884 and Matara a periodical named *Śrī Lankōttansaya* in 1895.[57]

Although the raison d'être for the *samāgam* was generally traditionalist and backward looking, their formation may be considered a vital feature of the social, political, and economic modernization of the Sinhalese community. In place of the primordial social relations based on tradition and sentiment, associative social relations were being

55. Roberts 1969:2.
56. Information from *Sarasavi Sañdaräsa*, January to December 1884.
57. Pannasekera 1965:376, 439; and Pannasekera 1966:278.

formed—based on reasoned deliberation and personal choice.[58] Of special significance in this connection was the formation of associations based upon occupational interests. One early indication was the formation of theater groups. C. Don Bastian, for example, who pioneered the Sinhala *nurti*, formed the Sinhala Nāṭya Samāgama (Sinhala Drama Society) in 1882 to work for "the honour of the Sinhala race." This was followed by several other similar associations in Colombo. One hears of the Sainhalabhāṣālankāra Nāṭya Sabhāva (Drama Society for the Adornment of the Sinhala Language), the Śrī Lankā Mātā Nāṭya Sabhava (Illustrious Mother Lanka Drama Society), the Sarasvatī (patron deity of performing arts) Nāṭya Sabhā, and the Sinhala Ārya Subōdha Nāṭya Sabhā (Drama Society for the Edification of the Sinhala Aryans)—the last organized by John de Silva.[59]

Following the example of these associations in Colombo several similar organizations sprang up in provincial towns, such as the Vinōdaranga ("entertaining plays") Sabhāva of Galle; the Śrī Vaiśākha Krīda ("illustrious vesak plays") Sangamaya of Ambalangoda, and the Trī Sinhala ("the three Sinhala regions") Nāṭya Sabhāva of Kandy.[60] It might be noted from the very names of these associations that the revivalist intent played an important part in their formation. Although there were several Christians among the dramatists of this period and a number of translations from English plays came to be produced along with translations from Indian plays, the dominant feature in the Sinhalese theatrical world, particularly during the first two decades of the twentieth century, was the nostalgia for the community's glorious past. Sinhalese history was the storehouse for the plot of many a play. Even where contemporary plots were used, the intent often was to deride the adoption of Western customs and uphold the traditional culture.[61]

This influence of revivalist ideology on the formation and functioning of drama associations owed much to the fact that these organizations were concerned with mass communication in a society where revivalism was the dominant ethic. Indeed, the revivalist ethic seems

58. This distinction is pointed out by Weber (1968:40–41). For similar developments in India, see Das Gupta 1970:74; and in Africa, see Hodgkin 1956:87.

59. Information obtained from *Sarasavi Sañdarăsa* and *Sihala Samaya* (*Si.Sa.*) of the 1880s and 1890s; Ratnayaka n.d.; and Hapuarachchi 1981.

60. Information obtained from Ratnayaka n.d. For Tri Sinhala, see Glossary.

61. For some of the Christian dramatists, see Don Peter 1964. For the intent of the majority of the plays, see Sarachchandra 1966:133–35.

to have affected all social activities in the Sinhalese society at the time. Hence even when other associations came to be formed, in spheres less loaded with cultural values, the inspiration from revivalist ideologies was unmistakably present.

Thus, there arose a Guru Sangamaya (Teachers' Association) of the Sinhala schoolteachers in 1891. It was established in Minuwangoda, a small town north of Colombo. A newspaper reporting on this stated that in the community's tradition the teacher was one who was highly respected in society, while under colonial rule he had been reduced "to a lowly position."[62] This association was expanded in 1913 to form the Śrī Lankā Mahā Guru Sangamaya (Great Association of the Teachers of Sri Lanka), and it was later to play a major role in promoting the cause of the Sinhala language.[63] At the turn of the century there was a strong association of the island's notaries public named Lakdiva Notāris Samitiya.[64] Most of these notaries were alumni of the *pirivena* seats of learning and formed a prominent section of the local elite engaged in the revivalist and social mobilization activities in early twentieth-century Sri Lanka.[65]

The associational activity mentioned above among the Sinhalese, although indicative of a responsive and enthusiastic population, was diffuse in form in that the activities of each association were confined to the region of its origin, even when the aims and aspirations had an all-island focus. A more ambitious project with such an all-island focus was the Bauddha Mahājana Sangamaya (Association of the Great Buddhist Populace) inaugurated by a group of English-educated Buddhists in 1903. It purported to "unite the Sinhalese people in order to present their grievances to the government."[66] Prominent among its founders were W. Arthur de Silva, a veterinary surgeon educated at the University of Bombay, D. B. Jayatilaka, a B.A. from the University of Calcutta, and Charles Batuwantudawe, a barrister-at-law of Grey's Inn. They represented a newly emergent stratum of nationalist activists who were

62. *DP*, 20 May 1891.

63. See chapter 7. For the role of the Sinhala schoolteachers in the language disputes of mid-twentieth-century Sri Lanka, see Wriggins 1906:337–39.

64. *Si.Sa.*, 26 March 1903.

65. For the "national elite" and the "local elite" in the early twentieth century, see Roberts 1969, 1977.

66. From the editorial in *Si.Sa.*, 1 October 1903, managed by the family of Dr. W. Arthur de Silva, a leading figure in the BMS.

to act as synthesizers of the European concepts of liberalism and utilitarianism with the primordial sentiments of group rights and historical prerogatives of the Sinhalese Buddhists.

It may be said that the advent of this stratum into national life held the potential for channeling the social mobilization that was taking place among the Sinhalese Buddhists into a unified and purposeful movement with explicit political ends. An opportune moment for this, although it was not fully utilized, appeared during the second decade of the twentieth century with the advent of the temperance movement.

The ill effects of the British policy of encouraging the opening of liquor shops with a view to increasing revenue was the focal point of criticism both by foreign and indigenous observers during the latter half of the nineteenth century.[67] But it was the reform of the excise law in 1912 and its consequence of more than doubling the number of licensed liquor shops which provoked a strong movement of temperance agitation.[68] It took place against the very appropriate backdrop of the Buddhist revival, where the past, prior to the advent of the Europeans, was idealized as one in which there was total abstinence from liquor in accordance with Buddhist ethics. The Sinhalese-Buddhist mobilizational activity described earlier provided an added stimulus to the emerging temperance movement. In 1912 a large number of public meetings, effectively enlisting popular participation, were held in Colombo; in Moratuwa, Aluthgama, Kalutara, Matara, Tangalla, and Chilaw along the seaboard; and in Mirigama, Hatton, Nuwara Eliya, and Kandy in the interior. In the same year the Colombo Total Abstinence Union (TAU) came to be formed, largely under the leadership of the English-educated Buddhists. Similarly, several provincial temperance organizations also came up, the most formidable being the Hapitigam Korale Temperance Union in the southwest led by the Senanayakas, a newly rich family in the area. This organization had eighty affiliated societies and a membership of nine thousand, and its public meetings were sometimes attended by twenty-five thousand or more.[69]

67. See n. 77 of chapter 2. Even Governor Sir William Gregory (1872–77) had observed: "English rule has given Ceylon many blessings but we have at the same time extended a curse throughout the island, namely, drunkenness" (Jayawardene 1972:87). Also see the editorial in *LMK*, 15 June 1881, and the reports about temperance associations in the 1880s already mentioned.

68. Fernando 1971:126.

69. Fernando 1971:141–42.

Although the temperance workers had among them several individual Christians – clergymen and members of the English-educated elite – the movement on the whole had a strong Buddhist flavor to it. Indeed, its success in enlisting an unprecedented mass participation on a single issue depended on this fact. At the forefront of the temperance agitation were English-educated Buddhists such as D. B. Jayatilaka, W. A. de Silva, C. Batuwantudawe, and F. R. Senanayaka,[70] who were evidently aware of the political potential of the religious coloration assumed by the movement.[71] In a situation in which there were strong inhibitions with regard to direct political action the English-educated elite used the temperance movement as a convenient issue to embarrass the government.[72] It may be said that the movement carried within it more than a streak of anti-British feeling. Thus, Anagarika Dharmapala wrote in *Sinhala Bauddhayā,* the newspaper founded and managed by him:

> It was "our-welfare-loving" and "just-in-all-respects" Englishman who paved the way for drunkenness among the Sinhalese people who had not partaken of any intoxicating drink for 2358 years. . . . The more the drinking of toddy and arrack increases to the same degree the Sinhalese race will go on the path of decline. . . . The Sinhalese, having sold his land, drinks toddy and arrack, becomes a slave of the white man and toils for him.[73]

The phrases "our-welfare-loving" and "just-in-all-respects" were used in sarcasm at some strands of native opinion which were loyal to the British raj. Unlike the Christians engaged in nationalist activities who also had crosscutting allegiances with the colonial rulers, or even other Buddhist national leaders for whom open confrontation with the authorities was impossible because of various professional and commercial interests,[74] Dharmapala was the "homeless" (*anagārika*) agitator who could freely indulge in activity that could even be categorized

70. See Fernando 1971. For details about these personalities, see Appendix.

71. See Fernando 1973b:336. For a similar development in the nationalist movement in colonial Burma, see Cady 1958:190.

72. K. M. de Silva 1973f:259.

73. *SB*, 3 February 1912.

74. For the Christians who joined the temperance movement and other nationalist ventures, see Roberts 1969, 1977: chap. 2.

as "seditious."[75] Thus, he personified the Sinhalese-Buddhist identity affirmation in a highly uninhibited form. Most notably, it was characterized by a strong antipathy toward anything that could be categorized as "alien," and this feeling was focused in particular on other ethnic groups found on the island.

The Sinhalese Buddhists vis-à-vis the Other Communities on the Island

For the Sinhala Buddhists the resuscitation of traditional arts and sciences and the cultivation of other symbols of traditional identity along with the rising awareness of the past achievements of Sinhalese civilization contributed in sum to a reformulation of the twin concepts of the *Sinhaladvīpa* (Island of the Sinhalese People) and the *Dhammadvīpa* (Island of the Buddhist Doctrine) found in the historical tradition.[76] These age-old concepts seem to have received a revalidation in the modern context as the Sinhalese Buddhists, who comprised the largest single ethnoreligious community in the island,[77] were gradually introduced to populist thinking. For a good example of this populist thinking, which formed the basis of Sinhalese-Buddhist self-assertion, we need to turn to Dharmapala:

> The island of Lanka belongs to the Buddhist Sinhalese. For 2455 years this was the land of birth for the Sinhalese. Other races have come here to pursue their commercial activities. For the Europeans, apart from this land, there is Canada, Australia, South Africa, England and America to go; for the Tamils there is South India; for the Moors . . . Egypt; the Dutch can go to Holland. But for the Sinhalese there is only this island.[78]

Sinhalese-Buddhist revivalism originated and found its most active form in the southern and southwestern seaboard, the regions most prone to the processes of modernization. A prominent feature of the modernization in social and economic spheres was the emergence of a

75. For the *anagārika* role, see Obeysekere 1970. Dharmapala was indeed charged for sedition and had to plead that he was a "loyal subject." See Dharmapala 1965:Intro.

76. See chapter 1.

77. In 1911, of a population of four million, the Sinhalese comprised 68 percent of whom 91 percent were Buddhist. See Denham 1912:196.

78. *SB*, 20 January 1912.

new entrepreneurial group, a category not found in the traditional Sinhalese social hierarchy. In their rise to economic influence these Sinhalese entrepreneurs had to combat the established power of foreign entrepreneurs—especially that of the traders of Moor and Indian extraction, who controlled most of the wholesale and retail trade in the island.[79] Although Europeans also owned some large commercial establishments, the Sinhalese masses seldom came into contact with them. Their contacts were with the ubiquitous Moor or south Indian (Tamil) trader, mostly the former. As the religiocultural revival gathered momentum, the class interests of the Sinhala entrepreneurs who provided the economic support for revivalist activities also became prominent.[80] This was especially evident in the antagonistic stance against alien traders taken by the mass media of the time.

The major newspapers and periodicals were managed by *samāgam*, which were largely if not solely associations of a rising urban elite;[81] these newspapers included the *Sarasavi Sañdaräsa* of the Buddhist Theosophical Society, the *Lankōpakāraya* of the Lankōpakāra Samagama, and the *Samaya Sangrahaya* of the Subhācāra Dharmadīpti Samagama. The class interests of the lay literary activists of the period, whether they be journalists, novelists, or dramatists, also seem to have approximated that of the rising urban elite.[82] Sinhalese entrepreneurs and professionals formed the *dāyaka sabhā* (supporters' associations), providing sustenance to Buddhist temples and *pirivenas,* which were in many ways hubs of journalistic activity.[83] Thus, the interests of the emerging Sinhalese-Buddhist elite, especially the trader element, often found expression in the journalistic and belletristic writings of the day. The *Sarasavi Sañdaräsa,* for example, from its inception in 1880 was a conspicuous agitator against the foreign domination of import-export and

79. Although many Moors would have come from India, a distinction needs to be made because the Moors were all Muslim by faith while the Indians were largely Hindu, with smaller groups of Zoroastrian, Baha-i, and Christian faiths.

80. As Stalin has observed (in the pamphlet *Marxism and the National Question,* 1912), "the market is the first school in which the bourgeoisie learns its nationalism."

81. Here I refer to the entrepreneurs and the professionals such as lawyers, doctors, teachers, and clerks who emerged under the new socioeconomic conditions.

82. For example, cases such as Dharmapala belonging to a prominent entrepreneurial family in Colombo and Sirisena being a protégé of Dharmapala; John de Silva being a lawyer; M. C. F. Perera, the editor of *Sihala Samaya* and a novelist, belonging to an entrepreneurial family from Moratuwa to which W. A. de Silva also belonged.

83. That is, by educating the would-be writers. Both Hikkaduwe and Ratmalane, the principals of Vidyodaya and Vidyalankara, respectively, were patrons to many a journalistic venture.

retail trade and gave prominent publicity to Sinhalese Buddhists who had embarked on various types of entrepreneurial activity. Its attacks were directed mainly against the Moors, who not only had large business establishments in principal towns such as Colombo, Kandy, and Galle but also controlled most of the retail trade in smaller towns and villages. The Sinhalese were exhorted to refrain from patronizing shops owned by the Moors, who were "greatly harming the Sinhala race."[84] The *Sinhala Bauddhayā*, managed by Anagarika Dharmapala and edited by Piyadasa Sirisena, frequently published reports of "dishonest" and "oppressive" trading by the Moors in various parts of the island: Padukka, Galle, Kandy, and Kurunegala, among others.[85]

The antipathy, first based on economic grounds, was later extended to the community per se. Negative traits, as far as the Sinhalese-Buddhist identity was concerned, were projected on the Moors. Thus, one writer in the *Sarasavi Sañdaräsa* elaborated on how the Moors were the polar opposite of the Sinhalese in every respect.[86] Another writer in the *Satya Samuccaya* stated that, compared with the Aryan Sinhalese, the Moors were "barbarians" (*mlēcca*).[87] Apparently, another reason for the escalation of the anti-Moor feeling by the Buddhists was their abhorrence of the practice of eating beef and the fact that a large number of the island's butchers came from the Moor community. Thus, when, as a corollary to the Buddhist revival, an anti-beef campaign was launched in the 1880s the Moors were naturally at the receiving end of Buddhist antagonism.[88]

Anagarika Dharmapala, who had more reasons than one for antipathy to the Moors, wrote:

> From the day the white man set foot on this island, the arts and the sciences and the Āryan customs of the Sinhalese have gradually disappeared and today the Sinhalese have to kiss the feet of the Moor [and] the dastardly Tamil.[89]

---

84. *Sa.Sa.*, 4 January 1884.

85. Reported in the issues dated 4 August, 25 August, 1 September, and 15 September 1906, respectively.

86. See "Marakkala Minissu" (The Moor people) in *Sa.Sa.*, 4 January 1884.

87. W. Arya Dharmawardhana, "Sinhala Caritra" (Sinhala Customs) in the issue dated 21 April 1891.

88. See "Asarana Gavaräla" (The Helpless Oxen) in *Sat. Sam.*, of 11 July 1884 and the petition for the ban of cow slaughter reported in *DP*, 11 November 1891.

89. *SB*, 6 April 1912.

Here we see the linking together of anti-Christian and anti-imperial feelings with the antipathy to the Moors along with the age-old antagonism toward the Tamils. For the advancement of these so-called aliens at the expense of the once powerful "sons of the soil" the blame is laid at the door of the imperial master.[90] Dharmapala's anti-Moor feelings would have originated in the economic field in his native Colombo and would have been accentuated with his visits to the ancient Buddhist sites in north India, which he saw as having been destroyed by "the sword and fire of Musalman spoilators."[91] He frequently gave vent to these feelings in his newspaper *Sinhala Bauddhaya* as well as in his itinerant preachings.[92]

In the midst of the newly crystallized antagonism toward the Moors which arose under the modernizing circumstances of late-nineteenth-century Sri Lanka, the age-old rivalry with the Tamils was not forgotten. Indeed, the revived image of past glories was concomitantly bound to rekindle a "retrospective hostility" to the Tamils:[93] In the popular mind they were the vicious destroyers of the ancient seats of Sinhalese-Buddhist civilization.

The Buddhist newspaper *Lankōpakāraya* spoke in its inaugural editorial of the glories of ancient Sri Lanka, which,

> although small in size was greatly advanced in all the arts and the sciences and was illuminated by the [Buddhist] religion. . . . However, because of the invasions by certain barbaric races of south India [the country] lost its former greatness and became destitute.[94]

The image of past greatness is contrasted with the present decline, and, like James D'Alwis thirty years earlier, the *Lankōpakāraya* falls back on the popular tradition in finding the Tamils the agents of destruction of the ancient Sinhalese civilization.

90. See his letter to the chief secretary in which he says, "Aliens are taking away the wealth of the country and the sons of the soil, where are they to go?" (Dharmapala 1965:527–28).

91. Dharmapala 1965:849.

92. See *SB*, 5 August 1911; 10 February 1912; and 23 March 1912. Also see the dossier on his activities prepared by the police, reproduced in Dharmapala 1965:LXV–LXX.

93. Chaudhuri (1976:235) mentions how Hindus in modern India harbor a "retrospective hostility" to the Muslims.

94. Issue dated 1 October 1884.

Again another Buddhist newspaper, the *Lak Miṇi Pahana,* invoking the glories of the time when the Sinhalese kings were ruling the land, stated:

> Although the cruel king named Elara came here hoping to uproot the Sinhalese nation and waged war, as the Sinhalese royal family remained safe in the southern region, the fortunate prince Dutthagamini came forth and destroyed the Tamils and constructed the great edifices which can still be seen in Anuradhapura, thus making it possible to be said that the Sinhalese were a great nation.[95]

Thus, in the hands of the manipulators of mass media the visions of past glory are invariably linked with the destruction by the Tamils. Just as D'Alwis did some time earlier, here the Tamils are viewed as the perennial enemies of the Sinhalese community. Indeed, the antagonism toward the Tamils seems to have provided a necessary contrastive tension for the Sinhalese-Buddhist identity to sustain itself. Dharmapala, for example, asserted that

> ethnologically the Sinhalese are a unique race, in as much as they can boast that they have no slave blood in them, and never were conquered by either the pagan Tamils or European vandals who for three centuries devastated the land.[96]

In this way the "harassment" by the Tamils and other "enemy" races has become an essential part of the Sinhalese-Buddhist view of history. It underlines the achievement of having survived such adversities as a distinct religiocultural as well as an ethnological entity.[97]

While the *Sinhaladvīpa* and *Dhammadvīpa* concepts were thus reformulated with additional ramifications, an opportunity arose for their application in a concrete circumstance. This was in connection with the retrieval from the jungle of the ancient Rajaraṭa, the heartland of Sinhalese civilization.[98] That the Sinhalese opinion leaders grasped the sig-

95. Issue dated 22 February 1896.

96. Dharmapala 1965:479.

97. It is the basis of a satisfaction like that of the "Jews who emerge time and again from seeming doom" (Dimont 1973:16).

98. *Rajaraṭa* means "royal territory" (see Glossary). This locality in the north central

nificance of asserting in this circumstance what they conceived as the community's ancestral rights is seen in an editorial of the *Sihala Samaya*. Urging the Sinhalese to go into those areas and "take posession of the land," it warned:

> If not, the Tamils will for certain capture these lands. There are lakhs of Tamils not only in Jaffna but also in south India . . . and if they start migrating here the Sinhalese people will have to face a great deprivation.[99]

Here we find expressed "the minority complex" of the Sinhala majority community, which has been a key factor in determining the island's interethnic relations in modern times.[100] For Dharmapala, whose conception of the greatness of the Sinhala Buddhists included the test of survival, the community appeared as if hedged in eternally by hostile races:

> During king Dutthagamini's time the Sinhalese had only one enemy. In the present day there are several races who are prepared to destroy the Sinhalese people: the English, Tamils, Muslim, Malay, Parsee, Bombay [*sic*] and Kabul.[101]

Thus, revivalist exhortations turned to paranoid rhetoric. For the Sinhala Buddhists the internalization of a "paranoid ethos"[102] was but the logical extension of the twin concepts of the *Sinhaladvīpa* and the *Dhammadvīpa*—placed as their small community was in the shadow of the Damocles sword of south India, not to mention other threats to their survival from other aliens in race and creed through the course of a history of over two thousand years. In fact, the Sinhalese literary tradition in its religious cum historical writings had kept an indelible record of these periodic devastations. Dharmapala himself once declared, "The

---

plains, which came to be covered in jungle with "the drift to the south-west," was again opened up after about six centuries in the late nineteenth century.

99. Issue dated 26 February 1903. In fact, the veracity of this warning became apparent later in the century when Tamil politicians started claiming the whole of the Northern and Eastern provinces as "traditional Tamil homelands" (see chap. 9).

100. See Farmer 1965:433. Conversely, the Tamil minority on the island seems to have a "majority complex." See K. M. de Silva 1986:368.

101. *SB*, 9 March 1912. "Kabul" probably referred to the Afghan moneylenders, a common sight in Colombo at the time.

102. For "paranoid ethos," see Schwartz 1973.

Sinhalese race during 2358 years has sacrificed more blood than the ocean in defence of this Lanka."[103]

Years of mobilizational activity in identity affirmation on the one hand and the solipsist excitation on the other had their behavioral repercussions. Thus, there were several clashes between the Buddhists and the Christians, ending in a major riot on 9 June 1903 at Anuradhapura, the first capital of the ancient Sinhalese kingdom and a sacred city of the Buddhists. This followed upon years of agitation by Buddhist leaders over the government's acquisition of land in the vicinity of Buddhist shrines for the purpose of extending the commercial center with liquor shops, meat stalls, and churches and mosques. While the Buddhists believed this to be the desecration of sacred sites, the government's perception was simply that "bare land" was being utilized for developmental purposes.[104]

As for the antagonism toward the Moors, fanned originally on economic grounds and later extended to other areas, initially there appeared Sinhala-Moor clashes in urban centers during the later nineteenth and early twentieth century.[105] Of these the incidents in 1907 at Gampola, a one-time capital of the ancient Sinhalese kingdom, which in modern times had come to shelter a sizable Moor population, was to have far-reaching consequences. Here the Sinhalese–Moor antagonism was based on a religious premise, the Moors objecting to an annual Buddhist *perehära* (a religious pageant accompanied by loud music) going past one of their newly erected places of worship. Government orders imposing restriction on the *perehära* were taken by the Buddhists as the denial of an inalienable right they had enjoyed from time immemorial, and the issue became a test case for the newly awakened Sinhala-Buddhist identity, with all its ramifications.[106] Sinhalese journalists played a key role in spreading the feeling that the traditional rights of the community had to be asserted. With these factors as the backdrop an incident in the nearby city of Kandy, another

103. *SB*, 16 December 1911. For details about the Sinhalese historical tradition in this respect, see chapter 1.

104. The main figure behind this agitation was Valisimha Harischandra. The new buildings mentioned above were targets of attack by the Buddhist mob during the riot. See *Si. Sa.* of 19 February, 2 April, and 18 June 1903. Also see Rogers 1987:185–86.

105. See reports of incidents in Colombo (*Sa. Sa.*, 7 November 1884); in Hambantota (in Woolf 1961:242–44).

106. There was a prolonged court case, which received wide publicity in the newspapers. See Blackton 1970.

holy center of the Buddhists, during the annual Vesak festival in 1915, triggered off an island-wide Sinhala-Moor clash of serious proportions.[107]

With regard to the interethnic relations between the Sinhalese and the Tamils, however, the consequences of Sinhala-Buddhist mobilizational activity were not so dramatic.[108] Its effect, on the other hand, was of deeper, far-reaching, and long-drawn salience. The image of the destructive vandal who was the spoiler of ancient Sinhalese civilization—a portrayal of the south Indian invader—resuscitated from the historical tradition and elaborated and widely circulated through mass media, contributed in the long run to harden Sinhalese attitudes toward the Tamils,[109] thwarting all attempts by moderates in both communities to forge a common "Ceylonese" or "Sri Lankan" identity in the twentieth century.

The Arya-Sinhala Identity and the Language Component of Revivalism

The strong identity affirmation by the Sinhalese, tinged with a deep mistrust of other ethnic groups in the island, was the culmination of several decades of intense religiocultural revivalism. Given the community's historical memories, this was but the logical outcome of the emphasis on indigenous authenticity, which had the dual purpose of internal integration and divergence from foreign ways. The singularity and the greatness of the ethnic group is underscored, as it were, by the exclusion and relegation of outsiders. Undoubtedly, prejudice toward the alien was functional insofar as it strengthened ties of group cohesion. Intensive attention given to such interactional procedures in emphasizing identity, however, led to the elaboration of a paranoid ethos, which had developed in the course of its history.

---

107. For details about the riots, see Fernando 1970. After the riots the *Sinhala Bauddhayā* and the *Sinhala Jātiya* (*SJ*) were proscribed, and eight editors of Sinhala journals were tried for sedition.

108. But there were sporadic expressions of antagonism. In 1910, for example, the Sinhalese railway workers in Colombo protested against the influx of Indian workers, and in 1913 they complained that the Indians were being given preference over them in employment (Jayawardene 1972:243).

109. Cf. With "the institutionalization of racial norms and values," according to William Barclay et al. (1976:7), they begin "to generate their own momentum," and they are "learnt by the members of the group in the way other social norms and values are acquired."

It is clear that such purposive developments in group sentiments and behavior originated and found their most cogent expression among the mobilizing populations in urban milieus and spread later to the outlying areas. Thus, as revivalist activity progressed, there arose, in conjunction with the interactional procedures, an attributional definition in the form of the "Ārya-Sinhala" identity. Its elaboration took place among the urban Sinhalese Buddhists, since among them were the community's intelligentsia, capable of visualizing the many implications of the contrast between the past and the present. Furthermore, these English-educated Sinhalese drew inspiration from European scholars such as Max Müller, who popularized the concept of an Āryan race.[110] The Ārya-Sinhala concept, among other things, contained a definite indication of the language component of the ethnic identity.

The Functional Validity of the Ārya-Sinhala Identity

The revivalist leaders, in their search for ethnically unifying and energizing themes from the community's historical tradition, found a most satisfying solution in the "paternity parameter of ethnicity," as represented by the belief of Āryan origins in northern India.[111]

The Authenticating Function

Prince Vijaya, the putative progenitor of the Sinhala race, was believed to have come from north India, the *Āryāvarta,* as it was called in Sanskrit texts. For the Buddhists, moreover, there were additional factors that intensified the appeal of the Āryan connection. The word *ārya* itself connoted meanings such as "noble," "worthy," and "honorable."[112] Indeed, in Buddhist texts the adjective *ārya* was used to refer to the central concepts of the Buddha's teachings: for example, *caturāriya sacca* (Pali: "the four noble truths") and *ariya aṭṭhangika magga* (Pali: "the noble eightfold path").[113] Hence the Āryan concept had enough in it to

110. See Gunawardena 1979:26–27. Gunawardena, however, overstates this influence. For details, see Dharmadasa 1989.

111. Fishman (1977b:17) defines the paternity parameter of ethnicity as "the recognition of putative biological origins."

112. Monier-Williams 1872:129.

113. See Monier-Williams 1872:129. Also see the meanings given the Pali equivalents *ayya* and *ariya,* in Rhys-Davids and Stede 1972:72.

recommend its choice to express the collectivity's highest (or deepest) cultural symbolism. Thus, Anagarika Dharmapala wrote:

> All the customs of Buddhists are different from those of European and Muslim false-believers. . . . Racially too the Āryan Sinhalese are different from the people of other races. . . . Hence is it proper for Āryans to act as killers of cows? Is it proper for Āryans to commit adultery? It is the bounden duty of Āryan Sinhalese Buddhists to refrain from lying, slandering, malicious speech and frivolous talk and from the drinking of intoxicating liquor.[114]

Here it is noted that the Āryan concept takes a racial *cum* ethical meaning. In Dharmapala's own belief "the Āryan race is the only race with noble customs handed down from tradition." Therefore, "the Sinhalese (who are Āryans) should cultivate ancient codes of conduct, Āryan customs and Āryan dresses and ornaments."[115]

Dharmapala expressed many of these sentiments, upholding the purity and nobility of the beliefs, values, and behaviors that characterized the ethnocultural aggregate, in an article entitled "The Sinhalese Nation Belongs to the Āryan Race."[116] That this focus on the Ārya-Sinhala identity of the community was persistently promoted by revivalist activists is evident from the "Ārya Subōdha Nāṭya Sabhā" of John de Silva founded in 1903; the compendium of verses *Ariya Vata* (The Āryan Ethic) purporting to "train the Sinhalese children in Aryan ways and customs";[117] the bilingual (Sinhalese and English) periodical *Āryayā* founded in 1909; and the weekly newspaper *Ārya Sinhala Vanśaya* (1912) published in Galle.[118] Indeed, as early as 1889, the *Sarasavi Sañdaräsa* office had published the *Ārya Sinhala Nam Pota* (The Book of Aryan-Sinhalese Personal Names), which purported to stem the tide of using European names. No doubt the emphasis on Āryan origins received a further impetus with the establishment of connections with India, particularly Bengal, under the guidance of the Theosophists from the 1880s on.

In the Ārya-Sinhala identity was implicit the belief in the commu-

114. *SB*, 13 January 1912.

115. *SB*, 10 February and 2 March 1912.

116. *SB*, 13 January 1912.

117. By an author named M. K. Wijeweera. It is reviewed in *Silumina* of September 1908.

118. See Pannasekera 1968a: 191, 294.

nity's origin in ancient north India. Thus, a writer named W. Arya Dharmawardhana, while upholding the Sinhalese customs declared:

> The progenitors of us Sinhalese were the Āryans of ancient India. . . . This is established by history. Our ways and customs are derived accordingly. The rituals and customs found among most of us are not different from those found among the Āryans of India.[119]

Dharmapala was more explicit:

> The Sinhalese first came to this country from Bengal and the Bengalis are superior in their intelligence to other communities in India.[120]

Apart from the psychologically pleasing prospects of the belief in Bengali connections, there was in it an inspirational relevance that became prominent at the turn of the century. Having established intimate contacts in Bengal, Dharmapala had set up the Indian headquarters of the Buddha Gaya Mahabodhi Society in Calcutta in 1892. The aim of this society was to liberate Buddha Gaya, the site where the Buddha had attained enlightenment, from the hands of a Hindu priestly landlord who had come to own it in the course of time.[121] Dharmapala's association with Bengali nationalists, such as the editor of the *Indian Mirror*, no doubt brought him in touch with the "Swadeshi movement," which was raging in Bengal at the time.[122]

The Dissociative Function

To return to the Sri Lankan context, the Āryan connection carried with it a further functional aspect in the current socioeconomic circumstances. That was in marking off the "negative reference groups" found within the island.[123] Evidently, conditions in the urban milieu of Colombo, where the Ārya-Sinhala identity was in the main nurtured,

---

119. *Sat. Sam.*, 31 January 1891.

120. *SB*, 13 January 1912.

121. Buddha Gaya was then in the province of Bengal. The president of the society was *bhikkhu* Hikkaduwe, and among its office bearers were Olcott and Bautwantudawe.

122. For Dharmapala's Bengali friends, see Sangharakshita 1964.

123. For this concept, see Lynch 1969:9.

forced the Sinhalese Buddhists to look for a definition of their identity which could effectively set them apart from the swelling ranks of aliens. No doubt the emergent Sinhalese elite was in great need of an emblem to distinguish them from the aliens, who were in competition with them. There was a need to clarify the division, without complications of crosscutting features of identity. In this connection, although many features of Sinhalese ethnicity would have proved to be satisfactory, there was a problem in the area of language which seems to have vexed the promoters of the Ārya-Sinhala identity. The Sinhala language shared many features, grammatical as well as lexical, with the Tamil language.[124] This was a disturbing phenomenon in that, through the history of the Sinhalese community, the Tamils represented the most negative reference group.

The implications of language consanguinity being what they were,[125] the strong urge for dissociative emphasis of ethnic identity made opinion leaders look for explanations other than "kin connection" to explain the linguistic similarities. Thus, we find Abraham Mendis Gunasekara, a leading Sinhalese journalist and the author of *A Comprehensive Grammar of the Sinhalese Language* (1891), asserting that,

> although the Sinhalese language is very close to Tamil and other southern languages, it has no kin connection with them. The reason for this closeness is the fact that the rules of southern languages have been modelled on the rules of those north Indian languages.[126]

In this way even the processes of language change are interpreted to suit the beliefs of the protagonists of the Ārya-Sinhala identity.

Obviously, there were more than mere language facts at stake here. In referring to the account in the historical chronicles that Vijaya, the first king of the Sinhalese, married a princess from Madura, who was consecrated as his queen, Gunasekara was anxious to state that this lady, although from a south Indian kingdom, would have be-

124. Because of the convergence of features (although the two languages belong to different "families") due to geographic proximity, as described by Emeneau 1956. The Dravidian features of Sinhala have been described by M. H. P. Silva 1961.

125. For "kin" connection carries with it deep moral obligations and is hence a "sacred" area in ethnicity. See Fishman 1977b.

126. "Sinhala Bahasava," *Sinhala Avurudu Saṅgarāva* 1915:15–18. Gunasekara was the editor of *Gñānāvabhāṣaya,* a leading scholarly journal.

longed to an Āryan lineage. "Otherwise," explained Gunasekara, "he (Vijaya) would not have asked for her hand and they would not have sent her down."[127] This emphatic affirmation of the Āryan connection was expected to establish, along with the broader cultural affinities, the all-important racial roots, while at the same time denying any blood relationship with the Dravidians.[128]

The preservation of the authenticity of the communal identity was viewed as crucial for survival. In Dharmapala's words, "The Sinhala nation has survived for 2450 years because of their pure ways and customs." "But," he warned,

> if they are to continue with the unseemly habits they have acquired recently for another ten years the Sinhala nation, would certainly perish.[129]

According to the logic of this belief, it was pointed out that the Sinhalese person who had embraced Christianity,

> because of his association with false-believers has come to adopt non-Āryan customs . . . and the families which have discarded Buddhism will perish before long.[130]

In this conception the Ārya-Sinhala identity is inexorably a Buddhist identity. Under revivalist pressures Buddhism assumes the form of an ethnoreligious system.[131] A Christian missionary reported in 1910 that Buddhism was identified with patriotism while Christianity was portrayed as the very opposite of this.[132] As Dharmapala put it, to an exemplary Sinhalese death would be preferable to living as a non-Buddhist.[133] So in order to avoid death of identity and to ensure the

---

127. "Karma Vibhaktiyehi *ṭa* Pratyaya," in *Sinhala Mitraya* 1, no. 12 (May 1913): 283–85. This observation is made during a discussion of a grammatical feature of literary Sinhala. Interestingly, modern historians, in explaining this incident, refer to the fact that Āryan influence had penetrated to Madura by this time. See Paranavitana 1959:94.

128. Although many Sinhalese scholars would have been inspired by European scholars such as Max Müller with regard to the Aryan theory (see n. 110), there was one notable exception among them. W. F. Gunawardhana believed that the Sinhalese were a "Dravidian race," and he was the only well-known scholar to hold this view. For details, see Gunawardena 1979:32–33.

129. *SB*, 7 May 1906.

130. *SB*, 26 August 1911.

131. For a parallel development in Burmese Buddhism, see von der Mehden 1974.

132. Cited in K. M. de Silva 1973d:212.

133. Dharmapala 1965:537.

continuity of the ethnocultural aggregate, the Sinhalese people are exhorted not to deviate from their "noble" Āryan traditions.

The Solidarity Function

The Ārya-Sinhala identity had an ideological potential, which was eagerly grasped by some opinion leaders. There was an urgent need for such a unifying ideology in the context of the intercaste rivalries that had burst upon the modernizing society of nineteenth-century Sri Lanka. Underneath the apparent unity that had emerged to tackle the task of confronting Western culture, and for corporate endeavors in revivalist activity, the Sinhalese society of the day was sharply divided due to vigorous caste competition. Indeed, a considerable part of the intellectual energies of the Sinhalese intelligentsia during the last decades of the nineteenth century and early years of the twentieth was spent on intercaste controversy.[134] In this context the Ārya-Sinhala identity could be invoked as a source of powerful cohesive meaning. Thus, Dharmapala, exhorting his compatriots to cherish "the Land, the Nation, the Religion and the Language," declared:

> The Āryan nationals belonging to the Govi caste, Kaurava caste, Durā caste, Vahumpura caste, Ulī caste, Berava caste and Radā caste should take it to heart to maintain Āryan codes of conduct . . . all men should wear white clothes . . . and women the *saree* . . . take Āryan names and adopt Āryan customs . . . and aspire to act in the manner of one community under the suzerainity of one monarch.[135]

At this time two journals, *Āryayā* (The Aryan, 1909) and *Ārya Sinhala Vaṃśaya* (The Aryan-Sinhalese Lineage, 1912), also worked for the same ideal. Apparently, it was hoped that by checking the fissiparous tendencies in the community and by uniting it under the banner of the Ārya-Sinhala identity, it would be provided with enough power and strength to withstand the ever-expected threats and dangers from other ethnoreligious entities.[136]

---

134. See the H. C. P. Bell collection in the Colombo Museum; Malalgoda 1976; and Roberts 1977:LXIII, LXVI.

135. *SB*, 2 March 1912. Also see Dharmapala's articles in *SB*, 25 March 1911.

136. Similarly, Tamil cultural nationalism in modern India emphasizes the overall Dravidian identity as against caste divisionism. See Barnett 1977.

The Language Aspect of the Ārya-Sinhala Identity

Necessary corollaries of the striving toward "strength through purity" are an antipathy to the introduction of alien blood into the racial stream and an abhorrence for the adoption of alien ways and customs in social life.[137] Hence in the field of language, which has a unique place in communal identity not only as "the conveyor of other ethnic symbols" but sometimes also seen as a part of nature, being "often taken as a biological inheritance,"[138] there is a parallel repugnance to alien elements. "Alienness," however, is a variable, dependent on the form of the accepted identity. Abraham Mendis Gunasekara, in consonance with the dominant Ārya-Sinhala identity of his day, thus declared:

> Because of consulting astrological and medical treatises in the Tamil language, and because of the influx and travel of Tamil people here from early times, and because of the arrival and residence here of Portuguese, Dutch and English nations for trade and other activity, many words of alien languages such as Tamil, Portuguese, Dutch and English have come into the Sinhala language. However, it is most befitting to leave them out as much as possible in books and other writings, and use instead pure Sinhala words or Pali and Sanskrit words, *which are necessarily related.*[139]

Judging from the stance of D'Alwis sixty-five years earlier, we find in Gunasekara a marked change in the attitude adopted toward the position of Sinhala vis-à-vis Pali and Sanskrit. There is an ideological shift.[140] This shift involved a redefinition of the authenticity parameter of language, a crucial ingredient of group identity.

James D'Alwis, having received an "English" education (in language as well as in other aspects of culture), was later in life induced to look for his cultural roots and found in the study of Sinhala language and literature a spiritual homecoming. For him the study of Sinhala was the rediscovery of a lost cultural legacy, and, although his intellectual

137. See the front page feature in *Si. Sa.* of 19 February 1903, entitled "Jati Braṣṭayo" (Spoilers of the Race), against marrying foreigners.

138. For this aspect of communal identity, see Fishman 1977b:19.

139. "Sinhala Bhāṣāva," *Sinhala Avurudu Saṅgarāva,* 1 April 1915, 15–18.

140. It is a shift rather than a completely new stance, and another such shift was to occur in the 1930s (see chap. 8). For D'Alwis the Europeans were the most relevant outgroup, but for Gunasekara the south Indians provided the contrast.

exercises encompassed the study of Pali and Sanskrit as well, his ideological commitment as far as his identity was concerned was to Sinhala alone—to be specific, to *Eḷu*, its pure form, as found in some classical writings.[141] This persistent concern for the "essence" of the linguistic heritage of the community evidently arose from the circumstances under which he sought for and found his cultural roots. Also like many an alienated intellectual in the modernizing Orient, D'Alwis was anxious about "cleansing the cultural inheritance from historically accidental accretions."[142] Thus, in his vision linguistic authenticity was given an elemental definition. Even Pali and Sanskrit borrowings, which so far had been considered part and parcel of the linguistic and literary tradition, were seen by him as alien elements. We must note here, however, that the *bhikkhus* and their associates, who spearheaded the religiocultural revival later, did not share this view with him. It was through the Sinhala language that D'Alwis was able to affirm his cultural identity. As a scholar, he delved deep into its form, and in his limited role as a political activist he attempted to promote its function. But unlike D'Alwis, the later revivalists did not have to undertake a strenuous search for cultural roots. The Sinhala language for them was one of the assumed "givens" of their social and cultural existence. Also in their case language was an essential yet subordinate corollary of their main concern, religion. The Sinhala language, in their vision, was an offspring of Pali and Sanskrit, and its classical literature, which was in the main a Buddhist literature, was written in *Miśra Sinhala,* Sinhala mixed with heavy doses of Pali and Sanskrit.[143] From time immemorial the tradition of learning among Sinhala scholars had encompassed the study of Pali and Sanskrit. Indeed, after about the twelfth century, Sanskrit had taken more of their interest than Pali, perhaps because of its potential as a gateway to a wider world of scholarship.[144] Gunasekara, in his *A Comprehensive Grammar of the Sinhalese Language* (1891), found that "almost the entire vocabulary of Sanskrit words is used in Sinhalese composition."[145] As for Pali, his observation was that only "a

141. See chapter 3.

142. For this anxiety by the intelligentsia of the Orient, see Shils 1972b.

143. Pali is the language of the Buddhist scripture. Cf. "In the *Sidat Sañgarāva* is delineated all the grammatical characteristics, except those peculiarities of Sinhala usage, in accordance with Sanskrit and Magadha (Pali) because the Sinhala language has originated mainly from the Sanskrit and Magadha languages" (*Sat Arunudāva* [*SA*], 1882. Quoted in Pannasekara 1965:393).

144. Wijesekera 1955.

145. Gunasekara 1891: 381.

smaller proportion of Pali words, generally religious terms," had come into Sinhala usage. Some of these revivalists, Gunasekara for one, being English-educated, were aware of the interest shown by contemporary European scholars to the study of Sanskrit. In any case the partiality for Pali and Sanskrit studies would have been perceived as a matter-of-course affirmation of the tradition. During previous cultural revivals the study of Pali and Sanskrit had been essential ingredients of the overall resuscitatory effort. Thus, in the Saranankara revival of the eighteeth century the revivalist leaders had to go through intense efforts to reestablish the study of Pali and Sanskrit.[146]

In the nineteenth century, however, when the first modern seat of Oriental learning was being established by *bhikkhu* Walane, the study of Sanskrit had again deteriorated. Because a knowledge of Sanskrit was greatly valued, Walane's senior pupil Batuwantudawe had to find recourse to obtaining tuition from a European missionary who evidently had learned Sanskrit in India before arriving on the island.[147] *Bhikkhu* Hikkaduwe, another pupil of Walane who later founded the Vidyōdaya Pirivena, went further and learned Sanskrit from an Indian Brahmin.[148] Similarly, *bhikkhu* Ratmalane Dharmarama, the chief pupil of the founder of the Vidyālankāra Pirivena, *bhikkhu* Ratmalane Dhammaloka, and who succeeded his teacher as its principal, also learned Sanskrit from an Indian Brahmin.[149] In Vidyōdaya and Vidyālankāra, and in the other seats of Oriental learning which followed them, the study of Pali and Sanskrit along with Sinhala and Buddhism comprised the core syllabus in the teaching program.[150]

The recognition of Pali and Sanskrit as essential ingredients of the Sinhala linguistic tradition did not by itself, however, lead to a policy of deliberate and large-scale "Sanskritization" of the language. This is because in the scholarly tradition itself was a strong conviction that the Sinhala language had certain unique features that made it distinct from those "parent" languages. The thirteenth-century grammar the *Sidat Sañgarāva*, for example, in discussing the category of gender, declares that,

146. Sannasgala 1961:481–86.
147. Pannasekara 1965:61.
148. Pannasekara 1965:109.
149. Buddhadatta 1950:134.
150. Ratanasara 1970:236.

although nouns may be categorized into three Genders according to the Sanskrit system of analysis, in Sinhala usage there are only the Masculine and Feminine Genders.[151]

Perhaps the emphasis on the uniqueness of the Sinhala language which characterized James D'Alwis's linguistic attitude may itself be traced to the material in the *Sidat Sañgarāva.*[152] Even the revivalist scholars who followed him, while accepting Pali and Sanskrit as so-called parent languages, were at the same time conscious of those peculiarities in Sinhala usage which gave it the status of a separate language. Hence even when guidelines for authentic Sinhala usage were being explored, and while the dominant ideology in regard to linguistic norms seems to have directed many scholars to Sanskrit models, there was a powerful rival strand of opinion which claimed to find such guidelines strictly within Sinhala usage.

151. Translated from *Sidat Sañgarāva,* ed. Dharmakirti Sri Dharmarama, 53. In modern Sinhala a three-term gender system is used as in Sanskrit, and the *Sidat Sañgarāva* statement has been the subject of many interpretations. See Wijayaratne 1956:56; and M. W. S. de Silva 1965:87.

152. That there is enough material in the Sinhala linguistic tradition to inspire such thinking was again demonstrated in the 1930s (see the work of the Heḷa movement described in chap. 8).

Chapter 6

Identity, Language, and Modernization

> A Sinhalese who has no knowledge of his own language and literature is a traitor to his country and a disgrace to his ancestry.
> —From an editorial in the *Sandaresa*, 27 October 1905

The Sinhala language was adapting itself to a new situation during the last decades of the nineteenth and early decades of the twentieth century. In this process of language modernization popular conceptions of the communal identity that emerged during the nineteenth-century revival were to play a crucial role. We have seen that a major ingredient as well as a mechanism of social, economic, and political modernization during the same period was the emergence of mass media, in particular the printed word in the form of journalistic and other belletristic writings. It needs mention that part and parcel of the rise of such popular literature was the emergence of a Sinhala-Christian literature. No less significant as a factor in this process of modernization was increasing literacy in the form of vernacular education. The spread of literacy and the rise of new forms of written expression was accompanied by a breaking down of traditional restrictions with regard to language function—and this in turn was to lead to changes in language form. Literary language was being put into more and different uses than before. Earlier the written word was on the whole connected with edification on lines prescribed by Buddhist thought. Now, apart from the necessity of using it for the spreading of the gospel of a new faith, Christianity, there was the need to employ the language in a whole range of new activities—polemics, entertainment, advertising, mass mobilization, and so on. This elaboration of function in Sinhala was concurrent with the contact with English, leading to an expansion on lines of intertranslatability with the language of already industrialized, secularized, and differentiated societies.[1]

Processes of language modernization, however, could hardly be uniform. Apart from the new strata of Sinhalese literati emerging due to advances in education and mass media activity on the one hand and the adoption of the vernacular writers' role by the Christian missionaries on the other, there arose controversies over the "correct" and "appropriate" literary norms. The power of the printed word, which could be used for an island-wide readership, was eagerly understood and in time enthusiastically exploited. This was taking place simultaneously with diverse forms of revivalist activity in which one sees, among other things, a deep concern about the authenticity and uniformity of the language component of communal identity. From this concern arose a pressing need for standardizing the literary medium. Although these activities of language development were the domain of the literary elite, the realization that the printed word had to reach as wide an audience as possible, pointed to the need for working at the same time for wider acceptance of the norm, which would involve "simplification" by means of "vernacularization."

All processes of modernization, however, had to be accommodated within a society that had restrengthened its contact with the Great Tradition. Indeed, the continued viability of the Great Tradition was being vigorously demonstrated, often by the utilization of new means to support existing ends. Identity affirmation was the order of the day.[2] In such a context language developmental activity was bound to be judged by its compatibility with the form of communal identity emphasized in other spheres.

The dynamics of language modernization under these circumstances may be ascertained from an examination of the impact of Christianity on the Sinhala language, the developments in the language of Sinhala journalism, and the problems arising in connection with the Sinhala school textbooks.

The Impact of Christianity on the Sinhala Language

It would have been apparent from the discussion above that Christianity in particular acted as a catalyst in the transformation of some

1. A "development" similar to that described by C. A. Ferguson 1968:32.
2. See chapter 4.

vital aspects of traditional Sinhalese culture, specifically the Sinhala language. We see that the production of a Sinhalese-Christian literature made special demands on the language and led in time to many linguistic novelties. First, there was the need to introduce the concepts of the Judeo-Christian tradition to the Sinhalese audience; second, in order to reach the largest possible readership, it was necessary to use as simple a literary medium as possible. "Simplification" here meant being closer to the colloquial idiom.[3] The strategies used by Sinhalese-Christian writers were not only innovative but, from the point of view of the traditions of Sinhalese scholarship, disruptive as well. Furthermore, the peculiarities of the idiom used in Sinhalese-Christian literature were accentuated by the fact that most of these writers did not have a sound knowledge of literary Sinhala. Also the fact that they were either Europeans or Burghers led to their Sinhala writing being subject to considerable linguistic interference from their first language.

Such peculiarities of Sinhalese-Christian literature were obvious from its early stages. To choose at random, for example, a citation from the late-eighteenth century translation of the New Testament:

> apē swāmīhu Yēsus Kristus vahansēge mahimatāvayat pitāvana deviyan vahansēge seneheyat suddavū sprītu vahansēge pangukamat um̆balā siyallō samaga vēvā.[4]
>
> (The majesty of our Lord Jesus Christ, the love of God who is the Father and the communion with the Holy Spirit may all these be with you.)

"The Heavenly Lord," "Holy Father," and "the Holy Spirit" were concepts novel to the Sinhalese mind. In order to render them in Sinhala, the writer, in the first instance, had to extend the meaning of an existing word *svāmī* (master); in the second, to borrow a Pali form *pitā* (father) not normally used in Sinhala; and in the third, to coin a new word *sprītu vahansē* (combining *sprītu*, meaning "essence" or "spirit," with the honorific title *vahansē*). Moreover, with the intention, apparently, of making the language as simple as possible, several forms from

3. Because the Sinhala language is characterized by a diglossia where there is a discrepancy between the spoken and literary languages and the mass readership was not highly conversant with the traditional literary usage. See M. W. S. de Silva 1967, 1974; Dharmadasa 1967, 1977.

4. Quoted by Sannasgala 1961:733.

colloquial Sinhala are used: namely *apē, uṁbalā,* and *pangukamat.* The use of the second-person plural pronoun *uṁbalā,* however, indicates the writer's ignorance of some finer aspects of the Sinhala language. For unlike in modern English, where there is only one second-person pronoun, in Sinhala there are a number of second-person pronominal forms, which are structured hierarchically, ranging from respect to disrespect, and in that hierarchy *uṁbalā* is a form used in disrespect. Also *pangukama,* here meaning "communion," is a new word, coined by adding *kama* (state of being) to *pangu* (share), an unusual combination. In addition to such features the writer's inadequate command of the norms of accepted literary usage is evident in the incorrect form of the suffix in *mahimatāvaya* (*-tāvaya* instead of *-tāva*) and in the use of the nominative form *siyallō* where the correct usage would have been the oblique *siyallan.*

As more and more material came to be produced by these writers, however, leading to an improvement in the knowledge of traditional literary usages, the language of Sinhalese-Christian literature came to be more in line with the accepted form of literary Sinhala.[5] Yet it was a long and slow process. The influence of the early form of missionary Sinhala was to remain for a long time in the works of Sinhalese-Christian writers even when they were dealing with nonreligious subjects. Thus, to cite an example from the writings of John Pereira, a leading Christian scholar in the mid-nineteenth century and a pioneer of Sinhala journalism:

> numut ingrīsingē nuvanin saha daksa kaminut käralivalaṭa mulkārayōva siṭiyavungen eka ekaa bägin allāgat bävin eṅdērek näti bäṭalu rälaval men käralivalaṭa bäṅdii siṭi ayaval manmulāva giyāya. (From the history of Lanka *Heladiv Rajaniya,* Wesleyan Mission Press, 1853:296)
>
> (But as the leaders of rebellious activity came to be captured one by one due to the intelligence and capability of the English, those who had joined the rebellion went astray like folds of sheep without a shepherd.)

Here, apart from the unidiomatic use of the instrumental case forms where the acceptable practice would have been to use a postposi-

5. Here criticism by Christians who had a better knowledge of literary Sinhala, such as James D'Alwis, was a contributing factor. See D'Alwis 1863; and Balding 1922:131–32.

tion (*nuvanin saha daksakaminut* for *nuvana saha daksakama nisaa*), the writer employs new coinages such as *mulkarayō* (to mean "leaders," instead of the Sanskrit borrowing *pradhānin,* which would have been the most appropriate) and *ayaval* for the concept "those people." The form *ayaval* appears especially inappropriate because of the employment of the *-val* suffix, which is normally used with inanimate nouns. Also the lack of a good command of literary grammar is evinced in the use of the nominative form *mulkarayō,* where the rules of syntax demand the use of oblique, *mulkarayan.* Similary, *rälaval* too is defective in that the *-val* suffix is used instead of the conventional zero suffix. Furthermore, the employment of the simile of the shepherd and the fold, which is quite foreign to the Sinhalese mind, is obviously inspired by Christian literature.

Undoubtedly, some features of this unorthodox literary idiom arose out of the need to expand the semantic range of the Sinhala language to suit modern circumstances. Also there was the need to present a "simpler" form of literary Sinhala for the benefit of the new and rapidly expanding readership whose level of literacy did not encompass a knowledge of the classics. Yet the attempts of these the early Sinhalese-Christian writers to "modernize" the literary usage appeared amateurish and naive because of their lack of an understanding of the accepted literary idiom. As a result, the Buddhist literati, who had a thorough training in the classical language, tended to look down upon the language used by Christian writers when they entered the field of mass media activity later in the nineteenth century.[6] Piyadasa Sirisena, for example, deplored the plight of the Sinhala language, which, he said, was being "debased" by "church Sinhala" (*palli hingala*), "Catholic Sinhala" (*katōlika hingala*), and "Bible Sinhala" (*baibal hingala*).[7] Here is evident not only the upholding of the "authentic" form of literary Sinhala but also a strong resentment of the "foreign" religion.

Similarly, M. Dharmaratna (1884–1925), a former *bhikkhu* and a leading Oriental scholar, who edited the newspaper *Lak Miṇi Pahana* from 1883 to 1924, was grieved to find that

> only a few pundits are available today who are competent to render a beautiful story from another language into Sinhala. The majority

6. See chapter 5. The early Buddhist editors of Sinhala periodicals such as Batuwantudawe and Koggala were very competent scholars not only in Sinhala but also in Pali and Sanskrit.

7. In the novel *Apaṭa Vecca Dē* (What Has Befallen Us) (Colombo, [1909] 1954), 39. The

> of such [translators] have been trained to write "Bible Sinhala." (*LMP*, 26 September 1903)

It was his fear that,

> just as much as the great Buddhist religion is declining because of [the influence exerted by] the Bible, the pure Sinhala language too will for certain disappear because of [the Bible] language. (*LMP*, 26 September 1903)

Thus, in an era where Buddhism was on the defensive any language innovation originating from the ranks of the Christians was viewed with suspicion, and, as the Buddhists had virtual control of the Sinhala literary establishment as it were,[8] such innovations had only a slender chance of general acceptance.

Indeed, Sinhalese-Christian scholars themselves who had gained a mastery of the Sinhalese literary tradition found many features of the current Christian literature both naive and inelegant. James D'Alwis, for instance, felt that the language of the Bible translations would "impoverish the Sinhalese language."[9] Criticism stemming from quarters such as this had some effect as far as the Sinhalese-Christian literature was concerned. But the wider community of Sinhala scholars was disturbed by the language usage of a much wider salience—namely that arising from the educational policy of the government and missionary authorities.

The Government's Literacy Program and the Problem of School Textbooks

While classical texts and the classical language were receiving the earnest attention of the revivalist elite, there was no prospect of this knowledge seeping down to the mass level. No doubt there had been a change of governmental policy with regard to education, and the spread of mass literacy in the vernacular had taken priority over the dissemination of the English language. But the intent of the government

word *hingala* (for *sinhala*), from the usage of the uneducated, denotes the writer's disparagement of the language used by Christian writers.

8. See the section "The Rise of the Scholarly Establishment," in this chapter.

9. See the section "The Concern for Authenticity" in chapter 3.

was to spread "rudiments of knowledge . . . to the people in their own tongue" and not "to promote the classics in the vernacular."[10]

In this connection the policy followed in government as well as missionary schools, which at the time formed the preponderant majority of the schools in the island, had been to avoid the use of classical Sinhala texts and instead use books prepared by missionary writers or government officials. Undoubtedly, one reason for avoiding the classics was religious—the Sinhala classics invariably contained Buddhist subject matter. Apart from the religious factor, the consideration that the textbooks should contain subject matter of contemporary relevance also lay behind this policy. In any case, it so happened that the writers of the new school textbooks were mostly Europeans, and sometimes Burghers, who lacked the native speakers' competence of the language. Furthermore, as a matter of policy, there was a general disregard for the rules of literary grammar, which was the concern of the traditional system of education. Hence when these books came out the leading Sinhalese scholars of the day found their language "more in line with vulgar usage."[11]

D'Alwis, engaged in a "struggle" in the cause of the Sinhala language, had brought to the notice of the Legislative Council in 1876 that the school textbooks then in use were "such as to do great damage to the Sinhalese language, a language which had existed for 2500 years."[12] At that stage, apparently, there was no popular concern about the matter. As the religiocultural revival gathered momentum, however, there were attempts to make the unsatisfactory state of the school textbooks a matter of wider social concern. Apart from the deeper awareness of and commitment to classical language norms brought about by endeavors in authentification and identity affirmation, there was a growing consciousness about the community's "rights" in making decisions abut its own language, especially in the education of the young. This consciousness was particularly strong in the organizational and agitational activity of the Theosophists.[13] Hence at the turn of the century there was a campaign in the newspapers and the periodicals against the Sinhala textbooks used in schools, in particular those prepared by one J. H. Leak, an Englishman, and Arthur van Culenberg, a Burgher.

10. *Sessional Paper VII* 1867, "Report on Education":9.

11. From a review in *Sarasavi Sandaresa,* 15 September 1882. The writer was Weragama Punchi Banda (d. 1892), an alumnus of Vidyodaya.

12. *Memoirs:*134.

13. See chapter 4.

The critics regarded Leak as one of that category of Englishmen who

> in their superior wisdom believe that the language of the Island which has evolved in the course of twenty-four centuries in accordance with the genius of the Sinhalese people can be improved upon English models.[14]

In this statement, which is indicative not only of the feeling of pride about the national heritage but also of the belief in the community's right to decisions about its own affairs, is found a distinct echo of D'Alwis's sentiments expressed about half a century earlier under other, but comparable, circumstances.

For those "would be improvers of our own language," the editor of the *Sandaresa,* the English newspaper of the Buddhist Theosophical Society, wanted to point out, there was "one great stumbling block" in their way, and that was "Sinhalese grammar." Therefore, what they have tried to do was "to abolish it altogether, and in no way recognize its existence in their writings." Thus, Leak was accused of "having no sympathy whatever for grammar and even sense." Examples were cited to illustrate how he had used faulty orthography, wrong morphological forms, and wrong syntactic combinations. Also it was pointed out that Leak displayed a deplorable lack of knowledge of the meaning of Sinhala words—for example, in using *makuṇa* (bug) to mean "spider" and *kakul* (legs) to mean "feet."[15] Similarly, van Culenberg was also accused of using wrong orthography and faulty grammar.[16]

A feature in these books which appeared most obnoxious to the Sinhalese scholars who were eagerly promoting classical norms in literary Sinhala was the preference given to the grammar of the current colloquial usage in place of the accepted norms of literary grammer. Instead of the three separate verbal forms, in accordance with the category of person in the indicative mood verbs found in the literary language, van Culenberg and Leak had used the common verbal form with the suffix *-vā* found in the colloquial language. That is:[17]

14. "The Degradation of the Sinhalese Language," pt. 2, editorial in the *Sandaresa* (English), 25 May 1906.

15. See n. 14. Incidentally, the orthographical mistakes pointed out contain the depiction of the colloquial equivalents of forms in the traditional literary usage.

16. See n. 14. The orthographical "mistakes" again depict the colloquial forms.

17. The material given in the following tabulation is taken from the criticism of Wer-

van Culenberg's Book	Accepted Literary Usage
bāla sahōdarī nidahas *venavā* (the younger sister gets free)	bāla sahōdarī nidahas *vey* (third-person singular)
num̆bat *enavā* (you too are coming)	num̆bat *ennehi* (second-person singular)
mama *situavā* (I thought)	mama *situvemi* (first-person singular)
Leak's Book	
māluvō saha kim̆bullu vaturē *pīnanavā* (the fish and the crocodiles swim in water)	māluvō saha kim̆bullu vaturē *pīnati* (third-person plural)

Other instances of the use of colloquial grammar were cited—for example, the use of the accusative suffix *-va* (as in *num̆bava, māva, leḍāva,* etc.). It was pointed out that such forms were "not found in any Sinhalese book written in the past" and that "they are being despised by Sinhalese pundits of the present day." Furthermore, it was considered pertinent that, even in the colloquial, such forms were "found only in the language of the vulgar populace in Colombo—the Sinhalese villagers themselves not using them." Evidently, the suggestion here was that, as van Culenberg was a town-dwelling Burgher and Leak an Englishman who had learned his Sinhala from people such as van Culenberg, they were unable to portray the authentic language of the Sinhalese people. As to the results of teaching the Sinhala language in schools by means of these textbooks, critics insisted that "these books are bound to vulgarize the language and degrade it to the level of the *patois*."[18]

With the steadily increasing awareness of the past achievements of the community, along with increasing attempts to emulate those achievements, especially in the field of Oriental scholarship, this disregard of linguistic norms was condemned as an "insult to the Sinha-

agama (n. 11) and the *Sandaresa* editorial (n. 14). For this particular difference between literary and colloquial Sinhalese, see Dharamadasa 1967:336.

18. N. 14. The following extract is also from this source.

lese people" and an "affront to Sinhalese scholarship." Were the Sinhalese people to be treated in the same manner as

> the savage races of Africa posessing no fixed language, no grammar, no literature of any kind, until the omniscient Englishman, the heaven-born civilizer of the world, appeared on the scene to supply these fatal defects?

This extract from an editorial in the English newspaper the *Sandaresa* shows how some English-educated Sinhalese were forging within themselves further motivations for nationalist endeavors by finding a contrast between the Sinhalese culture, with its past achievements, and cultures of "lesser development" elsewhere. Activists among them such as Anagarika Dharmapala, who often wrote in Sinhala, were to carry such messages to the masses.[19]

The critics of the new school textbooks, in addition to being either classical scholars themselves or admirers of classical scholarship, were ardent Buddhists as well. Hence they were not slow in observing the reluctance of the government (not to mention the missionary educational authorities) either to use classical Sinhala texts or to employ Buddhists, among whom obviously were the most competent Sinhala scholars, in the compilation of new textbooks. Thus, "P(iyadasa) S(irisena)," wondering whether the intention of prescribing these books for use in schools was to "help the progress of the Sinhalese people or to destroy them altogether," also ventured to ask:

> As all the important books in the Sinhala language are those written about Buddhism, is it not possible that these new books have been prepared with the intention of preventing those Buddhist books being read? (*SB*, 30 June 1906)

Evidently, the governmental and missionary educational authorities believed that it was impossible to find writers from among the Sinhala scholars of the day who could cater to contemporary educational

19. See, for example, his article in *SB* of 16 September 1911, where he compares the Anglicized Sinhalese to "the slaves of the Kaffir race in America"; and *SB* of 4 October 1911, where he exhorts the Āryan Sinhalese not to behave in the same "low-down blind and foolish" manner as "the Kaffirs of Africa who have embraced Christianity."

requirements. This was possibly why they decided to step in and write the textbooks themselves. As far as the Sinhala language was concerned, however, communicability suffered in these pioneering efforts. As for the subject matter, more often than not the products turned out to be attempts to replace the Buddhist content, as found in the Sinhala classics, with Christian subject matter.[20] Thus, along with the linguistic aspect, the religious aspect of the school textbooks also appeared to have a negative effect as far as the social implications of the educational policies were concerned—the Buddhists feeling doubly alienated.

Among Sinhalese scholars, the classical language form was cherished as a surviving element of the nation's glorious past. The fact that it had functioned as the vehicle of Buddhist thought also provided a strong motivation to treat it with zealous attachment. "The Sinhala language is an Āryan language," declared a *bhikkhu* correspondent writing on "The Preservation of the Sinhala Language,"

> which originated in our own island itself [*sic*], and is second to no other language. It is a truth known by all learned people that in it were written various explicatory works in accordance with the Buddha's own words. Also many beautiful literary works have been composed in it following rules of prosody and rhetoric. . . .

Viewed in such a context, it was a matter of grave concern that,

> when one considers the unseemliness of the language that is taught to Sinhalese children attending schools today, who can but not think that the little Sinhala extant will also soon disappear? (*Si.Sa.*, 16 July 1903)

The Buddhists, among whose ranks were the most competent Sinhala scholars of the day, were justifiably aggrieved that they were neither invited to help nor even consulted in the preparation of school textbooks. The *Sarasavi Sañdaräsa* raised this point in regard to the obvi-

20. Note, for example, *The Administration Report of the Director of Public Instruction 1879*, which stated that "the reading books used are full of the most dogmatic theological opinions which to an honest and intelligent Buddhist or Mahammedan are very offensive and calculated to do more harm than good."

ous failure to enlist Pundit Batuwantudawe's expertise for this purpose.[21] To remedy the situation in their own way the Buddhists proceeded to write textbooks themselves. Apparently, this was viewed as an essential corollary to their program of establishing a system of Buddhist schools.[22] Thus, *bhikkhu* Dodanduwe Piyaratana, a pioneer in the new Buddhist educational activity, published *Gñēyārtha Dīpanī* and *Jinadharma Vikāśinī*, and Thomas Karunaratna, an alumnus of Vidyōdaya, wrote *Varṇāvaliya.*[23] Without government support, however, these attempts could not proceed very far.

To remedy the situation themselves the Buddhists proceeded to include the study of Sinhala classics in their own schools. C. Don Bastian, another pioneer in Buddhist educational activity on modern lines, having established a Sinhalese school in Pettah in 1876, used classical literary works such as the sixteenth-century compendium of stories *Saddharmālankāraya* and the seventeenth-century collection of didactic verse *Subhāṣitaya* in his classes.[24] Evidently, the desire to propagate the knowledge of the classical language went hand in hand with the motive of keeping the students in intimate contact with the traditional religion. Furthermore, in order to supplement or even counteract the Christianity-based teaching imparted in government and missionary schools, the Buddhists started Sunday schools of their own. This practice, again being imitative of Christian institutions, was first tried in Colombo when C. Don Bastian founded the Bauddha Samayāvabhāṣa Paṭhaśālāva (School of Buddhist Religious Instruction) in Pettah in 1885. He was later followed by others, the movement spreading subsequently to the provinces.

The anxieties of the Buddhists as far as the religious aspect of education was concerned would have been largely abated as the number of schools under their management increased gradually. But the promotion of a literary usage based on classical models was no easy task. Apart from the fact that the government's educational policy with regard to mass literacy was not conducive to the fruition of such elitist expectations, the proliferation of popular journalism to meet a rapidly rising demand necessitated and hastened the vernacularization rather than the classicization of the literary medium.

21. "Don Andiris de Silva Batuvantudave Pandituma," *Sa.Sa.*, 19 December 1884.

22. See the section "A Buddhist Lay Educational System" in chapter 4.

23. Dharmarama 1965:2. Advertisement in *Lankōpakāraya*, 1 April 1882.

24. See "Punya Sanvarī Pāsāla," *Sa.Sa.*, 2 April 1885. Bastian's activities have been described earlier.

Sinhala Journalism and the Developments in Language

If at the dawn of the nineteenth century literary activity was mostly confined to elitist circles,[25] by its close there was every indication that this state of affairs would change drastically, for literature was becoming a mass concern. Expansion of educational facilities and the growth of literacy, the creation of new communicational networks linking the administrative and commercial centers with the countryside, and the increasing commercialization of society, which affected literary activity as well, all contributed to a tremendous expansion of mass media activity—particularly in the form of the printed word. For a language such as Sinhala, with its long-established classical tradition in literature, the demands of modernization meant specifically the removal of barriers between literary communication and mass communication. The exigencies of modernization, however, stood at cross-purposes with the indispensabilities of authentification—a prime need of the revivalist era. Here lay a dilemma for the Sinhalese literati, and it was to take a long time to resolve. This dilemma first became manifest in connection with the language of Sinhala journalism, the area in which burgeoning literary activity showed its most prolific form.

If the Sinhalese-Christian writers and the nonnative compilers of Sinhala school textbooks appeared far too adventurous in molding a literary idiom to suit the new circumstances, the Buddhist literati, especially at the early stages of their mass media ventures, appeared far too concerned about preserving the classical norms in the literary medium. Thus, for example, Batuwantudawe, the first Buddhist editor of a Sinhala journal, employed a highly Sanskritized literary idiom:

> lak div väsi sataratoraturu dänmehi adahas äti siyallan visin vimasā bäliya yutuyi. mē lankādvīpayehi magadha, sanskrta, eḷu yana bhāṣāvalin liyū dharma, vyākaraṇa candōlankāra tarka vaidyādī bohō śāstra pot tibiyadīt väsiyō ehi paridi nodänmen bohō seyin yuktāyukti tīraṇayaṭa asamarthava veset. (Editorial in *Yatalaba,* April 1854)
>
> (This should be examined by all in Lanka interested in learning about scholarly activity. Although there are many books found in this island written in *magadha* (Pali), Sanskrit and *Eḷu* (Sinhala) on

25. See the section "The Position of the Vernacular" in chapter 2.

> subjects such as the Buddhist doctrine, grammar, prosody, rhetoric, logic and medicine, the people live without the ability to ascertain which is proper and which is not as they are not conversant with those works.)

Here the writer follows the rules of classical literary grammar meticulously. As for the lexicon, he is careful to confine himself to literary forms even in the Sinhala words he has employed. Taken along with the large number of Sanskrit borrowings that have been used, Batuwantudawe's language is markedly different from that found in the other (i.e., Christian) journalistic writings of the day.[26]

With the Buddhists becoming increasingly aware, however, of the need for more regular involvement in journalistic activity, a field originally monopolized by the Christians, they also realized the importance of making adjustments in the literary medium to suit the new circumstances. Thus, to cite a passage from *Lak Miṇi Pahana* (1862), the first Sinhala newspaper of the Buddhists:

> mē bhāṣavē tibena visiturukama gänada rasavatkama gänada, mēka igenagannavunṭa utsāha danvanu sañdahā mehidī apa visin mē bhāṣāva praśansā kaṭayutu vūvat apēma bhāṣāvaṭa apima praśansā karanavāṭa vaḍā anun visin karana praśansāvak penvā dīmaṭa yōgya vey. (Editorial in *LMP,* 17 October 1862)

> (Although it is necessary at this juncture to praise this language as regards its beauty and its savour so that those who study it may be encouraged, it seems more appropriate to cite a complimentary remark made by someone else instead of praising our own language ourselves.)

The writer's vocabulary is on the whole confined to pure Sinhala. He retains a few Sanskrit forms—*bhāṣāva, praśansā,* and *yōgya*—which had obviously come into common Sinhala usage. The fact that he was keen to use some colloquial forms—*mēka, apēma, apima,* and *karanavāṭa*—evidently indicates the attempt to reach as wide a readership as possible.

The polemicist writings that appeared during the Buddhist-Christian confrontation were characterized by an even more "popular"

26. See chapter 4.

literary idiom.[27] The Christian writers, who obviously were not so conversant with the classical language, and their *bhikkhu* opponents, trying to reach as large an audience as possible, both tended to use a highly colloquialized language. Thus, to quote from a writing by Migettuwatte, the most prominent *bhikkhu* polemicist:

> api mē "satyamārgaya" nam lat patraya paṭangattē pradhāna koṭama āgama sambandha yahapat āranciya prakāśa karanṭay. ē atara lōkayāṭa prayōjanavat vū venat vädagat āranciyak läbunot prakāśa nokara arinnnē näta. innisā apē patrayaṭa ingrīsi-sinhala prasiddhapatrakārayō dos kīvā hari näta. (*Satyamārgaya* 1, no. 2 [1867])

> (We inaugurated this paper named *Satyamārgaya,* mainly for propagating the truth with regard to religion. But at the same time, if we obtain any other news which would be of use to people, we will not refrain from publishing it. Hence it is not proper for some English and Sinhala newspapermen to have found fault with us.)

Migettuwatte uses a large number of colloquial words: *paṭangattē, āranciya, karanṭay, läbunot, nokara, arinnē, innisā, apē, kārayō, kīvā,* and *hari.* Along with them he did use certain Sanskrit forms—*patraya, pradhāna, prakāśa, lōkayā, prayōjanavat,* and *prasiddha*—and these were obviously words that had come into common parlance; even the illiterate knew their meaning. Apparently, the language had to be softened by concessions to the colloquial idiom in this attempt to reach the popular readership, some of whom had only a bare minimum of literacy. Thus, the material of the public controversies between the Buddhists and Christians was published using approximately the same language used in the speeches made for the occasion.[28]

With the establishment of the two main seats of Oriental learning, Vidyōdaya (1873) and Vidyālankāra (1875) *pirivenas,* and the subsequent expansion of *pirivena* education and the number of readers with a sound grasp of the Sinhala classics, there arose a tendency among some journalists to return to classical linguistic norms. Thus, we have an editorial of *Sarasavi Sańdaräsa* written by an alumnus of Vidyōdaya:

27. See chapter 4.
28. For an analysis of the language of these, see M. W. S. de Silva 1967:14.

> sidat saṅgarāva mīṭa avurudu siya gananakaṭa ihata liyana laddaki. mēkālayehi siṭina sinhala panḍitayin sinhala vyākaraṇa igena gattet ē poteni. ē nisā sidat saṅgarāvē katrūgē mataya nivāradiyayi sitā ē matayehi ellī siṭīma yutu noveyi.[29]

> (The *Sidat Saṅgarāva* has been written some hundred of years ago. The Sinhala pundits of today learned the grammar of the language from that book. But to think therefore that the opinion of the author of the *Sidat Saṅgarāva* is always correct is not proper.)

The writer here uses very few Sanskrit forms—*vyākaraṇa* and *katrū*—and these were obviously ones that had come into common use in literary Sinhala at the time. While writing in a lucid style in the literary idiom he uses only one colloquial form, *gattet*. On the whole he has adhered to classical norms of grammar, although retaining a simple diction suitable for mass readership.

Obviously, a journal such as *Sarasavi Sañdaräsa,* functioning as "the mouthpiece of the two million Buddhists" of the island,[30] had to work more toward mass comprehension rather than the preservation of classical authenticity. It was indeed necessary to be so if the journal was to be an effective instrument of mass mobilization. Yet managed as it was by the religiocultural elite, its language had to retain the mark of authenticity. Hence a modus vivendi was achieved: The rules of classical grammar were retained, while at the same time in vocabulary a partiality was shown toward forms in common usage.

Vernacularization as an Incitement to Strive for Authentification

The processes of socioeconomic modernization led to a dramatic expansion of literary activity in Sinhala. First, there was a sharp increase in the number of journals in Sinhala during the last years of the nineteenth century: While only seventy-five newspapers and periodicals had appeared during the fifty-five years from 1832 to 1887, the twelve years from 1888 to 1900 saw the launching of eighty-eight new journals, in addition to the continued publication of some inaugurated earlier.[31]

29. *Sa.Sa.,* 15 September 1882. The writer is Weragama.
30. Bevan 1907:308.
31. The figures have been computed from Pannasekera 1965, 1966, and 1967.

With the expansion of journalistic activity many new writers appeared on the literary scene. Literary activity in Sinhala, other than that of the Christians mentioned above, had so far been confined to those trained in the traditional system of Oriental scholarship. But now many writers without such a background were coming into the field. These factors, in conjunction with the populist demands of mass media, seem to have led to a strong swing toward the vernacularization of the literary language. Thus, to cite a passage from *Siri Laka Situmina* (1893), published by a commercial establishment in Colombo:

> mē nam abhinava āranci patraya paṭan gannaṭa api muladī adahas kalē pasugiya pebarāvari māsēdī namut apē ē mul yōjanava assampūrnavū nisā bäri vunēya . . . velaňdāma karana api mebaňdu patrayak paṭan gattē apēma dänvīm nomilē pala karanṭa nova mēkālayaṭa mebaňdu pravurti patrayak paṭan gänma avaśyayenma onǟ bäv penī giya nisā dän api visin mē väḍē paṭan gatimu. (Issue dated 3 March 1893)
>
> (Although we originally expected to start this new journal in February we were unable to do so because our earlier proposal was not accomplished. . . . We who are engaged in commerce started a paper like this not with the idea of getting our own advertisements published free of charge but because it occurred to us that a paper of this nature is a necessity at a time such as today.)

In this passage there are mistakes in grammar (in the use of the direct nominal form *api* where the oblique *apa* is required and in the use of the active-voice verbal form *gatimu* where the passive construction *gannā ladī* is needed); also there is wrong orthography (in the use of the "dental" *l* in the word *pala* where "retroflex" *ḷ* should be used). In the second sentence the features of two sentence types are erroneously juxtaposed: The sentence begins as an emphatic construction and ends like a declarative one. The writer uses a colloquialized vocabulary and on the whole displays a propensity for the spoken idiom. In this attempt at vernacularization, however, he has ended with a literary form that is neither the accepted literary standard nor the written equivalent of the spoken language.

Problems and Typography

While journalistic output increased rapidly to meet a growing demand there was a proportionate neglect of the typographic niceties in text production. Assiduity with regard to the form of the texts in orthography, word division as well as grammar, left much to be desired. This was especially so because the new mode of text production, printing, had only recently been introduced to Sinhala society. As more and more texts with haphazard deviations from traditional language norms appeared on the literary scene, they naturally engaged the attention of the traditionalist literati. Deeply involved as they were in a religiocultural revival, such insouciance with regard to language, a crucial ingredient of the community's historical tradition, was indeed a matter of grave concern. Thus the editor of *Satya Samuccaya,* a journal published by Vidyālankāra, was to declare:

> Although in the past books were written with great care under the patronage of kings and ministers, in the present day many people whose motive is the finding of daily sustenance, have started writing books without any concern for matters such as spelling. (Editorial dated 15 April 1890)

Similarly, a correspondent to *Dinakara Prakāśaya,* one of whose coeditors was an examiner at Vidyōdaya, pointed to the damage done by careless journalists to the Sinhala language, which is honored by all Oriental people, chief among whom are inhabitants of Lanka.[32] The *Sinhala Bauddhayā,* managed by Anagarika Dharmapala, explaining the cause of this development, stated:

> Today the number of persons who write to newspapers and periodicals is very great indeed. . . . But some of these writers have not studied their own language by attending a school or a *pirivena.* (*SB,* 29 February 1908)

Again a Sinhala schoolteacher, deploring the standard of the printed material in the language, pointed out several glaring mistakes in orthography and word division in some contemporary texts and stated

32. "Pirimi Harak" in the issue of 10 June 1891. W. P. Ranasinghe, co-editor of this paper, was a lawyer by profession and an examiner of Vidyodaya Privena.

that "with the Sinhala people books which have been properly printed are rare indeed."[33]

It needs mention here that this concern with language form was much more than the solipsist opposition of a tradition-oriented literati to inevitable processes of modernization. While the utilization of printing opened the prospects for an unprecedented number of texts to flood the literary scene, a parallel increase in the concern about the form of the texts was essential if the stability of the code was to be preserved.[34] The fact that the literati were operating within the context of a religio-cultural revival gave a cutting edge to that concern, leading to value-laden stances concerning the processes and problems of language modernization.

Problems and Functional Expansion

In the journalistic literature of the time the Sinhala language was being utilized for functions above and beyond those with which it had hitherto been associated. Literary Sinhala, whose function had been quite limited, was now being put into more and varied uses. This language modernization, in the form of elaboration of function, was seen mainly in the sphere of journalistic literature. Thus, a special feature of journalistic activity at the turn of the century was the expansion into new areas of knowledge: While the traditionalist concerns were prominent, there was also a growing interest in new subject matter. This tendency may be elucidated thus:[35]

Subject Matter	*Journal*
1. Traditional	
religious propaganda:	*Bauddha Samaya Sangarava*, 1887
	Riviräsa, 1888
	Vidyā Darpanaya, 1893
Oriental scholarship:	*Gñānādarśaya*, 1896
ayurvedic medicine:	*Vaidya Śāstrālankāraya*, 1894
	Vaidyādhāra Sangarahava, 1896
astrology:	*Vidyādīpikā*, 1895

33. Piyadasa Ramachandra, *Sinhala Tarunaya*, October 1908.

34. Cf. "The heaviest demand for codification arises due to the spread of literacy and the technological demands of printing" (Haugen 1966b).

35. Information collected from Pannasekera 1965, 1966, and 1967.

2. Modern

light entertainment:	*Kav Kalam̆ba*, 1899
	Vivēka Kālaya, 1904
comic caricature:	*Kavaṭa Dūtayā*, 1889
	Kavaṭa An̆gana, 1902
commerce:	*Siri Laka Situmina*, 1893
	Velan̆da San̆garahava, 1895
modern agriculture:	*Pol Vävili San̆garāva*, 1887
	Govikam San̆garāva, 1896
modern education:	*Guruvarayā*, 1896
	Guru Śiṣya Sangrahaya, 1901
news and commentary:	*Dinapatā Pravurtī* (Daily) 1895
	Lak Rivi Kiraṇa (Daily) 1895
modern science:	*Vidyābharaṇaya*, 1907 (whose first number carried articles on modern mathematics, geometry, algebra, chemistry, and botany, etc.)

When these attempts at expanding the functions of literary Sinhala were taking place the attention of the traditionalist literati came to be focused on the form of the language used. The literati appear to have been very concerned as to whether, in these ventures into unchartered territory, the classical language norms could be maintained as well. Hence in literary reviews considerable attention was paid to flaws in orthography and grammar, while efforts to introduce the Sinhala readership to new areas of knowledge were encouraged. Sometimes doubts were expressed about the feasibility of the whole project:

> We are unable to say how far the attempt to teach Geometry and Algebra in Sinhala would be successful. Our opinion is that it is easier to learn the English language, even to some extent, and study these subjects through that medium.[36]

Such a feeling of inferiority could in itself prove to be a stimulus to identity affirmation. For "the intellectuals' feeling of continued dependence on . . . foreign cultures . . . and their awareness of the slow and painful course through which their nation must pass before

36. *Rivikiraṇa*, 25 September 1907, reviewing *Vidyabharanaya*.

its own language becomes adequate to the requirements of modern life cannot avoid touching their sensibilities." And the effort to assuage this hurt takes the form of "constant reaffirmation of their nationalistic attachment."[37] As for the Sinhalese intellectuals of the time, committed as they were to the Ārya-Sinhala identity, the reaffirmation of the nationalistic attachment was coterminous with the strategy adopted in language development. For having decided on "loan translation" and "rendition" (to the exclusion of "loan borrowing,"[38] which would lead to the "admission" of alien European forms), they turned invariably to the highly respected classical resource—the Sanskrit language. This source could, as had been demonstrated, provide enough sustenance in this regard because of its long tradition of literary activity in a wide range of subjects including speculative philosophy. At the same time this recourse to Sanskrit could be justified as a utilization of one's own ancestral resources and as essentially in conformity with the Ārya-Sinhala identity.

The practice of adopting Sanskrit forms in meeting the demands of language modernization,[39] however, was not accomplished without some misgivings. For the arena of this modernization, journalism, happened to be the domain of mass readership. Thus, the *Lak Miṇi Pahana,* commenting on the inaugural number of *Pol Vävili Sañgarāva* (Journal of Coconut Agriculture), suggested that the writers should "use very simple language without ambiguities in meaning" and went on to deplore the fact that "to find out the meaning of *ḍimba pōṣaṇaya* (cross pollination) one has to consult Sanskrit dictionaries."[40]

Such espousals of the cause of "simple language" did not, however, amount to unqualified demands for a highly vernacularized literary idiom. Dharmaratna, the editor of *Lak Miṇi Pahana,* was careful to follow the traditional rules of orthography as well as the norms of classical grammar, although with a partiality in lexicon to forms in common usage. The generality of opinion among the literati appears to have been that "vulgar language should not be propagated in the country by shouting 'simple language! simple language!' "[41]

37. Shils 1972c: 401–2.

38. For these three strategies in language modernization, see Haugen 1950.

39. This continues even today. For a comment, see M. W. S. de Silva 1974:80.

40. *LMP,* 17 August 1889. Incidentally, this word has become a freely used technical term today.

41. *Sinhala Taruṇayā,* reviewing *Rivikiraṇa* in the issue of January 1909.

The Viability of the Great Tradition

Although necessities of wider acceptance would have demanded the vernacularization of the literary medium, revivalist pressures that existed at the time apparently inhibited the adoption of such a policy. Of great significance in this regard was the revival of Oriental learning whereby the language of Sinhala classics became a lively academic concern of the literati. We have seen how traditional scholarly skills came to be mobilized in the new seats of Oriental learning, the *pirivenas,* and the way in which revivalist activists armed with those skills utilized printing, the newly introduced form of text production, to edit and propagate classical texts that were doubly important—for their Buddhist subject matter as well as for their classical language.[42]

As far as their linguistic interests were concerned, the classical text that engaged the literati's attention above all was the grammatical treatise, the *Sidat Sañgarāva.* Thus, during the period from 1850 to 1902 there were eight editions of this text, five of them with lengthy exegesis elucidating the rules of grammar given therein. Indeed, the *Sidat Sañgarāva* was the one classical text that repeatedly received the attention of the most eminent scholars of the day. Batuwantudawe wrote a new exegesis to it, which was published in 1857, and edited and published its old exegis, which dated back to about the thirteenth century in 1877. *Bhikkhu* Hikkaduwe, the founding principal of Vidyōdaya, published his own exegesis to it in 1884, and *bhikkhu* Ratmalane Dharmarama, the second principal of Vidyālankāra, published his exegesis in 1902. In addition to these works there were two editions of the text by James D'Alwis (in 1850 and 1852). The esteem in which this text was held by the literati of the day may be gauged from the following statement of W. F. Gunawardhana, who had received his education in classical Sinhala during the heyday of revivalism:

> For a man to say "when I was having the *Sidat Sañgarāva* expounded to me" was as much honour and pride as saying "when I was reading for my Degree."[43]

Along with the *Sidat Sañgarāva* other Sinhala classics were being edited and printed, enabling scholars to be more readily conversant

42. See the section "The Pirivenas as Centres of Revivalism" in chapter 4.

43. Introduction to *Siddhānta Parīkṣaṇaya* (Colombo 1924), 17, which is one of the most elaborate companions to the *Sidat Sañgarāva.*

with classical language models. As much as being edificatory reading matter, they would have contributed, so far as their language was concerned, to an effective reinforcement of classical language norms.

The search for authenticity in language matters was dramatized at the turn of the century in the "*n,ṇ,l,ḷ* controversy" where the scholars attached to the two prime seats of Oriental learning, Vidyōdaya and Vidyālankāra, confronted each other. The point at issue was orthographical—where to use the letters for retroflex *ṇ* and retroflex *ḷ* as against those for dental *n* and dental *l*. While the Vidyōdaya school tended to look for guidelines in Sanskrit usage, the Vidyālankāra school believed that there was a specifically Sinhala set of rules, which they sought to unearth by careful study of classical Sinhala writings.[44] In addition to this major controversy there were frequent debates between scholars over topics of grammar found in the *Sidat Sañgarāva*. The "*karma vibhkti* controversy" and the "*ukta vastu* controversy" during the late 1880s and the "*aa nä pasa* controversy" during the first decade of the twentieth century were some of them.[45] The most prominent characteristic of these controversies was the citational utilization of material from the classical works to support one's standpoint. Here the community's language and literary heritage was being mined and refined in search of authenticity.

Such authenticating devices for finding, claiming, and utilizing the community's cultural heritage had other behavioral concomitants. In the current context particularly, they took the form of criticizing what were deemed unorthodox usages and deviations from conventional norms. There was indeed enough material in this connection to engage the sustained attention of the traditionalist literati. As we have seen, this was the period in which the impact of Christianity on the Sinhala language was perhaps at its strongest. New textbooks were being prepared and used in the expanding vernacular educational system, and burgeoning journalistic activity had led to deviations from classical literary norms. The latter development was particularly disturbing. Thus, some of the traditionalist writers considered it necessary to codify the "scholarly norms" of literary usage. A pioneer in this regard

44. See *Satya Samuccaya* of 15 April and 15 May 1890. Also see Sannasgala 1961:738; and Pannakitti 1965. *Bhikkhu* Ratmalane Dharmarama, the second principal of Vidyalankara, claimed that he unearthed these rules after intensive research (Pannakitti 1965).

45. See *Satya Samuccaya,* 15 May and 15 June 1889; and *Dinakara Praskasaya,* special supplements of 27 June and 20 July 1891. Also see Pannasekara 1965:386–96; Pannakitti 1965; and K. D. P. Wickramasinghe 1965: chap. 3.

was *Pundit* Thomas Karunaratna, an alumnus of Vidyōdaya.[46] In the journal *Gñānāvabhāṣaya* (August 1881), which he edited, the first number itself carried two articles by him, one on "Correct Orthography" and the other on "Sinhala Verbal Conjugation." A contemporary journalist, welcoming Karunaratna's effort, hoped that by its means would be found "a most honourable way of illuminating the Sinhala language."[47] Similarly, *bhikkhu* Mahāgoda Gnanissara, the second principal of Vidyodaya, was to write on "Proper Usage" (*śiṣṭa vyavahāra*) in language to the journal *Siḷumina* (1908).[48] In this journal, edited by W. F. Gunawardhana, there were regular articles criticizing "wrong" usage and pointing out their "correct" counterparts.[49]

Modernizing the Sinhala language to meet the demands of the wider functions assigned to it involved, along with the structural modifications in language already mentioned, the disruption of the established diglossic pattern and its restructuring on a new basis.

The Prospect of a New "High" Variety

Rather than confine serious scholarly activity to an exclusively classical language form, many journalistic writers, even those with a thorough academic training along traditional lines, ventured to use a colloquialized literary idiom in some of their writings. Prominent among such writings were those produced during the various scholarly controversies in the latter half of the nineteenth and early part of the twentieth century. Thus, to cite a passage from the contribution of a *bhikkhu* participant in the "Kav Miṇi Koňḍola" controversy of 1905–6:

> kav miṇi koňḍolehi "saňgagaṇaṭa-sangaṭa" yayi sampradānadvya yedunā vāgē guttila kavehit "saňga satu-saňgasatu" yayi padadvayak yedī tibunā nam samarasēkera unnähēṭa gajavāsiy. itin dän tamangē pihiṭa pinisa tibunu guttila sākṣyayat samarajīva tumāṭa pakṣa vecca. itin samarasēkera unnähēṭa vūyē mahat värädday.[50]

46. With Weragama he was in the first group of students at Vidyodaya.

47. From a comment in *Satyālankāraya*. Quoted in Pannasekara 1965:359.

48. Vol. 1, no. 1 (July 1908); 25–26.

49. Those by Piyadasa Ramachandra, a schoolteacher, and Sri Vijaya Kaviraja, a journalist, in vol. 1, no. 1 (July 1908); articles by "J. S.," in vol. 1, nos. 8 and 9; another by Ramachandra in vol. 1, no. 9. The *Siḷumina* was praised for these attempts to promote the "correct" language by *Satya Samuccaya* in an editorial of 15 September 1908.

50. The writer is *bhikkhu* Welipatanwila Dipankara (1872–1944), alumnus of Saila-

(If in the same manner as the two Dative forms "saṅgagaṇaṭa-sangaṭa" had occurred in the *Kav Miṇi Koṅḍola,* the two words "saṅga satu-saṅgasatu" had occurred in the poem *Guttilaya,* it would have greatly profited Mr. Samarasekera in his argument. So, now the *Guttila* evidence which he hoped for, has turned out to be supportive of Mr. Samarajiva. Hence, Mr. Samarasekera has fallen into a grave difficulty now.)

Here although the norms of the classical language are strictly adhered to in the use of case suffixes (*koṅḍolehi, kavehi*), some verbal forms (*vūyē*), and in the choice of Sanskrit lexical items (*sākṣyaya, sampradānadvaya*), the writer has opted to employ a considerable number of features from the colloquial idiom: the invariables *vāgē* and *itin;* the verbal form *vecca;* the lexical item *unnähē;* and the idiomatic expression *gajavāsiya,* literally meaning "elephantine profit."

The acceptance of colloquial grammar and lexicon in the practice of literary Sinhala in this manner would have amounted to a recasting of the "High-Low" distinction maintained in the Sinhala diglossia so far. Features of the "low" language had traditionally been admitted only in documents of a personal and informal nature, and only the "high" variety with its strong classical flavor was used in serious writings.[51] But so far such serious writings were confined to religious and quasireligious subject matter. Now when, in the scholarly controversies, new subject matter came to be treated in literary Sinhala, and that too in the platform of mass media, a linguistic compromise was made—between the classical and the colloquial idioms.

The Reaffirmation of the Classical "High" Variety

If the newly emergent intermediate literary variety came to be generally accepted in the treatment of scholarly subject matter, it did not become institutionalized as the high variety in course of time, although there had been some prospect that this would happen. The sociocultural pressures of that revivalist era were to lead to a strong reaffirmation of the classical-based high variety. Thus, by the time the "period of con-

---

bimbārāma Pirivena of Dodanduwa, who later became the principal of Galaturumula Pirivena of Devundara and Gauthama Vidyālaya, Tangalla. The quotation is from *Kav Miṇi Koṅḍola Vadaya,* ed. Palita, 102.

51. For details, see Sugathapala de Silva 1967:11.

troversies" was drawing to a close in the early 1920s, the polemicists appear to have become meticulously careful in retaining the classical flavor in their writings. To cite a contribution to the "*Siddhānta Parīkṣaṇa* controversy" of 1924 as an example:

> sidata vanāhi mīṭa varṣa hasiyayakaṭa pamaṇa pera siyabasä vibat-niraṇaya sañdahā nipadavana laddaki. eheyin ē kālina sarva sid-dhāntayangen samupētayay kiyanu nohäka. kālāntarayaka siṭa atinataṭa ena grantayaka pramādabhramada ätiviya häka.[52]

> (*Sidata* was compiled about six hundred years ago, for the elucidation of nominal cases in our language. Therefore, it cannot be considered as being comprehensive of all the linguistic rules of that time. Also the possibility is there of imperfections arising in a text which has continued in use for a long period through the system of manuscript copying by hand.)

The writer here uses exclusively classical grammar and lexicon. Furthermore, he infuses an "elevated" flavor to his composition by the use of such archaic features as the specifying particle *vanāhi* and the locative case ending *ä* (*siyabasä*) and by employing uncommon lexical items, such as the Elu form *hasiyayakaṭa* and the Sanskrit *samūpēta,* and, in particular, by employing compounds such as the Sinhala *vibat-niraṇaya* and the Sanskrit *pramādabhrama.* This return to classical models may be categorized as another case where a "more L-like variety" was considered as "threatening" the functions of the "H-like variety."[53] Since the "H(igh)" variety was identified with the past glories of the community, such a threat had to be resisted. The threat was perceived in several spheres: in the field of Sinhala journalism, in the Christian Sinhala literature, and, more important, in the Sinhala school textbooks.[54] As regards the last, evidently, in the conception of the literati, the two goals—"the mastery of H by all students" and "good education for all students"—were considered identical. Hence the option for a more "vernacular distant" form as the standard.

52. Acarya Aryasena, "Sinddhanta Pariksana Parisksanaya," *Sri Saddharma Śāstra Latā* 1 (2 August 1924). For *Siddhānta Parīkṣaṇaya,* see n. 43. The *Sidat Sañgarāva* remained a source of perennial research and controversy.

53. For the H(igh) and L(ow) varieties, see Ferguson 1965.

54. These aspects were discussed earlier in the chapter.

The Emergence of a Neoclassical Standard

Although there was a return to the classical models in the manner described above, the vernacularization of the literary medium, which was affected during the early polemical period, was not to disappear without first making a lasting impact on the literary language. The potentialities of the vernacularized literary medium to serve new functions had been effectively displayed. Indeed, the literary language had been rendered "a more plastic instrument" in the treatment of new subject matter.[55] This development was a major factor in the formation of modern Sinhala narrative prose. Its early manifestations were seen in Albert de Silva's *Arābi Nisollāśaya* (1895, a translation of an English version of *Arabian Nights' Entertainments*), which in its "fluent and easy style deserves the place of a classic,"[56] and C. Don Bastian's *De Soysā Caritaya* (1904, the biography of a contemporary business tycoon), "a triumph both of biographical narrative as well as of the art of printing."[57]

Once the novel became a very popular literary genre during the early years of the twentieth century the use of a popular form of literary language received an added and very powerful impetus. Thus, with the writing of A. Simon Silva, Piyadasa Sirisena, and M. C. F. Perera there was a constant attempt to mold a new literary medium that, while it retained basically the classical rules of grammar and orthography, preferred to use the lexicon from common usage.

Modernization of language, however, involves much more—the processes of language development should extend further: "to cover topics and to appear in a range of forms of discourse including nonliterary prose."[58] Indeed, the measure of the highly differentiated functions the language must fulfill in modern society is gauged by "the achievements in the realm of information, not imagination."[59] As indicated above, by the turn of the century, a start had been made in this direction: particularly in the journals whose interests covered modern agriculture, modern education, news and comment on contemporary affairs, and modern science. Those attempts brought to the fore the inevitable tension between the requirements of modernization and those

55. Sarachchandra 1950:68.
56. Sarachchandra 1950:68.
57. Wickramasuriya 1975:119.
58. C. A. Ferguson 1968.
59. Kloss 1967:35.

of authentification. The pull of the past, the straining toward more authentic expressions of the heritage of yesterday and of long ago, seemed more alluring as far as the literati were concerned.

Literature and writing in general, however, were no longer activities confined to elitist circles alone. The written medium was becoming more and more a mass concern with the progress in education and increase in the rate of literacy.[60] Forms of mass media were growing rapidly to meet the rising demand,[61] and the language of written communication perforce had to adjust itself to new circumstances. In this regard it is apparent that there was a lively interaction between the language of journalism and the language of prose narrative mentioned above—particularly because almost all the early Sinhala novelists were leading journalists as well.[62] Hence what might be termed a second compromise came to be made between the classical and the colloquial language forms,[63] whose peculiarities are exemplified in the following excerpt from a periodical published in 1921:

> kolam̆ba nagarayē pamaṇak pravurtipatra tibīmen muḷu raṭaṭa väḍa sidu novē. lakdiva anit nagarayanhi da dhanavat mahatvaru ugat mahatunṭa anubala dī pravurtipatra paṭan ganṭa sitvalaṭa gatahot in mahajanayāṭa ätivana prayōjanaya pramāṇa kaḷa nohäka. esē prayōjana gena denṭat patra katrūvaru usas adahas äti vyakta aya viya yutuy.[64]
>
> (The whole country does not benefit from having newspapers only in the city of Colombo. If the wealthy gentlemen in other towns take it in heart to start newspapers by encouraging educated gentlemen to do so, the benefit to the people at large cannot be

60. The percentage of male literacy rose from 42 percent in 1901 to 56.4 percent in 1921; female literacy from 8.5 percent to 21.2 percent; and the overall literacy from 26.4 percent to 39.9 percent (Panditaratne and Selvanayagam 1973:301).

61. During the period 1908–18 185 new journals appeared and from 1919 to 1924 another 198 began publishing. Although many of them did not last long, their appearance alone indicates a rising demand. (Figures computed from Pannasekera 1968a and b). Also see Rajakaruna 1970 on the novel; L. D. A. Ratnayaka n.d. on drama; and K. D. P. Wickramasinghe 1965 on literature in general.

62. For example, Piyadasa Sirisena, M. C. F. Perera, and W. A. Silva. For details, see Wickramasuriya 1975; and Sarathchandra 1950.

63. See previous discussion of the first compromise.

64. F. D. Vikrama Sri in *Siri Sara Sangara*, 1 April 1921. This journal was edited by W. A. Silva, the most popular Sinhala novelist at the time.

measured. To render such benefits it is also necessary that the newspaper editors be clever persons with elevated thoughts.)

Here the writer is careful to follow assiduously the conventional rules of orthography. Also he maintains the classical flavor in his composition by the utilization of classical sentence-ending devices. In dependent clauses, however, he sometimes ventures to use a colloquial device—for example, the infinitive (in *paṭanganṭa* and *denṭa*)—instead of the conventional dative verbal noun (*paṭan gänīmaṭa* and *dīmaṭa*).

It is evident that this second compromise between the classical literary idiom and the colloquial language is heavily biased toward the former and hence may be termed a "neoclassical" form. As described earlier, this bias was the result of the impact of revivalist activity on the processes of language modernization.

It was this neoclassical form that became established as the standard language of mass media, particularly in the popular newspapers and periodicals. The more erudite sections of the literati preferred, however, to utilize a literary form with a highly classical flavor, especially in dealing with their scholarly concerns, and this invariably contained a heavy load of Sanskrit borrowings.

In the "acceptance" of the neoclassical variety as the commonly usable standard literary language, it is apparent that "quality" in the form of past "authenticity" was generally considered the most important criterion.[65] In the aftermath of a revivalist era, where the masses had been mobilized into an awareness of and responsiveness to the communal cultural heritage, the criterion of acceptance itself seems to have taken a peculiar form—for the preservation of language authenticity as a natural and necessary part of the collective continuity appears to have been of utmost importance. Apparently, this view was shared by the scholarly elite and the masses. There is no record of an attempt to promote a more "L-like" variety. It was by and large another instance where "classicization" had been "misconceived as being synonymous with standardization."[66] Here, however, the masses were ready to follow the lead given by the elite.

Nevertheless, it needs to be pointed out that the result of this

65. For "acceptance" and "quality," see Haugen 1966b; and for "authenticity," see Fishman 1972c:7–10.

66. For the theoretical possibility of such a development, see Ray 1963:125.

policy was not a wholesale classicization of the literary idiom. For as seen in the above excerpt, some flexibility had been allowed for what might be termed "modifications in line with culture change."[67] The limits of this flexibility were a matter of debate over the years.[68] For the time being, however, the prospects for a "counter-elitist" effort with regard to language standardization were so limited as to be considered nonexistent.

The Rise of the Scholarly Establishment

As we have seen, the propagandist efforts of the Christians had inaugurated the processes of language modernization in one way or the other, as, for example, in the introduction of new religious concepts; in the "simplification" of the literary idiom; and in the introduction of colloquial language features into school textbooks. Although the Buddhist literati also saw the necessity for vernacularization, especially the language of mass media, their efforts in this regard were restrained and inhibited, in contrast to the adventurousness of the Christian writers. The Christians were again involved in the crucial step of attempting to discuss modern science in Sinhala—the *Vidyābhraṇaya,* the first journal to do so being edited by two Christian clergymen.[69] No doubt, the fact that the Christians, unlike the tradition-oriented Buddhist literati, had better access to and contact with Western knowledge explains their headway in this regard. The acquiescence of the Buddhist literati, however, was essential for such modernizing steps to achieve wider social acceptance. The *bhikkhus,* who formed a major element of the Sinhala literati, had emerged by the early twentieth century—by processes of dynamic adjustment—as a "strategic elite" in modern Sri Lankan society,[70] and the Buddhists by the turn of the century had outdistanced the Christians in journalism and other mass media activity. Also the Buddhists apparently were most vigorously involved in the associational activities of different *samāgam.*[71]

The mass media, as instruments of social mobilization, and the

67. I borrow this phrase from Garvin (1964:521), who discusses the theoretical possibilities in such situations.

68. Later developments in this regard are dealt with in Dharmadasa 1977.

69. Rev. W. J. Wijesinghe and Rev. Theodore G. Perera. The latter was also the author of *Sinhala Bhāṣāva,* a grammar of Sinhala which became a widely used school textbook.

70. For the concept, see Keller 1963.

71. See chapter 5.

voluntary associations, as avenues thereof, appear, by and large, to have been under the guidance and control of an elitist circle comprised mainly of the leading *bhikkhus* and their close lay associates. The names, for example, of the *bhikkhus* Hikkaduwe Sumangala, Ratmalane Dhammaloka, Ratmalane Dharmarama, Migettuwatte Gunananda, and Dodanduwe Piyaratnana and the laymen Pundit Batuwantudawe, M. Dharmaratna, Anagarika Dharmapala, Piyadasa Sirisena, John de Silva, Walisinha Harischandra, C. Don Bastian, and D. B. Jayatilaka, to mention a few, often appear in connection with many of the social mobilizational activities that occurred during the period from about 1850 to about 1920.[72] Indeed, it was under their leadership that the religiocultural revival took place. And as far as the language component of revivalism was concerned, the concept of Ārya-Sinhala identity and, following upon it, the adoption of classicization as the major strategy in language standardization may be traced to this elitist leadership.

Of great symbolic significance in consolidating the status of this elite was the government's involvement, although on a limited scale, in the promotion of Oriental scholarship. A crucial step in this regard was the formation of the Committee of Oriental Studies in 1902 under the chairmanship of the director of public instruction. The aim of this committee, which consisted of the principals of the leading *pirivenas* and other eminent Oriental scholars, was the coordination and systematization of Oriental studies on the island.[73] This may be considered the crowning point of the government's interest in Oriental scholarship, which began in the 1870s when, accepting a proposal made by James D'Alwis and Muthu Coomaraswamy in the Legislative Council, a grant of six hundred rupees was made to Vidyōdaya.[74] This grant, made first under Governor Sir William Gregory (1872–77), was raised to one thousand rupees under the administration of Sir Arthur Gordon (1883–90). Gregory and Gordon both displayed a keen interest in Buddhism and Oriental studies.[75]

72. For a general discussion of elite formation in British Sri Lanka, see Roberts 1968 and 1974. While following that analysis, I am recognizing a special strand in the elite leadership.

73. For the formation of this committee and its functions, see *The Annual Report of the Director of Public Instruction* 1903; and Ratnasara 1970:210–20.

74. Ratnasara 1970:264.

75. Gregory made a contribution to the repair of the ruined Buddhist shrine Ruwanweli Dagaba at Anuradhapura, donated two lamps to the Temple of the Tooth in Kandy, and established the Colombo Museum. Gordon was instrumental in the granting of the Vesak holiday.

The government finally took the positive step of establishing the Committee of Oriental Studies, under which a system of three examinations came to be instituted, the final being "of a high standard equivalent to a General degree in Oriental languages."[76] Soon the certificate of *Prācīna Pundit* offered at the successful completion of the final examination came to be the highest scholarly aspiration of the Sinhala literati, and the membership of the Committee of Oriental Studies came to be considered the badge of the highest scholarly distinction in Sri Lanka.[77] Apart from the systematization and coordination of *pirivena* education, which the committee was able to accomplish, its very establishment seemed to provide a much wanted imprimatur to the scholarly activities of the Buddhist literati. Thus, in whatever form, the involvement of the government was greatly appreciated and sought after. *Bhikkhu* Ratmalane Dharmarama pointed out that "this was the first time since the days of the ancient Sinhala kings" that such encouragement by the state was taking place.[78] Viewed from the perspective of the community's traditions, this patronage was of the utmost significance. As a further step in this encouragement, the annual grant to Vidyōdaya was doubled in 1917. By this time, as a result of revivalist endeavors as well as a response to governmental recognition, there were sixty-two *pirivenas* of recognized reputation in the island.[79] Also, in 1919 the government provided for a post of inspector of *pirivenas.*[80]

Thus, on the one hand, governmental involvement in activities that were functional ingredients of their status placed the scholarly elite in a more favorable position than before, and, on the other, the institutional basis and the system of examinations paved the way for the crystallization of a definitive concept of Sinhala scholarship. *Pirivena* education, with its Buddhist base and a high degree of partiality to Pali and Sanskrit, had become the means to formally recognized scholarly distinction.

These factors, in sum, led to the formation of what might be termed a scholarly establishment. Buddhist leaders, in particular the *bhikkhus,*

76. *The Annual Report of the Director of Public Instruction,* 1903.

77. See the report on the annual distribution of certificates reported in the *Sandaresa,* 20 October 1905.

78. Speech at the annual distribution of certificates reported in *Sat. Sam.,* 15 June 1908. Ratmalane was the principal of Vidyālankāra.

79. *The Annual Report of the Director of Public Instruction,* 1917:4.

80. *The Annual Report of the Director of Public Instruction,* 1919. The first appointee was Pundit W. A. Samarasekera, an alumnus of Vidyōdaya.

comprised its major segment. With regard to language, their preference was for *Miśra Sinhala* with heavy Sanskrit and Pali borrowings. Furthermore, it came to be universally accepted that, "in order to use Sinhalese correctly, knowledge of Sanskrit and Pali is compulsory." [81]

With regard to the language affairs of the Sinhala community, the emergence of this scholarly establishment was the end result of years of revivalist activity and attempts to affirm the Ārya-Sinhala identity. As a result of authentification endeavors, the classical norms of literary grammar had come to be considered inviolable. At the same time a conviction had taken root that "the Sinhala people whose original motherland is the Āryavarta should in particular learn that cultured (Sanskrit) usage."[82]

Sinhala scholars from early times had considered the study of Pali and Sanskrit to be part of their intellectual training and vocation. But significantly, Sanskrit received a boost in the late nineteenth century due to a European inspiration. Scholars such as Max Müller elevated Sanskrit to a special niche among the classical languages, a move that was eagerly accepted by scholars in India and Sri Lanka. It gave them a respectability that, as subjects of the British empire, they greatly appreciated.[83] The linguistic innovations introduced by agents of modernization, particularly Christians, had little chance of receiving wider acceptance in this new situation. As noted above, the attitude of the British administration toward Buddhism and Oriental learning had begun to change as early as the 1870s. Although this change had come to be firmly established by the first decade of the twentieth century, much was left to be desired as far as Sinhalese-Buddhist aspirations were concerned. With regard to the language component of the communal identity a matter of crucial importance was the fact that the government's policy on mass literacy remained unchanged.[84] In addition to the problems concerning language form, another factor, this time concerning language function, was emerging. It was another result of modernization arising from the introduction and growth of democratic principles to the political institutions of the island and the widening of the elec-

81. Editorial, *S.B.*, 12 May 1906. This view has persisted even in modern seats of learning. Thus, at the University of Peradeniya a paper in Sanskrit was compulsory for aspirants to the Special Arts Degree in Sinhala until 1978.

82. *Bhikkhu* Mahagoda Gnanissara, "Śiṣṭa Vyavahāra," *Siḷumina* 1, no. 1 (July 1908): 25–26.

83. See Poliakov 1974:209–10.

84. See above for details of this policy and its unacceptability to the elite.

torate, culminating with the introduction of universal suffrage in 1931. Following upon it, there was the need to give more functional as well as symbolic space to "the language of the people" as against English, the language of the foreign master. A greater concern about the "national language" arose from among the political leadership in the island, a leadership that was itself the product of the processes of modernization brought about under Western rule.

Chapter 7

Political Developments and the Position of the Vernacular

> The skin is Sinhalese, the name English
> And the food too indeed English
> The country is Sinhalese, the language English
> And the clothing too indeed English
> The father is Sinhalese the mother Dutch
> And thus a thorough mixture of both
> This for certain is one
> Aspiring to the post of the Sinhalese Councillor
> —Verse by Pundit Thomas Karunaratna (circa 1920)

The second and third decades of the twentieth century saw notable changes in the island's political structure. These changes, in the form of liberalization of the political structure, were to have repercussions on the position of the vernacular vis-à-vis English. As a prelude to the examination of these developments, it is useful to understand the position of the two languages at the turn of the century.

A Language-Based Class Stratification

As would be characteristic of a colonial situation, an "out diglossia" came to be institutionalized in Sri Lanka society under British rule.[1] The "higher" functions of social, political, and economic life were conducted in the medium of the English language, while the vernaculars—Sinhala and Tamil—were confined, in terms of the dominant value system, to functions of "lower" significance. These circumstances led to the emergence of a class stratification based on language criteria.

English, as the language of the rulers, was the avenue of upward

1. For the concept, see Kloss 1966.

social mobility. While employment and other socioeconomic opportunities open to those educated in the vernacular were narrowly restricted, English education brought with it access to a range of occupations more lucrative and more prestigious, precisely because the new and high status occupations were all creations of modernization brought about under British rule. With an English education one could aspire to be a clerk in a government department or a large mercantile firm, a surveyor, a lawyer, an advocate, a doctor, or an engineer. The employment opportunities of the vernacular educated were confined to those of schoolteacher, notary, *āyurvedic* physician, and the less-esteemed posts in the public service and in private sector employment.

Apart from its overt value in "social advancement," English was, as typical of a colonial situation with unequal power relations, the "language of power."[2] Thus, while the vernacular was used in domains such as family, friendship, religion, and elementary education and in the lower rungs of administration, English was the language of higher administration and officialdom, higher education, and dominant elite status. Clearly, in the allocation of power English carried much more weight than the vernaculars.[3] Furthermore, from the beginning of British rule in the nineteenth century a scarcity value had come to be attached to English. At the early stages of British administration the benefits of English education came to be largely confined to the higher strata of the native society.[4]

There were those—very few, in fact—who argued that there should be a wider diffusion of the benefits of Western education, but circumstances and policy decisions prevented the adoption of such a program. A lack of resources, human as well as financial, prevented a large-scale spread of English until the mid 1850s. Very soon the influence of a policy decision in favor of vernacular mass education formulated for British India by Wood's dispatch of 1854 came to have its impact on thinking in Sri Lanka as well.[5] Consequently, government schools in Sri Lanka also concentrated on the spread of vernacular literacy, leaving English education largely to private enterprise, which often meant missionary enterprise. The missionaries recognized the value of English in the modernizing society of the day—that "the ener-

2. For this concept, see Mackinon 1977:28–32.

3. Cf. "There is nothing more real than the allocation of power in social relationships. This allocation so frequently follows language lines or invites language demarcations corresponding to it" (Fishman 1976a).

4. See the section "The Position of the Vernacular" in chapter 2.

5. For Wood's dispatch, see Tiffen and Widdowson 1968:7.

getic and aspiring among the people will not be content without a knowledge of English." Hence they were all too aware that "the great desire for English" could be used to entice the children to attend their schools.[6] While the demand was thus rising, however, there arose simultaneously misgivings about the desirability of spreading mass English education. A British inspector of schools found the English schools in the island turning out

> a class of shallow, conceited, half-educated youths, who have learnt nothing but to look back with contempt upon the conditions in which they were born, and from which they conceive that their education has raised them and who desert the ranks of the industrious classes to become idle, discontented hangers-on of the courts and the public offices.[7]

Again British officials of the 1870s often complained that English was leading to village youths abandoning "ancient paddy fields," setting their sights on "some small government post, the demand for which just now is far in excess of the supply."[8] Even some missionaries themselves warned about the "evil of educating individuals above . . . their probable sphere in life."[9] As time passed, perhaps the colonial administration itself was to become wary of the "ideological baggage," subversive of imperial interests, which followed English education. For there was "the potential for agitation inherent in Western types of education on the colonies."[10] Indeed, after the Indian mutiny of 1857 there was discernible a concerted social policy of imperial exclusivism, very much a contrast to the utilitarian doctrines enunciated by policymakers such as Colebrooke a few decades earlier.[11] In such a context language could be utilized as a cogent symbolic barrier, an instrument of social distance.[12]

---

6. *Report of the Wesleyan Methodist Missionary Society for 1867*. Quoted by Wickramaratne 1973:180–81.

7. W. J. Sendall, *Report of the Central School Commission, 1862*. Quoted by R. Pieris 1951–52.

8. Administrative reports for Kegalla and Puttalam districts for 1876 and 1877, respectively. Quoted by Wickramaratne 1973:181.

9. The Rev. S. O. Glenie, archdeacon of Colombo, writing on "Hints towards the Promotion of Education of Ceylon," in *Ceylon Magazine* 2 (1842). Quoted by Ludowyk 1966:127–28.

10. For these observations on colonial education policy, see von der Mehden 1963.

11. For Colebrooke, see discussion in chapter 2. For the change of policy, see Park 1967:19.

12. For such use of language in other colonial territories, see Whiteley 1969:61.

All in all it may be said that choice as well as chance led to the restriction of English education to a select few among the native population. The English schools were confined to the few urban centers, and they levied fees for attendance.[13] These factors, along with the policy of the colonial government of creating a loyalist support base from the higher strata of native society, and possibly its desire to maintain an elitist sanctity for English, all combined to produce the result of restricted English education.[14] Thus, in 1878, after more than fifty years of English education, James D'Alwis remarked that "there is not . . . above 50 Sinhalese men in the whole island who can write to the English newspapers."[15] By 1911 only 1.8 percent of the native population was considered literate in English. In terms of communities it amounted to 4.9 percent of the Tamils, 3.5 percent of the low-country Sinhalese, and 0.7 percent of the Kandyan Sinhalese.[16] It was this small stratum of the native population which had, in relation to its less fortunate compatriots, access to "national elite" status.[17]

As mentioned above, English education, as against education in the vernacular languages, conferred on individuals access to lucrative and "prestigious" occupations. Geared as the economy of the island was to colonial needs, it created inadequate employment opportunities beyond the administrative needs of the infrastructure. Thus, "the chief industry in Ceylon was the Government service,"[18] which under the impact of overall modernization expanded considerably in the nineteenth century. In a society that was undergoing transition from traditional to modern "old status values were transferred from the feudal society to the colonial government,"[19] and, as "government service was valued more than self-employment in private industry," even a clerical job carrying with it the symbols of Westernization—English language and European dress—inevitably conferred on an individual a highly

13. In 1911, while there were over 3,500 vernacular schools, the number of English schools was only 242. Of these only a handful in Colombo, Kandy, Galle, and Jaffna had "collegiate" status. See Wickramaratne 1973; and R. Pieris 1964. For "colleges," see n. 24.

14. For the policy of creating a loyalist enclave, see chapter 2. A policy of restricting the metropolitan language to a select few among the natives was also followed by the Dutch in their eastern colonies. See Stevens 1973.

15. *Memoirs*:103–4. This to some extent could be an exaggeration. See the quote from the same source given at the head of chapter 2.

16. Statistics based on the census figures of 1911 and computed for this purpose by Kearney 1967:70.

17. For a detailed study of elite formation in British Sri Lanka, see Roberts 1974.

18. Jayaweera 1969:89.

19. Ryan 1961:474.

"respectable" status.[20] Then there were the other byways of elite employment produced under the *Pax Brittanica:* the "genteel professions" of law, Western medicine, engineering, English teaching, and the like. These areas of employment, also being dependent upon and symbolic of English education, carried prestige similar to government employment mentioned earlier. In this way a new pattern of hierarchical relations, based on English education, came to be established.

Because of the limiting factors connected with access to English education mentioned above, it was only the already highly placed strata of society which could, by and large, educate its children in English. Since university education was not available in the island until 1921, aspiring families who had the economic wherewithal could send their young to universities in England or India. Elite status was thus self-perpetuating, and what might be termed a local "mandarinate" had come into being by the early decades of the twentieth century.[21] As late as 1946, which was two years before the island achieved political independence, a Select Committee of the State Council found that "it is possible to attain the highest post in the island, amass wealth and wield influence, without learning a word of the national languages."[22]

Incidentally, the supremacy of English had a religious aspect to it. From the early days of English education in the island the missionaries had control of modern as well as English education.[23] Their sway over the field of English education was further strengthened with the decision of the government in the latter half of the nineteenth century to confine its activities to the field of vernacular education, leaving English education to "private," that is, missionary, enterprises. Thus, Buddhist, Hindu, and Islamic youth seeking English education had no choice but to attend a missionary school; hence the majority of students in the missionary schools belonged to these religions. By the turn of the century the prestigious English schools, known as "colleges," almost all belonged to missionary organizations of various denominations: for example, St. Thomas, Wesley, and St. Josephs in Colombo; Trinity in Kandy; Jaffna Central and Jaffna College in Jaffna; and St. Johns in Panadura.[24] Although the Buddhist revivalist movement led to the es-

---

20. R. Pieris 1949:408.

21. For a similar situation in colonial Africa, see van den Berghe 1968.

22. *SP,* XXII 1946:11.

23. The difference between traditional and modern education in the island has been dealt with in chapters 2 and 3.

24. See n. 18 of chapter 2. "Colleges" in Sri Lanka compare with what are called

tablishment of a rival system of schools, the Buddhists had by this time only three schools that could aspire to "collegiate" status: Ananda in Colombo, Dharamaraja in Kandy, and Mahinda in Galle. For a long time to come, however, Christians, especially Protestant missionaries, dominated formal education in the island. When a Ceylon Board of Education was created in 1895 to advise the colonial government on education it was dominated by Christian interests: Thus, for example, even in 1926, of its twenty members fifteen were Christians (including missionaries), and ten were Europeans.[25]

Educational activity per se reflected the role of English as the language of power and prestige. In the school system—whether governmental, missionary, Buddhist, or Hindu—great attention was paid to the maintenance of the special status of the English medium colleges.[26] In the school system as a whole English schools commanded the highest prestige; next came the Anglo-vernacular schools; and vernacular schools were at the bottom of the prestige scale—vernacular education being "regarded as something derogatory and akin to an admission of inferiority."[27] Thus, it may well be said that the relationship between the two languages within the school system symbolized and epitomized power relationships in the society at large.

There was thus little motivation for study in the vernacular medium in the modern schools system, the better students escaping into the Anglo-vernacular schools or English schools, and others often becoming dropouts. In 1922, for example, only 0.6 percent of those who began their education in the vernacular schools remained in the eighth standard, which was the year before they were to take the school-leaving examination.[28]

Related to the counterprestige attached to vernacular education was its poverty of content. Except for a handful among them which provided a two-year "postelementary" course in the Oriental languages, the vernacular schools remained truncated at the elementary

"High Schools" in the United States, except that most Sri Lankan colleges have classes from kindergarten and up.

25. Jayaweera 1973:462.

26. While, for example, the government paid only 36 percent of the bill of other English schools, its grant to Royal College was 56 percent (Jayaweera 1973:467).

27. J. J. R. Bridge, an official sent from England, reporting in 1912. Quoted in Jayasuriya 1976:336.

28. Jayaweera 1973:466.

level.[29] An educator of the time stated that this education was intended to prepare a rural boy for the "humble career which ordinarily lies before him."[30]

As was common in a colonial situation, there emerged a bifurcation of society based upon language criteria: An upper crust of English educated elitism came to be constructed over the Sinhalese society.[31] There was a class cleavage between the two social strata discernible in power and ritual dimensions. Most conspicuously, there was a great cultural divide.

Two Cultures: English Education–Based and Vernacular Education–Based

As we have seen, there was in the principal educational system a high-low status dichotomy based on language: English education was associated with power and prestige; vernacular education, on the other hand, was characterized by their relative absence. Concomitantly, the latter was also characterized by poverty of content—with barely any progress beyond the elementary stage. To be specific, in 1914 the curriculum of vernacular schools comprised the "three R's" (Reading, Writing, and Arithmetic), geography, history, needlework, drawing, drill, and gardening, while to these were added in 1922 hygiene, physiology, linen embroidery, and lace making. The whole content of this education was apparently intended to impart basic instruction for living in a community with very limited horizons.[32] Although no specific policy directives can be quoted in this regard, there is indication that some sections of opinion among the English-educated native elite were aware of this propensity and endorsed it. Thus, for example, J. P. Obeysekere, the Sinhalese representative to the Legislative Council from 1878 to 1881, supported the decision to close down some of the schools, stating that, by limiting their education, village children would be allowed to "follow such vocations as they are fitted by nature."[33]

29. Jayaweera 1973:466.

30. Charles Bruce, the director of Public Instruction in the 1880s. Quoted in Wickramaratne 1973:185.

31. For similar developments in India, see Kohn 1929:172; and in colonial Burma, Malaya, and Indonesia, see P. T. M. Fernando 1973. Alexandre (1972:86) finds the process continuing in postcolonial Africa.

32. Jayaweera 1973:466.

33. Quoted in Wickramaratne 1973:185.

That educational activity expanded nevertheless, and more and more schools came to be opened in the following decades,[34] did not, however, lead to a concomitant mass dissemination of modern knowledge. The curriculum of the vernacular schools, which catered to the larger mass of the school-going population,[35] was extremely limited. Whatever higher education was available in the vernacular lay outside the school system, in the *pirivenas*. Here the curriculum consisted of the study of the classical literatures of Sinhala, Pali, and Sanskrit and was of little use in terms of modern economic and social opportunities.[36] Moreover, the only source from which modern ideas and information on current affairs could be obtained was the periodical literature, which, although it expanded rapidly in the early decades of the century,[37] had a largely literary and tradition-oriented bias. Hence the form of social mobilization they engendered tended to emphasize primordial bonds and sentiments.

Thus, the content of the available education, formal as well as informal, was suggestive of the political culture that could arise within the vernacular-educated populace. Limited as its intellectual horizons were, it could be mobilized in support of traditionalist movements launched by opinion leaders, who were either themselves religious personages or closely associated with the ancestral religion. The Sinhala language in this context may well have had the characteristics of a "restricted code" in relation to English.[38]

Education in the English medium opened the door to a more "elaborate" intellectual world—modern science and technology as well as Western ideologies on social, political, and aesthetic life. All in all, as compared with the English educated, the Sinhala-educated group was less intensively mobilized. For the former had come into more di-

34. For the increase in the number of schools, see n. 13; and for the figures relating to the rise in literacy, see n. 60 of chapter 6.

35. In 1912 among the school-going population, except for 14.3 percent in the English schools; all the others were in the vernacular schools.

36. The only exception was the school established in Colombo to train vernacular teachers, the "Normal School," which functioned from 1870 to 1884. Later a government teachers training college, established in 1903, trained a limited number of vernacular teachers until a Sinhalese teachers training college was established in 1919, enrolling twenty students biannually.

37. See n. 61 of chapter 6.

38. Robinson (1971) suggests this characterization of the vernacular in relation to the metropolitan language (elaborate code) in colonial societies.

rect and intimate contact with the modernity of the West. Their literacy in the metropolitan language, their vigorous participation in the dominant mass media activity with direct contact with what was happening and what was said in Europe, their almost total shift to nonagricultural wage labor occupations, and their urban provenance all pointed to this distinction. Of particular significance for the present discussion are the political orientations and behavior of this group.

The Political Dimensions of the English Education Culture

In assessing the impact of colonial rule on Sinhala society a distinction can be made between "Westernization" and "modernization."[39] Whereas Westernizing influences led to negative reactions in the form of nativistic strivings, the modernizing influences were by and large welcome—the fact that some such modernizing features were adopted in the nativistic resistance to Westernization was proof that such a conceptual distinction between the two was available.[40] This distinction needs to be kept in mind when examining the English education–based culture that came to be superimposed upon the indigenous mass culture. It facilitates an understanding of the political role, on the one hand, and the social role, on the other, of the English-educated elite.

English education, among other things, for a section of the Sinhala community brought about an awareness of the principles underlying the European concept of democracy, such as equality before the law and government by consent. Those who had the opportunity to receive further education in Europe obtained firsthand experience of liberal democracy in action. Thus, for example, James Pieris wrote to his cousin on his arrival in Cambridge in 1878, where he was later to be the president of the student union and was to obtain a first class in the moral science tripos:

> You cannot at all imagine the manner in which the greatest men treat us here. It is so totally different from what we get from Englishmen in Ceylon. Here the greatest man shakes hands with

39. For this distinction, see Ames 1973.
40. See especially the careers of D'Alwis and Migettuwatte described earlier.

you, offers you a seat as high as his own, and talks with you most familiarly, as if you were his friend.[41]

But when he returned to his home country the Western-educated native faced an embittering experience. He was denied the privileges enjoyed by Europeans, despite the years and money spent on a laborious process of imbibing a Western education and life-style. He was discriminated against in appointment to higher government posts and was subjected to many symbolic slights. Indeed, it was the ideological baggage that followed English education which made those who were socialized into the new culture aware of their humiliating situation. And, of course, the immersion experience in England was not necessary to feel and to resist that injustice. This was proved in the career of James D'Alwis. But after a sojourn in "the mother country" with a day-to-day life of being "English in tastes, in opinions, in morals and in intellect,"[42] and, above all, in political behavior, a return to the native land to be confronted with a form of caste exclusion and to be treated as a mere "native" seems to have goaded many a colonial intellectual to fervent nationalistic activity.[43] Indeed, the first expression of "civil politics" among the Sinhalese was spearheaded by such an elitist group. Whereas the traditional elite, led by the *bhikkhus*, invoked primordial sentiments to combat Westernization, the modern elite, who were the English-educated intellectuals, many among them with educational experience in England, utilized political weaponry discovered during their own modernizing experience to agitate in the cause of the liberalization of the colonial administration. In the colonial situation it was only the Westernized group who were linguistically equipped and intellectually competent to conceptualize the ramifications of the new legislative and administrative system, and they naturally assumed the role of political leaders in native society. At this stage they comprised the sole "participants" in the political structure in contradistinction to the larger population, who were predominantly "parochials" and had not even graduated to the stage of being "subjects."[44]

41. Letter dated 11 November 1878. Reproduced in Keeble and Suryasena 1950:7–8.

42. As Macaulay expected: "A class of persons Indian in blood and colour but English in taste, opinions and in morals and in intellect." Quoted in Majumdar et al. 1965:46.

43. Cf. Colonialism "produces the intellectuals and yet, by its very existence, it frustrates them and hence arouses their opposition" (Kautsky 1962:49).

44. For this tripartite distinction, see Scott 1965.

The Constitutionalist Aspirations of the English-Educated Elite

The English-educated elite, who had received the "demonstration effects" of democratic and liberalist ideologies,[45] were not slow to understand the contradictions between those ideologies and the actual Western-created institutions under which they lived.[46] With the growth of a sizable group of these intellectuals various forms of political agitation were to emerge.

In the first instance a few expatriate Europeans had given the lead in liberalist agitational activity. The *Colombo Observer,* edited by Christopher Elliot, campaigned in the 1840s for reform in the Legislative Council to make it representative "of the people at large." Writing an editorial on 3 July 1848, Elliot declared that

> the Sinhalese people, as British subjects, ought generally to be remained of the important principle that all who pay taxes have an inherent right to a voice in the disposal of these taxes. . . . Millions in Europe have lately acquired these rights, and, enlightened Ceylonese, who have heard of the onward movement, were in hopes of sharing in the boon.[47]

Elliot's anticipations came too early, however, as an "enlightened Ceylonese" stratum with enough ideological commitment and self-confidence to make such demands was still in its embryonic stage. The first constitutional challenge to imperial administration in the island was led in 1864 by another European, George Wall, in the Legislative Council, and in it were associated the Sinhala representative James D'Alwis and the other Ceylonese, C. A. Lorenz, the Burgher representative. Subsequently, in 1864 an organization called the Ceylon League was formed to agitate for "reform." The league was dominated, however, by European planters and merchants. And an acting governor pointed out in his reply to the league's demands:

> Until the large majority of the people can be enabled by education to understand their true and proper spirit . . . and until they can

45. I have borrowed the concept from Deutsch 1975.
46. For this phenomenon in colonial societies, see Worseley 1972:57.
47. Reproduced in K. M. de Silva 1973e:237.

> appreciate and be made equal to the benefits of representative institutions, the power and responsibility of ruling the country must be entrusted to the government.[48]

It was the classic response of the colonial administration to the early demands for the liberalization of the political structure. Evidently, it was justifiable in the light of the possibility of foreign (European) entrepreneurial interests forming an oligarchy over the mass of the native population if the former were granted the power to make policy decisions. The same principle was applicable, however, even when, over fifty years later, a demand for elected representation came from English-educated natives who pointed out that there was an electorate,

> a highly intelligent one, composed of members of the Government service, professional men, graduates, landed proprietors and merchants of all races who . . . could be safely entrusted with the task of electing their representatives in Council.[49]

No doubt, there was a social and cultural gulf that divided the English-educated elite from the popular masses whom it wished to represent. But there were also many personal and social ties, notably family and caste, which enabled the two strata to have identities of interests, and, all in all, the English-educated elite was more qualified to be the "platonic guardians" of the country's masses than the imperial administrators and their protégés appointed to the Legislative Council.

The political demands of the English-educated elite were exceptionally moderate and based on the principles they had imbibed from the British political culture. They asked for the utilization of the elective principle in making appointments to the Legislative Council, the abolition of communal representation in it, the shifting of representation therein from the Europeans to the natives, and the inclusion of two "unofficials" in the Executive Council. While making these demands, their loyalty to the British empire was emphatically affirmed. They were always anxious to call themselves "an eminently loyal people

48. *Addresses Delivered in the Legislative Council of Ceylon by Governors of the Colony, 1860–77* (Colombo: Government Press, 1877), 2:166–67.

49. Memorandum to the Colonial Office in 1908 from James Pieris. Reproduced in the *Handbook of the Ceylon National Congress* (*HCNC*):6–16.

deeply sensible of the benefits of British rule." And the demand for elected representation was posed as an aspiration, "to win the full measure of British citizenship."[50]

It needs to be noted that these demands were aimed at the rights of representation for the English-educated elite as an element that could be safely entrusted with political responsibilities and not the rights of the masses at large. For even as late as 1928, when the Donoughmore Commission was ready to grant universal adult suffrage, some English-educated politicians such as James Pieris and E. W. Perera, who incidentally were at the forefront of the agitation for "reform," argued against the enfranchisement of the masses.

The tepidity of the political demands of the English-educated elite was understandable. First, it had a strong interest in maintaining the economic, and possibly the social, status quo—because of its professional and property interests.[51] Second, its political aims and ideas, having been drawn from the models of "Anglo-Saxon liberalism," could not extend any further than the concepts enshrined therein.[52]

The Need to Affirm the National Identity of the English-Educated Elite

At the dawn of the twentieth century the English-educated elite in Sri Lankan society was a stratum seeking access to decision-making areas in the political structure. While making this demand on behalf of the "people of Ceylon," this elite was laying great emphasis upon the "liberal capacity" of its exclusive circle. Thus, when demands for constitutional reform were being addressed to Whitehall, a prominent figure among the elite affirmed:

> We are not all *goiyas* (farmers) and villagers. It is not only the *goiya* who requires to be represented. It is time that the educated members of the population should have their opinions represented to the government. Sober and responsible people should guide their less educated fellows. . . . Who is there who dare say that the

50. E. W. Perera 1907:60.

51. Jayawardene 1972:137.

52. As Roberts (1977:XCVI) puts it, they were "thoroughly brainwashed in a milieu infused with the incense of British liberalism."

> people of Ceylon are not loyal and peaceful? . . . We are not inclined to sedition. . . . But we want our rights.[53]

Here the demand is based squarely on the "rights" of a group with "the liberal capacity." Indeed, the tone of the affirmation suggests a strong conviction of that capacity—and that conviction would have arisen from the self-confidence gained in the successful socialization into metropolitan culture. By this categoric distancing of itself from "the *goiyas* and villagers," it was apparently hoped that the group's equality in this respect with the "white sahib" would be emphasized.[54]

The English-educated elite was thus appealing to its rulers in the premise of an ideal that the latter had long decided to forgo and forget.[55] "The ward had come of age," however, although "the guardian" was reluctant to accept that fact.[56] The ward was using the same metaphors as was the guardian: He was not using "the Asian language of *sirita* (custom)" but the Western language of "rights."[57]

Thus, unlike the amorphous and narcissistic religiocultural revival,[58] the demand for constitutional reform posed an immediate problem and a direct challenge that had to be dealt with by the colonial administration. Justification to encapsulate the attitude of "fervid hostility" of the colonial officials to such liberalist aspirations were, however, not hard to come by.[59] Governor Sir Henry McCallum (1907–1913), in a dispatch on the subject stated:

> All these memorials emanate, not from "the people of Ceylon" as is claimed by the memorialists, but from certain well-defined classes of the native population . . . which represent a small minority of the whole . . . who have assimilated an education of a purely Western, as opposed to Oriental type. . . . Hardly any of them, to the best of my information, have any wide or intimate experience of the Colony as a whole, any close and authoritative

53. E. W. Jayawardene, a leading lawyer in Colombo and scion of a *mudaliyar* family. Quoted in Martinus 1941:34.

54. As Ludowyk (1966:136) puts it, "These gentlemen politicians were as patronizing to the poor as officialdom was to them."

55. That is, the ideal enunciated by Macaulay, Colebrooke, and others in the nineteenth century. See n. 42.

56. K. M. de Silva 1973g:386.

57. Roberts 1977:69.

58. See chap. 4.

59. K. M. de Silva 1973g:386.

> knowledge of the rural population which form the bulk of the native inhabitants.[60]

In the eyes of the colonial administration, then, that which was conceived as an asset by the elite turned out to be a liability. A tone of cynicism was not lacking in the governor's remark that

> this demand . . . is a natural result of . . . the exotic training and education to which this class of native community has been subjected.[61]

And it was his belief that

> the Oriental who has studiously forced himself during the most malleable years of his life to discard the native tradition in favour of that of the European, who has consciously taught himself to think as Europeans think, to adopt theories of life and government which are the exclusive product of the European intellect, character and civilization has . . . ceased to be in any sense a typical Oriental, and thereby has forfeited the right to speak with authority on behalf of the Orientals who form the immense bulk of his countrymen.[62]

While the internalization of European culture had made these natives aware of and qualified for the liberal experience, the same factor had also made them "marginally ethnic in their personal lives" and hence deprived them of the right to represent their nation.[63] As they were destined to remain "provincial,"[64] the only alternative open to the English-educated natives was first to go through the "agonizing process of re-making themselves," if they hoped to embark on projects of "re-making their peoples."[65] Indeed, the more perceptive among them had come to this realization much earlier—as the career of James D'Alwis demonstrated. But at that stage his was an exceptional case.

60. Reproduced in *HCNC*:46–59.

61. Reproduced in *HCNC*:53.

62. Reproduced in *HCNC*:59. This was a typical response. Before him in India Governor General Duffrin had characterized the agitating educated stratum as "a microscopic minority" (Ghose 1975:13).

63. For this predicament of the elite in modernizing societies, see Fishman 1972c:17.

64. For this characterization of the Asian intellectuals, see Shils 1972b:367.

65. Fishman 1972c:17.

A few years before the shock of McCallum's arrogance, a small group of English-educated native intellectuals had launched a "Self-Respect" movement in the form of the Ceylon Social Reform Society (1905) and the Ceylon University Association (1905). The leading figure in the former was Ananda Coomaraswamy (1877–1947), the son of a prominent Tamil lawyer, Sir Muthu Coomaraswamy, and his English wife.[66] Thus, born with a crisis of identity as it were, Ananda received his education in England, where he came under the influence of Fabian socialism, English liberalism, and the Utopianism of William Morris and John Ruskin. He returned to the island to embark on a short but dynamic career of attempting to "inculcate national sentiment by historical method."[67] Through public speeches, articles to periodicals, and participation in the Social Reform Society he made an eloquent appeal for the preservation of the country's indigenous arts, crafts, and social traditions, including language. It was his conviction that

> in exchange for this world of beauty that was our birth-right the nineteenth century has made our country a "dumping ground" for all vulgar superfluities of European over-production.[68]

Coomaraswamy was a typical representative of the Asian intellectuals, "alienated from the indigenous authorities of their own traditional society . . . and from the rulers of their modern society—the foreign rulers and the 'Westernized' constitutional politicians," and thus found "only the 'people' . . . as support in their search for salvation" of their own souls and their own society.[69] Coomaraswamy's fervent concern was for what was authentically national, and he found it in the past before foreign conquest, traces of which were also discovered in the present in remote villages, uncontaminated by foreign culture. His monumental *Medieval Sinhalese Art* (1908) was a typical example of this approach. To inspire him, and to supplement his

66. The mother Elizabeth Clay Beeby (1851–1939). Sir Muthu was himself educated in England and was the first South Asian to be called to the bar in England. Apparently, the marriage was not favorably viewed by the British expatriates in the island.

67. See Crouch 1973; and Lipsey 1974. His interest in the field of culture drew him away from his original training as a geologist and made him an aesthete, art historian, and metaphysician. When he died in 1947 he was the Fellow for Research in Indian, Persian, and Muslim Art at the Museum of Fine Arts, Boston.

68. Quoted in Sen 1952:255.

69. Shils 1972c:405.

efforts, the religiocultural revival in Sri Lanka at the time was in full swing. The inspiration was indeed reciprocal. Several English-educated Buddhists who were actively engaged in the revival, such as D. B. Jayatilaka, W. A. de Silva, and F. R. Senanayaka, joined Coomaraswamy in the Ceylon Social Reform Society.[70]

The same personalities were involved in the Ceylon University Association. Its leadership devolved upon Ponnambalam Arunachalam (1853–1924), a cousin of Coomaraswamy, who, having studied at Christ College, Cambridge, became the first Sri Lankan to be admitted to the elite Ceylon Civil Service. Denied any of the highest administrative posts because of his ethnicity, he retired from government service to become in time a leading figure in the agitation for constitutional reform.[71]

Those who were involved in the Social Reform Society and the Ceylon University Association were aware of the "imposing array of discontinuities between the masses and those normally expected (and expecting) to be their leaders."[72] Arunachalam declared:

> It will the chief aim of the Ceylon University which while making efficient provision for the study of English and the assimilation of Western culture, to take care that our youth do not grow up *strangers to their mother tongue and their past history and traditions.*[73]

Coomaraswamy was more forceful in his condemnation of colonial educational policy. Characterizing it as being "motivated by an *intention* to destroy existing cultures," he found it "sapping the very foundation of these peoples' individuality." He called the products of this education a group of "intellectual parasites" who had become "strangers in their own land."[74] Here one notes a recurrence of the theme outlined by D'Alwis. As with D'Alwis fifty years earlier, it was the em-

70. For further details of this society, see Roberts 1977:XC–*XCI.*

71. He would have acted as colonial secretary had he been European, and Sir Alexander Ashmore, the colonial secretary from 1903 to 1907, is reported to have told him so directly. Arunachalam left government service and in 1917 became the first president of the Ceylon National Congress, the major forum of elite politicians during the early twentieth century.

72. This feature of the native elite in colonial societies has been pointed out by Fishman (1972c:41).

73. Arunachalam 1906:126; emphasis added.

74. For details, see Wickramasuriya 1976.

phasis on "authenticity" which lay behind the concern of these elite activists at the turn of the century.[75] Coomaraswamy sought to demonstrate "what difficulties are surmounted in Ireland, Wales, Poland and Finland" in the cause of indigenous language and culture.[76] "Every separate race," he declared, "has its own special character and virtue, a something which . . . it alone can contribute to the glory and greatness of the world."[77]

It was again the defensive reaction of those of the intelligentsia who were shocked into the realization of their mistake at having "cut themselves adrift from their past and become hangers-on of a ruling race that in the main despises them or at best misunderstands them."[78] Coomaraswamy's reaction can be categorized as an attitudinal glorification of the indigenous tradition. Just as D'Alwis glorified Sinhala language and literature through works such as the *Sidat Sañgarāva* translation and the *Catalogue of Sanskrit, Pali and Sinhalese Literary Works of Ceylon,* Coomaraswamy produced the monumental *Medieval Sinhalese Art* and a large number of articles on the arts and crafts of traditional Sri Lanka.[79]

In this search for national honor and self-respect the indigenes were supported by a handful of Europeans who, like Olcott earlier, had chosen to cast their lot with the native people, such as Ethel Coomaraswamy, the wife of Ananda, Museaeus Higgins, and F. L. Woodward, who were all active in the Social Reform Society. Woodward, who was the principal of Mahinda College of Galle, a Buddhist Theosophical Society school (during the period 1903–19), wrote:

> Empires have flourished and passed away with languages and civilizations but the East has still the password to the common treasures of all, enshrined in a great literature of science and metaphysics written in Pali and Sanskrit, Tamil and Sinhalese.[80]

---

75. See chapter 3. Incidentally, similar ideas were expressed in India after D'Alwis and before Coomaraswamy. See McCully 1940:242–43.

76. Letter to the editor, *Sandaresa,* 20 October 1905.

77. "Swadeshism in Ireland," in *Sandaresa,* 8 December 1905.

78. Coomaraswamy, "Anglicization of the East," *Ceylon National Review,* 2 July 1906, 181–95.

79. For details, see Crouch 1973; and Lipsey 1974.

80. "The Advantages of a Knowledge in the Mother Tongue," *Sandaresa,* 23 March 1906.

Thus, the return to one's own cultural roots could be viewed as a sacred mission—a falling back on one's own spiritual heritage. Perhaps such a conceptual formulation was urgently needed in the context of the counterprestige attached to the vernacular culture. In the same way as English education led to the "estrangement" of people "from their traditional inheritance,"[81] it was believed that by means of a "national education" the indigenes could

> take up [again] the threads of [their] ancient civilization and thus give the soul of [their] people the momentum to start on its pilgrimage.[82]

A deputation from the Social Reform Society met Governor Sir Henry Blake in Colombo on 2 July 1906 and made representations for the inclusion of the "mother tongue" and the "history of the motherland" as compulsory subjects in all schools.[83] Although it took some time for such attempts to bear fruit, pressure was building up in elitist circles for the "indigenization" of the content of education. As found in many nationalist movements, it was "a characteristic nationalist assertiveness . . . tinged with a heavy dose of romanticism."[84]

Decidedly, the English-educated class was in dire need for internally generated coherence and identity. Theirs was a desperate search for remedies to the "terrible soul sickness"[85] with which they had become afflicted by undergoing a process of subtractive bilingualism.[86] More significant, at the same time they were formulating preventive prescriptions for the benefit of their compatriots, the "illiterate" many, who were "better off than we, for they have only to learn. . . . We have a great deal to unlearn."[87] This paternalistic concern about the masses appeared to loom large in the formulation of the first major political decision with regard to the role of the vernacular in national life.

81. Coomaraswamy, "Kandyan Art: What It Meant and How It Ended," *Ceylon National Review* 1, no. 1 (January 1906): 1–12.

82. Peter de Abrew, *Eastern Learning* (Colombo, 1919). Quoted in Roberts 1977:92.

83. Report in *Sandaresa*, 6 July 1906.

84. For this general observation, see Coleman 1965:45.

85. Coomaraswamy 1946:32.

86. For "subtractive" and "additive" bilingualism, see Lambert 1967.

87. Coomaraswamy n.d.:174.

A Structural Change in Education: From English to the Vernacular

The English-educated elite, the upper crust of the intelligentsia in Sri Lankan society, was thus a group that had recognized its own alienation from the mainstream of national tradition. The cause was seen in the education its members had received, and the blame was placed at the door of the colonial master: "The export of your 'education' is even more nefarious than your traffic in arms."[88]

It was in the logic of this stance that, when the native intelligentsia, as the political leadership of the community, obtained a measure of control over legislative functions, it would attempt to arrest the continuance of that educational policy. Such a step was taken in 1926. As this occurred under circumstances where the indigenous political leadership had acquired substantial control of legislative activity, it is necessary at this juncture to trace briefly how this development came about.

The English Educated Elite Gain Access to Legislative Power

The demand for constitutional reform could not be ignored for long; a change in the constitutional structure was long overdue. Since 1833, when the Legislative and Executive Councils were set up, making Sri Lanka the most constitutionally advanced colony in the British empire, no structural change had been introduced, and in the meantime other colonies had left the island far behind the constitutional development.[89] The rapid expansion of the governmental system during the nineteenth century was felt by the early years of the twentieth century to be causing severe strain on the existing constitution.[90] Furthermore, the strategy of the English-educated intelligentsia in making direct appeals to Whitehall was proving to have some effect.[91]

Thus, in 1912 a minor but notable change was made in the constitution. For the first time the elective principle, although on a very restricted basis, was introduced in the appointment of unofficial members

88. Coomaraswamy 1947:9.

89. See K. M. de Silva 1973e:240.

90. Wilson 1973:360.

91. The Secretary of State for the Colonies and his Parliamentary Undersecretary were both agreeable to the granting of concessions to the "educated Ceylonese," in spite of opposition from the authorities in the island. See K. M. de Silva 1973g:387.

to the Legislative Council. In this body, consisting of eleven officials and ten unofficials, four of the latter were to be elected: two Europeans, one Burgher, and one "educated Ceylonese."

Among the native population the Burghers were considered a special element, closer to the ruling race and given a separate electoral seat.[92] The educated Ceylonese seat, on the other hand, was meant for the others – Sinhalese, Tamils, and Muslims – and, among them, the English educated. The requisites were a pass in Senior Cambridge or its equivalent and an income of Rs 1,500 per annum. This electorate comprised only about 1.8 percent of the total population.[93]

The concessions thus grudgingly granted fell far short of the expectations of the native political leadership. They had been given only one seat in a Legislative Council of twenty-one. In it the officials were in the majority, and among the unofficials six were nominated by the governor compared to the four who were elected. Furthermore, these six were nominated on a "communal" basis – two low-country Sinhalese, two Tamils, one Kandyan Sinhalese, and one Muslim. Thus, the principle of "communal" representation, which the native political leaders wanted removed, had been retained – in the elected seats as well as in the nominated seats. Moreover, no unofficials were included in the Executive Council.

Two opportunities arose during subsequent years for the political leadership to give vent to their dissatisfaction with the status quo. One was the agitation against the Excise Ordinance of 1912, leading to a large-scale temperance movement with ideological and behavioral links with the religiocultural revival; the other was the agitation against the excessive measures taken by the government in subduing the 1915 communal clashes between the Sinhalese and the Muslims.[94]

In the former, the English-educated elite, Christian as well as Buddhist, skillfully utilized the potential of an issue that could generate mass enthusiasm and thus prove to the authorities that its members were the legitimate leaders of their people. In the latter the government had overreacted to a clash between two communal groups, interpreting it as a mutiny against British rule, and the excesses committed by some European volunteers who believed themselves to be

92. Not only by being Christian but also by having European connections because of their Portuguese and Dutch ancestry. See P. T. M. Fernando 1972.

93. Jayawardene 1972:71.

94. For details, see P. T. M. Fernando 1970b.

> leaders of posses of vigilantes sent out to deal with desperadoes in the manner depicted in the cinema shows and dime novels of the wild west . . . [95] [had created a] feeling of horror throughout the country.[96]

The English-educated elite rose to the occasion and mounted a campaign demanding an official inquiry into these incidents. Prominent in this group were the lawyers, who collected evidence and carried on a persistent agitation for about two years by public meeting and newspaper in the island and by enlisting support in England—of personalities such as Lawrence Ginnel, Colonel Josiah Wedgwood, F. Booth Tucker, Leonard Woolf, and T. W. Rhys Davids; of journals such as the *New Statesman* and the *Review of Reviews;* and of organizations such as the Anti-Slavery and Aborigines Protection Society and the Native Races and Liquor Traffic Committee.[97] If this campaign was not very effective in influencing opinion among the authorities of the Colonial Office in London, it nevertheless provided the English-educated elite with an opportunity for leadership on an issue over which popular feeling had been aroused. With the temperance movement a good many of the elite had established an unprecedented rapport with the "mobilized" sections of the peasantry. And in the postriots campaign for justice, where several among the English-educated elite were imprisoned, they appeared to be martyrs of a national cause that they alone could conceptualize elaborately and advocate effectively.

The political agitation of the English-educated elite subsequently assumed a more determined form. This was partly the result of confidence gained in the two previous campaigns and partly the arousal of fresh hopes and aspirations following the statement made by the secretary of state for India in 1917 that the British government hoped for "the increasing association of Indians in every branch of administration."[98]

It was realized that a political organization with nationwide appeal and support, similar to the Indian National Congress, was a prerequisite for obtaining any substantial measure of political responsibility. At first there was some hesitation, as the streak of conservatism arising

95. From a dispatch of the governor of the succeeding period to the authorities at the Colonial Office. Quoted in Hulugalle 1963:164.

96. From the diary of a Christian priest. Quoted in Jayawardene 1972:167.

97. See Jayawardene 1972:182.

98. For details, see Roberts 1977:XCVII.

from self-interest was quite strong, but eventually the Ceylon National Congress (CNC) was formed in 1919. The CNC, however, lacked the crucial feature of mass participation, which was often displayed by its Indian counterpart, and remained, in spite of the attempt of a handful of enthusiasts to infuse it with such a quality, "an elitist organization dominated by conservatives."[99]

In the following years there ensued a tug-of-war between the political leadership, which demanded "vigorous development of self-governing institutions," and the governor, who claimed that such a demand was "extravagant."[100] Eventually, the agitation reached such a high pitch, "since the infection of political reform had reached Ceylon from India," that the governor had to concede that some reform was necessary.[101] Hence in 1921 a new constitution was granted. It had a Legislative Council with an unofficial majority (fourteen officials as against twenty-three unofficials), most of whom were elected: three communal (two Europeans and one Burgher), two from special electorates (from mercantile and plantation interests), and eleven from territorial electorates (nine from Sinhala-speaking areas and two from Tamil-speaking areas). The Executive Council was to include three unofficials nominated by the governor.

Yet this constitution too fell far short of the expectations of the native political leadership. The government still seemed to command the majority in the legislature, for the seven members who were nominated by the governor could be expected to vote with the fourteen officials, as against the elected sixteen. Also the unofficials in the Executive Council were "Governor's men," and not elected representatives of the people. The congress rejected the new constitution on the grounds that it did not signify even the beginnings of self-government.

As a result of further agitation, the constitution was amended again in 1924. Now the Legislative Council had twelve officials and thirty-seven unofficial members. Of the latter twenty-three were elected territorially, eleven communally, while three were nominated by the governor. Thus, for the first time the elected membership was in an overall majority in the legislature. As another concession to liberalist demands, provision was made for the post of an elected vice presi-

99. K. M. de Silva 1977:77.

100. See Jayawardene 1972:195–96.

101. The confidential dispatch of the governor dated 7 February 1919. Quoted in Jayawardene 1972:196. The Indian connections of the nationalist movement of Ceylon were more prominent from about 1919 onward. See Roberts 1977:LXXVI–LXXVII.

dent who would chair the ordinary meetings of the council in place of the governor, who had so far been its ex-officio chairman. Yet the membership in the Executive Council was not substantially altered—with that existing under the former constitution now carried over to the latter.

The constitution of 1924 thus created a situation of "power without responsibility." In the legislature the elected representatives were in a clear majority; the executive was in "a definitive minority while it continued to remain responsible for the good government of the country."[102] That this situation did not lead to a series of constitutional deadlocks, falling into the more common colonial pattern of "oppositional and agitational, and often merely obstructive" politics,[103] may be attributed to the restrained and cautious outlook of the bulk of the native elite deeply steeped in British liberalism.

The Espousal of the Vernacular by the English-Educated Elite

As outlined above, by the 1920s the British colonial authorities—at Whitehall as well as in the island—had accepted the need for sharing power on a formal basis with the elected representatives of the native population. The Legislative Council of the colony, the majority of whose membership comprised councillors elected on a restricted franchise, could now initiate legislation on a wide range of topics.[104] Since the representatives of the people so elected belonged to the English-educated stratum,[105] it was in the order of things that they would initiate legislation that would prove their identity of interests with the masses. One such concern, engaging their attention for some time, had been the position of the vernaculars vis-à-vis English in the educational system.

On 25 February 1926 A. Canagaratnam, the elected member for Northern Province, Southern Division, moved a motion in the Legislative Council that,

102. Wilson 1973:365.

103. For this general observation, see Shils 1972d.

104. See Weerawardana 1951:6–9.

105. In the 1920 constitution those literate in the vernacular were also enfranchised if they had certain property qualifications as well. But only those who could speak, read, and write in English and who had a higher property qualification could be members of the Legislative Council. See Jennings and Tambiah 1952:24–25.

> as the educational policy of *maintaining two sets of schools for the people of the island, English and vernacular,* has resulted in . . . the vernacular languages being reduced to the level of teaching pupils just to read and write and not proceeding much further; [and therefore] the vernaculars having no chances of development as vehicles of modern thought . . . [and] the training given in English schools [was] alienating the pupils from traditions . . . [etc.,] this Council recommends that the policy adopted in most civilized countries of having only one set of public schools graded according to the standard of instruction imparted in them, be adopted in Ceylon too; and that *English, Sinhalese and Tamil be made language subjects in all schools, the mother tongue of the students being gradually adopted as the medium of instruction* in schools of all grades. (*Debates, LC* 1926: 317; emphasis added)

The adoption of the mother tongue of the student as the medium of educational instruction was thus Canagaratnam's motion's intent. It was axiomatically believed that education through the medium in a foreign language alienated the children so taught from their own cultural traditions. It was hoped that educating them in the mother tongue would, in Canagaratnam's words, enable them "to utilize their own ancestral culture and [its] advancement[s] as foundations upon which to build further intellectual progress." Indeed, the text of the motion contained in sum the full range of anomalies that, it was believed, had resulted from confining higher education to the English medium and in having the socioeconomic system structured in such a manner that education in English conferred a higher status than that in the vernacular.

Canagaratnam's motion deplored the plight of the vernaculars, Sinhala and Tamil, which "in spite of their being cultured languages," were "having no chance of development as vehicles of modern thought" because their utilization as media of education was confined to primary stages. The obvious result of this limited role assigned to the vernaculars was the bleak prospect of "modern knowledge" becoming "the common property of the Ceylonese people just as it is the common property of all other civilized nations." In this regard it could be said that the educational system prevented the vernaculars from growing into vehicles of modern knowledge: "their literatures . . . had come to a dead stop" (Canagaratnam's motion).

The fact that the vernaculars were not provided with the necessary preconditions for modernization and functional expansion was seen as being very prejudicial to native interests: "the people were being deprived of originality of thought and of culture in their own language." Furthermore, educating the native children in the medium of a foreign language was seen as bringing in its wake a train of undesirable results. Thus, Canagaratnam's motion complained that

> the environment in the English schools encouraged the indiscriminate adoption of Ceylonese youths of European modes of living which are unsuited to their own traditions and the conditions of the (country's) climate.

Connected to this was the fact that English education was "causing social irregularities and increased cost of living." Elucidating the above, it was pointed out that those who gained the benefits of an English education tended to consider themselves "a superior class," and the concomitant "false sense of dignity" resulted in a "distaste of manual labour."[106]

Apart from such wide socioeconomic implications, it was believed that education in an alien language was dysfunctional from a pedagogical point of view. "The necessity under which . . . the children are placed to acquire knowledge of a new language in their infancy," said the motion "is creating an undesirable mental strain on them and leading to considerable waste of time and energy." Also the language discontiguity between home and school was considered a serious deterrent to intellectual development. Canagaratnam claimed that

> children whose mother-tongue is Sinhalese or Tamil . . . are unable, when sent to English schools where alone some substantial knowledge is imparted, connect ideas imparted to them at school . . . and therefore the natural and progressive growth of their intellect is checked.

We have seen how from the early years of the twentieth century a vociferous section of the English-educated elite was critical of educating the country's young through the medium of the English language. The ideological commitment for attempting a change in the educational

106. For such alienating effects of colonial education, see Le Page 1964:24.

system was thus already present. Also a similar issue was being raised in other colonies at this time. In India, for example, a Calcutta University commission report of 1919 had declared:

> All people have an inherent right to their own language. It is the means of expression to their own personalities . . . and no greater injustice can be committed against a people than to deprive them of their own language.

The conclusion arrived at in the report was that the "forcing" of its own language by a "controlling" nation on a "native" people, "whatever the motives" be, was "unwise and unjust." Indeed, the motion presented to the Sri Lankan Legislative Council seems to have been grounded on a wish similar to that of contemporary Indian nationalists, who sought "to make education 'national' by using it to create a love for the mother country rather than loyalty to the British Raj."[107]

Supporting the motion, D. B. Jayatilaka, one of the few individuals who were involved in both the Buddhist revival and the constitutional agitation of the elite, declared:

> It is impossible for a people to grow to their full manhood, to their fullest stature, unless the individuals that compose that people have a language of their own, in which they give expression to their highest and best thoughts. (*Debates, LC* 1928:367)

Jayatilaka, with his background of cultural nationalism, with its strong emphasis on authenticity, was apparently advocating the move as a step in forging national self-respect. He too was convinced that originality of thought was inextricably bound with "one's own mother tongue." Thus, he asked:

> We have had English education in this country over a century . . . but has any one left a single book in English verse or prose which will survive a generation? (*Debates, LC* 1928:368)

Sometime back Ananda Coomaraswamy too had expressed a similar sentiment: "I believe no Indian ever has produced, or ever will pro-

107. Myrdal 1968:1655.

duce, immortal literature in English."[108] If we are to compare the stance taken by the English-educated elite in the early twentieth century with that of their predecessor James D'Alwis about half a century before, we may note that their ideas were based substantially on the same premise. D'Alwis was single-handedly engaged in a struggle in the cause of the vernacular, on the grounds of its antiquity and the cultural load that accompanied it. Also the vernacular, in his view, embodied the essence of the indigenous ethos—hence his prescription to the colonial administrator to study it.[109] In D'Alwis's time there was, moreover, a genuine fear of a language shift, and he was perturbed by the "degeneration" that had set in the Sinhala language, possibly a forewarning of the ultimate collapse—hence his emphasis on classical linguistic norms. Indeed, D'Alwis had a more encompassing vision in the cause of the vernacular than that envisaged by the elitist politicians of the 1920s. D'Alwis was able, because of his special talents, to cater to the "ideological" as well as the "technological" aspects of national language policy.[110]

Possibly, the fact that by the 1920s institutional means such as *pirivena* education had appeared to take up the technological aspects of the vernacular language interests might explain the specialized concern of the motion of 1926. It is a fact, however, that the 1926 generation of the English-educated elite, except for a few individuals such as D. B. Jayatilaka and W. A. de Silva, lacked the intimate knowledge of the indigenous culture which enabled D'Alwis to envision a broader cause in the interests of the vernacular.

If, in James D'Alwis's days, there was a threat of a language shift, with the vernacular being replaced by English, by the 1920s it had disappeared. With the religiocultural revival one observed a determined effort to "render the present a rational continuation of the past."[111] Aspects of the traditional culture had become rallying points for mobilizational activity. The language component of this mobilization in the urban centers, and to a lesser extent in the countryside, comprised the vernacular. These developments had occurred on the whole separate from the movement among the English-educated elite for the liberalization of the political system. But from the 1920s on pressure began to mount to combine the two movements.

108. *Ceylon National Review*, 2 July 1906, 185.

109. See chapter 3.

110. For this distinction, see Whiteley 1969:116.

111. This phrase characterizing revivalist movements is borrowed from Bromage. Quoted in Fishman 1972c:8.

The Emerging Political Salience of the Vernacular Culture

In the 1921 constitution literacy in the vernacular was recognized for the first time as a qualification for civic rights. In spite of the fact that some property and income qualifications also had to be satisfied and that only males were entitled to the right, this recognition led to a substantial widening in the electorate. From 3,013 (when only literacy in English was recognized) in 1917 the voting population rose to 54,207 in 1921 and to 189,335 in 1924 (with the enfranchisement of the vernacular literates).[112] The tremendous increase in 1924 compared with 1921 was probably due to the eagerness of more vernacular-educated individuals for political participation, a clear index to the sociopolitical change that was taking place. It was a change in the direction of greater distribution and reciprocity of power. The stage was now set for the transformation from elite "constitutionalism" to mass politics.

If the English-educated elite politicians so far had been concentrating their energies on eloquent and courteous political bargaining with the British authorities, now there was a need for paying equal or more attention to nursing the local electorate. The need became even greater with the announcement in 1927 that a commission of inquiry would be considering further liberalizing changes in the constitution. The attitude of the British authorities had changed by now. Sir Hugh Clifford, the governor in 1926, wrote a confidential memorandum to Whitehall stating that a great measure of responsible government was the next logical and inevitable step.[113]

The Sri Lankan political leadership now had to concentrate more on establishing its "legitimacy," especially in the eyes of the British authorities and the Donoughmore Commission, from whom political concessions were to be obtained. Also, as far as the local society was concerned, the leadership had to find ways and means of consolidating and preserving its political hegemony and its legitimacy under new circumstances.

No doubt, it was still the English-educated elite that had the necessary linguistic access and the intellectual competence to participate actively in the political process. But the broadening of the electoral foundation from which the leaders had to derive their power meant a concomitant shift in the attributes of leadership. If political leadership earlier rested more on intellectual achievements and the ability to pre-

112. The statistics are from Roberts 1973:275–76.
113. K. M. de Silva 1973h:489–91.

sent cogent constitutional arguments, those attributes would now be of no avail unless they were supplemented by the capacity to inspire a mass following. Hence the urgency in the national elite's efforts to expand its influence and to control the political periphery.

As indicated earlier, a strong conviction had appeared among these political leaders that their Western type of education had alienated them from their compatriots. Now the time had come to follow this conviction with practical measures to ameliorate the situation. For the aspiring political leader it meant seeking issues that functioned to project his image across the cultural gulf distancing him from the masses.

At the early stages of this elitist effort to penetrate into the political periphery the usual strategy was based on patrimonialism. Thus, the aspiring political leader appeared as "the friend of the poor."[114] Evidently, the patrimonialist claim to leadership had a cogent appeal in the context of the tradition-oriented Sinhalese society of the day, used as it was from time immemorial to show deference to ascribed status.

The process of political participation would inevitably lead, however, beyond patrimonialist politics. Vernacular journals were steadily disseminating the message of popular civic rights. The word *mahajanayā*, meaning "the masses," and its derivations were for the first time being extensively used in periodical literature.[115] Hence the aspiring political leader was forced to find means to fraternize with the larger society, which in the current context amounted to the establishment of rapport with the vernacular literati and similarly mobilized sections among the masses.

A further inducement for working in this direction was the emergence of the urban working class as a strong political force. This process, which began in the latter half of the nineteenth century, had reached maturity in the 1920s with the working class becoming organized and politically vociferous.[116] The rising political, social, and economic aspirations of the working class could hardly be contained in the conceptual structure of middle-class constitutionalist politics. For

114. See, for example, this appellation given to aspiring politicians in the Sinhala pamphlets *Mahajana Mitrayā* (Friend of the People), December 1930; and *Sinhala Sevakayā* (Servant of the Sinhalese), May 1930.

115. Thus, for example, see the journals entitled *Mahajana Mataya* (People's Opinion), 1921; *Mahajana Hañḍa* (Voice of the People), 1921; and *Sri Lanka Mahajana Hañḍa* (People's Voice of Sri Lanka), 1923.

116. Jayawardene 1972:XV.

more often than not the interests of the elitist politicians came into head-on conflict with those of the working class.[117]

This polarity of interests was being dramatically demonstrated within the newly formed Ceylon National Congress (1919) – an organization that, although superficially similar to the Indian National Congress, was far less militant in its activities due to the "conventional and stodgy" outlook of the elite politicians who dominated it from the outset.[118] A handful of radicals led by Alexander Ekanayake Goonesinghe (1891–1967) were attempting unsuccessfully in the 1920s to orient it more in the line of its Indian counterpart. Goonesinghe, having been educated in one of the Buddhist schools and coming under the influence of Anagarika Dharmapala, had by the early 1920s become the undisputed leader of Colombo's working class. Having formed the Ceylon Labour Union as a leading member of the Young Lanka League (1915), established in cooperation with several radical-minded English-educated youth, Goonesinghe entered the Ceylon National Congress – the acknowledged forum of national politics of the day. Within the congress Goonesinghe and his associates engaged themselves in an incessant effort to goad that organization to radicalize its demands as well as its tactics regarding constitutional reform. One of his principal objectives, which the CNC establishment viewed with undisguised disfavor, was the need for universal adult franchise.[119]

Under the system of franchise introduced in 1921 literacy qualifications (in English or the vernaculars) were supplemented by property or income qualifications.[120] Thus, the urban working class, most of which was literate in the vernacular, was denied the vote, and this in turn led to an apalling lack of social legislation to cover minimum wages, hours of work, and other welfare measures in the interests of labor. Economic dislocation and concomitant hardship in the aftermath

117. Because almost all the constitutionalist politicans were large property owners and/or entrepreneurs. Thus, for example, D. R. Wijewardene, a prominent figure in the congress, ruthlessly crushed a strike in the newspaper business he owned. See Jayawardene 1972:321. Also see Roberts 1974 for a discussion of the property and business interests of the elite.

118. K. M. de Silva 1973g:395.

119. "Goonesinghe emerged as almost the sole advocate of universal suffrage before the Donoughmore Commission" (K. M. de Silva 1973h:493). Also, see the discussion below.

120. When the franchise was introduced in 1911 only adult males literate in English had the vote. In 1921 the property qualifications were *either* a clear annual income of Rs 600 *or* immovable property worth not less than Rs 1500 *or* occupancy as owner or tenant

of the First World War led to a series of industrial disputes in the 1920s through which the working class demonstrated unequivocally its presence in the sociopolitical life of the island.[121]

It was Goonesinghe's belief that universal adult suffrage would be a "sort of panacea" for the problems facing the working class, for it would ensure that their demands were heeded in the legislature.[122] His campaign for widening the franchise made very little headway within the Congress, but nothing daunted Goonesinghe, who next carried his battle outside that body to a wider public. His moment of triumph, although a very brief one, came when the Donoughmore commissioners were in the island. Goonesinghe appeared before the commission to advocate universal adult suffrage. In striking contrast to Goonesinghe, the deputation of the congress, led by its president, E. W. Perera, and its joint secretaries, S. W. R. D. Bandaranaike and R. S. S. Gunawardena, opposed a major extension of the franchise and argued that it should be confined to "the competent adult population who were fitted for the franchise."[123]

The radicalist challenge to the conservative congress leadership was taken to the journalistic platform as well. In addition to the campaign carried out by the English journal *Young Lanka* there appeared a number of Sinhala journals—*Lankā Kamkaru Prabōdhaya* (1922), *Kamkaru Hañḍa* (1928), *Kamkaru Balaya* (1928), and *Kamkaru Dhvajaya* (1930)—and the daily newspaper *Vīrayā* (1929), launched by Gonnesinghe himself, to agitate in the cause of the working class. As could be expected, Goonesinghe and his associates used this popular platform to castigate the elitist politicians who controlled the congress. This leadership was referred to as "political scarecrows" and "miserable purse-proud poltroons" who were "pawning the sacred liberties of the land."[124] Goonesinghe urged the worker and the common person to assert their individuality by repudiating the authority of that "class of men who, calling themselves leaders, want you to follow like dumb driven cattle."[125]

The significance of the career of Goonesinghe lies in that it marked

---

of houses valued at Rs 400 or Rs 200, according to their urban or rural situation, respectively.

121. K. M. de Silva 1973g:404.

122. Jayawardene 1972:266.

123. Jayawardene 1972:264–65.

124. *Young Lanka*, 13 February 1920.

125. *Young Lanka*, 17 September 1922.

the first populist challenge to the domination of the island's politics by the English-educated elite. Although he himself belonged to the latter social category, Goonesinghe was taking up the cause of "the real people" of the country, the masses, by denouncing the legitimacy of the "fossilized old fogeys" in the congress establishment.[126] The vernacular journals disseminated these ideas among the popular readership. Thus, it was an instance where changes in the social structure, conflict within the political leadership, and the influence of mass media were all merging to effect a shift in the structure of political participation.

With regard to the breakthrough of the working class into the political arena, intra-elite factionalism merely added momentum to an inevitable process. The beginnings of the political self-assertion by another disadvantaged yet mobilized group, the vernacular schoolteachers, was taking place at the same time but without the abetment of elite factionalism. In 1923 the defunct Sri Lanka Guru Sangamaya, the national organization of the vernacular teachers based in Colombo,[127] was revived to focus attention, among other things, on the need for higher wages and the use of the vernacular in government offices and courts of law.[128] A more militant provincial organization, the Swabhasa Guru Sangamaya of Galle, appeared before the Donoughmore Commission to present a number of grievances, the most important among them being the fact that the majority of the vernacular teachers were denied the right of franchise—obviously due to lack of income qualifications. Also the association took the opportunity to speak of the low wages paid to them compared with those paid to English teachers, the lack of facilities for higher education in the vernacular, and the paucity of employment opportunities for those educated in the vernacular.[129]

All in all, the democratizing and rationalizing processes of political development were thus contributing to the emerging salience of the vernacular culture. Meanwhile, the institutional broadening of political participation by the extension of the franchise, on the one hand, and the rising importance attached to the popular will, on the other, were setting the stage for the buildup of the "language of the people" as a political cause. The beginnings of this process could be seen in the 1920s. As if to provide a backdrop for the manifestation of language as the

126. From an article in *Young Lanka,* 7 July 1918.

127. See section "Voluntary Associations" in chapter 5.

128. For details, see *Sri Lanka Guruvaraya* 1 (1 May 1927).

129. See the editorial of *Guruvadana* 1, no. 1 (1929).

symbol of group identity par excellence—"the conveyor of all other ethnic symbols"[130]—we notice a shift in the focus of Sinhalese national identity.

A Shift in the Focus of Sinhalese National Identity: From Religion to Ethnicity

With regard to the rising political salience of the vernacular culture, the threads of revivalism were picked up again to receive added significance in an era of democratization. But there was a crucial shift of focus taking place. The religious factor, which had received unequivocal emphasis in the identity affirmation endeavors of the earlier era, was now gradually receding to the background. The greater urgency during the 1920s appeared to be that related to the broader ethnic cohesion of the Sinhalese community—the overarching unity irrespective of caste, creed, or regional differences. Exerting external pressure in favor of this cohesive propensity, as it were, there appeared at the time a political competition with the Tamil community and a threat to the indigenous working class from Indian immigrant labor.

Intra-Ethnic Cohesion among the Sinhalese

Two major causes may be adduced to explain the receding salience of religion as a feature of the Sinhalese identity. First, the success of the Buddhist revival in molding an ideology as well as an infrastructure to counter Christian proselytism would have contributed to slowing down the competitive spirit of the Buddhists, although not eliminating it altogther.[131] Second, the political climate of the early twentieth century, the result of the traumatic experience of the Sinhala-Muslim conflict of 1915, the political struggle for the liberalization of the administration, and the emerging interethnic rivalry with the Tamils in the age of political democratization, appears to have been more conducive to intra-ethnic cohesion than competition.

Thus, except for a brief factionalist threat posed by a "Kandyan nationalism" espoused by a few English-educated scions of feudal fami-

130. I borrow this phrase from Fishman 1977b:25.

131. Hence this was only a period of hibernation as proved by later history. For the accumulated grievances, see *The Betrayal of Buddhism*, prepared by the Buddhist Committee of Inquiry (Balangoda: Dharmavijaya, 1956).

lies and encouraged by a British governor,[132] the 1920s witnessed intense efforts to consolidate intra-ethnic unity among the Sinhalese. Although similar sentiments had been expressed earlier as well, there was now a strong political motivation. Indeed, Kandyan factionalism tended to provoke a negative reaction, intensifying endeavors in the cause of a united Sinhalese community. In this regard the preceding era of revivalism provided not only the ideological motivation but also the mobilizational apparatus in the form of the journalistic platform and the *samāgam* structure.[133] Thus, *Situmiṇa*, a journal published in Kandy, declared:

> The disunity among the Sinhalese people today will adversely affect future generations and they will for certain go further and further in the path of decline. It is no secret that the Sinhalese today live in an unfortunate disunity due to religious conflict, caste conflict and regional conflict. . . . A human community called the Sinhalese exist only in this island. It is appalling even to imagine that such a community is living in discord. (Editorial in *Situmiṇa*, 21 February 1929)

Similarly, *Samagi Sañgarāva*, published in the cause of the "land, nation and religion," pointed to a past in which

> the Sinhalese people because of their unity lived in splendour, developing their land, nation and religion. Now when that unity has disappeared, due to the machinations of foreigners and the jealousies among the Sinhalese themselves, the land, nation and religion is going from decline to further decline. (Editorial in *Samagi Sañgarāva*, February–March 1931)

Unlike during the revivalist era, however, the connection between Sinhalese ethnicity and Buddhist religion was not often emphasized, and the Sinhalese journals regularly stressed the fact that they were working for national unity and campaigning against caste and religious divisionism.[134]

---

132. The governor was Sir William Henry Manning (1919–25). For details, see K. M. de Silva 1973g:402–3.

133. See chapter 5.

134. See, for example, the inaugural statements of *Loku Siñgho* (1926), *Rāma Säraya* (1926), *Sañda Miṇa* (1926), *Mudalāli* (1927), *Lanka Taruṇayā* (1927), *Lak Väsiayā* (1928), and *Sin-*

Apparently, the increasing possibility of the indigenous political leadership gaining a greater share of political control was a powerful factor in motivating efforts toward intracommunal unity. "If our aim is home rule," declared one journal, "the only way to attain that is by sinking all caste and creed prejudices." And referring to the political leadership, it said:

> We know that the majority of our leaders have hailed from Christian institutions, and so far Christian influence has not failed. So why take up cudgels against the Christians? (Editorial in *Swadēsha Prabōdhaya* [Sinhala and English] 1 November 1921)

Such remarks denote a shift in priorities. Political aspirations were becoming matters of great urgency. The Buddhist component of traditional Sinhala ethnicity was being played down in the context of a compulsive need for an all-encompassing intra-ethnic concord. Also there was a marked eagerness on the part of the Sinhalese Christians to affirm their ethnic identity. Thus, in 1914 an organization called the Sinhalese Young Men's Association, prominent among whose membership were Christians such as E. T. de Silva and Rev. J. B. de Silva, organized a "national day" on the Sinhala New Year's Day. Declared E. T. de Silva:

> It was felt by the nationalists that the sentiment deep rooted in their breasts should receive a visible manifestation, and that one day in the year should be set apart for introspection by the Sinhalese of themselves as Sinhalese. . . . We the Sinhalese wanted "just one day" set apart for the celebration of our past glory and to breathe our hopes for the future. (*Nationalist Monthly of Ceylon* 1 [1917])

Evidently, the recognition of their increasing marginality created in the minds of the more politically conscious Christians a compelling need to emphasize their ethnic identity. Here one may note again a motivation similar to that of D'Alwis earlier, perhaps now more widely prevalent due to the catalytic intervention of the Buddhist revival.

---

hala Balaya (1928) given in Pannasekera 1969 (vol. 6) and 1970 (vol. 7). The "nation" referred to was the Sinhalese nation.

Aspirations of intra-ethnic cohesion were further strengthened as a result of the consistent cooperation between the elite political leaders of the two religions. Buddhist leaders such as D. B. Jayatilaka, W. A. de Silva, and F. R. Senanayake worked hand in hand with the Christians James Pieris, E. W. Perera, and H. J. C. Perera to agitate for constitutional reform. Indeed, together they comprised the "establishment" in the Ceylon National Congress after the departure of the Tamils from that organization in 1922. In the first regionally based elections of 1921, where the majority of the electorate consisted of the vernacular-educated group, both Pieris and E. W. Perera secured predominantly Buddhist electorates. Commenting on this, a Buddhist journal congratulated these "champions of the Ceylonese" and observed that their victories "clearly shows that the Congress represents the people."[135]

If the age of political democratization thus witnessed strong tendencies of internal cohesion within the Sinhalese community, the converse was taking place with regard to the larger multiethnic conglomeration of the island. The third decade of the twentieth century witnessed a rift between the Sinhalese and Tamil leaders, who had so far acted together in the constitutionalist agitation.

Interethnic Cooperation in the Constitutionalist Agitation and Its Subsequent Dissolution

The camaraderie that existed between the Sinhalese and Tamil political leaders during the early stages of the agitation for constitutional reform was to break down, ironically enough, during the period when the reforms were gradually being made. As a prelude to the examination of these developments, it is useful to understand the early visions of an integrated "Ceylonese" identity.

The English-educated elite in early twentieth-century Sri Lanka were deploring the alienating effects of the English education its members had received. But such an education also had its more positive effects. This secondary socialization had resulted in an outlook that stretched beyond their individual ethnic perspectives toward a broader national unity rising above those separate loyalties. The vision of the political leadership of the early years of the century in their demands

135. Editorial in *Young Buddhist* 1, no. 3 (1921).

for constitutional reform was the creation of a Ceylonese society, in which liberal institutions united the "Sinhalese, Tamils, Burghers and Mohamedans as one race [*sic*] in their love for this land."[136]

These elite politicians were aware that a crucial component of "the liberal capacity" in the British political tradition was the ability to rise above "communalism." Hence strong and consistent affirmations were made of the Ceylonese identity. H. J. C. Pereira, as president of the Ceylon National Congress, for example, declared in 1925:

> The salvation of Ceylon depended not on the growth of communalism or racialism but on the growth of the true national spirit which the Congress . . . would always foster. (*HCNC*:501)

When the congress was formed in 1919 with the aim of carrying on systematic and organized agitation for constitutional reform the Sinhalese and Tamil politicians worked together as representatives of the two major communities in the island. The first president of the congress was Ponnambalam Arunachalam, one of the most prominent Tamil political leaders. A successor of his, C. E. Corea, a Sinhalese, declared to the congress in 1924:

> I wish to disavow in the name of the Ceylon National Congress all responsibility of Congress for the so-called Sinhalese-Tamil split; I disavow all racial partiality; all discrimination in the national brotherhood. (*HCNC*:646).

Such pious sentiments notwithstanding, the conflict potential of a pluralistic society is high, especially one with a long history of intercommunal rivalry and mistrust. Theoretically, "almost any difference between two groups can become politically significant."[137] Ironically enough, it was a central liberalist aspiration that epitomized this difference in the Sri Lankan context.

---

136. E. W. Perera, quoted in Roberts 1977:LXXXIII. The word *Ceylonese* was coined in the mid-nineteenth century by the liberal-minded Burgher group led by C. A. Lorenz (Roberts 1977:LXXXII).

137. For this theoretical possibility, see Zolberg 1968.

The Politicization of Ethnic Interests and Communal Polarization

The elitist politicians, in their demand for constitutional reform, considered the perpetuation of the principle of communal representation an affront to their liberal capacity. Hence the removal of the communal principle and the institution of territorial electorates was one of their major political aspirations from the very start. But an exclusively territorial representation would inevitably lead to the Sinhalese community securing an overwhelming majority of seats. From a communalistic angle this revealed to the Tamils the inescapable eventuality of becoming a political minority, if and when the liberalist ideals were transformed into institutional realities. Thus, in 1921, soon after the introduction of the principle of territorial electorates, the larger component of Tamil membership in the congress, along with the president Arunachalam, having failed to secure from the Sinhalese the concession of a Tamil "reserved" seat in the predominantly Sinhalese Western Province, made their exit from the congress. Immediately, a Tamil Maha Jana Sabhai came into being, seeking to promote the political interests of the Tamils.[138]

The Sinhalese on their part, "with the confidence and security of superior numbers, could insist on the simple and familiar devices of democratic government."[139] But not so the Tamils. Hence the Tamils, now transformed from a "majority" community into a "minority," consequent upon the liberalizing change from communal to territorial representation, joined hands with other minority groups such as Muslims, Burghers, and Europeans in demanding constitutional "safeguards" against the overwhelming majoritarianism of the Sinhalese. In this way the politicizing, and thereby the freezing and strengthening, of existing parochialisms followed inevitably upon the political developmental process in an unintegrated pluralistic society with deep historic antagonisms brought into sharper focus by a contemporary cultural revival.

From the viewpoint of the Sinhalese the Tamil breakaway from the mainstream nationalist movement would have only confirmed a long-standing sense of group mistrust. A time-worn hostility had now

138. For details, see K. M. de Silva 1972.

139. Kearney 1967:32.

been transformed into a contemporary political rivalry, and it was to remain so.

As an added impetus to the revival of rancorous memories from the past, there appeared in the 1920s a threat of "de-stabilizing" Indian influx into the island.

Sinhala Fears of the "Indian Menace"

The importation of plantation labor from south India had been the mainstay of the development of British plantation capitalism in the island in the nineteenth century. Thus, until the early twentieth century migration increase in the form of south Indian labor influx constituted over 50 percent of the increase in the island's population. In 1921 the population percentage of Indian Tamils was 13.4 percent as against 11.5 percent Sri Lankan Tamils and 67.0 percent Sinhalese.[140] The south Indians were principally concentrated in the Kandyan territories, where the major plantations were located. They constituted an ethnocultural enclave that appeared to receive the care and attention of British rulers, while the Sinhalese peasantry in the same region was being virtually neglected and was also being hemmed in by the large tea and rubber plantations. In addition to the laborers there was a sizable Indian trader element in Colombo and other commercial centers. The social mobilization taking place along with the cultural revival were bringing the "Indian menace" gradually into focus, particularly due to the work of activists such as Anagarika Dharmapala. It was in the 1920s, however, with the politicization of the urban working class and the franchise question, which followed, that Indian immigration came to be viewed as a potent threat to Sinhala interests.

The 1920s were years of economic depression, characterized by unemployment, low wages, and high prices.[141] When in the attempt to win higher wages the earliest organized labor group in the island, Colombo's predominantly Sinhalese working class, resorted to strike action, the typical countermove adopted by employers in this case took the form of the importation of south Indian workers. This happened, for example, in the railway strike of 1912, the harbor strike of 1927, and the Lake House strike of 1927. Significantly, even without the provoca-

140. For the nineteenth-century immigration figures, see Balakrishnan and Gunasekera 1977:110. For the 1921 figures, see *Census of Ceylon, 1921* (Colombo: Government Press, 1923), 191.

141. See K. M. de Silva 1977:78.

tion of a strike, south Indian labor was becoming preferable because of its relative low cost.[142]

In this context the visitation of the failures and frustrations of the Sinhalese working class on the historically culpable Dravidians was a predictable development. A contemporary journal, referring to the "Indians in Ceylon," stated:

> Ceylonese are being ousted from every sphere of activity gradually, but surely. . . . We cannot permit the outsider to take the bread out of the mouths of the sons of the soil. (*Searchlight* 6, no. 51 [21 January 1928])

This defense of the interests of the *bhumiputras,* the "sons of the soil," a familiar theme found in many multiethnic societies, was elaborated into a warning that stirred the embers of a historical fear:

> The day will come when Ceylon will be completely swamped by the Indian hordes, unless something is done to put an effective check. (*Searchlight* 6, no. 51 [21 January 1928])

At this juncture a transformation was witnessed in the policies of the "undisputed leadership" of the working class. From being the spokesman of the laboring classes in general Goonesinghe became the champion of the Sinhalese workers, and, here we should remember that the Sinhalese working class of the day was "not above a touch of National Socialism with its contempt for lesser breeds."[143]

In an era where the colonial authorities seemed to be keen on sharing power with the local population the Sinhalese community was beset by anxieties arising from deeply ingrained historical memories. Obviously, "the minority complex" of the majority Sinhala community motivated its political leaders to find means of putting an effective check on the possibility of being swamped by the Indian hordes.[144] Notwithstanding its liberalist orientations, the congress leadership was irrevocably against the granting of universal adult franchise, which Goonesinghe and other radicals sponsored. The motivation was partly the elitist mistrust of "the great unwashed" and partly the communal

142. Jayawardene 1972:286, 218–19.
143. Ludowyk 1966:152.
144. For the concept, see Farmer 1965.

fear, openly expressed by congress stalwarts such as D. S. Senanayake and D. R. Wijewardene, that, for example, as Senanayake put it,

> unless we stem the tide of this growing domination of Indians in Ceylon in our economic and political life, our extinction as a Ceylonese nation is inevitable.[145]

Feelings among the Sinhalese political leadership against the granting of franchise to Indian emigrant labor, which by 1930 comprised about 700,000 out of a total population of 5,306,871, were so strong that the leaders preferred to reject the recommendations of the Donoughmore Commission granting a very large extent of constitutional power to the indigenous political leadership if it also meant granting the franchise to the Indians on the same terms as the Sri Lankans in general. Governor Sir Herbert Stanley (1927–31) recommended the imposition of restrictions on the franchise qualifications of the Indians in a bid to win enough support for the commission's recommendations in the legislature.[146]

The rising salience of communal issues among the elite politicians may be adduced to several factors. First, in spite of secondary socialization on Western lines, traces of primordialism still lingered in the psychological makeup of these leaders. Second, the inevitable broadening of the base of political participation should have made, at least to a limited degree, the temptation to court the masses by appealing to traditional loyalties virtually irresistible. Furthermore, there was taking place in the 1920s a gradual change in the congress leadership: The Christians were being slowly replaced by Buddhists. Thus, by the 1930s Buddhists such as D. B. Jayatilaka and D. S. Senanayake, with their early background of involvement in the religiocultural revival, had undisputed authority over congressional affairs and the mainstream political movement in the island. Here they had replaced Christians such as James Pieris and E. W. Perera. The political elite, however, working as it was in a context in which political concessions had to be won from

145. Quoted in Roberts 1977:CXVI. Senanayake was in the island's legislature, from 1924 until his death in 1952. And he was the first prime minister of independent Sri Lanka (1945–52). Wijewardene owned the Lake House group of newspapers comprising the most widely read and stable newspapers in Sinhala, Tamil, and English in the island. Paradoxically, he did not hesitate to import Indian labor to break up a strike in Lake House. See Jayawardene 1972:322–23.

146. K. M. de Silva 1973h:495–96.

the colonial authorities by demonstrating a "liberal capacity," had to display moderation in any articulation of communal interests. Hence even if the leaders wished so, they were not in a position to increase their effectiveness by open and vigorous commitment to ethnic or religious exclusivism.

Added to this was the fact that the outlook of conservatism continued to persist among the congress hierarchy, even after the leadership change mentioned above, and the flavor of elitist politics remained characterized by a disinclination for mass arousal and violent agitation. Indeed, the inhibitions of the elite regarding universal adult franchise were grounded on the group's distaste for, if not fear of, the potential it held for political radicalization.[147] At a time when the political participatory base was being broadened such an outlook among the leadership held prospects for the development of counterelitist sentiments at the popular level.

The Beginnings of Counterelitism: A Demand for Behavioral Affirmation of Ethnic Identity

As mentioned, regret for having lost its cultural patrimony was prompting the English-educated elite to engage in identity affirmation endeavors during the early years of the twentieth century. Their self-criticisms reached the mobilized sections of the populace. Added to these were the examples of revivalists, such as Anagarika Dharmapala, who in spite of having received an English education engaged themselves in a crusade against Westernization among the Sinhalese. In a typical invective, written in English, Dharmapala declared:

> A patriot's blood boils with indignation at the sight of the present Anglicized Sinhalese who loves neither his country nor nation. Fancy the descendants of Vijaya having names like Pereras, Silvas, Almeidas, Diases, Liveras. . . . (*Buddhist* 4 [October 1892])

He continued this campaign in the Sinhalese press. It was his opinion that

> there is only one other idiotic and loathsome human group in the whole world who indulge in such bovine stupidity. That is the

147. See K. M. de Silva 1973h:492–93.

> small Kaffir element in Africa who have embraced Christianity. The Sinhalese who follow European ways and those Christianized Kaffirs, both are found behaving in the same manner. (*Sinhala Bauddhaya* [14 October 1911])

Dharmapala evidently had struck a responsive chord among the vernacular literati of his day. The local vanguard in the temperance movement and the later "link men" in the more politically oriented Mahajana Sabha (People's Association), both spearheaded by the English-educated elite, consisted mostly of persons inspired by Dharmapala's activities.[148]

The Mahajana Sabha movement was launched by the elite politicians in 1918 "to reach as large proportion as possible of people who (spoke) the vernacular."[149] It had the dual objective of proving to the British authorities that the political demands of the elite had popular backing and also of making the vernacular-speaking masses aware of their own political rights. Thus, by 1927 there were at least twenty-seven Mahajana Sabhas established in different parts of the island, and these, as a special command post under the former temperance leader F. R. Senanayake, were affiliated with the Ceylon National Congress. The central elite had penetrated to the periphery largely by means of a patrimonial linkage system.

The vernacular language was a sine qua non in reaching and mobilizing the masses. Since Senanayake's Mahajana Sabha movement was confined to the Sinhala-speaking areas, the proceedings of the branch organizations and the head organization in Colombo were in Sinhala. But the Ceylon National Congress, the organization of the national political leadership, continued to work in English. Here we note that, with the emergence of the Mahajana Sabha movement, a breakthrough had been achieved: The vernacular was now accepted in the discussion of purely political issues. Soon the elite politicians themselves had to make some concession at least, and Sinhala came to be used along with English at some conferences organized by the congress in the mid 1920s, as a sizable section of the participants were Sinhala monolinguals.[150]

The recognition given to the vernacular proved to be a stimulant

148. See Roberts 1977:CIX.

149. Roberts 1969:23. The following description is based on this source.

150. Roberts 1977:CX.

to aspirations for its functional expansion. In the final analysis it may be said that in their attempt to penetrate to the political periphery the English-educated leaders rendered their own social stratum more vulnerable to egalitarian demands. The cause of the vernacular came to be promoted by the vernacular-educated intelligentsia, often in the form of chagrin about the language behavior of the national elite.

"In the high class families today," noted one prominent *bhikkhu*, "the children study English without even a modicum of regard for our own language. . . . One has to ponder on the fact whether they will be of any service to the Sinhalese nation, our own language or religion."[151] The editor of a Sinhala journal deplored the fact that "in upper-class families it is indeed rarely that even the parents are addressed in Sinhala."[152] Exhorting the upper-class Sinhalese to follow the example of the Bengalis, who have given "the national language and culture pride of place," another journal drew their attention to a statement made about them by a European writer: "they [the upper-class Sinhalese] are all 'Europeans' . . . only the menial servants speak Sinhalese."[153]

Members of the English-educated elite were being reminded of the fact that one's behavior, in particular one's language behavior, is a truer reflection of one's ethnic allegiance than one's cultural heritage as determined by birthright. Indeed, their legitimacy as political leaders was coming to hinge on their behavioral demonstration of that allegiance. The enfranchisement of the vernacular educated in 1920 was having its political consequences. Thus, the editorial of one Sinhala periodical stated that, when electing members to the Legislative Council,

> we must elect only those who, while being thoroughly conversant with English and other areas of foreign knowledge, are able to think, write and speak well in Sinhala and who have studied Sinhalese history and who respect Sinhalese ways and customs. (*Sinhala Siri* 1, no. 1 [2467 B.E., A.D. 1923])

Although such expectations had not become widespread and by no means had the force of mass demands, the fact that they appeared at all is quite significant. There was an emerging awareness of the politi-

151. Karandana Jinaratana Maha Thera, "Siya Basa," *Siya Basa* 1, no. 3 (1925): 50–53.
152. *Satyartha Sangrahaya* 2, no. 9 (1920).
153. *Manorama* 1, no. 5, (September 1926).

cal importance of traditional culture, particularly its language component.

The Articulation of Language Interests: The Urgency of Developing the Sinhala Language

A demand was rising from the mobilized sections of the Sinhalese people that the Anglophile political leadership demonstrate behaviorally their allegiance to the traditional culture. It would appear that there was an underlying class rivalry motivating this demand. The vernacular literati, in particular the Sinhalese schoolteachers and other Sinhalese-educated groups employed in low income professions, were acutely aware of the allocation of power along language lines. What demarcated their own lower status vis-à-vis the higher status attributed to some others was the special value attached to the English language in economic and social terms. If the value attachment could be reversed—the vernacular attaining the position now enjoyed by English—there would be a status reversal, and supremacy would be theirs. Although homilies could be heard, however, in the cause of national culture and even national language from the Anglophile upper class, there was little or nothing done in practical terms to provide the vernacular with recognition or status. Evidently, the dominant class did not want a change of status after all.

In this context the vernacular literati were aware that there was one powerful argument that could be used against the vernacular vis-à-vis English. That was the fact that all modern knowledge was available only in English and that the vernacular lagged far behind in this respect. Hence there arose among the vernacular literati a great concern for language development: to make Sinhala a viable medium for functioning in a modern society. A *bhikkhu* principal of a *pirivena,* writing on "Developing Our Language," declared:

> It is extremely difficult to achieve national development without a language which is complete in all respects so that the country can be administered through it. For example . . . the savants of Bengal, in their love for the people . . . developed their language so that it could be utilized easily for all purposes. Similar developments took place in many other lands. The only nation which tries

> to advance itself while leaving behind its own language is the present day Sinhalese nation.[154]

The imputation here was that the political leadership was neglecting the most important aspect of national identity. In prescribing a course of action for language development the above writer declared:

> Lovers of our nation should further develop whatever Sinhalese writings there are which contain in succinct form material on science and technology; and they should prepare and publish books on the well known, important, and useful sciences in the modern world. It is the rich and the learned gentlemen who should engage themselves in this virtuous endeavour.

Similarly, a Sinhalese schoolteacher pointed to the fact that "the measure of a nation's progress is the degree of development its language has reached." He cited the example of the English nation and its language, exhorting his compatriots to develop a love for their own language and to work toward mending its deficiencies with regard to lack of books on modern knowledge.[155] "A language is considered to be a well developed language," wrote another scholar-*bhikkhu*, "when books have been written in it on different religions, on different arts and sciences, and on different languages. Thus, for example, the English language."[156]

It is evident from such statements that contact with English was proving to be a stimulant for aspirations of developing the vernacular on similar lines. Significantly, these aspirations were emerging at a time when prospects for change from subject community status to self-governing community status appeared in the political horizon.

While the urgency for language development by means of a foray into "new forms of discourse" was being expressed, there was also an awareness of the fact that concomitantly an "expansion of lexicon" was also necessary.[157] Although some strands of opinion among the ver-

154. Pundit K. Sri Dhammananda Thero, principal of Gnanodya Pirivena of Kotmale, "Swabhasa Vardhanaya," *Samagiya* 1, no. 1 (1921): 4–6.

155. S. P. Rupasinghe, "Swabhasa Mamatvaya," *Siybasa* 1, no. 3 (1925): 50–53.

156. Polwatte Buddhadatta Thero, "Ape Adupadu," *Sri Kavi Dhvajaya* 1, no. 3 (1921): 56–58.

157. For this aspect of language development, see Ferguson 1968.

nacular intelligentsia had it that Sinhala was and always is self-sufficient in this regard, in other quarters there was also recognition of the need for a special technical vocabulary to deal with areas of modern knowledge unknown to traditional learning. The chief incumbent of a Buddhist temple in Colombo, who was also a highly respected Sinhalese scholar, argued that: "A language is considered rich not by having a large number of synonyms to refer to one thing but by being adequately equipped with separate words to refer to everything possible." He recommended therefore that:

> We must replenish our language by including in it enough words from whatever possible source so as to make it capable of expressing unambiguously the various ideas which are current in modern times.[158]

In this way sections of the vernacular literati, in particular those in the major urban centers who had come into intimate contact with the English language and the modern knowledge that accompanied it, were expressing strongly the need to expand the resources of the Sinhala language. These intellectuals were concerned about the fact that they had to depend continuously on a foreign language for the acquisition of modern knowledge. And the recognition of the "slow and painful course through which their nation must pass before its own language becomes adequate to the requirements of modern life"[159] were touching their sensibilities—hence the urgency for language development.

A Language-Related Groupness Perception

In the nineteenth century a lone individual, James D'Alwis, perceiving an extreme disregard for the vernacular in the dominant social ethos, struggled single-handedly for its maintenance, reinforcement, and enrichment. By the 1920s, however, circumstances in Sri Lanka had changed substantially. A religiocultural revival had taken place. Institutionalized efforts in the cause of national culture had come into being. There was now a widespread concern for the community's cultural

158. *Bhikkhu* Pälāṇē Srī Vajiragñāṇa, of Vijairārāmaya, Colombo, "Sabdārtha Chitā," Sāhitya Taranginī 1 (April 1929): 35–56.

159. For this general observation, see Shils 1972b:401–2.

heritage, and language was emerging as one of the most salient features of that heritage.

In this period, when the masses were being gradually drawn into political participation, ethnicity was becoming a powerful nucleus for crystallizing group interests. The breakaway of the Tamils from the Ceylon National Congress marked the debut of communalistic politics. It also added momentum to the concern among the Sinhalese about intracommunal solidarity. In this regard the formerly emphasized religious component of historical ethnicity was being downplayed, leaving language as the most compelling symbol of group cohesion.

The demand made on the Anglophile elite for behavioral affirmation of their ethnic loyalty, particularly in language-based activity, and the urgent concern that was being expressed for language development were unmistakable signs that a "language-related groupness perception" was emerging in the Sinhalese community,[160] precisely among its more mobilized sections.

Unlike in the days of D'Alwis, now there was no fear of a language shift. On the contrary, the fundamental democratization of society which was taking place held brighter prospects for the vernacular. Those among the vernacular literati who were gradually becoming aware of its political potential were searching for ways and means to promote its cause. An editorial in one Sinhala journal declared in 1923:

> It is the leadership in our society who are responsible for the present depreciation of our own language . . . We must use our own language in all our activities, make our classics readily available, and produce new books on the technological subjects. Every Sinhalese person should resolve to ponder on the present degradation of his language and strive for its advancement. (*Śrī Dharma Śrī* 4 [3 September 1923])

Such affirmations of nationalistic attachment to language per se required further elaboration, invigoration, and dissemination if they were to be transformed into an effective political force.

160. The above phrase is from Fishman (1971a), who says, "We have little systematic information concerning the circumstances under which language consciousness, language knowledge and language-related groupness–perceptions–do or do not enter into reference group behaviour in contact situations."

Chapter 8

The Politicization of Language Loyalty: A Bid to Make Sinhala the Official Language

> The power of the vote you have reached, O Sinhalese!
> Is an incomparable weapon to vanquish your meniality
> If however, you were to give it away through fear, persuasion or for money
> Ponder intelligently, what succor will there be for your country.
> —Verse by Munidasa Cumaratunga, 1934

With the adoption of the Donoughmore Constitution in 1931 the larger portion of the island's internal government was passed onto Sri Lankan hands. Equally significant was the introduction of universal adult franchise. These substantial changes in the political structure spurred the political leadership to adopt more and more "popular" issues, among which were further efforts to seek expansion and symbolic elaboration of vernacular language functions as against English, the language of colonial administration. Four resolutions presented to the State Council, the island's legislature under the new constitution, demonstrate this attempt: the first in March 1932 concerning the use of the vernaculars in the debates of the council; the second in July of the same year concerning vernacular proficiency of the administrative personnel; the third in 1936 concerning the use of the vernacular in the administration of justice; and the fourth in 1943 for the adoption of Sinhala as the official language of the state.

It is noteworthy that in the two resolutions of 1932 and in that of 1936 the reference was to Sinhala as well as Tamil, as against English. But the original resolution of 1943 purported to make Sinhala *alone* the official language, although in the course of the debate that followed an amendment was accepted, with some members dissenting, that Tamil too should be given an equal status with Sinhala. The significance of the shift in content in relation to the original resolution of 1943 must be looked at in the context of the events that preceded and followed it. As for those that followed, the most vehement outburst of language nationalism in the island occurred in the mid-1950s over the demand for "Sinhala Only"—the Sinhalese pressing for this demand while the Tamils agitated for a parity of status for Sinhala and Tamil. Sinhala was made the one official language in the aftermath of the 1956 general election where popular support for Sinhala Only was unequivocal. Since that day Tamil opposition to this legislation has escalated, and in the early 1970s a secessionist movement, which subsequently resorted to violence for the achievement of its aspirations, emerged.

Seen in this light it would appear that the original resolution of 1943 is one of the most important landmarks in the intergroup relations between the Sinhalese and Tamil communities in Sri Lanka. Indeed, it signifies the parting of the ways between the two communities as far as language-related group interests are concerned. Where the Sinhalese are concerned, it signifies the first political attempt at the institutionalization of language-based group interests. These efforts to change the functional allocation of languages within the polity can best be understood with reference to the socioeconomic context in which they arose.

The Ethnolinguistic Group Vitality Configuration of the Sinhalese, 1931–43

According to Howard Giles, R. Y. Bourhis, and D. M. Taylor the vitality of an ethnolinguistic community in relation to corresponding groups in the polity may be measured by three main structural variables: status, demography, and institutional support. The utility of this analysis for the present study lies in the premise that,

> given the particular pattern of strengths and weaknesses of a group in terms of its dimensions of group vitality, one may be able to predict over which structural variables group competition may be most likely to occur between ingroup and outgroup.[1]

Although in this case the events have already taken place, the framework provided by Giles, Bourhis, and Taylor helps us to better

1. Giles et al. 1977:308.

understand the group dynamics in the Sri Lankan society of the 1930s and 40s which prompted the language resolution of 1943. The pressures and agitation of the Sinhalese ethnolinguistic group have to be assessed in relation to the two relevant out-groups, the Tamils, who are a comparable ethnolinguistic community, and the nebulous category, the English-educated community in the island, made up of elements from the indigenous ethnic groups (the Sinhalese, Tamils, Moors, and Burghers) as well as the small European expatriate segment.

As Giles, Bourhis, and Taylor have shown, there are four pertinent factors in the assessment of the group vitality of an ethnolinguistic collectivity: economic status, ascribed status, sociohistorical status, and language status.[2]

Economic Status

While British entrepreneurial interests dominated the commanding heights of the economy—the major plantations and the bulk of the import-export trade—the most highly placed situations in public and private employment were also reserved for the Europeans. As for non-European plantation ownership, the Sinhalese were the foremost group, making up 75.3 percent of the principal plantation owners by 1917.[3] Among the non-Europeans engaged in import-export trade, however, the Moors and the Indian Tamils taken together appeared to be ahead of the Sinhalese. It was in government service and the "select professions" such as law, medicine, engineering, and surveying that the lower economic status of the Sinhalese, who were the majority of the population, was markedly apparent. In 1921, for example, while the Sinhalese, comprising 76 percent of the total adult population, with the exclusion of the Europeans, held only a total of 46 percent of the select professions; the Sri Lankan Tamils, constituting only 13.3 percent of the same total, had a 31.9 percent share of these jobs; and the Burghers, forming only a minute 0.7 percent of the total, held a totally disproportionate 17.7 percent.[4] The Tamils were markedly dominant in the medical profession. In 1921, while 34 percent of the physicians and medical practitioners were Sinhalese, the Tamils' share was as high as 44 percent of the total.[5] The Tamils could generally make headway in the

2. Giles et al. 1977:308.
3. Roberts 1977:xxxv.
4. See table 4 in Roberts 1973.
5. K. M. de Silva 1986:90.

professional field because they were ahead of the Sinhalese in English literacy.

By 1946, however, when independence was only two years ahead, the Sinhalese were gradually catching up in English literacy and thus asserting their majority status in the professional fields.[6] Thus, for example, in the civil service which was the topmost layer of the bureaucracy, the Sinhalese held 69 posts, the Tamils 31, and the Burghers 16; and in the medical profession there were 205 Sinhalese doctors compared to 115 Tamils and 25 Burghers. While these gains were being made steadily, there was a growing apprehension among the Tamils that their advantageous position in public life was threatened; some Sinhalese, on the other hand, were feeling that the gains were not coming quickly enough.

Ascribed Status and Sociohistorical Status

In the colonial setting the Sinhalese, although numerically a majority, were a subordinate group, not only politically but in socioeconomic terms as well. By the dawn of the twentieth century, however, revivalist endeavors had succeded in instilling a distinct vision of what might be termed "historical events as symbols of struggles, oppression . . . and moral and physical valour" in the community as a whole.[7] Beginning with the late nineteenth century the unearthing of the community's cultural heritage provided visible symbols that could inspire a heightened status within the group as well as for it in relation to other groups.[8]

Language Status

English was the language of "high culture" as the medium of technology, science, larger business, and governmental activity. Sinhala, however, with a long literary history and a substantial body of classical literature, proved to be a source of pride, particularly for the traditional intelligentsia. Here was a painful status discrepancy. The vision of former greatness compared with contemporary deprivation held the potential for stimulating what might be called "a belief structure of social change."[9]

6. The following account is based on K. M. de Silva 1986:87–95.
7. As enumerated by Giles et al. 1977:312.
8. See chapter 4.
9. As envisaged in the formula of Giles et al. 1977:312.

Demographic Factors

For the Sinhalese ethnolinguistic group their demographic vitality in relation to other ethnolinguistic groups in the same geographical environment would have constituted a structural factor conducive to a perception of alternatives to the existing status relationship. In the national territory, which was the island of Sri Lanka, they comprised 65.4 percent in 1931 and 69.4 percent in 1946 of the total population, in comparison with the next largest ethnolinguistic group, the Tamils–Sri Lankan and Indian–who made up 26.7 percent in 1931 and 22.7 percent in 1946. Contributing further to the vitality factor was the group's long history in the national territory–the island of Sri Lanka–which during that period became conceptually linked with ethnic and religious ideology.[10]

The presence, however, of elements inharmonious with and disruptive to the above conceptualizations, the most prominent among which was the Tamil community–concentrated in the northern part of the island, in settlements along the east coast, and, more disturbingly, in the central plantation areas as well as having a strong presence in neighboring south India–would have contributed to a gnawing doubt and fear by the Sinhalese community about its own demographic strength. Contributing further to these apprehensions was the immigration policy of the British authorities, which permitted the free influx of people from India and which tended to grant them civil rights very liberally, the most important of which was the franchise. Thus, the demographic vitality of the Sinhalese was affected by doubts and fears, which led to paranoia.

Institutional Support Factors

In institutional settings such as the national legislature, called the State Council (1931–47), the courts of law, the administration, and in higher levels of modern learning, the supremacy of English was unequivocal. Apart from the fact that the spreading of egalitarian ideologies in the wake of the political democratization demanded that English be replaced by the vernaculars in a wide range of domains, the supremacy of English itself had created glaring socioeconomic imbalances. There were uneven rates of the spread of English between the low-country and the Kandyan Sinhalese, between the Jaffna and Eastern Province

10. See chapter 1.

Tamils, between the "urban" and "rural" populations, and so on. Where the two main ethnic groups were concerned, however, it was clear that, as a community, the Tamils had received a disproportionately favorable share in the opportunity structure.

A good index to the relative sociopolitical strengths of the Sinhalese and the Tamils was available in the ethnic composition of the "educated Ceylonese" electorate of 1911 where proficiency in English and specific income and property qualifications were the criteria for enfranchisement. While the Sinhalese, comprising 75.1 percent of the indigenous adult male population, were represented by only 56.4 percent, the Tamils, only 14.5 percent of the same, made up as much as 36.4 percent of this electorate.[11] The census report of 1921 made an illuminating observation in this regard: "The Ceylon Tamils were ahead of the Low Country Sinhalese [the most modernized section of the Sinhalese community] in English literacy, though they were behind them in literacy generally."[12] This statement, among other things, provides the key to a consequential development in the years that followed: the further progress of vernacular literacy among the Sinhalese; rising aspirations among the burgeoning Sinhala-educated stratum, whose socioeconomic mobility was blocked by a language barrier; the perception of cognitive alternatives to the existing status relationship; and the adoption of the strategy of functional reallocation of languages within the polity to give an advantage to the majority community.

The Dynamics of Group Vitality Factors

It would have been evident from the above description of the pattern of strengths and weaknesses of the Sinhalese community in terms of its dimensions of group vitality factors that pressure might develop for greater institutional support. The relative strengths and weaknesses of three vitality factors—demography, institutional support, and economic status—makes this clear.

Under the circumstances high demographic vitality in the national territory could be utilized to tip the balance in other relevant areas in favor of the in-group:

Demographic Strength > Institutional Support > Status

11. Roberts 1973:283. The Indian Tamils, who were in the main estate laborers, generally did not have these educational and income qualifications.

12. *Census Report 1921*, vol. 1, pt. 2, 29.

Such a cognitive alternative to the existing status relationship became highly plausible in the context of the political changes taking place.

Political Developments and the Progress of the Language Problem: From "Sinhala and Tamil" to "Sinhala Only"

As described, opportunities for greater mobility and the distribution of power in socioeconomic terms pointed unequivocally to the supremacy of the English language over the vernaculars.[13] It was to be expected, however, that, with the sociopolitical transformation that followed social mobilization and the democratization of the political structure, "language problems" would crop up, specifically the demand for the reallocation of power and resources in favor of the indigenous languages.

The growth of literacy, the spread of mass media activity, and the emergence of voluntary associations in Sinhalese society during the late nineteenth and early twentieth centuries was followed by a substantial democratization of the political structure. The most momentous of all these events was possibly the "voting participation," having its maximum effect after 1931 when universal adult franchise was instituted. By bringing people out of the isolation of their localities into the participatory process at the national level it set the stage for mass political activity. As in many a new state during the early years of political activity along democratic lines, primordial loyalties provided the strongest and most reliable base for political action or appeal. Perhaps it was inevitable that some form of political transformation of ethnic interests was necessary at first to motivate populations that were used to traditionalist thinking. Thus, aspiring politicians found issues of language, religion, and alien immigration, for example, the best way to inspire a popular following. Mobilization meant in effect the mobilization of tradition – and in the process language became a powerful factor, the symbol of all other ethnic symbols.

Apart from such symbolic value, language was the key to positive economic and social resources, for it could very well be said that "the struggle of the languages is the struggle for jobs." Hence language could be the means by which the majority community might assert itself, politically and economically.

13. Also cf. "The social and economic structure of the country is still such that post-primary education in English continues to have high utility value . . . whereas social and economic conditions in the island render a post-primary education in Sinhalese and Tamil profitless" (*Administration Report of the Director of Education* 1944:6–8).

But what prospects did the Sinhalese community perceive for itself at the moment? During the recent cultural revival the Sinhalese had become aware of and responsive to their high sociohistorical status. At the same time, however, they had also become aware of their low economic status in relation to the aliens – European and Indian – and the fact that, as it was, the Sinhala language offered hardly any prospect in terms of conferring socioeconomic mobility. The demographic factor, as far as the national territory was concerned, was in their favor, but there lurked the eternal demographic threat from south India. In the dimension of group proportions the fact that the Sinhalese community was confined to the island of Sri Lanka while the most relevant out-group, the Tamils, had a massive camaraderie in the adjoining subcontinent appeared to negate the demographic vitality of the Sinhalese community.

These perceptions of group vitality and weakness had already appeared when the opportunity for mass political participation emerged. There were now available the means for group preservation through legislative and administrative processes. Although the British authorities still kept in their own hands crucial governmental functions such as finance and law enforcement, along with the power of veto over any legislation, virtual control over the larger area of internal government had passed to Sri Lankan hands.

From a communalist viewpoint the Sinhalese were an uneasy majority, despite their definitive conceptions of a "historical right" to rule the island of Sri Lanka.[14] And, after 1931, the next "logical and inevitable step" was to "self-government."[15] In the State Council, out of the total of fifty-eight seats, thirty-eight in 1931 and thirty-nine in 1936 were held by the Sinhalese, while others held twenty and nineteen seats, respectively. There was also the Indian issue to contend with: The franchise rights of those immigrating from India remained in place, although in a modified form, thus indicating the possibility that the Sinhalese could be outnumbered in some parts of their own national territory, especially in the plantation districts. Indeed, some Sinhalese politicians made no secret of their concern about the Sinhalese interests in this regard – for example, S. W. R. D. Bandaranaike and such congress stalwarts and senior members of the legislature as W. A. de Silva and Siripala Samarakkody.[16]

14. See chapter 1.
15. Governor Clifford, quoted in K. M. de Silva 1973h:489.
16. See Russel 1976:492–93.

As far as the majority of the Sinhalese political leadership was concerned, however, there was no possibility of open, vigorous, and full-scale advocacy of sectarian interests. Apart from their ideological inclinations—having been politically socialized under the aegis of British liberalist thinking—they had to tread with caution in a situation where the necessity to convince the British authorities of their "liberal capacity" assumed paramount importance.

All in all, then, for the Sinhalese politicians it was a difficult task to balance communal interests with egalitarian commitments. The State Council granted equal rights to Sinhala and Tamil in the language resolutions of 1932 and 1936.[17] But sociopolitical pressures would soon bring to the surface the latent disjunction between the two communities, and in this the predicament of the Tamil politicians was no better than that of their Sinhalese counterparts. The parting of the ways was briefly but unequivocally demonstrated in 1943, although faith in consensus politics was still strong enough, at least for the time being, to effect a compromise.[18] Yet the political expression of exclusive ethnolinguistic group interests had manifested itself in no uncertain terms.

In 1943 political developments in Sri Lanka had entered the crucial stage when a decision concerning the transfer of power was imminent. For those engaged in the cause of independence, political caution was extremely necessary—to put up a united effort by allaying minority fears on the one hand and by convincing the British authorities of the island people's liberal capacity on the other. Hence the concession to Tamil interests came to be granted without much hesitation in the official language resolution of 1943. Independence was achieved in 1948. Several years passed, and signs that institutional support and the status structure were being transformed in favor of the vernaculars and away from English were hardly visible. Indeed, the governing elite, drawn from the English-educated stratum, adopted a policy of very slow progress in these spheres. By the mid-1950s the Sinhalese intelligentsia was extremely discontent. This was the opportune climate for language to play a most salient political role, and, as could have been expected from the dynamics of the group vitality characteristics of the Sinhalese community, Sinhala Only as the official language became the most potent political slogan. It was a major issue and one by which the Mahajana Eksath Peramuna, led by S. W. R. D. Bandaranaike, was

17. See the discussion below.
18. See the discussion below.

voted into power by a large majority in April 1956. Two months later Bandaranaike presented to Parliament the Official Language Act—"to prescribe the Sinhala language as the one Official Language of Ceylon"—and it was passed by an overwhelming majority.

The language policy enactments moved by Sri Lankan politicians in the national legislature thus follow a sequence—from the balancing of Sinhalese *and* Tamil interests to an emphasis on the exclusive interests of Sinhala alone. That is:

1926	= Sinhala and Tamil
1932 (March)	= Sinhala and Tamil
1932 (July)	= Sinhala and Tamil
1936	= Sinhala and Tamil
1943	= Sinhala (later amended to include Tamil as well)
1956	= Sinhala Only

Legislative Attempts to Expand the Functional Use of Sinhala and Tamil

As mentioned, the processes of broadening political participation on an institutional basis and the rising importance attached to the popular will, which began in the 1920s, set the stage for the buildup of the "people's language" as a political cause. A precondition for these processes to reach their maximum potential came into being in 1931 with the granting of universal adult franchise. The number of voters registered jumped from about 4 percent of the population in 1924 to nearly 30 percent of the total in 1931 and nearly 50 percent of it when the second general election was held in 1936.[19]

For the aspiring politicians the concept of "the people" became a model and a standard. Since a seat in the legislature now depended on one's "closeness to the people," in an atmosphere of competitive politics the politicians could both *represent* the popular demand as well as *generate* it. Among other things, language was a salient issue in this regard, especially because the Sinhalese community was considerably mobilized at the time. It was a primal issue to sensitize the politically active sections of the populace—the vernacular intelligentsia including the *bhikkhus,* the Sinhalese schoolteachers and journalists. Hence the issue of giving more functional space to the "language of the people"

19. *Report* 1945:54.

as against the language of the colonial master was taken up in the legislature.

The Use of Sinhala and Tamil in the Debates of the State Legislature

On 9 March 1932 G. K. W. Perera, a Buddhist leader and an alumnus of the prestigious Buddhist school, Ananda College, in Colombo, who had received the bachelors of arts and laws in London and had entered the State Council as the member for Matara in the Southern Province, moved a resolution in the State Council that the council's standing orders be amended to allow Sinhala or Tamil to be used in conducting business in the council. In the course of the debate that followed Perera stated, in answering an objection that some members would not be able to understand the speeches made in Sinhala and Tamil:

> I think it would be very fine to encourage the study of Sinhalese or Tamil, to insist on the electorates returning people who know the languages of the country. . . . We do not want people to come here and represent—to claim to represent—the interests of the people of this country if they do not understand the language. (*Debates, SC* 1932:3118)

Here we see a repetition of a nationalist stance taken by James D'Alwis in the mid nineteenth century: that for good government the governing elite should know the language of the governed. In an era of democratic politics the claim had an irresistible appeal. Indeed, G. K. W. Perera claimed, in replying to an objection on constitutional grounds:

> We want to assert our elementary rights to carry administration and legislation in this house . . . in the language the people understand. (*Debates, SC* 1932:3220)

Similarly, senior politician E. W. Perera asserted:

> It is the inherent right of every representative assembly . . . that they should have the right to speak in the language which the majority of the people know. (*Debates, SC* 1932:3222–23)

To support his claim, E. W. Perera cited the cases of the Canadian legislature, where the representatives have the right to speak in French or English, and the South African assembly, where they have the right to speak in Afrikaans or English. Another councillor, E. A. P. Wijeyeratne, mentioned how in 1901 this right was asserted in the British House of Commons with regard to the Irish language and how in New Zealand the Maori language was permitted in the deliberations of the legislature. Councillor A. Ratnayake pointed out that in India in the Bihar and Orissa legislative assembly no fewer than three languages were spoken. In this way the English-educated elite were bringing in their knowledge of nationalist struggles elsewhere to advocate the cause of the vernacular. And, of course, they were concerned about the exigencies of the political developmental process and the place of the people's language in it. Thus, Wijeyeratne declared:

> I think a beginning has to be made if we are serious, really serious, as regards the future government of this country. *If it is the intention of the people of this country that the government should be a national government,* responsible to the people of this country, I think it is but necessary that the *government should be conducted in the two national languages known to this country—Sinhalese and Tamil.* (*Debates, SC* 1932:3326; emphasis added)

G. K. W. Perera's resolution failed, however, to change the standing orders of the council; although it obtained a majority vote, it failed to secure the necessary two-thirds majority.

Sinhala and Tamil for Administrative Functions

A second resolution presented by G. K. W. Perera for the functional expansion of the vernaculars, which was tabled in July 1932, came up for debate on 16 February 1934. This resolution sought to carry the functional allocation of the vernaculars further—to affect the administrative machinery as well as the legal structure. Its intent was:

1. To ensure that appointment into the Civil and Clerical Services be restricted to persons who had reached a "high standard in Sinhalese or Tamil."

2. To limit future promotions in both above services to those who "showed proficiency in Sinhalese or Tamil."
3. To ensure that appointments to the posts of Police Magistrate and President of higher criminal courts be limited to persons of "proved . . . ability to conduct and record proceedings in Sinhalese and Tamil," and
4. To establish the right of lawyers "to conduct criminal trials in Sinhalese or Tamil."

(*Debates, SC* 1934, 1:224)

This resolution too harked back in its content to the views of James D'Alwis. It was evident that the question raised by this nineteenth-century nationalist concerning vernacular proficiency in the administrative and legal service still remained unsolved. By the time G. K. W. Perera's resolution appeared in the legislature, apart from the broader egalitarian principle involved, there was a new dimension to the problem. English-educated Sri Lankans were now pressing for the indigenization of the administrative service. The employment interests of "the sons of the soil" could now be promoted under the guise of a democratic principle—proficiency in the language of the people. For as late as 1923 the twenty-three highest positions in the administrative service were still reserved for British expatriates, together with twenty-two out of the twenty-seven at the second highest level. Hence there was by the 1930s mounting pressure for the "Ceylonization" of these higher positions, called the Civil Service. A year before Perera's resolution the State Council resolved that the appointment of non-Ceylonese to the service should cease. A program of Ceylonization was introduced subsequently.[20]

The fact that the indigenous languages were being used in a way as instruments for promoting the interests of Sri Lankans against foreigners does not cancel the fact that in many areas of government the use of English placed the bulk of the population at a tremendous disadvantage. Indeed, G. K. W. Perera's second resolution was addressed to such a grievance—this was in the sphere of the administration of justice. Like the non-Magyar peasant in imperial Hungary, the

20. For the 1923 figures, see Ludowyk 1966:80. For changes in the 1930s, see Warnapala 1973:415–16.

Sri Lankan peasant too stood "like an ox before the courts of his native land."[21]

The Use of Sinhala and Tamil in the Administration of Justice

The cause of the Sri Lankan masses came to be taken up more vigorously by the Marxist politicians, who appeared on the scene in the mid-1930s. Launched by a small group of intellectuals who had returned to the island after university and professional education in Europe, the Marxist movement assumed institutional form in 1935 with the establishment of the Lanka Sama Samaja (Equal Society) party. Two Marxists entered the State Council at the 1936 elections: Philip Gunawardene (1900–1972), who had studied at the University of Wisconsin, and N. M. Perera (1905–79), a Ph.D. from the London School of Economics. With their strong espousal of egalitarian causes the Marxists took up, among other things, the right of the people to use their mother tongue in dealing with the government. The specific area that they selected for the assertion of this right was the sphere of the administration of justice. Thus, Gunawardene presented a resolution on 3 July 1936 which was addressed to two issues: first,

> in view of the frequent defeat of the ends of justice caused by inaccuracy in recording police station entries in English by policemen and sergents, who are proficient neither in the vernacular nor in English . . . that entries made at police stations . . . be recorded in the language which they were originally stated. (*Debates, SC* 1936, 1:881)

Second,

> in view of the grave hardship and injustices attending the loss of accuracy in interpretation and re-interpretation of questions and answers in Court proceedings . . . in the Municipal and Police courts of the Island the proceedings should be conducted in the vernacular. (*Debates, SC* 1936, 1:881)

21. For the Magyar situation, see Inglehart and Woodward 1967, from which this phrase is borrowed.

This resolution was passed after a lengthy debate, with thirty-four assenting, four opposing, and one declining to vote. Gunawardene succinctly put the aim of his resolution as the freeing of "the villager" from "the oppression and injustice that he suffers from daily at the hands of Magistrates and Lawyers and Interpreter Mudaliyars."[22] Thus, for the Marxists there was a strong instrumental reason for taking up the issue of the medium of administration. Especially in the administration of justice in imperial territories, the use of the metropolitan language amounted to what might be termed "a structured linguistic blackout,"[23] as far as the large mass of the population was concerned. It was a blackout extending from the time the complaint is made to the police until its resolution in the courts of law. If G. K. W. Perera's earlier proposal for the use of Sinhala and Tamil in government administration reflected more of a symbolic assertion in the cause of the indigenous language, Gunawardene's emphasized the legal-rational implications of modern governmental activity.

It has been noted that in the early stages of political development the paternalistic orientation of the leadership tends to consider "government *for* the people . . . many times more important than government *by* the people."[24] The older generation of Sri Lankan political leaders, who appear to have had such an outlook, now found a strong challenge to their position in the "political education" of the masses by the Marxists.[25] Much of the Marxist invective on the old-guard politicians could be directly linked to the counterelitist sentiments of earlier years. As before, the neglect of the national languages by the elite was a prominent theme in these accusations.[26]

The Mobilization of Sinhalese Ethnicity and the Emergence of Sinhalese Exclusivism

Viewed from the perspective of language-related legislation in the 1920s, the resolutions of 1932 and 1936 reflected a continuation in policy

22. *Debates, SC* 1937, 2:189.
23. Kidder (1976:236) about colonial India.
24. Clerk 1974:24.
25. Lerski 1968:27–28.
26. For example, N. M. Perera's indictment of Francis De Zoysa and Bandaranaike in *Debates, SC* 1937, 2:165–66, 175–78.

by the Sri Lankan political leadership of promoting the cause of the indigenous languages, Sinhala and Tamil, in favor of English.

In the context of the interethnic relations between the Sinhalese and the Tamils this orientation, while falling in line with precedent, shared the optimistic anticipations of the Donoughmore commissioners, who framed the 1931 constitution. They denounced the principle adopted so far of communal representation, calling it "a canker in the body politic, eating deeper and deeper into the vital energies of the people, breeding self-interest, suspicion and animosity." Their argument was that "only by its abolition will it be possible for the various diverse communities to develop together a true national unity."[27] The fact that the post-1931 era witnessed the emergence of political configurations along noncommunal lines was evidently a fulfillment of this expectation. The Marxist LSSP, which in its structural characteristics was the first modern political organization in the island, had a program of political, social, and economic development catering to all ethnolinguistic communities, and its membership was drawn from all the communities in the island.[28] At this time, even in an organizationally much looser forum, the Ceylon National Congress, reaffirmations were being made of "Ceylonese Nationalism." [29]

Such fulfillments of the hopes of the Donoughmore commissioners, however, did not constitute the dominant tendency in the political process of the day. As noted earlier, some time before the adoption of the new constitution there appeared, with the liberalizing changes in the political structure, unmistakable signs that communal interests would be politicized. Ethnicity was emerging as the most effective resource for political mobilization, becoming a strategic site from which to face the uncertainties of sociopolitical change. For from the 1920s onward Sri Lanka entered a crucial stage of political development in which basic power relationships within the polity were fundamentally altered in unpredictable ways. In such a situation the eruption of deep communal anxieties was inevitable. Although the first signs of these alterations had become apparent by the early 1920s, it was with the adoption of the Donoughmore Constitution in 1931 that the most vital period of the transfer of power began.

In the context of the group dynamics of the Sri Lankan society of

27. *Report* 1928:39, 99.

28. Lerski 1968:27–28.

29. See Roberts 1977:1126, 1156, 1241.

the day ethnicity seemed to provide the strongest and most reliable base for political action. Thus, there emerged the All Ceylon Moors Association of 1935, the Sinhala Maha Sabha (Great Association of the Sinhalese) established in roughly 1934 to 35, the Burgher Political Association of 1938, and the Ceylon Indian Congress of 1939, all of which were "updatings" of ethnicity to suit the new circumstances. As noted earlier, the emergence of the Tamil Mahajana Sabhai in 1921 had signaled the rise of political organizations on ethnic lines, but it was an isolated incident. What happened in the 1930s amounted to a significant change in the sociopolitical system.

It has already been pointed out that "organized manipulation of ethnicity" not only produces "heightened ethnic consciousness" but also heightens "language consciousness and language loyalty."[30] The effect would, in fact, be reciprocal. The catalysts in bringing about these consequences are the "cultural entrepreneurs," who enlarge "the solidarity resources of the community," in particular those resources connected with language, and "political entrepreneurs," who proceed to mobilize ethnicity by focusing on collective aspirations in the sociopolitical realm.[31] In Sri Lanka the sequence of these developments was such that the activities of the political entrepreneurs became significant somewhat earlier than those of the cultural entrepreneurs.

The Sinhala Maha Sabha and the Politicization of Sinhalese Ethnicity

The Sinhala Maha Sabha (SMS), which was formed in 1934–35, was the brainchild of S. W. R. D. Bandaranaike (1899–1959), a scion of a low-country aristocratic family who had graduated from Oxford and returned to the island in the mid-1920s to enter politics. Bandaranaike described the aims of the organization as a very desirable form of communalism, where all that is valuable to a community—its traditions, its culture, its literature, its language—is fostered; where an attempt is made *"to obtain the true advancement of a community by composing the various differences of caste, religion, and so on within the community, while not forgetting the higher unity, that of [all] communities."*[32]

The ideological antecedents of this stance could be observed in

30. Fishman 1977b:17.
31. Young 1976:46; Rabushka and Shepsle 1972:59.
32. Bandaranaike 1961:67; emphasis added.

some early concomitants of the modernization process. Sociocultural modernization in the nineteenth century had led, among other things, to the mobilization of tradition, in that parochial loyalties such as caste, region, and religion had become bases for mobilization.[33] As their initial fervor was subsiding somewhat and power relations between communities were becoming the central issue of the day, there emerged a compelling need for unity and solidarity within the Sinhalese community. Apart from that, the mobilizational potential of Sinhalese ethnicity would have been quite obvious to the ambitious political aspirant who was just entering the political arena and was set on making a place for himself in an already crowded platform of political leadership. Furthermore, with a highly Westernized and Christian family background, Bandaranaike belonged to a social category that was steadily becoming outdated among the political leadership; thus, a personal identity crisis also played a part. Open and vigorous commitment to the cause of Sinhalese ethnic nationalism would have addressed both these problems. Not long after returning to the island Bandaranaike became a Buddhist and started wearing the newly designed national dress.[34] The founding of the Sinhala Maha Sabha may be considered a further step in this program.

In its original agenda the Sinhala Maha Sabha seems to have resembled other ethnicity-based and mobility-conscious movements in colonial societies such as the "Getting Up" movement in Igboland and the Self-Respect movement in south India,[35] which sought by means of communal mobilization to further the interests of the group on several fronts. Thus, when the SMS was inaugurated three panels were instituted: a religious panel, where the majority were *bhikkhus;* a literary panel, composed of literary men and scholars; and a political panel, headed by Bandaranaike himself who was also the president of the SMS and remained so during its lifespan. Soon the SMS shifted into an exclusively political function, and the other panels withered away.

Bandaranaike, while remaining a member of the Ceylon National Congress, devoted his time and energy to the development of links with the political periphery—the rural areas and the vernacular intelligentsia—through the SMS. He was in a tremendously advantageous

33. See chapter 5.

34. In 1921 P. de S. Kularatna, the principal of Ananda College, introduced the "national dress" that is popular today.

35. For these organizations in other societies, see Young 1976:99; and M. Singer 1972:383.

position in this regard by being the president of the All Ceylon Village Committees Conference, a post he held from about 1930 for over two decades. Indeed, Bandaranaike's success in penetrating and mobilizing rural Sri Lanka was demonstrated convincingly in the 1950s.[36] The Sabha no doubt provided a national platform for the politically active local elite such as Sinhala schoolteachers, *ayurvedic* physicians, Sinhala traders, and other village-level political activists, more so because, with the gradual decline of the Mahajana Sabhas after the demise of F. R. Senanayake, there was no similar national platform for this rapidly expanding stratum with rising aspirations.

The efforts of the SMS leadership to make a political impact were facilitated by the availability of a mobilizational groundswell created during the religiocultural revival of the late nineteenth and early twentieth century. That revival had created a communicational and ideological infrastructure, which had become a self-sustaining factor even after the initial revivalist fervor had subsided. Mass media in the form of newspapers, periodicals, theater, and belletristic writings continued with great vigor and were steadily expanding with the increase in literacy. The conceptualization of the Arya-Sinhala identity and the reaffirmation of the *Sinhaladvīpa* and the *Dharmadvīpa* concepts were salient features of the updated communal identity.

As noted earlier, however, the ideological orientations of the national political leadership, deeply steeped as they were in British traditions, had prevented the utilization of this mobilizational groundswell for explicit political purposes. There was a socially mobilized Sinhalese intelligentsia: journalists, schoolteachers, *ayurvedic* physicians, and Buddhist monks who could provide excellent material for specifically political mobilization. The advantages of tapping these resources would have been obvious to any political entrepreneur after the grant of universal franchise in 1931. It was to Bandaranaike's credit that he, more than any other, perceived this potential. While the older generation of political leaders were mostly involved in "national politics" concerning the transfer of power, Bandaranaike was busy forging links with the political periphery in rural Sri Lanka and utilizing the mobilizational potential of the underlying substratum of religiocultural nationalism.

---

36. Bandaranaike founded the Sri Lanka Freedom party in 1951, merging the SMS with other similar interest groups. Bandaranaike's resounding electoral victory in 1956 and the party's later successes are attributable to its solid power base in the rural areas.

Geertz has pointed out that "the institution of universal suffrage . . . [makes] the temptation to court the masses by appealing to traditional loyalties virtually irresistible."[37] In Sri Lanka universal suffrage had been introduced to a society where traditional loyalties had been updated by revivalist activity. A distinct set of custodians of tradition had emerged, and the Sinhala Maha Sabha was able to attract this segment of the Sinhalese community. Thus, the Sabha catered to a cogent need of the day as far as the Sinhalese community was concerned: In an atmosphere of political conceptualization on ethnic lines, the Sabha came forward "to work for and defend their interests."[38] The "defence" of the crucial desiderata of communal identity, a very potent rallying call for nationalist endeavors would have suited the Sinhalese interpretation of the situation more than anything else.

The importance of the Sabha has to be understood also in relation to the stratum of the populace it was able to mobilize. As one of the first major attempts at political mobilization of the rural areas, it contributed to the implanting of ethnically biased political thinking in a relatively unexploited political terrain. The simultaneous foray of the Marxist LSSP into rural areas was limited to certain localities,[39] and the Sabha's links with the villages was more extensive. One important distinction has to be made, however. The Sabha was never an organized political party, and its effect was more in conceptual formulation than in behavioral manifestation. Yet the political conceptualizations prepared by the Sabha may be considered the foundation upon which Bandaranaike, the political entrepreneur, and Sinhalese language nationalism, the political movement, raised their triumphant edifices in the 1950s.

As we have seen, Bandaranaike chose to remain within the congress fold while organizing and utilizing the Sinhala Maha Sabha. This was possible because the congress never was an organized and regimented political party. The SMS too was not a neatly structured organization. The ideology it envisaged, however, attracted much attention and some opposition. For it was the first island-wide association giving political expression to specifically Sinhalese ethnic interests. Hence it was condemned by many as a communal organization. The (Tamil) Youth Congress of Jaffna saw it as "avowedly communal";[40] and the

37. Geertz 1963:123.

38. Bandaranaike, quoted in Youth Congress 1939:84.

39. Lerski 1968: chap. 2. Also see Jayawardene 1971; and Roberts 1969.

40. Youth Congress 1939:9.

Marxist state councillor Philip Gunawardene referred to it as "the most rabid, the most narrow minded, most chauvinist organization . . . not a national organization but a tribal one . . . appealing to the basest instincts of the people."[41] Such criticisms were probably indicative as much of the ideological orientation of the critics as of the Sabha's ideology. Also among the higher political circles of the day, inspired as they were by European concepts of national integration and liberalism, ethnic and tribal loyalties could be viewed as "divisive, barbarous and vile . . . symbols of pollution and all that was politically detestable."[42] Hence Bandaranaike, while exploiting the mobilizational potential of Sinhalese ethnicity, tended to be moderate in his demands. Indeed, we see him more often on the defensive. In replying to his critics, he had to work out a formula based on the acceptance of and deference to the fact that the island population was structured in cultural segments. "If national unity is the aim," he declared once,

> surely the best method was to start from the lower rung: firstly unity among the Sinhalese and secondly, whilst uniting the Sinhalese, to work for the higher unity, the unity of all communities.[43]

Bandaranaike seems to have believed that, if it were posed in such a form, the program of the Sabha would be a feasible political proposition. The mobilization of Sinhalese ethnicity, however, in the name of defense, while parallel mobilizations were taking place in other ethnic groups, was fraught with the danger of reinforcing and updating traditional polarizations—particularly in a context where the masses were being suddenly thrown into the political arena. The mutually reinforcing effects of the politicization and ideologization of ethnicity resulted in the creation of barriers to the building up of a cohesive all island national consciousness.

As far as the Sinhalese community was concerned, the ideologization of ethnicity had already been largely accomplished. The religiocultural revival witnessed a weaving together of traditionalist ideological strands into a comprehensive solidarity system. The integrated interpretation of the past included a definitive image of Sinhalese-Buddhist rights over the island and the triumphant defense of the Sin-

41. *Debates, SC* 1939, 2:138.
42. Roberts 1978.
43. Quoted in Roberts 1978:360.

halese people and the Buddhist dispensation against aliens, the most salient among them being the south Indian invaders.[44]

Thus, whatever the conceptual ramifications of working for Sinhala unity and the defense of Sinhalese interests would have been to the Oxford-educated Bandaranaike and the small English-educated hierarchy of the Sinhala Maha Sabha, it possibly could not have been the same in the minds of the rank-and-file member drawn from the vernacular-educated stratum. Translated into the rhetoric of the vernacular language culture, working as it was within the confines of abrasive and anxiety-ridden history and mythology, the Sinhalese group mobilization would have simply amounted to the relating of identity to conflict.

In this way the 1930s witnessed the first signs of organized political activity by the Sinhalese on communal lines. The mobilizational groundswell of the revivalist era had been tapped for political purposes by leaders such as Bandaranaike, particularly in the unexploited ground of the political periphery. It must be emphasized, however, that this mobilization of communal interests was not confined to the Sinhalese ethnic group. There were parallel communal mobilizations among others, particularly the Tamils. In spite of the preliminary constraints, which precluded open and vigorous espousal of communal interests, the groundwork had been prepared for the articulation of communal interests. Perhaps it is inherent in the very process of political development in new democracies that such moderation and restraint be only a passing phase. The next inevitable stage is that of heightened ethnic passions and the ethnicization of public affairs. The push into that stage is provided by the "outbidders," who promise "more,"[45] ideologically as well as in the supply of political goods.

As for the Sinhalese community, there emerged in the late 1930s a movement that sought to inject Sinhalese ethnicity with an unprecedented ideological tenor, thus transforming it into a rallying call, a cause worthy of fighting for and even dying for. The most important factor with regard to this movement was its emphasis on language as the focus of group mobilization. This movement was the work of a small band of enthusiasts led by a charismatic figure named Munidasa Cumaratunga.

44. See chapter 5.

45. These concepts have been borrowed from Sartori 1966.

The Heḷa Movement and the Ideological Pinnacle of Language Nationalism

The Heḷa movement, whose high tide was observable from about 1939 to 1944, was characterized by a rare and advanced ideological commitment in the cause of the Sinhala language. While the Sinhala Maha Sabha tended to view Sinhalese identity as componentially and experiantially multifaceted, the affirmation of group identity by the Heḷa movement was emphatic on the placement of language squarely at the emotional and intellectual center of ethnic identity. Hence in spite of the fact that this heightened and integrated behavior toward language was confined to a small group of activists, the inexorable emphasis on the language component of the communal identity by the Heḷa movement seems to have exerted a profound influence on the group assertive activity of the Sinhalese people in the years that followed.

Cumaratunga, "The Great Helese"

Munidasa Cumaratunga (1887–1944), the son of an *ayurvedic* physician, was born at Dikhena in the Matara district of the Southern Province. He received his primary education in Oriental languages in a *pirivena* in the vicinity and in English at St. Thomas College, Matara. Hoping to be a schoolteacher, he arrived in Colombo and entered the Government Teachers Training College.

As a student in the training college, Cumaratunga made himself conspicuous by his propensity to question the views of teachers there. His challenge to authority was observable throughout his career: for example, his condemnation of *bhikkhu* Sri Rahula of the fifteenth century, one of the most esteemed among the classical Sinhala scholars and the author of the poem *Kāvyasēkharaya,* which resulted in a public controversy in the 1920s;[46] his relentless criticism of the Sinhalese dictionary project, headed by the veteran politician and Oriental scholar D. B. Jayatilaka;[47] and above all, his repudiation of the Ārya-Sinhala identity with its Indic orientation, in order to uphold an exclusively indigenous, Heḷa, identity.[48]

46. See Weerasekera 1938.

47. This project, inaugurated in 1927, was criticized by Cumaratunga for its conservative policy and slow progress. Only in February 1992 did the dictionary office claim that its work had been completed.

48. See the discussion below.

The relentless consistency of Cumaratunga's nationalistic approach prompted him not merely to challenge the dominance of English but also to reject, in the name of the same principle, the dominance of Pāli and Sanskrit, which his compatriots considered an honor and a privilege to retain. In his opinion:

> Of late we have been committing a great mistake. That is, using in our writings as many borrowings as possible from Sanskrit. In the same manner as it is considered fashionable today to lean towards English, those who lived sometime ago thought it very cultured to lean towards Sanskrit. . . . Now we have a duty to perform. That is, to do our best to emancipate the Sinhala language. Without impairing our conviction we must attempt, wherever possible, to use pure Sinhala. We must attack the mean idea that without borrowing from Sanskrit, Pāli, Tamil or English it is not possible to express the thoughts of the Sinhalese. (*Subasa* 1, no. 3 [1939]: 29)

The principle of linguistic independence was thus pursued to its logical conclusion. Cumaratunga thus represents a certain type of nationalist ideology – uncompromising and ruthless in the pursuit of the ideal of cultural insularity.

Cumaratunga joined the education department as a teacher and was soon promoted to the post of inspector of Anglo-vernacular schools. But in 1922 he left government service to embark on a career devoted to the pursuit of his nationalist ideology. This career of freelance journalism, teaching, and organizational activity reached its climactic phase with the inauguration of the Sinhala journal *Subasa* (Good Language) in 1939 and the English journal *The Helio* in 1941 and the founding of the Heḷa Havula (Pure Sinhala Fraternity) in 1941. In the eyes of his followers he assumed messianic proportions and was given the appellations *Guru Devi* (Teacher Divine), *Cumaratuṅgu Muni* (Cumratunga the Sage), and *Maha Heḷa* (the Great Helese).[49]

The Exclusivist Emphasis on Communal Identity

The premise on which Cumaratunga launched his endeavor was the same as that envisaged by the religiocultural revivalists of the preceding era – the avowed rationale for nativistic activity being the desire to

49. For these appellations, see Ahubudu 1957; D. V. R. de Silva 1969; and Gunawadu 1957.

"restore" the ethnic uniqueness and cultural greatness of the community which, they believed, existed in a remote past and from which a decline had occurred only in the recent past. Although he may thus be considered as heir to Migettuwatte and Dharmapala,[50] there was a marked difference in Cumaratunga's stance which at first might tend to eclipse the ideological continuity. The communal authenticity, as envisaged by Cumaratunga, was exclusively indigenous, and in this light all features of the accepted identity which came from outside, including the origin myth connecting the Sinhalese people to Āryan India and the Pāli and Sanskrit linguistic heritage, were considered anathema to the uniqueness of the Heḷa national identity.

The Heḷa identity upheld by Cumaratunga was, in effect, a repudiation of the Ārya-Sinhala identity forged during the religiocultural revival. Speaking of the religious component of the national identity, Cumaratunga declared:

> One can change one's religion as many times as one likes. But even the gods cannot change one's nationality without changing one's birth. Let all be Heḷa in nationality, caste, language and religion. Heḷa religion is that which a person professes according to his conscience. (*Helio* 1, nos. 7 and 8 [1941]: 56)

Being a Buddhist himself, Cumaratunga ventured to consider religion (i.e., Buddhism as envisaged in the Ārya-Sinhala identity) as an extraneous factor as far as the unity emanating from the communal birthright was concerned. As for that authentic heritage, it was believed that the community was autochthonous, without any ancestral obligations to an external source. Thus, speaking of the generally accepted idea of Vijayan colonization, Cumaratunga declared:

> It is a slur on the Helese nation to say that the arch robber Vijaya and his fiendish followers were its progenitors. Many thousands of years before their arrival we had empires greater and mightier than the greatest and mightiest that any other nation could claim to have had. (*Helio* 1, nos. 11 and 12 [1941]: 87)

The reiteration, although in a highly exaggerated form, of a belief held by James D'Alwis about a century earlier, is obviously indicative

50. For these nationalist activists, see chapter 4.

of a strand of opinion—a subconscious fancy, as it were—found among certain sections of the Sinhalese intelligentsia. Cumaratunga, however, is the first nationalist ideologue to have elaborated it and give it wide publicity.

Furthermore, it needs to be noted that the Heḷa conception of the community's history differs markedly from that held by D'Alwis. In the case of D'Alwis pre-Vijayan antiquity was sought for the purpose of establishing direct and immediate connections with Indo-Āryan sources. For Cumaratunga, on the other hand, pre-Vijayan antiquity bespoke of an unobliged authenticity—a Fichtean *Ur-volk* status. In his opinion,

> those who consider that we, our language and our customs etc. are derived from someone else do indeed disparage us. There is perhaps no other nation older than we. How can we therefore accept the idea that everything of ours is derived from outside? (*Subasa* 1, no. 4 [1939]: 43)

According to the Heḷa theory of the island's history, long before the beginning of the lineage of kings recorded in the *Mahāvaṃśa* Sri Lanka was populated by the Heḷa people who built up a great civilization. The land itself was much larger, extending over to Madagaskar. Great monarchs such as Tāraka and Rāvaṇa, who could effectively challenge the military might of the mightiest of Indian empires, ruled the Heḷa kingdom. This great civilization came to an end due to the treachery of "Heḷa traitors" such as Vibhīṣaṇa and Kuvēṇi, who fraternized with the Indians, and, consequently, Indian influences swept over the kingdom, debasing and corrupting, among other things, the language of the Heḷa people.[51]

The same convictions of Heḷa preeminence underlies Cumaratunga's attitude toward Pāli and Sanskrit, which D'Alwis was eager to consider as closely allied with the original Sinhala language and which were held in high regard as *matṛ bhāṣa* (parent languages) by the

51. The Heḷa interpretation of the community's history is found scattered in a number of writings. See Cumaratunga's speech in 1931, recorded in Cumaratunga 1962:71–80; and his contributions to *Helio* 1, nos. 11 and 12 (1941): 87; and nos. 14 and 15 (1941): 124–25; and in *Subasa* 2, no. 25 (1941): 392–95. These ideas were further elaborated by his associate R. Tennakoon in "The Hidden History of the Helese," which appeared in several installments in *Helio*, vol. 1. Tāraka and Rāvaṇa appear in the Hindu epic *Rāmāyaṇa* along with Vibhīṣaṇa, and Kuvēṇi appears in the *Mahāvaṃśa*. The bias in favor of India found in these works has been turned the other way by the Heḷa historiography.

promulgators of the Ārya-Sinhala identity. In Cumaratunga's conception, however,

> Pāli, one of the so called mothers of the Helese language has been fathered by the Helese themselves. How far the Sanskrit language has been enriched by the ancient Helese language, only time will disclose. (*Helio* 1, nos. 11 and 12 [1941]: 87)

With such vehement repudiations of the accepted theory on the origins of the language, culture, and genes of the community, the exclusivist emphasis of the Helese identity was complete. "The myth," as has been pointed out by Georges Sorel, "must be judged as a means of acting on the present; any attempt to discuss how far it can be taken literally . . . is devoid of sense."[52] The Heḷa myth, as we shall see, had a cogent sociopolitical purpose. Its assertions were evocative of a compelling need in the communal consciousness to sharpen the boundaries, particularly with regard to India. Thus, it can be said that the Helese myth, like the nationalist myths pointed out by Joshua A. Fishman, sought "to mobilize and motivate, to clarify (even by distorting) and to activate (even by over-dramatizing)."[53]

The material from which the Helese ideology was constructed was present in the community's ideological tradition. Some time back, D'Alwis, writing the history of Sinhalese literature, had shown an unmistakable partiality to the "genuine Sinhala" (Eḷu, or Heḷa) language, deploring its historical "decline" due to admixture with Sanskrit and Pāli. After D'Alwis there was the religiocultural revival, whose major emphasis was the country's Buddhist heritage; in it was evident a strong partiality for Indic connections—Buddhism itself being an Indian legacy. Furthermore, there was the theory of Vijayan colonization, as promulgated in the Sinhalese historical chronicles, which were consulted over and over again in the course of revivalist enthusiasm; and then the fascination for Pāli and Sanskrit, deeply embedded in the scholarly tradition, all of which fitted together neatly in the Ārya-Sinhala identity, as actively promoted under the guidance of traditionalist scholars, most of whom were *bhikkhus*.

The Heḷa identity, on the other hand, epitomized a straining toward purer and more genuine expressions of the communal heritage.

52. Sorel 1961:125.
53. Fishman 1976b:21.

Hence like the self-respect movement emphasizing the Dravidian heritage in contemporary south India, the Heḷa movement sought a fundamental detachment from all extraneous traditions.[54] The repudiation of the theory of Indic origins and the denial of any importance to the Buddhist religion were obviously means to such an end.

Significantly, the keystone of the Helese identity was the pure Sinhala (Eḷu, or Heḷa) language. In place of the ethnoreligious trinity "land, nation and religion" (*raṭa, jātiya, āgama*) upheld during the religiocultural revival,[55] Cumaratunga insisted on the adoption of "language, nation and land" (*basa, räsa, desa*) as the symbols of nationalist endeavor. The selection as well as the shift in emphasis of elements found in the latter trinity are of crucial significance: *Religion* has been replaced by *language,* and *language* has been given precedence over *nation* and *land* by placing it first. *Language,* the emblem of communal authenticity par excellence, in Cumaratunga's usage specifically referred to its most genuine phenomenological manifestation.

The Language Component of the Heḷa Ideology

The Eḷu, or Heḷa (Helese), idiom upheld by Cumaratunga bespoke of what is unique in the historical phenomenon that is the Sinhalese language. Amid its diversity in time as well as space Cumaratunga found the Heḷa idiom the most authentic embodiment of the ancestral genius of the community.

Considered historically, the Heḷa language form represents the individual and separate development of Sinhalese from its Indic origins. In the historical evolution of Sinhala clear indications of this separate development were manifested by about the sixth century. A distinctly Sinhala (Eḷu) linguistic element is thus discernible in the stone inscriptions of this "proto-Sinhalese" period.[56] Those specifically Sinhala features became more numerous as time went on. They were prominent in the literary compositions that appeared about two centuries later. The most notable among the latter were the verse compositions, whose

54. For the "Self Respect" movement, see M. Singer 1972:383–441. I have no evidence of a direct influence of this movement on the Heḷa ideology.

55. For example, in Dharmapala's writings. See *SB*, 30 September 1911; and 2 March 1912.

56. The evolution of the Sinhala language from Indic roots is traced through four stages as Sinhala Prakrit (ca. 2d c. B.C. *to* A.D. 3d c.); Proto-Sinhalese (c. 3d c. to 8th c.); Middle Sinhalese (ca. 8th c. to 13th c.); and Modern Sinhala (ca. 13th c. onward). See Jayatilaka 1933; and Geiger 1938:3–4.

earliest examples were the Sigiri graffiti written during the period from about the eighth to the tenth centuries.[57] Because of a convention that had come to be established during this period, it became customary to use Eḷu as the exclusive medium of verse composition while employing *miśra Sinhala,* which was Sinhala mixed with Pali and Sanskrit borrowings, as the standard medium of prose compositions. This convention continued, by and large, to modern times.

The first exception to this arrangement appeared in the fifteenth century when, in a new verse genre of royal panegyrics, Sanskrit, Pāli, and Tamil words came to be included in verse compositions, evidently for onomatopoeic purposes.[58] Such compositions, however, were few and far between. The first generation of modern poets, in the late nineteenth century and early twentieth, followed the traditional convention, but gradually it was abandoned and is no longer considered essential.

In the maintenance of separate linguistic forms for verse and prose compositions, then, a conventional restriction applied only to the language of verse. Thus, it is found that during the classical period of Sinhalese literature (i.e., from about the eighth to about the fifteenth century A.D.), while *miśra Sinhala* remained the commonly used medium of prose composition, writers sometimes resorted to an exclusively Eḷu idiom, specifically in passages with a highly poetic content. Such code switching illustrated the accepted conventions and the association of Eḷu with poetic expression. In this way Eḷu while it represented the most authentic, unique, and hence maximally contrastive manifestation of the Sinhala language, was, as far as traditional literary conventions were concerned, an idiom confined to verse.

Cumaratunga, however, was to repudiate this convention regarding the use of Eḷu. Although he employed *miśra Sinhala* in his prose writings up to about 1940, thereafter he adopted an exclusively Eḷu idiom in prose as well as in verse. This linguistic shift is illustrated below in two passages representative of the two periods—one he wrote to a journal in 1926 and the other from a correspondence in 1941 to *Subasa,* the journal he edited:

1. vanmālāva gē nairmalyaya da, arthayā gē vaiśadyaya da śiṣyayan gē sukhāvabōdhaya da, patannā vū samikṣyakārī

57. Of this graffiti 680 have been deciphered. See Paranavitana 1956.
58. For details, see M. W. S. de Silva 1970.

madhyastha sudhīhu karuṇā pūrvaka vä apa gē prayatnayehi sārthatva vyarthatva viniscaya keret vā. ("ä yanna," *Swadēsa Mitrayā*, 24 August 1926)

(Let the discriminating and impartial savants, who desire purity of language, clarity of expression and ease of comprehension by students, kindly make judgment on the success or otherwise of our effort.)

2. basa nam däyekä ayitiyeki. ehi däyē muhuṇuvara purā peniyä yutu yä. Sakuyehi hō vañguyehi hō hindiyehi hō maha gorahäḍi vadan vū paliyaṭa mä heḷayā gē da heḷa basé da ūruva gananaṭa no genä, ē gorahäḍi vadan e sē mä gänima däyaṭa maha mañdi kameki. ("vaḍu vadan väla," *Subasa* 2, no. 22 [1941])

(Language is a property of a nation. In it should be fully mirrored the distinct character of the nation. Just because coarse and jarring words are found in Sanskrit, Bengali, or Hindi it is utterly demeaning to borrow those words in the same form without consideration for the distinct character of the Heḷa man and the Heḷa language.)

In the first passage it is evident that Cumaratunga uses a heavy dose of Sanskrit borrowings, displaying his erudition in that language, as it were. Thus, even when the more common purely Sinhala or hybrid (half-Sinhala and half-Sanskrit) forms were available, he prefers to use the pure Sanskrit form. For example:

nairmalyaya	instead of	*nirmala bava*
vaiśadyaya	instead of	*pähädili kama*
sārthatva vyarthatva	instead of	*sārthaka asārthaka bava*

In the second passage, on the other hand, Cumaratunga goes to the other extreme. As if to establish unequivocally that any meaning could be expressed in the Eḷu idiom, without any resort to borrowings, from Sanskrit, Pali, or any other language, he omits even those borrowed forms that had become accepted usages in the literary Sinhala of the day and replaces them with "authentic" Sinhala (Eḷu/Heḷa) forms. For example,

basa	instead of	*bhāṣāva*
däyekä	instead of	*jātiyaka*
sakuyehi	instead of	*sanskrutayehi*
vadan	instead of	*vacana*

Viewed from the perspective of the directional drift in language planning activity in modern Sinhala, this ultimate shift into the most authentic Sinhala idiom may be considered the culmination of a process set afoot in the eighteenth century at the initial stages of the present diglossic situation in the language.[59] Scholars, who were intent on reviving the literary tradition after a period of decline due to political instability, utilized the linguistic features of about the thirteenth century as the standard to be followed in prose writings, thereby establishing the principle of falling back on classical models for the authentification of the literary idiom.[60] This principle remained to exert a directional grip on subsequent corpus planning activity. As noted, in the aftermath of several waves of purism it appeared to Sinhalese scholars by the early years of the twentieth century that they had achieved the highest point of classical perfection—the *miśra Sinhala* prose standard of about the thirteenth century. It was upheld by the scholarly establishment and taught in the *pirivenas* and other schools, and it was the basis for the neoclassical standard that emerged in popular literature.

Cumaratunga was not prepared to be satisfied, however, with this conception of the authentic linguistic heritage—the heart of the national identity which should be cherished and upheld. His concern was for the exclusive and unique features of Sinhala which did not have anything in common with the linguistic heritage of another community. He invoked the pure Sinhala (Heḷa, Eḷu) idiom, free of Pali, Sanskrit, Tamil, or any other "contamination." Like D'Alwis in the nineteenth century, Cumaratunga expressed an adverse judgment on the history of the community. "A great blow fell on our language from the *Sidat Sañgarāva,*" he declared,

> for it inaugurated the practice of relegating Sinhala usage to a secondary place, or of ignoring it altogether, for the purpose of teaching grammar on lines suggested by Pāli, Sanskrit and other

59. See M. W. S. de Silva 1967; and Dharmadasa 1967.
60. For details, see M. W. S. de Silva 1967.

languages. ("Sinhala Grantha Vaṃśaya," Cumaratunga [1962]: 71–80)

Here we see Cumaratunga going a step further than D'Alwis. The latter, while upholding the Eḷu idiom and reproaching his forebears for neglecting it because of their fascination with Sanskrit, was at the same time emphatic in recognizing the *Sidat Saṅgarāva* as the ultimate authority of Sinhala grammar. This view indeed had become an article of faith with the scholarly establishment by the early twentieth century. Cumaratunga proceeded to carry the authentification endeavor further—to its logical conclusion, as it were. Thus, by the time he inaugurated the journal *Subasa* (Good Language, 1939) for the "upliftment of the language," Cumaratunga had shifted to the Heḷa idiom, which, as the above excerpt from one of his writings illustrates, was characterized by phonological and morphological features peculiar to the Eḷu idiom found in some of the literary compositions of about the twelfth century.[61]

Not only was the Heḷa idiom totally free of borrowings from any other language, including Pāli and Sanskrit, which were highly respected by traditionalist scholars, claim was also made of its exclusive history. Cumaratunga declared:

> Know that the Helese language is *not a daughter of any language now in existence.* Her idiom is her own. The Helese people . . . must realize that their beautiful language is not the same as the debased jargon now in use among ignoramuses whose names have been variously appendaged. They must begin to feel proud of their language *by finding its singularities which they must uphold and cherish.* (*Helio* 1, nos. 11 and 12 [1941]: 87)

Thus, authenticity in language, as envisaged by Cumaratunga, meant to uphold the Heḷa language, like von Grimmelshaugen's German, "a language of heroes existing for and by itself."[62] It was to pursue this particular emphasis on linguistic and national authenticity that Cumaratunga and the few scholars who joined him in the Heḷa movement proceeded to employ the Heḷa idiom. Language was thus to per-

61. The most striking examples of such *Eḷu* prose are found in some passages in *Dharmapradīpikāva* and *Butsaraṇa* of the twelfth century.

62. I borrow this phrase from Poliakov 1974:92.

form a separatist function—as a symbol of the separate and exclusive national identity of the Sinhalese people.

The Behavioral Manifestation of Heḷa Authenticity

We notice in the Heḷa movement a zealous commitment to promote what was believed to be the genuine Sinhalese heritage in many aspects of communal life. With regard to language the main concern was grammatical explication and codification as well as the production of texts utilizing that grammar. Then there was, in other areas of culture, a calling forth of all "genuine" ethnic activity. All these involved the stimulation and mobilization of the vehicles of that authenticity. Here it was mandatory to "win over the Helese to the cause,"[63] which, incidentally, involved a challenge to accepted authority and a direct confrontation with the scholarly establishment, as described earlier.[64]

Grammatical Codification and the Production of Texts

Cumaratunga, identifying the Heḷa idiom as the essence of national identity, sought to promote it by behavioral implementation. Thus, he and his associates proceeded first to sort out the rules of Heḷa grammar, codify them, and produce as many texts as possible using them. Cumaratunga edited a large number of classical texts, appending copious notes where the authentic grammatical rules were explained. He also wrote several treatises of Sinhala grammar, prepared a considerable number of school textbooks and student guides to prose and verse composition, and produced a substantial volume of creative literature.

Among Cumaratunga's grammatical treatises are: a critical examination of the *Sidat Sañgarāva* (*Sidat Sañgarā Vivaraṇaya,* 1934); a treatise on the Sinhala verb (*Kriyā Vivaraṇaya,* 1935); and a comprehensive grammar of Sinhala (*Vyakaraṇa Vivaraṇaya,* 1937). He also edited thirty classical texts in which the extensive elucidatory notes concentrated largely on grammar.[65] Cumaratunga, like the Norwegian scholar Ivaar Asen, sought to establish the fact that a creative literature could be produced in the language he sponsored, so as to inspire others to follow him.

63. This was the aim of the organization Heḷa Havula founded in 1941 by Cumaratunga. See *Subasa,* 2, no. 18 (1941): 278.

64. See the section "The Rise of a Scholarly Establishment" in chapter 6.

65. For details, see Cumaratunga 1961: Introduction; and Cumaratunga 1962: Introduction.

Thus, mention may be made of his short stories and poems, particularly the latter, among which are some highly praised by critics. He also wrote two plays, *Doraṭa Väḍuma* and *Nikam Häkiyāva*. The two series of school textbooks (*Śikṣā Mārgaya* and *Kiyavana Nuvaṇa*) and the student guides to prose and verse composition (*Prabandha Sangrahaya*, 1938; *Prabandhōpadeśaya*, 1938; *Kavi Śikṣāva*, 1939; and *Virit Väkiya*, 1938), which he compiled, indicate that he realized the importance of working through the school system in language planning strategy.

Other prominent scholars in the Heḷa movement were Raipiel Tennakoon, Jayantha Weerasekera, and Jayamaha Wellala. Their large literary output, aimed particularly at an audience in the school system (teachers as well as students), constituted a heavily labored behavioral accomplishment for the resuscitation, maintenance, and enrichment of Heḷa, the authentic Sinhala language.

The Calling Forth of Other "Genuine" Ethnic Activities

Connected with Cumaratunga's search for language authenticity in its most fundamental form was a determined effort to find, claim, and utilize the authentic national heritage in other spheres of culture as well. It was his conviction that

> Helese is one of the oldest nations in the world. There is evidence to show that they had a wonderful literature which is now lost to us. What now remains does not . . . represent even one thousandth of what our people have been producing. (*Helio* 1, nos. 15 and 16 [1941]: 124–25)

Hence there was an urgent need to mine and refine the available tradition in order to arrive at the substance of greatness which lay concealed in it. One may note, for example, the changes Cumaratunga effected in his own name, each time to be in conformity with a new insight into the authentic Sinhalese tradition, which he sought to resuscitate. First known as Munidasa Cumaranatunga, he subsequently dropped the letter "ṇa" and called himself Munidasa Cumaratunga; later he observed that the traditional Sinhalese custom was to be known by the family name first then by the personal name, thus he changed his name again to Cumaratunga Munidasa; finally, in consonance with the Hela idiom, which he adopted in 1941, his name appeared as Cumaratuñgu Munidas.

Similarly, he ventured to resuscitate the authentically Sinhalese music (see his *Hela Miyäsiya*, 1941) and theater (see his introduction to *Nikam Häkiyāva*, 1941). It needs to be mentioned, however, that his claim in these two instances that what he presented comprised "the lost tradition" of Helese is not substantiated by any proof. Be that as it may, his zealous effort in search of the genuine ancestral authenticity is noteworthy. In the same vein he attempted to resuscitate Hela industry, Hela cuisine, and other "lost traditions."

Group Mobilization in the Cause of Language

Although the Heḷa endeavor at authentification thus concerned itself with many aspects of the community's culture, the feature that engaged it most was language. Language was indeed the authentificating device in the search for the intergenerational essence in other spheres. Language–specifically its genuine phenomenological manifestation–was relied upon to enact, celebrate, and call forth all other genuine ethnic activity.

"Language is the life-blood of a nation," declared Raipiel Tennakoon, a lieutenant of Cumaratunga,

> It is the highest heritage of any community. The national feeling, the national honour, the national pride and all such things of a human community stand firm on the solid base of language. (*Helio* 1, nos. 7 and 8 [1941]: 59–60)

In the logic of the thinking, language planning in the form of winnowing out "impurities," had a cogent purpose in the context of other types of national plannings. The Heḷa philosophy in this regard was based on a kind of linguistic determinism. "A base, corrupted, inelegant and insipid language," declared Cumaratunga, "will produce a mean and miserable mentality."[66] Starting from this premise, he constructed a program of communal upliftment. His line of thinking is best summarized by one of his close associates, who wrote his biography:

66. *Helio* 1, nos. 9 and 10 (1941): 74.

> It is accepted by learned scholars that the life-blood of a nation is its language. This is universal truth. Munidas (i.e., Cumaratunga), who believed it whole-heartedly, surveyed the world with his keen intellect, taking guidance from history. What he saw everywhere was that whenever language became weak, the nation deteriorated. To Munidas, who pondered over the past and the present of the Helese nation, one truth became obvious. That is, the one unmistakable way of fortifying the nation was to fortify the language. (Gunawadu 1957:87)

In this way the resuscitation of the classical linguistic idiom was the crucial ingredient in a formula designed to recreate the complete situation in which the nation's great ancestors had lived. One cannot characterize the Heḷa movement, however, as merely a pathetic endeavor to circumvent the remorseless flow of Time by going back into a dead or buried past through a literary door. Cumaratunga and the others who joined him in the Heḷa movement believed that the solutions to many, if not all, of the community's current problems had to be inaugurated by linguistic reform.

From the early stages of Cumaratunga's concern for the "good language" to the founding of the Heḷa Havula (Pure Sinhala fraternity) in 1941 one notes the progressive development of a strategy aimed at the mobilization of the Sinhalese intelligentsia in the cause of language, for the inauguration of a program of national upliftment. "Signs are appearing," he declared in 1936,

> that Sinhala will become an uncivilized language of the worst kind. . . . With a civilized people what becomes civilized first is their language. . . . Need it be said that a people who use an uncivilized language are themselves uncivilized? . . . The time has arrived for us to correct this. This is not a malady that cannot be cured. ("Sinhalayē Abhāgyaya," *Vidyōdaya* 1, no. 1 [1936])

Thus, he urged the adoption of good language not only in writing but in speech as well. It was his contention that, if grammatical standards are meticulously maintained in writing as well as in speaking English, there was no reason why it was not possible to follow the same principle with regard to Sinhala. "The Sinhala teachers can," he said, "make the spoken language grammatical, at least in the schools, within one week."[67] A serialized language lesson that he wrote to the weekly newspaper *Lak Miṇi Pahana* in 1934, under the pseudonym Guru (teacher), was designed to teach grammatical Sinhala in writing and speech.

By 1936 Cumaratunga had outlined the course his national rejuvenation program should follow. "It is urgently needed," he wrote,

> to institute a society, with its headquarters in the capital and with branches all over the country, which is *devoted to the development of the Sinhala language,* and which seeks to *purify its usage,* to bring out its hidden potentialities, to disseminate the useful knowledge found in Sinhala books, *to generate a love for our own language and to intensify the love for it which already may be there.* ("Sinhalayē Abhāgyaya," *Vidyōdaya* 1, no. 1 [1936], emphasis added)

With the newspaper *Lak Miṇi Pahana,* which he edited during the period from 1934 to 1936, and later with the periodical *Subasa,* which, unlike the former, was totally devoted to the "upliftment of the Heḷa language," Cumaratunga was able to win over a considerable section of the Sinhalese intelligentsia to his cause. This group was drawn mainly from among the rank of Sinhalese schoolteachers—for whom, as a social category whose work involves the use of language, the Heḷa ideology, with its strong emphasis on language matters, would have held a strong fascination. Another reason why they were attracted to the Heḷa movement had to do with their socioeconomic status. The Sinhalese schoolteachers were a group with an acute sense of relative deprivation. When compared with their counterparts who taught in English, they were poorly paid and ranked far below in social status. These factors, no doubt, would have made them highly susceptible to self-assertive endeavors with the Sinhala language as a mission and a cause. Furthermore, the Heḷa ideology, as manifest in Cumaratunga's writings and public lectures, contained a specific effort to uplift the self-esteem of the Sinhalese schoolteacher. Starting with the series of articles entitled "Śikṣakaka Vruttiya" (Teaching Profession) to the newspaper *Swadēśa Mitrayā* in 1930, a special striving could be observed in all his mobilizational activities to make the Sinhalese schoolteacher "free

67. Cumaratunga 1961:26.

of slavishness and meniality, and endow him with the capacity to speak with head held high in front of any powerful authority."[68]

By the early 1940s the time seemed ripe for launching the pure Sinhala fraternity, the Hela Havula. Cumaratunga declared at its inaugural meeting, attended by some three hundred members:

> If a certain language in undeveloped, the land in which that language operates is also undeveloped. . . . It is impossible for a single individual to develop a country, to develop a language, or to uplift a nation. . . . Therefore, let us form an association, spread its branches all over the country, and win the Helese over to our cause. (*Subasa* 2, no. 18 [1941]: 278–79)

Significantly, it was "the Helese" that needed to be won over. In Cumaratunga's conception the Helese had to be distinguished from the "others." Apart from the more obvious cases of the Tamils, the Moors, and such, who would be excluded on the more patent ethnic criteria, there were others within the Sinhalese community who had to be marked out. These latter were the "degenerate Helese"—"the Sin-Helese" (as Cumaratunga called them in his English writings), or the "sii-Heḷa" ("despicable Hela," in his Sinhala writings). Like Fichte's characterization of the true heirs to the *Ur-volk* as those retaining the *Ursprache*, Cumaratunga identified the Helese as those upholding the Heḷa idiom. All others stood excluded and condemned.

The Challenge to the Scholarly Establishment

The Heḷa movement, with its emphasis on unique ethnic patrimony and the unconventional views on the language, history of the community, and other cultural traditions, appearing as it was in a society already intensively mobilized in accordance with conventional ideologies, was bound to come into conflict with established authority. The unyielding criticism of time-honored beliefs and the relentless attack on the established leadership, many among which were held in very high esteem in Sinhalese society, appear to have produced more negative than positive results as far as the popularity of the movement was concerned.

---

68. An observation by a leader of the schoolteachers' trade union movement. See D. P. Silva 1969:83.

Prominent among those most vituperatively condemned as "Sin-Helese" by Helese activists was the scholarly establishment, which appeared in the wake of the religiocultural revival. "The pundits of the temple and the university," declared Cumaratunga,

> have created a language of their own which is at once debased, insipid and inelegant. . . . It is difficult to learn, difficult to understand and difficult to follow. (*Helio* 1, nos. 13 and 14 [1941]: 105)

Their "crime" was the "lack of purity" and "inauthenticity" characterizing their language, which in the eyes of Helese protagonists stemmed from the ethnical lapses in having invited foreign (particularly Indian) linguistic "contaminations." Thus, in the pages of *Subasa* and the *Helio* (the English journal of the Heḷa Havula) such "pundits of the temple and the university" as *bhikkhu* Welivitiye Sorata, a teacher in the Vidyōdaya Pirivena and a well-known scholar; *bhikkhu* Medauyangoda Vimalakitti, a reputed Oriental scholar; *bhikkhu* Bambarende Siri Sivali, a teacher in the Vidyālankāra Pirivena and author of many books; and G. P. Malalasekera, the professor of Pāli, Sinhala, and Sanskrit at the University College, were regularly marked out for attack. "Our bitterest complaint," declared Cumaratunga, "is against men who do not know our language well enough to write a good essay in it, and pose as the highest scholars" (*Helio* 1, no. 1 [1941]: 1).

The Heḷa activists were also relentless in their chastisement of Bandaranaike, "the presumptuous leader of the Sin-Helese" (Tennakoon, in *Subasa* 3, nos. 21 and 22 [1941]: 321), who happened to be their rival in mobilizing Sinhala ethnicity. Again Sir Baron (formerly D. B.) Jayatilaka, a veteran politician and Oriental scholar, who had been appointed editor-in-chief of the Sinhalese dictionary project (launched in 1927), was severely reprimanded for making that undertaking an "ignominious fiasco." Furthermore, it was said:

> The Sinhala language is trying its best to get itself freed. It has a right to ask for your assistance. But what assistance are you rendering it at present? Instead of rendering it every assistance to free itself from bondage you yourself are supposed to be holding it tight. . . . I have heard it freely said that had you but released this unfortunate Dictionary from your relentless grasp, it would have appeared in its entirety before the public long ago.

(Cumaratunga, "An Open Appeal to Sri Baron Jayatilaka," *Subasa* 1, no. 7 [1940])

It needs to be noted that this section of the elite which came under virulent criticism of Heḷa activists was closely linked with the hierarchy of the Buddhist dispensation. Mention was made earlier of the prominent *bhikkhu* scholars—Welivitiye, Medauyangoda, and Bambarende—who were the butt of Helese criticism. Sir Baron was a distinguished alumnus of Vidyālankara and the president of its Dayaka Sabhā (Supporters' Association), and Malalasekera, an alumnus of Vidyōdaya, and a Ph.D and D.Litt. from the University of London, was highly respected in *pirivenas* as a scholar in Pali and Buddhism. Provoked by continuous vexations, an organization of *bhikkhus* named the Bhikṣu Sammēlanaya called for an island-wide campaign against the Heḷa Havula in 1941.[69] Although the campaign did not come about, the opposition of the Buddhist hierarchy and the Buddhist lay leadership was a key factor in the failure of the Heḷa movement to attract the support of the bulk of the Sinhalese literati and hence the population at large.

The Dogmatic Elitism of the Heḷa Movement and Its Failure to Win Mass Support

Heḷa activism was characterized by the repudiation of established authority, in language as well as in other spheres of sociocultural activity. Furthermore, the Heḷa ideology contained many dogmatic positions, which would have been most offensive to the traditionalist intelligentsia. Thus, for example, the iconoclastic view that Pāli, rather than being a parent language and the medium through which the Buddha preached his doctrine, had been created by the ancient Sinhala (Heḷa) people themselves; that Sanskrit, the other parent language, instead of enriching Sinhala had itself been enriched by the latter (*Helio* 1, nos. 11 and 12 [1941]: 87); and that the universally respected historical chronicle the *Mahāvaṃśa* was "only a clumsy file of fragmentary documents written by cunning mendicants" (*Helio* 1, no. 4 [1941]: 28).

Furthermore, the "blasphemous" stance taken in repudiating the preeminence of Buddhism among the historically inherited group symbols would have amounted to the rejection of a fundamental "given" in the Sinhala identity as it had received categoric reaffirmation in the

69. For details, see Ahubudu 1957:10–13.

preceding religiocultural revival. Indeed, in the current context, religion was the most highly mobilized aspect of the Sinhalese identity. Hence an attempt to repudiate its priority of status to replace it with a new mobilizational symbol, language, although the latter was a compelling cause for some among the literati, would not have been popular with a large mass of the Sinhala population. Another important factor in the Heḷa movement's failure to gain mass appeal was its repudiation of the established leadership and its opposition to the religious and political elite of the day. The Heḷa movement in itself held elitist rather than populist appeal. "Painters, musicians and writers," wrote Cumaratunga, in reply to a query about the difficulties faced by the ordinary man in following the highly classicized Heḷa idiom,

> are great artists. Their sole aim is to bring their great art as near perfection as possible. *The duty of the ordinary man,* if he is not false to himself, *is to try his very best to follow the great masters and not to complain against the inaccessibility of their performances.* (*Helio* 1, no. 5 [1941]: 37; emphasis added)

With its avowed commitment to preserving the sanctity of the authentic communal heritage the Heḷa movement could not accede to populist pressures on language matters. Indeed, it was Cumaratunga's conviction with regard to all sociocultural activity that "cultured people ought to lead the masses" (*Helio* 1, no. 5 [1941]: 74).

Characterized by such elitist emphases, the Helese movement could catch up with only one particular group of cultural custodians. This group, as mentioned earlier, was drawn largely from among the Sinhalese schoolteachers who came to be involved in language issues not only because their work involved the use of language but also because of the predicament of their being relegated to a low status because English, the language of the colonial master, not Sinhala, was still the dominant language and thus the more valuable in socioeconomic terms.

A further reason for the failure of the Heḷa movement to win wider support was that, in discarding the *miśra Sinhala* idiom in favor of the Heḷa idiom, it was ignoring or failing to appreciate the powerful system linkages involved. *Miśra Sinhala* was the medium in which almost all the extant prose classics, mainly Buddhist in content, had been composed. The recognition of this functional prerogative of *miśra Sinhala* was a deep-seated feature of the communal consciousness. In the religiocultural revival classical *miśra Sinhala* models were universally adopted as the ideal in the standardization of the literary idiom. And the instrumental as well as the symbolic value of *miśra Sinhala* was reinforced with the printing, dissemination, and study of the classics. In the postrevival period, then, *miśra Sinhala* had become—like classical Hebrew after its resuscitation—"a living factor." In the Sinhala ethnic experience of the day, if one single language form could be conceived as the recorder, the expressor, and the carrier of national identity, it was truly the *miśra Sinhala* idiom.[70]

Thus, the system linkages between language, ethnicity, and religion, which had been enlivened and reinforced during the revival, had strong and deep roots in the communal consciousness—too deep for the Heḷa movement to effect a change. Rather than a positional change involving a mere redistribution, it was a structural change, involving a basic change in categories, that was envisaged by the Heḷa movement. Indeed, the failure of the Heḷa movement to win popular support, in spite of its strong assertive stance in the cause of the Sinhala language, was in large part due to the miscalculation of the power of religion as a source of mobilizational appeal which had been proven unmistakably in the preceding decades. The potency of religion was to be proved again in the 1950s, when the decisive triumph of political mobilization in the cause of the Sinhala language was in large measure due to the injection of a religious content in ideological as well as behavioral terms.[71]

Thus, the Heḷa movement failed in terms of getting wider societal commitment to its programs. The highest recorded membership of the Heḷa Havula is about five hundred.[72] This figure, although a very considerable one in the context of Sinhalese voluntary associations in general, would have represented the hard core of the movement—those who had been "won over" to the Heḷa cause. Furthermore, when judged in relation to the forces the movement had to contend with, particularly those involving the social and political elite, the scholarly establishment, and the Buddhist clergy, such a membership, drawn particularly from among the intelligentsia, was an impressive achievement. With the loss of the charismatic leadership of Cumaratunga with

70. For details, see chapter 6.
71. For details, see K. M. de Silva 1986:196–200.
72. For details, see Dharamadasa 1972.

his untimely death in 1944, however, the movement suddenly lost its former élan and was soon on the path of decline.

The Place of the Heḷa Movement in the Annals of Sinhalese Language Nationalism

In spite of its failure to ignite a mass response, the Heḷa movement may be considered a landmark in the rise of Sinhalese language nationalism. On the one hand, it gave expression, no doubt in an unconventional form, to a pressing need in the Sinhalese communal consciousness for authenticity and distinctiveness; and on the other, in its importunate emphasis on the language component of ethnic identity it heavily influenced the course of group assertive strivings of the day and in the decades that followed. It gave forceful expression to the sense of ethnolinguistic uniqueness of the Sinhalese community, and with it was reached the ideological pinnacle of Sinhalese language nationalism. It had a profound impact on the corpus planning activities in Sinhala, and, more important, it inspired hopes and strategies for status planning endeavors in the cause of the Sinhala language.

The Emphasis on Ethno-Linguistic Uniqueness

In the religiocultural revival of the late nineteenth century and early twentieth century historical links with the Indic Great Tradition came to be reinforced sentimentally as well as instrumentally. In the language sphere, in particular, revived interest in Sanskrit resulted, among other things, in a strong Sanskrit influence on the processes of language standardization. Also, taken as a whole, the form of group identity associated with the Ārya-Sinhala identity was essentially Indic in inspiration.

By the 1930s, however, there seems to have emerged a need for a contrastive emphasis on the Sinhalese identity *even with regard to India.* The factors involved were as follows: There was, on the one hand, a strand of opinion, starting with the Theosophist movement and more emphatically formulated by Dharmapala, that Sri Lanka should be closely allied with the "Big Brother" India in the movement for freedom from the British yoke. Thus, among the older generation of the political leadership, those such as C. W. W. Kannangara, as well as in the emerging younger generation thereof, the Marxists as well as others, such as J. R. Jayewardene, there was a distinct preference for Indian inspiration, guidance, and even a federated merger.[73]

On the other hand, however, there was the opposite viewpoint, which reflected a deep-seated fear in the Sinhalese historical consciousness: that the Sinhalese people should be vigilant of their own individual interests, particularly with regard to the possibility of being overwhelmed by the tremendous numerical strength of the Indians. Several prominent politicians, such as D. S. Senanayake, had given public expression to this fear.

Both those viewpoints found reflection in the mass media. Of particular interest for present purposes is the anti-Indian invective. The newspaper *Sinhala Bauddhayā,* in opposition to the proposal for a federated merger with India, stated in 1940:

> If such an idea existed among our forefathers there would have been no need for them to soak Mother Lanka with their own blood, and they could easily have come under one of the various Indian empires which arose from time to time. . . . On the contrary, during its golden age in king Dutugemunu's time, when it sat in splendour among all the great nations of the day, as well as in other less glorious times, Lanka always remained unconstrainted by India. It was never submissive and struk back, blow for blow. (Editorial, 24 August 1940 [the editor was Hemapala Munidasa])

Thus, historical memories were being resuscitated to outline one of the most relevant negative reference groups of the day: for the relevant "others" of ethnocultural self-definition are prone to change, not only over time but also from subgroup to subgroup at one particular time. For the Sinhalese people a few decades earlier the most prominent negative reference group were the Westerners, and the Indians were considered in some way as belonging to the in-group. Now the focus was shifting: While for some Sinhalese the older definition was still valid, in the conception of some others the Indians were coming to the fore as the most relevant negative reference group.

---

73. For the idea of federation, see Edwin Wijeratne's presidential address to the congress in 1940 (Roberts 1977:1389). George E. de Silva (president of the congress in 1930) referred to India as "our mother country" in 1939 (Roberts 1977:1348). For Kannangara's and Jayewardene's eulogies of Indian nationalists, see Roberts 1977: sec. 6. For Marxists and the Indian nationalist movement, see Jayewardene 1971.

It was this emergent contrastive dimension that came to be reflected in the Heḷa ideology. The Sinhalese, whose identity affirmation during the preceding revivalist era centered upon the Ārya-Sinhala identity with its heavy Indian emphasis, were now being brought to an awareness of their own *singular identity,* not interlocking and not overlapping with any other identity. As emphatically maintained by Heḷa protagonists, the spirit of the Heḷa culture was a totally indigenous one without ancestral obligations to any other culture. Thus, all ideological strands of the Heḷa identity were directed toward the establishment of its authenticity, singularity, and preeminence. Hence the repudiatory stance taken even with regard to Buddhism, the assertion of indigenous historical roots for the total dismissal of Indian origins, and, above all, the insistent emphasis on the purity and authenticity of the Heḷa language, a factor that could be demonstrated behaviorally.

The contrastive self-identification promulgated in the Heḷa identity pertaining to the Indian context was not directed against the Tamils alone. If the Tamils were the sole focus of contrast, the Ārya-Sinhala identity with its north Indian genesis and inspiration would have been sufficient. But as reflected, for example, in an editorial of the *Sinhala Bauddhaya,* cited above, the need had arisen for a complete dissociation from the Indian subcontinent, and this need manifested itself in the Heḷa identity.

The Ideological Pinnacle of Language Nationalism

The Heḷa ideology purported to bestow upon language the inordinate supremacy among the desiderata of communal identity. Hence the trinity of language, nation, and land. Significantly, the Heḷa ideology was constructed solely on language foundations. The very label *Heḷa,* to begin with, was the designation of a linguistic form. It was utilized, in extension, to designate the race, land, music, cuisine, and so forth.

Again the Heḷa (re)construction of history, like its Turkish counterpart,[74] for example, each purporting to establish unequivocally the glory and the grandeur of the community's past, was a fabrication in which everything depended on words. Being essentially linguistic, the material was at the very tongue and fingertips of highly articulate

74. For the Turkish "Sun Language" theory, see Heyd 1954.

manipulators such as Cumaratunga and Tennakoon, and whatever conceptualization was wished for was provided by that bountiful "mother," language.

Thus, it was through language that access was had to all other valued desiderata of authentic communal identity. Language was here the substantial hub of nationalism. "The true national spirit," declared Tennakoon, "is the eldest son of the mother tongue" (*Helio* 1, nos. 7 and 8 [1941]: 59). A categorical recognition was made of the authentic language form, which was to be celebrated as the indubitable mark of national identity. The Hela idiom, autonomous and without ancestral obligations to any other language, was thus considered the true embodiment of ancestral genius, holding "sentimental and behavioral links between the speech community of today and its counterparts yesterday and in antiquity."[75]

In the context of a servile present such consciousness and accessibility of national authenticity led to a strong compulsion to meet the responsibilities incumbent upon the carriers of that intergenerational essence. "Our patient is our mother tongue," declared Cumaratunga,

> she is being deliberately neglected, abused, degraded, starved, spoiled and poisoned. Her own children have already forgotten the fact that she was their own mother. Some even have engaged secret murderers to poison her, pretending all the while that they are only attending on her to bring her back her old life . . . and liberty. (*Helio* 1, nos. 9 and 10 [1941]: 71)

This kinship metaphor was reflective of the sense of deep moral obligation which characterized the intense commitment of the Heḷa movement to the cause of language. Significantly, the theme of the symposium held at the inaugural meeting of the Heḷa Havula was: "If a certain language is undeveloped the land in which that language operates is also undeveloped" (*Subasa* 1, no. 18 [1941]: 278–79). Significantly again, at the second general meeting of the Heḷa Havula the discussion centered on the theme "The re-making of the Heḷa language."[76]

If the kinship metaphor included within it deep moral obligations in the cause of language, the conception of revived authenticity held promises of "glory yet to come," and the purified and sanctified Heḷa

75. For this typical feature of language nationalism, see Fishman 1972c:43.

76. Personal communication by the late Sri Charles de Silva, a founding member.

identity, based solidly on the "purified" and sanctified foundations of language, was to be the solidifying, stimulating, and energizing conceptual focus of group assertive activity.

The uninhibited criticisms and categoric denunciations of the established authority in its various forms – the British administration, the Sri Lankan political leadership, the scholarly establishment, including members of the Buddhist clergy – all indicate a combative stance befitting such an orientation. In one of his patriotic poems Cumaratunga declared:

> May that life which does not integrate within itself the Language, the Nation and the Land, Depart
>
> (*Hela Miyasiya*, 1941:74)

Those in the Heḷa movement were exhorted to be prepared for any sacrifice, "be it friend, relation or even mother and father," in the cause of the "Heḷa Trinity" (*heḷa teruvana*) of language, nation, and land (*Subasa* 1941, 3:279).

Although D'Alwis may go on record as having first conceived of language as the central feature of national identity, it was Cumaratunga who gave that conception an intellectual elaboration and behavioral expression so as to make it a potent social factor. First, Cumaratunga's role, unlike that of D'Alwis, was not confined to being a cultural leader, for he went further and became an organizational leader as well. Second, D'Alwis, as a Christian and belonging to the English-educated stratum and writing mostly in English, was a conspicuously "marginal" individual and could hardly have inspired a mass enthusiasm. Cumaratunga, on the other hand, coming from a Buddhist background and with strong ties with the Sinhalese intelligentsia, particularly the Sinhalese schoolteachers, could readily establish rapport with a politically relevant group through his prodigious writing and impressive oratory. Third, timing was opportune in the case of Cumaratunga. He appeared at the scene of an already mobilized ethnicity that, although not prepared for the structural change in ideology which he attempted, was in the mood for the self-assertive activity in the cause of the Sinhala language which he envisioned.

Seen in historical perspective, Cumaratunga may be regarded as having provided the ethnic self-assertive activity of the Sinhalese not only with a highly satisfying ideological content but also with a potent symbol that could function as a common focus for the whole community in a modern milieu. In spite of the refusal to accept the traditional view, which conceded to Buddhism the preeminent place among national symbols, the Heḷa ideology contained an extremely attractive vision of the community's cultural heritage.

Thus, although the Heḷa movement failed to obtain mass commitment, its effect in terms of energizing and boosting the morale of the Sinhalese population cannot be overlooked. Again, by deflating the power of religion among the desiderata of group identity, to crown language as the integrative and instrumental symbol par excellence, ethnic ideology was updated, for it facilitated the ready involvement of Christian Sinhalese in goal-oriented ethnic activity. The Heḷa identity in this way brought within the ethnic fold the one section of the Sinhalese community which had been left out by the Ārya-Sinhala identity. No doubt there had been sporadic involvements of Sinhalese Christians in nationalistic activities earlier. But the ideological base provided by the Heḷa movement now facilitated a stronger commitment. Many Sinhalese Christians, particularly from the teaching profession, took an active part in the Heḷa movement, and during the 1950s, when the national language question became a political issue, they were as much involved as the Buddhists in the cause of the Sinhala language.

Heḷa Impact on Corpus Planning

In the Heḷa movement language was conceived as the key to the vitality of the nation. In Tennakoon's words:

> Almost all the enslavers of our nation tried to crush our mother tongue with all their might. . . . *Once the language was crippled, the nation became a set of fools like a flock of sheep.* (*Helio* 1, nos. 7 and 8 [1941]: 59–60; emphasis added)

Again Cumaratunga, viewing the Department of Education as a "malicious contrivance to push the people into slavery" (*Swadesa Mitraya,* 7 September 1930) believed that it

> has done and are [*sic*] still doing everything to make the language lawless, graceless, powerless and worthless. *Language without dignity produces men and women without dignity.* Men and women with-

> out dignity are as base as beasts and can be made to stoop to any meanness. (*Helio* 1, nos. 9 and 10 [1941]: 70; emphasis added)

Thus, the path to national rejuvenation lay with language. The Hela view on the matter was neatly summarized by Cumaratunga in verse:

> Whatever anyone may say we will never obtain freedom if we
> despoil our own language. Begin therefore with language.

The language form that could inspire dignity and self-reliance was the Heḷa idiom. Speaking of the concern of the day with status planning activity, Cumaratunga was to declare:

> We clamour for court proceedings in the Sinhala language. We long to listen to Sinhala speeches in the State Council. In short we want Sinhala to be made the official language at least in the Sinhalese provinces. But *how many of us pay attention to the language itself, its form, its purity, its forcefulness, its elegance?* (*Subasa* 1, no. 18 [1940]: 266–67. Emphasis added)

Posed in terms of language planning strategies, Cumaratunga's stance amounted to an insistence that the work in developing the language had to be completed before the promotion of its functional utilization could be undertaken. Language development in his conception, however, was a development to end all development—a going back to the perfect status of classical purity. Nevertheless, the pure Sinhala form thus sponsored failed to gain wider societal acceptance. Its use was confined to those actively engaged in the Heḷa movement, and, as far as the bulk of the Sinhalese literati was concerned, the literary medium remained the *miśra Sinhala* idiom. The Heḷa linguistic philosophy was generally considered as extremist.[77] But this did not mean that the Heḷa movement was a passing phase without any impact on corpus planning. The Heḷa activists were forever vigilant in their role as custodians of authentic linguistic usage, and they were relentless in their criticism of others' lapses in this regard.

77. In its subeditorial on the day following Cumaratunga's death, for example, the Sinhala daily *Dianamina,* while appreciating his immense services to Sinhala language and literature, remarked that his desire to restore classical grammar went so much beyond limits as to deserve the epithet "fanatical" (*Dinamina,* 3 March 1944).

In sum it can be said that the Heḷa movement functioned as a strong inhibiting factor in all populistic pressures on corpus planning during the 1930s and the 1940s. Were it not for its intervention, in fact, the societal drift toward populism during this period, when self-government was the national goal, would possibly have led to large-scale simplifications of the literary language. Indeed, there were several proposals for simplification.[78] The fact that they were rejected outright, thus reinforcing conservative tendencies, making the literary idiom strongly resilient in the face of populistic pressures, was in no small measure due to the intervention of the Heḷa movement.

It was, however, not the intention of the Heḷa movement to be content with corpus planning alone. While believing that corpus planning should come before attempts were made at status planning, the Heḷa movement had in its agenda concrete strategies in the latter sphere as well.

The Heḷa Impact on Status Planning

In the current context of democratically oriented politics the national political leadership was the special target of Heḷa indignation about the low status of the Sinhala language. Cumaratunga believed that "the English nation . . . would have given us full freedom long ago had it not been for the treacherous conduct of some of our own so-called leaders" (*Helio* 1, nos. 15 and 16 [1941]: 125). He observed that those leaders,

> who aspire to make Sinhala the language of the courts, the medium of State Council debates and the language of government administration, themselves write in English the address of a letter they send to a relative who does not know a word of English, and sign their names in English. (Editorial in *Lak Mini Pahana,* 1934; reproduced in Cumaratunga 1961:26–29)

In his own way Cumaratunga took steps to remedy the situation. He is on record as the first to send a telegram in Sinhala and to use Sinhala to fill in the postal order forms, which were printed in English. Apart from such individual performances, corporate efforts were launched to sponsor the use of the vernacular in governmental activity.

78. See the discussion below.

"Let us take a new stand in the next general election," suggested Cumaratunga in 1941;

> let us declare beforehand that we shall not give our vote to anyone who does not promise to speak exclusively in Sinhala in the Council. Let us be determined in putting this into practice . . . and see if our hopes will not be fulfilled. (*Subasa* 3, no. 1 [1941]: 35–38)

With his uninhibited opposition to establish authority, Cumaratunga was able to suggest a strategy that only a few among the Sinhalese intelligentsia would have ventured to propose. No doubt, there had been criticisms of the English-educated political leadership earlier, and the older generation of leaders had been challenged by younger ones.[79] But it was Cumaratunga who linked the vernacular language interests with the challenge to the political leadership, thus inspiring an emergent group of language custodians for mobilizational activity in the cause of the Sinhala language, and the political force they could harness was amply demonstrated in the 1950s.

The Heḷa movement, it is clear, epitomized an unprecedented concern with language. Its conceptual elaboration of the language component of national identity, and its activities in the cause of language, although confined to a numerically small section of the population, seem to have had immediate as well as long-term effects on the course of Sinhalese language nationalism. As far as corpus planning was concerned, it tended to strengthen the classicist inclinations in language standardization. And as for status planning, it was functional like many an expressionistic movement in that it fertilized the soil of discontent and planted there the seeds of unity, organization, and hope. By injecting an avowedly exclusivist and determinedly self-assertive content into the social mobilizational activities of the Sinhalese intelligentsia, the Heḷa movement became the forerunner of its aggressive organizational behavior in the 1950s.

As for its immediate effects, the Heḷa movement, with its persistent "struggles" in the cause of the Sinhala language, along with the activities of the Sinhala Maha Sabha, with its political mobilization of Sinhalese ethnicity, provided the sociopolitical backdrop for the attempt in 1943 to make Sinhala the "official language" of Sri Lanka.

79. Especially the Marxists. In the congress, too, "Young Turks" such as Dudley Senanayake and J. R. Jayewardene were doing so. See Roberts 1977.

The 1943 Resolution to Make Sinhala the "Official Language"

On 22 June 1943 J. R. Jayewardene (b. 1906), the state councillor representing the Kelaniya electorate and a joint secretary of the Ceylon National Congress, gave notice in the State Council of the following resolution:

> That with the object of making Sinhalese the official language of Ceylon within a reasonable number of years, this Council is of the opinion–
>
> (a) that Sinhalese should be made the medium of instruction in all schools;
>
> (b) that Sinhalese should be made a compulsory subject in all public examinations;
>
> (c) that legislation should be introduced to permit the business of the State Council to be conducted in Sinhalese also;
>
> (d) that a Commission should be appointed to choose for translation and to translate important books of other language into Sinhalese;
>
> (e) that a Commission should be appointed to report on all steps that need be taken to effect the transition from English into Sinhalese.
>
> (*Debates, SC* 1943, 1:1024)

When the resolution was formally moved on 30 November 1943 Jayewardene stated that it was his wish to include Tamil also in it so that both Sinhala and Tamil would be official languages (*Debates, SC* 1943, 1:2588). Later, when debate on the resolution began on 24 May 1944, he declared that on representations by his Tamil friends he had decided to "include Tamil also as an official language" (*Debates, SC* 1943, 1:2588). According to the Standing Orders of the Council, however, the original resolution could not be reformulated at that stage, and an amendment by V. Nalliah (councillor for Trincomalee-Batticaloa) was subsequently accepted, whereby the words *and Tamil* were included "right through the motion wherever the word 'Sinhalese' occurs," and it was this amended motion that was accepted by the State Council in May 1944 (*Debates, SC* 1944, 1:760).

The original resolution proposed by Jayewardene signified the parting of ways between the Sinhalese and the Tamils in the process, which began in the 1920s, to replace English with the country's native languages, Sinhalese and Tamil. In the previous resolutions brought before the council both languages were promoted in favor of English. In the original resolution of 1943, however, only Sinhala was mentioned. This was not an oversight but, rather, the result of a deliberate choice. Matters were rectified subsequently, in any case, by the inclusion of Tamil when the resolution was finally accepted by the council, which had an overwhelmingly Sinhalese membership. Of the fifty elected members thirty-nine were Sinhalese compared to ten Tamils. But this change from Sinhala Only to Sinhala and Tamil engaged the attention of some custodians of Sinhalese ethnic interests, who ventured to elaborate upon the implications of the move. This expression of language-related group interests among the Sinhalese community was found within the council as well as outside it.

Sinhala Only against Sinhala and Tamil

As mentioned earlier, the articulation of Sinhalese group interests, especially with regard to the Sinhala language, was observable by the early decades of the twentieth century. Concomitantly, there emerged a language-related groupness perception. The drastic changes in the political structure leading to mass participation in political affairs set the stage for the buildup of the so-called people's language as a political cause. The people's language was at first conceptualized as Sinhala or Tamil. Upholding Sinhala and Tamil was part and parcel of the populistic political strategy that emerged in the era of mass politics. The organized manipulation of ethnicity produced not only heightened ethnic consciousness but specifically heightened language consciousness and language loyalty as well. Indeed, with some sections of the population the "ideological pinnacle" of language nationalism had been reached. In such a context it was to be expected that the language-related group interests of the Sinhalese community would be jealously guarded, particularly when those interests appeared to be threatened by similar interests of the most relevant out-group, the Tamils.

It is apparent that the Sinhalese members of the State Council, who acceded to the pressure of the Tamil members that Tamil too should receive official language status with Sinhala, were themselves aware of the deeper implications of their compromise and the anxieties that could arise because of it within the Sinhalese community. This understanding is evident in the speech of Jayewardene, the mover of the original resolution to make Sinhala the official language, who later agreed to the position that Tamil also "be included on equal terms with Sinhalese" so that both will be official languages. "As two thirds of the people of this country speak Sinhalese," explained Jayewardene, "I had the intention of proposing that only Sinhalese should be the official language of the island" (*Debates, SC* 1944, 1:748).

Apparently, this majoritarian consideration received a much needed endorsement from the example of neighboring India. This was the time when the freedom movement in the Indian subcontinent was finding strong reverberations in the island, and many Sri Lankan politicians were turning to India for inspiration and guidance. The movement for the promotion of Hindi as the *rāṣṭra bhāṣa* (state language), whose main aim was the anti-imperial turning of the tables, would have been an example that invited emulation. Indeed, Jayewardene himself was in no small measure fascinated by the Indian nationalist movement and was a member of the Ceylon National Congress delegation to the Ramgarh sessions of the Indian National Congress in 1940. Thus, the inspiration from India is obvious. Also Jayewardene would have been aware of the idea that the Hindi language—for India the "one national language"—was to be the basis of national unity in a multilingual society.[80]

This particular aspect of the promotion of native languages as against the language of the colonial master was cogently outlined by Bernard Aluvihare, council member, who held steadfastly to the idea that Sinhala alone should be the official language. Aluvihare had been in India for a long time, taken part in the activities of the Indian National Congress, and was a personal friend of Gandhi and Nehru.[81] On his return to the island he entered the State Council as member of the Kandyan seat of Matale, his home region. And in the council he was a staunch proponent of the cause of the Kandyan peasant who was being hemmed in by British-owned plantations heavily populated by south Indian labor. Speaking on the resolution on the official language, Aluvihare stated that "the fundamental condition for national unity,"

80. As a student of the Law College, Jayewardene had defied the authorities by hanging a portrait of Gandhi on the college premises. For his Indian connections as a member of the congress, see Roberts 1977: sec. 9. For the "one language" formula of Gandhi and Nehru, see Das Gupta 1970:109–12.

81. Aluwihare (1902–61) was married to a Bengali lady and even wore the national costume worn by Nehru and other Indian leaders when he attended council sessions.

as envisaged by the leaders of the Indian National Congress, "was the existence of what is called a national language, a common language" (*Debates, SC* 1944, 1:749).

Therefore, he suggested that, while Tamil might function as the language of administration in Jaffna, Sinhala should be made a compulsory subject in schools there, so that "those people will be able to communicate and to keep in touch with the rest of the population and to feel that they are one with the rest of the population in this country" (*Debates, SC* 1944, 1:749–50). It was no doubt a powerful argument in favor of sociocultural and political integration. At the same time Aluvihare was also expressing his concern about the propensity of certain sections of the Tamil population to consider south India as their primary land of allegiance.[82] Furthermore, as a representative of the Kandyan peasantry, he had expressed his apprehensions about the tremendous increase of south Indian labor in Kandyan areas, making the Kandyans "a minority in their own territory."[83] Thus, Aluvihare, in urging the adoption of Sinhala alone as the official language, was no doubt thinking of preventing the Sinhalese people from being overwhelmed by the numerical might of the Tamils in Sri Lanka and south India.

The opposition to the two-language formula was more explicitly expressed by Dudley Senanayake (1911–73), council member for Dedigama. Dudley, the elder son of D. S. Senanayake, had completed his law studies at Cambridge University and returned to the island to enter politics during the 1930s. He was for some time associated with Bandaranaike's Sinhala Maha Sabha, and, with some other young activists such as Stanley De Zoysa and J. R. Jayewardene, he had been carrying on a movement within the Ceylon National Congress for more militant action in the struggle for political freedom. In Dudley Senanayake's opinion Sri Lanka was "too small a place" to have two official languages. He affirmed:

> It is very essential that there should be only one official language. And I ask what could that language be other than Sinhalese? (*Debates, SC* 1944, 1:769)

82. Not only Indian Tamils but also Sri Lankan Tamils have expressed this view—for example, R. Sri Pathmanathan (councillor for Mannar-Mulaittivu), who in one of his speeches declared: "All of us Tamils owe allegiance to India" (*Debates, SC* 1934:833).

83. Statement in 1940. Quoted in Russel 1976:319.

This statement is indicative of the fact that the Sinhalese could insist on "the familiar devices of democratic government" because of their "confidence and security of superior numbers."[84] At the same time it was an overt manifestation of the *Sinhaladvīpa* concept, which had to be reinforced time and again in the face of the ever-present demographic threat from south India.

As for the Tamils, from the 1930s there was an increasing apprehension about being overwhelmed by the Sinhalese majority in the eventuality of a transfer of power from British to Sri Lankan hands. In 1937 they complained to the British authorities that

> the conception of corporate unity in the mind of the Sinhalese is in the nature of a merger, an absorption, of the minorities in the majority community.[85]

Perhaps the "integrationist" ideas put forward by Aluvihare, quoted earlier, provided another instance to substantiate this fear.

By the mid-1930s the Tamils had found their own ideological means to counter the ethnocentric musings of the Sinhala Maha Sabhā and the Heḷa Havula. Thus, in 1935 a Tamil memorandum to the governor claimed:

> The Ceylon Tamils were the original inhabitants of this island and the Sinhalese people of old had regarded themselves as an offshoot of the Tamil nation. (Quoted in Russel 1976:223)

How this claim would have injured the susceptibilities of the Sinhalese community, living as it was in the euphoric aftermath of a religiocultural revival, needs no elaboration. To add insult to injury, as it were, one leading Tamil politician declared in a public speech in 1939:

> The greatest Sinhalese kings are Tamils. The Tamils had an unparalled history and an unequalled traditional culture . . . [whereas] the Sinhalese were a nation formed from the hybridization of a small class of people from north India; they were a nation of hybrids without history. (Quoted in Russel 1976:234)

84. Kearney 1967:32.

85. Memorandum from the All Ceylon Tamil Conference to the Secretary of State for the Colonies in England, 14 July 1937. Quoted in Roberts 1978:359.

The speaker was G. G. Ponnambalam (1902–77), a Cambridge-educated lawyer who had emerged by this time as the most dynamic of Tamil politicians in the island, who, because of his "fluent tongue, multitudinous connections in the north, energy and ability to speak colloquial Tamil (unlike the old guard politicians)," had emerged as the chief spokesman of the Tamil cause.[86] The speech we refer to above was made at Nawalapitiya, a Kandyan town hemmed in by tea plantations with large concentrations of south Indian laborers. Ponnambalam's remarks provoked as a riposte, an invitation to Bandaranaike to form a branch of the Sinhala Maha Sabhā in Nawalapitiya, which was done in the following month. A. E. Goonesinghe, on his part, organized a boycott of Tamil shops in Colombo, which was his stronghold.

Political mobilization on communal lines served to foster mutual prejudices and intergroup suspicions. Thus, some statements of Tamil leaders tended to touch a most sensitive spot in the communal consciousness of the Sinhalese. R. Sri Pathmanathan (the councillor for Mannar-Mullaitivu), for example, claimed in the course of a debate in the State Council that

> all of us Tamils owe allegiance to India and we are thankful to her for the spiritual gifts and privileges she gave to us. . . . As a Tamil I am proud of the history and civilization of my people. . . . The civilization of this country to a great extent is Tamil in origin and character. (*Debates, SC* 1934:833)

This statement acknowledged a traditional prejudice, which tended to view the Tamils in the island as a fifth column. Again it was reported in the *Sinhala Balaya,* a newspaper sponsored by Bandaranaike, that V. Nalliah (the councillor for Trincomalee-Batticaloa) had stated in a speech in Jaffna that, as the Sinhala people were a most communal-minded nation, all Tamils should strive to make Sri Lanka a part of India (Editorial, 8 July 1944).

Such statements seem to have sparked off the deep-seated anxieties in the Sinhalese communal consciousness regarding the demographic threat posed by south India. In this context the so-called 50-50 demand associated with Ponnambalam, whereby it was sought to devise checks and balances in the representative system so that no single

86. Russel 1976:295.

ethnic group could outvote a combination of others,[87] was seen as a direct threat to the Sinhalese majority. One newspaper called it a "design to wipe out the Sinhalese race and to take complete control of the land of Lanka into Dravidian hands" (Editorial, *Sinhala Bauddhayā*, 12 August 1944). The ingrained "minority complex" of the Sinhalese people was clearly manifest in the elaborations upon this theme. "If they obtain the '50-50' demand," warned the *Sinhala Bauddhayā* in the above quoted editorial, captioned "The Future of the Sinhala Race,"

> they will next ask for half of the island of Lanka; and then design to bring from India numbers to exceed the Sinhalese population, make war, and annihilate the Sinhalese race.

It was in such an atmosphere of mutual prejudices, suspicions, and fears between the Sinhalese and the Tamils that the official language resolution was presented to the State Council. Indeed, J. R. Jayewardene, who moved the resolution, was himself fully aware of the specific interests of his own community when he sought to replace the language of the colonial master with the language of the people. Thus, while suggesting later at the formal moving of the resolution that he wished at that stage to include Tamil along with Sinhala as the proposed official languages, Jayewardene made it quite clear why Sinhalese Only would have been preferable:

> The great fear I had was that *Sinhalese being a language spoken by only 3,000,000 people in the whole world would suffer, or may be entirely lost in time to come, if Tamil is also placed on an equal footing with it in this country*. The influence of Tamil literature, a literature used in India by over 40,000,000 and the influence of Tamil films and Tamil culture in this country, I thought, might be detrimental to the future of the Sinhalese language. (*Debates, SC* 1944, 1:748; emphasis added)

Sri Lanka at this juncture was on the eve of political independence, and once the imperial hand of Britian was removed the island was to fend for itself, particularly as the tiny neighbor of the vast state of India, which too was to be independent. What then would be the fate of the Sinhala language if Tamil, with its vast resources in south India, was

87. For this controversial proposal, see K. M. de Silva 1986:103–5.

given equal status with Sinhala, which was confined to a small community of people in the island? Could the language survive, and could the people survive as a distinct ethnic group?

Jayewardene was unequivocal in recognizing the role of language in maintaining ethnicity:

> Language . . . is one of the most important characteristics of nationality. Without language a nation stands a chance of being absorbed or losing its identity. It is because of our language that the Sinhalese race has existed for 2400 years. (*Debates, SC* 1:784)

Jayewardene was voicing opinions whose conceptual formulation had been achieved earlier by custodians of language-related group interests such as James D'Alwis and Munidasa Cumratunga. Indeed, two prominent ideological themes found in the writings of those language loyalists were the crucial role of language in maintaining ethnicity and the anxieties raised by the demographic threat to the Sinhalese from south India.

In Jayewardene's statement quoted above we find an explicit statement of the deep-seated fears of a small community living in the shadow of a mighty neighbor. Seen in this light, it is obvious that the original official language resolution of 1943—to make Sinhalese the one official language—was not by way of oversight. On the contrary, it was a deliberate choice, which was based on two considerations: a majoritarian principle ("as two thirds of the people of this country speak Sinhalese"); and the desire to safeguard the interests of the Sinhalese ethnic group, which was confined to the island of Sri Lanka, or, to put it more strongly, to ensure its very existence on the face of the earth (so that these "three million people would not suffer or . . . get entirely lost in time to come"). In a context where the crucial step of political independence for both India and Sri Lanka was imminent the Sinhalese people were anxious to guarantee by institutional means the safety and viability of their own language and, through it, their ethnic group.

Apart from the explicitly stated anxieties of the Sinhalese community with regard to the granting of equal status of Tamil as official language along with Sinhala—in the speeches of J. R. Jayewardene, Bernard Aluvihare, and Dudley Senanayake—there appears to have been a strong undercurrent of opinion against changing the original resolution. Jayewardene, while expressing his own support for the amendment to give Tamil official language status along with Sinhalese, stated that certain members (most likely Sinhalese) urged him to retain the original resolution to make Sinhala the one official language (*Debates, SC* 1944, 1:748).

It appears, however, that at this time, when the British were envisaging the transfer of power to Sri Lankan hands and the Sri Lankans on their part were anxious to display their "liberal capacity," the concession to Tamil demands was made without much ado. "If it is the desire of the Tamils that Tamil also should be given an equal status with Sinhalese," declared Jayewardene, "I do not think we should bar it from attaining that position" (*Debates, SC* 1944, 1:748).

Indeed, the principle of distributive justice, which was invoked as the most powerful argument for the displacement of English, "from the position it held for over one hundred twenty-five years as the official language of the country," was applicable in the case of the Tamils in the same way as with the Sinhalese. "This country," declared Jayewardene,

> is always in danger of being governed by a small coterie who go through . . . the English schools, whereas the vast majority who go through the Sinhalese and Tamil schools must always be in the position of hewers of wood and drawers of water. (*Debates, SC* 1944, 1:747)

The statement of S. W. R. D. Bandaranaike (the councillor for Veyangoda, minister of local government, and leader of the Sinhala Maha Sabhā) in whom some custodians of Tamil interests saw Hitlerian propensities,[88] was perhaps representative of the publicly expressed attitude of many Sinhalese political leaders at this point. "While . . . there are certain advantages in having one language . . . as the official language," he declared,

> it would be ungenerous on our part as Sinhalese not to give due recognition to the Tamil language. (*Debates, SC* 1944, 1:810)

Possibly the ethics of British liberalism, which had been imbibed by them during their secondary socialization, came to the fore when these elite politicians adopted such an accommodating attitude.

88. See Russel 1976:248.

Although such a conciliatory stance was generally seen with the English-educated political leadership, the opinion outside the council, particularly among the Sinhalese intelligentsia, was for the establishment of the unequivocal supremacy of the Sinhala language. Thus, the *bhikkhu* principal of a *pirivena* declared:

> The Sinhalese have a right of possession over the Sinhala land. The majority of the people living in it are also Sinhalese. If we, the Sinhalese, go and settle down in another land, the governmental system of that country will not adjust itself to suit our needs. It is a crime if we expect in another country that the government there should be changed to suit our requirements. (Ambalangoda Śāstrōdaya Parivenadhipati Paṇḍita Ambalangoda Dhammakusala Sthavirayan Vahanse, "Sinhalaya," *Annual of the Colombo Oriental Studies Society* [1946]: 24–26)

Here the basis for the supremacy of Sinhala is explicit. The Tamils are reminded that they are living in *Sinhaladvīpa,* the land of the Sinhalese people, and that they have their own land (in south India) where they could expect similar supremacy of status for the Tamil language.

In a similar vein the Sinhalese newspaper *Vīrayā,* in its editorial two days after the commencement of the debate on the official language resolution in the State Council, stated:

> The language of the majority race in Lanka should be the language of government, and the smaller races should learn the language of the majority race. It is stupid on the other hand for over eighteen varieties of other smaller races in this country to demand that their languages should also be languages of government. (Editorial in *Vīrayā,* 26 May 1944)

A correspondent to *Sinhala Bauddhayā* had already declared that,

> as almost all minorities in Lanka know at least how to speak Sinhala, they should be very happy about making Sinhala the language of government. (G. M. Jinadasa, *Sinhala Bauddhayā,* 17 July 1943)

The insistence, therefore, was that the language of the host community, which was also the majority community, be the lingua franca of the island. Measures to achieve this end were also suggested. A *bhikkhu* correspondent wrote to *Sinhala Bauddhayā*: "Sinhala should be made a compulsory subject for all races in the island of Lanka" (Bataduve Sumedha bhiksu, letter to the editor, 28 August 1943).

The promotion of its own exclusive language interests in this way was to be expected from a community as mobilized as the Sinhalese at the time. It needs to be noted, however, that such language consciousness and activism in the cause of language was confined to a small group, particularly the Sinhalese intelligentsia, prominent among whom were the Sinhalese schoolteachers and Buddhist monks. That there was no widespread concern about the language-related interests of the community, as witnessed later in the mid-1950s, was largely due to the fact that the political leadership at this stage resisted the temptation to court the masses by appealing to ethnic loyalties. Compared with the high tide of language nationalism which existed during the mid-1950s, with a strong ideological and behavioral commitment to making political boundaries coincide with linguistic ones, the articulation of Sinhalese interests in the mid-1940s was confined to sporadic ideological elaborations without the accompaniment of any mobilization. Apart from the restraint of the elite politicians, another reason for the lack of focused attention regarding the issue of status planning, particularly among the Sinhalese literati, was the fact that in the 1940s, they were more interested in issues concerning "corpus planning."

Populistic Pressures on Literary Sinhala

The 1940s witnessed, along with a concern for status planning, as found in the official language resolution, endeavors in corpus planning, which sought to "simplify" literary Sinhala. Like the former, the latter behavior toward language also arose from the populistic tendencies of the day. Thus, for example, a writer named Ariyadasa suggested in an article in the popular Sinhalese weekly *Siḷumiṇa* in 1940 that, instead of making Sinhala "almost a dead language" by using an archaic idiom for literary purposes, steps should be taken to adopt the equivalent of the spoken idiom in writing as well.[89] Similarly, *bhikkhu* Bambarende Siri Sivali (1908–85), a teacher at the Vidyālankāra Pirivena, wrote in the same year to the popular daily *Dinamiṇa* promoting the idea that books

89. See Dharamadasa 1977.

be written in the equivalent of the spoken idiom. Bambarende had just returned to the island, having studied at Kasi Vidyapeeth in Benares, India. Citing the cases of English and modern Bengali, he urged Sinhalese writers to adopt this "progressive" (*pragatiśīlī*) attitude to language. He suggested furthermore that the archaic linguistic philosophy of the Heḷa Havula was detrimental to the progress of the Sinhala language.[90]

Another well-known writer who was partial to this progressive attitude was Martin Wickramasinghe (1891–1976), a leading novelist and literary critic who had functioned as editor of two leading Sinhalese newspapers, *Dinamiṇa* (1920–27 and 1932–46) and *Siḷumiṇa* (1931–32). In the foreword to the play *Chitrā* which he published in 1940, Wickramasinghe declared about the language he used in the dialogues:

> Although what befits drama most is the spoken idiom, as Sinhalese literature is not developed in various aspects to be strong enough to surpass the limitations enforced by the servants of our phalanx of pundits, it is only very slowly that the learned language has to be eliminated.[91]

Similarly, a resolution was moved at the All Ceylon Congress of Literary Associations (Samasta Lankā Sāhitya Sammēlanaya) in 1944 that the Sinhala language should be modified to suit modern circumstances. This was to be accomplished by such means as the "simplification" of grammar and the removal of "unnecessary" letters in the alphabet.[92]

These expectations, it appears, were rising in the context of growing popular participation in public affairs – a tendency discernible from the 1920s which gathered momentum with the granting of the universal adult franchise in 1931. By 1940 it was evident that the next "logical step" in constitutional development was self-government. Even in this era of democratic politics, however, populistic pressures on language development had to contend with deeply entrenched notions about the standard form of the language which was to be the literary medium. As

90. The Hela Havula launched a prolonged attack on Bambarende. See *Subasa* 1, no. 21 (1940): 317–18; 1, no. 25 (1940): 387–90; 2, no. 5 (1940): 79–80.

91. Foreword, *Chitra* (Galkissa: Mount Press, 1940). For Hela criticisms of Wickramasinghe, see *Subasa* 1, no. 25 (1940): 385–86; and 2, no. 5 (1940): 67–69.

92. No specific changes were suggested. The resolution was on the principle. See "Sinhala Sāhitya Sabhāvak," *SB*, 17 July 1944.

indicated earlier, archaism had been the dominant tendency in all language standardization efforts so far. This propensity received further reinforcement from the Heḷa movement in the late 1930s and the early 1940s. And as could be expected, Hela activists appeared at the forefront of the campaign to preserve the classical literary idiom in the face of populistic pressures.

A major theme running through the defense organized by the "language gatekeepers" of the Heḷa movement against the progressive onslaughts was the notion that it was only through strict adherence to the norms of classical grammar that ideas could be expressed lucidly, rationally, and without ambiguity. It was contended that the progressives were advocating "confusion in language" because of their ignorance of the rules of good language. Examples of confused meaning were drawn from the writings of these progressives. Prominent among those quoted were *bhikkhu* Bambarende and Martin Wickramasinghe. One Hela writer advised Bambarende to leave everything else and engage himself in the study of good Sinhala for three months.[93]

Apart from the Hela critics, there were other defenders of the neoclassical literary idiom. The weekly paper *Sinhala Bauddhayā*, for example, admonished those would-be reformers of the Sinhala language to utilize their energies in "developing the Sinhala language instead of trying to hew and chop it" (*SB*, 24 June 1944). Similarly, the *Sinhala Balaya*, whose editorship was assumed by Hempala Munidasa, a forceful writer and himself a target of attack by Hela activists for being a supporter of Bandaranaike, deplored the attempt by the progressives to

> divest mother Sinhala of her fine and magnificent jewellery, and remove her silken garments, to dress her up only in a "simple" loin cloth. ("Toraturu," *Sinhala Balaya*, 22 June 1944)

Such strong defenses and emotion-ridden pleas in the cause of the neoclassical literary idiom may be taken as indicating "the mission, the glory, history and authenticity" characterizing the traditional literary language in many diglossic situations.[94] It appears that, among the Sinhalese literati of the day, corpus planning engaged greater attention than the status planning attempted by the official language resolution. A major reason for this was the fact that the Sinhalese literati were not

93. *Subasa* 1, no. 18 (1940): 269–70.
94. Fishman 1973.

yet greatly involved in political activity, and their attention was mostly confined to literary pursuits. In the political arena the Sinhalese literati still remained a local elite—confining themselves to positions as aides and adjutants of the national elite, drawn from the English-educated stratum.[95]

In a decade's time, however, the social and economic pressures developing in independent Sri Lanka were to force the erstwhile local elite into making their presence felt among the ranks of the national elite, and the rise of the Sinhala language as a highly potent political cause was part and parcel of those developments. Then the Sinhalese literati—Buddhist monks, Sinhalese schoolteachers, notaries public, ayurvedic physicians, and Sinhalese journalists—were to enter the political arena as "language militarists," battling to bring about the triumph of Sinhala Only as the official language as against Parity of Status for Sinhala and Tamil.

The Aftermath of the Official Language Resolution of 1943

As noted, the original official language resolution of 1943 was later amended to give equal status to Sinhala and Tamil as official languages. Nevertheless, apprehension about the implications of this particular arrangement upon the Sinhalese community was explicitly stated, even by some who had agreed to the amendment. Unlike the earlier resolutions aiming at the functional reallocation of linguistic codes within the polity, this occasion witnessed the surfacing of Sinhalese individualism, which in effect sought to confine the benefits of the move to Sinhala alone. This was because the question of official language involved the most vital sociopolitical considerations, and, as far as the Sinhalese were concerned, the placement of the Sinhala language on an equal official status with Tamil suggested potentially dire consequences, even regarding their national survival.

Nevertheless, it appears that the Sinhalese political leadership chose not to elaborate extensively upon these implications, and no attempt was made to utilize the issue for political advantage—largely because Sinhalese political leaders, including those such as Bandaranaike and Goonesinghe, who had usually been vociferous about Sinhalese interests, were finding the need for political caution in those crucial years leading to the transfer of power. The virtue of caution with regard

95. For details about this distinction, see Roberts 1974.

to ethnic politics was perhaps more in demand from the Sinhalese, the majority community, than from the minority communities. Thus, while we see the Sinhalese politicians such as Jayewardene and Bandaranaike asking for "fairness" and "generosity" from their community, leading Tamil politicians did not reciprocate with similar pleas to their own community. The prominent response was alarmist, and the official language resolution was used to draw the conclusion that the Sinhalese were intent on undermining "the position of the Ceylon Tamils in the professions and the administrative services."[96] Here was one of the most sensitive points in Tamil anxieties—that the advantageous position held by the Tamil community in the professions, when English was the official language, was to be drastically undermined once English was removed from that dominant position.[97]

The fact that the Sinhalese political leaders chose to be cautious and moderate at this juncture did not mean that communalistic political opinions were absent among the Sinhalese populace. There were instances in the mid-1940s when the exclusive interests of the Sinhalese ethnic group were sponsored, even at the expense of the "Ceylonese nationality" that some politicians were eager to promote. Two incidents might be cited involving Jayantha Weerasekera (1895–1949), who assumed leadership of the Heḷa Havula after the demise of Cumaratunga in March 1944 and who was a colleague of Jayewardene and Bandaranaike in the Ceylon National Congress, as a member of its Working Committee since 1943 and one of its joint secretaries in 1946. At the Twenty-Fifth Annual Sessions of the Congress in 1945 (a few months after the passage of the official language resolution) a Declaration of Fundamental Rights was discussed. Article 3 of the proposed declaration read as follows: "The culture, language and script of the minorities shall be protected."

Weerasekera proposed, at a meeting of the Congress Committee held subsequently, that the words *language* and *script* be deleted. This was seconded by P. Galloluwa, but the amendment was nevertheless rejected by a majority vote.[98]

Again, where article 25 of the declaration stated that "the official

96. For details, see Russel 1976:473.

97. For a detailed examination using statistics, see K. M. de Silva 1986:84–95.

98. Galloluwa was a representative of the Māradana Association in Colombo and possibly a close associate of Weerasekera. This and the following incidents are cited from Roberts 1977:CLXIV.

language shall be Sinhalese and Tamil," Weerasekera proposed that the words *and Tamil* be deleted. This proposal was also defeated after a lengthy discussion. These incidents show that, even after the passage of the official language resolution in the State Council, there were custodians of Sinhalese ethnic interests who were not prepared to compromise their position regarding the right of the Sinhala language to assume dominant status. Most significant, it was with a Heḷa activist, one with a strong ideological commitment to the Sinhala language, that this singular and exclusive interest manifested itself.

Thus, even after the passage of the "Sinhalese and Tamil" language resolution of 1943 the "Sinhala alone" voice remained undiminished in certain quarters. Perhaps the following statement from a commemorative article on Cumaratunga, written two years after the passage of that resolution, was a forewarning of the struggle that was to ensue in a few years time:

> This is the land of the Heḷa people. It is the Hela language that should be used here. To add Tamil to it is to start another disputation. Therefore, Tamil should not be a state language. (Liyanaheva Tilakaratne, "Viśrādayekugē Guṇānusmaraṇaya," *Sinhala Balaya,* 9 March 1946)

This statement seems to demonstrate that the official language problem impinged heavily on the historically inherited self-image of the Sinhalese people—a self-image that had been mined and refined in multitudinous ethnoreligious activities during the period from about 1815 to 1943.

Even in 1943 and 1944, however, when the national language question first arose, there was no sudden upsurge of defensive language nationalism. Even though some custodians of Sinhala interests were pointing out the "dangers" that would follow the adoption of a two-language formula, there was no significant attempt to elevate Sinhala in the country at large or in the legislature.[99] And when the question of recognizing Tamil along with Sinhala as an official language was put to the State Council in May 1944, twenty-nine members, of whom twenty were Sinhalese, voted for it. It was opposed by only eight,

99. For a perceptive study of the background to the language resolution of 1943–44, see Russel 1978.

among whom were four Sinhalese, one Sri Lankan Moor, one Burgher, and two Europeans.[100] The last three, in any case, were opposed to the idea of replacing English.

By the mid-1950s, however, when the official language issue came up again, there was a dramatic change not only in the political structure but also in the intergroup relations between the Sinhalese and the Tamils. Part and parcel of these changes were the mobilizations of ethnicity that were taking place within the Sinhalese community as well as the Tamil community. These transformations resulted in 1956 in the reversal of the two-language formula in favor of Sinhala Only.

100. Namely B. H. Aluvihare, A. Ratnayake, Dudley Senanayake, U. B. Wanninayaka, A. R. A. Razik, G. A. H. Wille, J. H. Griffith, and J. W. Oldfield. The Moor A. R. A. Razik, while stating that the languages of his community were Arabic and Arabic-Tamil, contended that making Sinhala the official language would "bring unity to our people" (*Debates, SC* 1944:812).

Chapter 9

The Aftermath, 1943–90

At this moment we are . . . trying to restore to the Sinhalese people a rightful inheritance which had been taken away from them.

—K. M. P. Rajaratne, member of Parliament for Welimada, during the debate on the Official Language Act, 1956

Whereas throughout the centuries from the dawn of history the Sinhalese and Tamil nations have divided between them the possession of Ceylon . . . this convention calls upon the Tamil nation . . . to come forward to throw themselves fully into the sacred fight for freedom and to flinch not till the goal of a sovereign socialist State of EELAM is reached.

—From the Vadukkodai Resolution of the Tamil United Liberation Front, 1976.

India achieved political independence from the British empire in 1947, and Sri Lanka followed suit in 1948. Although the island polity, largely due to the restraint exercised by its political leadership, did not experience the bitter communal conflict that characterized the transfer of power in India, it too, within a decade, experienced an intense communal rivalry between the majority Sinhalese (who formed 69.3 percent of the population in 1953) and the largest minority, the Tamils (who were divided into two groups, as Sri Lankan Tamils, 10.9 percent and the "stateless" Indian Tamils, 12 percent). Specifically, the problem arose in the mid-1950s over the choice between Sinhala Only and Sinhala and Tamil as the official language(s) of independent Sri Lanka. In spite of the principle of egalitarianism invoked in support of the two-language formula, especially by the Marxist Lanka Sama Samaja party and the Communist party, whose majority membership was Sinhalese, the advocates of Sinhala Only insisted on their position for several reasons:[1]

1. The following is a summary of the views expressed in this regard at the debate on the Official Language Bill of 1956. See *Parliamentary Debates* 1956.

1. The use of one official language is more efficient and economical than two, as it was being done in India, and Sinhala, which is the language of nearly 70 percent of the people, is the obvious choice.
2. Sinhala is a language found only in Sri Lanka, whereas Tamil has its own homeland in south India, where it enjoys official status, and it is unfair that Tamil, which is only the language of a small minority (the 10.9 percent Sri Lankan Tamils and 5.7 percent Moors), be given parity of status with Sinhala.
3. If Tamil is placed on an equal footing with Sinhala concerning its use in government administration, education, job opportunities, and so on, Tamil, having the advantage of a massive base in neighboring Tamilnadu, with the support of over fifty million speakers and having large literary and scholarly resources, will soon become the dominant language, eventually eliminating Sinhala, which has only ten million speakers who are confined to the island of Sri Lanka.

The language issue seemed to take precedence over everything else during the general election of 1956. With the conclusive victory of the coalition, the Mahajana Eksath Peramuna (People's United Front), led by S. W. R. D. Bandaranaike, upholding the cause of Sinhala Only, the institutionalization of Sinhala interests seemed guaranteed. Bandaranaike brought before Parliament an "Act to Prescribe the Sinhala Language as the One Official Language of Ceylon" (*The Official Language Act No. 33 of 1956*), and it was carried with an overwhelming majority. But the matter did not rest there. A process began of interethnic mistrust and rivalry, maneuverings by politicians for partisan advantage, extremist violence, and foreign intervention, all contributing to an ever-deepening crisis, which has not been fully resolved.

After the passage of the Sinhala Only legislation the government of 1956 and subsequent governments made various attempts to allay the grievances of the Tamil-speaking community. But these attempts failed to satisfy Tamil interests. The long delay in coming to a consensus on the language problem led to the emergence of other problems: namely those concerning employment, higher education, land settlement, devolution of power, and national security. Thus, even a far-reaching recognition of the language rights of the Tamils by the constitution of 1978, creating a virtual parity of status for Tamil with

Sinhala, failed to bring about a lasting settlement.[2] Indeed, by this time the language problem had been transformed into one about national and territorial rights, and a powerful secessionist movement had emerged, intent on setting up a separate Tamil state in the north and east of the island.

The Language Issue: The Failure to Bring about a Political Settlement, 1957–1975

The language problem not only worsened, but also the tensions and fears it generated were soon extended to other areas of national life during the period from 1957 to 1975. Since the passage of the Official Language Act of 1956 two major attempts were made to resolve the issues arising from this Sinhala Only legislation: one in 1957, the Bandaranaike-Chelvanayagam pact (B-C), and the other in 1965–66, the so-called Senanayake-Chelvanayagam pact. Neither of these agreements, arrived at after lengthy consultation between the Federal party (FP), the most representative political grouping among the Tamils, and one of the two largest Sinhalese parties (the first with the Sri Lanka Freedom party [SLFP] and the other with the United National party [UNP]), could be fully implemented. That is primarily because the UNP and the SLFP in turn resorted to fanning up communal anxieties as the other was trying to come to a lasting agreement with the Federalists.

One part of the Tamil-speaking population, the Moors, gradually came to agree to work within the premise of Sinhala as the official language with provision for "the reasonable use of Tamil."[3] The Tamil community, on the other hand, with the Federal party (better known as Ilankai Tamil Arasu Kadchi [Lanka Tamil State party] in Tamil areas) as its chief mouthpiece, gradually came to place greater emphasis on territorial demands and drifted more and more into an intransigent position.

According to the provisions of the Bandaranaike-Chelvanayagam pact, two important steps were to be taken in order to recognize the language rights of Tamil speakers. First, a Regional Councils Bill was drafted with the purpose of devolving power to regional units. Second,

---

2. For details, see K. M. de Silva 1986:287–303. It needs to be noted that the political situation did not permit the full implementation of these provisions.

3. As envisaged by Bandaranaike in 1957; also see the discussion below.

the Tamil Language (Special Provisions) Act was carried through Parliament in 1958, providing for the use of Tamil in prescribed administrative activities in the Northern and Eastern provinces. Furthermore, it recognized the right of the Tamils to have their children educated and to take examinations for entry into public service in the Tamil medium. The enactment of regulations under this act was, however, left for a future occasion, thus delaying its effective implementation.

With regard to the Regional Councils Bill the prime minister could go no further than publishing a draft of the bill in the government gazette in July 1957. Immediately, a massive campaign was mounted against it, alleging that it was an attempt to "divide the country." Much of the strongest and most effective opposition to the bill came from within the prime minister's own party, the SLFP, and he was forced to abandon the bill and declare the B-C pact null and void. The UNP, then in the political wilderness, also campaigned against it. It was argued by these critics that the implementation of a scheme of regional councils along the lines suggested by the pact would preclude the Sinhalese from settling in the Northern and Eastern provinces, while the Tamils would have no restriction in settling in any part of the island. It was also argued that the powers the regional councils in these areas would hold regarding the settlement schemes—that is, settlement of persons on state lands for agricultural purposes—could well be used for an expansionist drive that would threaten the position of the Sinhalese community. These fears were expressed in the context of the ascendancy of the Dravida Munnetra Kazagam (Dravidian Progressive Organization) and other extremist groups in south India with political ambitions stretching over peninsular India into northern Sri Lanka and encompassing the cause of the large group of Indian Tamils in the center of the island.[4]

Having failed to get the support of the SLFP for their demands, the FP next turned to the UNP, which had set up a minority government after the general election of March 1960. When the UNP refused to comply, obviously because of its reluctance to estrange Sinhalese opinion, the FP joined hands with the SLFP to defeat the government. At the next general election held in July of the same year the SLFP returned with a clear majority. Again there was no response to the demands of the FP. Instead, the government appeared intent on the implementation of the Official Language Act of 1956, and this time without promul-

4. For these sentiments, see *Parliamentary Debates* 1956; Ratnatunga 1988:70–104; Jayakody 1967:317–74; and Sumatipala n.d.:81–89.

gating any regulations under the Tamil Language (Special Provisions) Act of 1958. Thus, the Language of Courts Act of 1961 provided for the progressive replacement of English by Sinhala in courts of law.

With the implementation of the Official Language Act public servants appointed after 1956 were required to obtain proficiency in Sinhala if they were to retain their posts. Under these circumstances it appeared as if the government was not ready to give any recognition to the Tamil language, and, consequently, the career opportunities of the Tamils were adversely affected, and very severely at that. The FP launched a civil disobedience campaign in 1961, and the government responded by declaring a state of emergency. The FP campaign fizzled out. Within Parliament it moved into a position of opposition to the SLFP government. When in late 1964 the government—then in alliance with Marxist parties in a coalition—was defeated through the defection of a large group of SLFP, as well as other progovernment members of parliament, the Federal party was a key element in the opposition campaign. The FP had voted with the UNP to bring down the government. Interestingly, the two major Marxist parties, the Lanka Sama Samaja party (LSSP) and the Communist party (CP), gradually abandoned their former language policy, for parity of status for Sinhala and Tamil, and by the early 1960s drifted to a Sinhala Only policy.[5] Their alliance with the SLFP underlined their commitment to this new language policy.

Before the general election of 1965 the FP came to an agreement with the UNP. The UNP agreed to: enact regulations under the Tamil Language (Special Provisions) Act of 1958, thus giving legal recognition to the use of Tamil for specific official purposes; decentralize administration under a scheme of district councils; and give priority to local landless people and to Tamil-speaking persons in the land settlement schemes in the Northern and Eastern provinces.[6]

The FP joined the UNP in forming a government in 1965, and the first part of the pact was fulfilled by legislation in 1966. But the devolution of power to district councils had to be abandoned in the face of the opposition initiated by the SLFP, which took a strong pro-Sinhalese line, and the Marxist parties too joined the opposition campaign. Furthermore, there was pressure from within the UNP as well, and the

5. See Jayawardene 1985:102–13. Horowitz (1985:336) gives an early date for this change.

6. For the full text, see K. M. de Silva 1986:402.

prime minister was forced to abandon the envisaged legislation. Any proposal for devolution could be used to rouse the susceptibilities of the Sinhalese electorate, and both the major parties in the Sinhalese areas, the UNP and the SLFP, have resorted to such political "outbidding" in turn.

In the general elections of 1970 the governing UNP was defeated, and the United Front (UF), whose main component was the SLFP, in coalition with the two major Marxist parties, the LSSP and the CP, came to power with a two-thirds majority in Parliament. Among other things, the coalition of the UNP with the FP was used during elections to discredit the UNP in the Sinhalese areas. One of the major undertakings of the new government was the enactment of the Republican constitution of 1972, which embodied the political ascendancy of Sinhalese-Buddhist interests and a downgrading of minority rights. Not only was Sinhala recognized as the official language, but it was also specifically stated that the regulations under the Tamil Language (Special Provisions) Act of 1958, approved by Parliament in 1966, were subordinate legislation and therefore amenable to amendment and even abrogation. This meant, first of all, that the use of Tamil for official purposes had no constitutional guarantee. Second, the minority safeguards in the former constitution were absent in the new constitution. Third, departing from the principle of religious neutrality, Buddhism was accorded "the foremost place" in the polity, making it "the duty of the state to protect and foster Buddhism" while assuring to all religions the "rights of practice, assembly, etc." Furthermore, the upper house of the legislature, called the Senate, which in the previous constitution had acted as a deterrent to hasty legislation, was abolished. The legislature, in the form of the National State Assembly, elected by popular vote, was made supreme, and no law made by it could be questioned in courts of law. Further strengthening the hands of the legislature and the executive, which was the cabinet of ministers, the public service was brought under that body's control, leading to open assertion of political partisanship in appointments and promotions. Another significant development was the extension of governmental control over the Lake House group of newspapers, the largest newspaper concern in the country, by legislation in 1974, placing it under a board of management appointed by the government. Also in 1974 another group of newspapers, the Davasa Group, was closed down by government order. All these moves in sum not only affected minority rights but also imposed severe restrictions on political dissent, thus weakening the very foundation of democracy.[7]

During the period of the UF government a drastic change was also made in university admissions policies. Under pressure from the Sinhalese districts, whose students formed over 70 percent of the student population at the primary and secondary levels, the government introduced a system of standardizing marks and a district quota system for entry into the universities.[8] From the viewpoint of the Sinhalese students in the less-developed areas of the country, where educational facilities were poor, this action eliminated a system of perpetual deprivation, also giving them the chance for entry into the universities.

For the Tamils, on the other hand, this meant a dramatic change for the worse. While the national proportion of Sri Lankan Tamils in 1969 was 12.9 percent, for example, they held as much as 48.3 percent of the places in the engineering courses in the universities. But with the changes in the admissions system their numbers fell to 24.3 percent in 1973 and 14.2 percent in 1975.[9] This drastic change in university admission policy, although it could be justified, was one of the primary factors in the radicalization of Tamil youth in the north and east of the island, which was to cause so much harm to Sri Lankan public and political life in subsequent years.

The Religious Issue: Assertive Buddhism, 1948–72

While the main arena of communal rivalry in postindependent Sri Lanka was language, religion too played a powerful role in exacerbating communal tensions. While religious rivalry during the early years of independence was mainly between the Buddhists, who formed 64.3 percent of the population, and the 8.9 percent Christians,[10] who continued to hold many privileges as part of the colonial heritage, competition in the religious sphere affected ethnic relations as well. Although the preponderantly large majority of Tamils were Hindus by religion, there were strategically placed Tamil Christians who were confronted by the Sinhala-Buddhist assertiveness.[11] Although some observers believe that Hinduism, being closer to the syncretist Buddhism practiced

7. For details, see K. M. de Silva 1986:247–54.
8. For details, see C. R. de Silva 1987:241.
9. In C. R. de Silva 1987.
10. The figures are from the 1953 census.
11. For some such instances, see Horowitz 1980: chaps. 2 and 9.

by the Sinhalese today, does not appear so alien as Christianity,[12] one cannot assume that historically created phenomenology would always mold ideological stances and control behavioral manifestations.

Earlier in the present study we saw how resurgent Buddhism in the nineteenth century witnessed the emergence of the *bhikkhu* as a social and political activist.[13] Twentieth-century Buddhist assertiveness was mainly spearheaded by the *bhikkhus*, who became effective mobilizers of popular opinions.[14] Buddhist assertiveness on the eve of independence was focused upon the school system, which was regarded as a major source of Christian dominance in public life. After a series of public campaigns, in which *bhikkhu* influence over the masses was unmistakably displayed, a bill curtailing some aspects of Christian supremacy in the educational sphere was carried through the legislature in May 1947.[15] *Bhikkhu* involvement in politics was justified on the grounds that an interest in public affairs was part of the altruistic role of the *bhikkhu* from the early days of Buddhism. And it was claimed that this interest continued all along the history of the *Sāsana*.[16] In the mid-1950s the triumphant campaign to establish Sinhala as the one national official language, and to ensure the primacy of Buddhism in the island polity, established the *bhikkhu* as an unmistakably legitimate opinion leader.[17]

The three-year period of the Bandaranaike government, from 1956 to 1959, saw the peak of *bhikkhu* influence in public affairs.[18] But in September 1959, with the assassination of the prime minister by a *bhikkhu*, there was a sudden and dramatic change of opinion. The orthodox viewpoint that *bhikkhu* political involvement was contrary to strict adherence to *vinaya* (ecclesiastical code) rules asserted itself, and, although individual *bhikkhus* entered the political arena from time to time, *bhikkhu* politics has never recovered from this setback.

The political pressure built up by Buddhist opinion leaders, however, resulted in many notable achievements for the Buddhist side. The establishment of two *pirivena* universities, Vidyōdaya and Vidyālan-

12. For example, see Committee for Rational Development 1984:45.

13. See chapter 4.

14. See Dharmadasa 1988:115–16.

15. See Dharmadasa 1988:111–16.

16. These arguments were cogently put forward by one of the leading *bhikkhu* activists (in Rahula 1946). It has been translated into English as *The Heritage of the Bhikkhu* (New York: Grove Press, 1974).

17. For details, see D. E. Smith 1966.

18. Phadnis 1976:127ff.

kāra,[19] and the setting up of a government Department of Cultural Affairs, which later became a separate ministry with priority being given to Sinhalese and Buddhist cultural activities, were notable achievements in the 1950s. With the state takeover of all "assisted" schools in 1962 Christian influence over the educational system was finally removed, paving the way for the extension of Buddhist influence in this vital sphere of public life.[20] Other events in the early 1960s strengthened Buddhist ascendancy. In the aftermath of an abortive coup d'état in 1962, led by a group of Christian army officers, the opportunity was taken for a purge of the armed forces. The opportunity was also taken to limit as much as possible the recruitment of non-Sinhalese to the armed forces.[21] In the same year the governor general, the head of state who happened to be an Anglican, was replaced by a Buddhist. In his way by the mid-1960s the primacy of Buddhism and Buddhists in the Sri Lankan political system became a hard reality.[22]

Change of governments, however, did not affect the ascendancy of Buddhist influence over public affairs. In 1972, with the adoption of the first Republican constitution, the primacy of Buddhism in the island polity was given constitutional recognition. Chapter 2 of the constitution read as follows:

> The Republic of Sri Lanka shall give Buddhism the foremost place and accordingly it shall be the duty of the state to protect and foster Buddhism while assuring to all religions the rights guaranteed by section 18(1)(d).

This provision was left unchanged when the second Republican constitution was adopted by the succeeding government in 1978. There were other pressures from certain Buddhist activists to make Buddhism the "state religion," as in Burma and Thailand,[23] but these were unheeded.

The constitutional imprimatur given to the primacy of Buddhism in public affairs became another grievance of the Tamils. In the Vadukkodai Resolution of the Tamil United Liberation Front (TULF) in 1976, in which it was agreed to launch a separatist struggle for the establishment of a Tamil state, one of the instances adduced to prove that "suc-

19. The origin of these two institutions was described in Chapter 4.
20. For details, see Dharmadasa 1988:121–22.
21. See Horowitz 1980:53–75 193–216.
22. K. M. de Silva 1986:196–206.
23. *Report* 1978:272, 275.

cessive Sinhalese governments since independence . . . encouraged and fostered an aggressive Sinhala nationalism," was the granting of the foremost place to Buddhism, "thereby reducing the Hindus, Christians and Muslims to second class status in the country."[24]

Apart from the particular achievements of the Buddhist lobby, a factor that would have perturbed minority interests, was the uncompromising stance taken by Buddhist opinion leaders on the language issue; most of them would brook no compromise on the rigid Sinhala Only formula. They were also strong opponents of the proposals to decentralize administration viewing in such projects as the beginning of the possible dismemberment of the island polity. No doubt these apprehensions arose in the context of the territorial demands of the TULF and its political antecedents and the threat posed by the Dravida Munnethra Kazagam ideology in south India. But one may well notice here the lingering potency of the *Sinhaladvīpa* and *Dhammadvīpa* concepts. Thus, in spite of the sobering influence of Buddhist ethics on ethnic strife, Buddhist activism has had a negative effect on attempts at compromise and consensus.[25]

Separatism and Violence

With the failure to bring about a political settlement of the ethnic problem and the frustrations faced by a sizable section of the Tamil population, especially the youth, due to difficulties in employment and in higher education, the aim of a separate Tamil state "moved away from the wild imagination of the lunatic fringes of Tamil politics into the centre of Tamil political calculations."[26] A youth movement named Liberation Tigers of Tamil Eelam (LTTE) was formed in 1975 to carry out an armed struggle for the establishment of a separate state on the island. It was to be named Eelam, and its territory was to be the Northern and Eastern provinces. The emergence of the LTTE marked a dramatic change in the political situation in Sri Lanka. Now the state had to contend with a group that resorted to violence for political secession. The LTTE indulged in planned acts of violence such as robbing banks, damaging state property, and assassinating members of the police and the army as well as others, ranging from Tamil politicians who sup-

24. For the full text, see K. M. de Silva 1986: app. 9.
25. See Matthews 1985:85.
26. Arasaratnam 1979:156.

ported the two main national political parties, the UNP and the SLFP, to persons considered to be police informers. Soon several other militant groups emerged: the Tamil Eelam Liberation Organization, Peoples' Liberation Organization of Tamil Eelam, Eelam National Democratic Liberation Front, Eelam Revolutionary Organization of Students, Eelam Peoples Revolutionary Liberation Front, and so on. By the mid-1980s there were no less than thirty-six such groups.[27] Originally, their acts of violence were confined to the Northern and Eastern provinces, but soon they extended their activities to other areas as well.

Indian Intervention and the Gandhi-Jayewardene Peace Accord, July 1987

Beginning in about the mid-1970s Tamil separatist groups have been battling the Sri Lankan armed forces. The task of containing this guerrilla war has been difficult because the Tamil militants had bases and training facilities in south India as well as in other parts of India. It has been revealed that agents of the Indian government have been involved in the training and arming of certain guerrilla groups.[28] In 1983 the opportunity arose for India to intervene openly when widespread rioting by the Sinhalese led to over five hundred deaths and the flight of over thirty-five thousand Tamils to south India as refugees.[29] At the initial stages of this intervention India's role was constructive insofar as it acted as the intermediary in bringing the representatives of the Sri Lankan government and the Tamil militants to a conference table.

While such attempts were being made to arrive at political settlement the struggle went on in the north and east of Sri Lanka, the terrorist groups making sporadic attacks on Sinhalese villages in the Northern and Eastern provinces as well as on Sinhalese villages in the North Central Province, including the massacre in May 1985 of one hundred forty-six people in the sacred city of Anuradhapura, along with some *bhikkhus* at the Temple of the Sacred Bo Tree. Finally, in mid-1987 there was a strong offensive by the Sri Lankan army, which appeared to be going in for a decisive victory by the end of June. Agitation in Tamilnadu, in response to the accusation that the Sri Lankan army of inflicting heavy casualties on Tamil civilians, led to the government of

27. Ratnatunga 1988:249–57; Gunaratna 1987:27.

28. Weaver 1988; Marks 1987.

29. For details about this incident and other related problems, see K. M. de Silva 1991, Kodikara 1989, and Tambiah 1986.

India intervening, and the offensive was abandoned.[30] Negotiations were undertaken between the Sri Lankan and Indian governments, and conditions to bring an end to the civil war and establish a political settlement were agreed upon.

On 29 July Prime Minister Rajiv Gandhi of India and President J. R. Jayewardene of Sri Lanka signed a peace agreement. It was agreed that: (1) the Northern and Eastern provinces were initially to be a single unit in a devolved political structure with the whole country being divided into regional administrative units called provincial councils; a plebiscite in the Eastern province one year later was to decide whether the amalgamation of the two provinces was to stay; (2) the Tamil language was to be recognized as a national official language along with Sinhala; and (3) Tamil militants were to hand over their arms and Indian troops were to be stationed in the Northern and Eastern provinces to act as a peace-keeping force.[31]

On 9 October 1987 the government placed before Parliament two bills entitled the "Thirteenth Amendment to the Constitution of the Democratic Socialist Republic of Sri Lanka." The first bill was to recognize Tamil along with Sinhala as an official language, and English was designated as the "link language." The second, the Provincial Councils Bill, sought to provide for the setting up of provincial councils and clarified the procedures to be followed in the process, thus giving constitutional recognition to the devolution of power to these provincial units of administration. By the Provincial Councils Act no. 42 of 1987 nine provincial councils were set up: namely Western, North Western, Uva, Sabaragamuva, Central, Eastern, Southern, North Central, and Northern. The Thirteenth Amendment, which was passed by a two-thirds majority in Parliament on 12 November, was a landmark in the history of language and language-related problems in Sri Lanka. After thirty-one years of bitter conflict there was a return to the compromise reached in 1944. Tamil received equality of status with Sinhala as an official language, and, as a pragmatic arrangement, English, whose importance as a language of administration and higher education could not be denied, was recognized as the link language—a term that was not specific and whose definition was obviously left open to personal interpretation.[32]

30. Weaver 1988; Marks 1987.

31. For a detailed analysis, see Kodikara, ed., 1989.

32. See *Parliamentary Debates* (12 November 1987).

The novel feature, the setting up of provincial councils, it was hoped, would transfer enough power to the local areas, especially the Tamil-speaking localities, for them to be satisfied that they were being allowed to manage their own affairs. Some difficult problems remained, however, namely the question of land settlement—whether the regional units should have absolute control over the choice of settlers and the question of police and armed forces in the provinces—and how much control the center should have in this crucial area of national security.

Problems and Prospects

Indian intervention, particularly the presence of the Indian peacekeeping force (IPKF), in Sri Lanka has led to dramatic changes of opinion, in Tamilnadu and in Sri Lanka. The Tamilnadu government in 1987, led by then chief minister M. G. Ramachandran, which earlier had sympathized with the terrorist groups, joined the Delhi government in the formulation of the peace accord. It was generally agreed that the accord was an affirmation of the supremacy of Indian interests in the region. Hence even in Tamilnadu the mood was reconciliation under its conditions. Among the Sri Lankan Tamils, however, particularly those espousing the cause of Eelam, there was a sense of betrayal, specifically because India was looked to for support in achieving Eelam. The more moderate politicians, and even those of the TULF hierarchy, expressed their satisfaction with the accord, since it guaranteed the devolution of power to an amalgamated Northern and Eastern provincial unit. But soon they had to contend with the supremacy of the LTTE and other terrorist groups in these regions. Subsequent to the signing of the peace accord, several TULF politicians, including its leader, A. Amirthalingam, were assassinated by gunmen now known to be members of the LTTE.

From the point of view of Sinhalese interests the Gandhi-Jayewardene Accord was seen as a definite setback. Apart from the vitiation of the *Sinhaladvīpa* concept, crucial economic and political factors were involved.[33] First, the granting of a large measure of autonomous power, substantial enough to satisfy Tamil interests that have campaigned for a separate state, to two regions that constitute 28 percent

33. For appraisals, see Kodikara, ed., 1989; C. R. de Silva 1987:234, 268; and the Sinhala publications *Vivaraṇa* (April 1988) and *Rāvaya* (April 1988).

of the total land area of the country could severely curtail the spatial mobility and economic interests in general of the Sinhalese community. The problems might become more acute as time goes by, since most of the high-density population areas are in the Sinhalese districts, and land available for settlement is in the Northern and Eastern provinces. In fact the possibility that the Sri Lankan Tamils, who are only 12.6 percent of the population, could have a dominant position in a territory that would be nearly one-third of the island has been one of the arguments put forward against the amalgamation of the two provinces. Apart from that, the concept of a "traditional Tamil homeland," a theory of recent origin and dubious validity, appeared to have achieved recognition.[34]

There has been widespread resentment against the arrival of the Indian army, expressive of the age-old fear of domination by India. The sudden threat of violence posed by the Sinhalese militant organization the Janatha Vimukti Peramuna (JVP) (People's Liberation Front) and its armed wing, the Deshapremi Janata Vyaparaya (Patriotic People's Movement), against the state, the politicians of the ruling party, and others who did not contribute to their nationalist ideology appears to be partly due to this sense of frustration.[35] The ideology of this movement has not yet been understood in detail. It appears to contain a haphazard mixture of egalitarianism and Marxism with Sinhalese ethnocentrism. One thing is clear, however. There has been no religious (Buddhist) content in this ideology. In that, as well as in its strong anti-Indian stance, the JVP has a parallel with the Heḷa movement. Here we are reminded of the fact that James D'Alwis also did not subscribe to a Buddhist ideology in his expressions of Sinhalese ethnocentrism.

34. For a critical appraisal, see G. H. Peiris 1991; K. M. de Silva 1987; and Samarasinghe 1988.

35. The JVP has been a factor in Sri Lanka's political scene since 1971. During 1987–89, with its assassinations, work stoppages, and destruction of public property, it posed a serious threat to the government. But by the end of December 1989 the movement had been crushed with the killing or arrest of all its leaders. For a perceptive analysis of the JVP, see "The JVP Insurrection, 1987–89," by C. A. Chandraprema, serialized in a number of articles in the daily newspaper the *Island* from January 1990. Also see R. Gunaratna 1990.

Appendix: Biographical Notes on Important Personalities Mentioned in the Text

Aluwihare, Bernard (1902–61)

A graduate of Oxford University, he was a lawyer by profession. He entered the State Council in 1936 as member for Matale, his home area in the central hills. He had intimate contacts with the Indian nationalist movement, being a personal friend of Gandhi and Nehru. He joined Bandaranaike in the formation of the SLFP in 1951 and entered parliament again in 1952. He left the SLFP, however, to join the UNP in 1956 and was defeated in the general elections. Aluwihare is remembered for his struggles in the cause of the Kandyan peasantry.

Arunachalam, Sir Ponnambalam (1853–1924)

Having studied at Royal College, Colombo, Arunachalam won a scholarship to the University of Cambridge. On his return to the island he entered the prestigious Ceylon Civil Service and soon rose to one of the highest posts given to Ceylonese – registrar general and fiscal of the Western Province. Arunachalam, however, was more interested in the agitation for political reform and retired in 1913 to enter politics. He was a leading figure in the formation of the Ceylon National Congress (1919) and was elected its first president. In 1921 he and many Tamils left the congress over the dispute over a Tamil reserved seat in the Western Province. Arunachalam was a pioneer trade unionist and a key figure in the demand for a University of Ceylon.

Bandaranaike, Solomon West Ridgeway Dias (1899–1959)

Born into a low-country aristocratic family that was Anglican by religion, Bandaranaike studied first at St. Thomas' College, Colombo. Later he entered Christ Church College, Oxford, and was the first Sri Lankan to be the secretary of its student union. After graduation he returned to the island, embraced Buddhism, and practiced as a barrister for some time before entering politics as a member of the Colombo Municipal Council. In 1931 he entered the State Council as member for Veyangoda, his hometown, and retained that seat until his death. From 1936 to 1947 he was minister of Local Government, and he was minister of Health and Local Government and leader of the House in the first parliament of independent Sri Lanka. He left the governing UNP to form his own party, the SLFP, in 1951 and, along with some smaller parties, led it to a resounding victory in 1956. His brief administration, from 1956 to 1959, is remembered for several notable socialist measures, including the nationalization of bus transport and the paddy lands legislation, giving security of tenure to tenant farmers. Above all, Bandaranaike is remembered for his sponsorship of the Sinhala language and Buddhism as political forces.

Bastian, Calutantrige Don (1852–1921)
Dramatist, educationalist, and journalist. Having produced the play *Rolina* (1876), he introduced the *nurti* theatrical form (in imitation of a contemporary north Indian opera) to the Sinhalese audiences. Bastian was a pioneer in the Buddhist schools movement, having founded the Punya Samvari school in Colombo Pettah in the early 1870s. He was editor of *Lak Rivi Kiraṇa* before inaugurating *Dinapathā Pravurti,* the first daily newspaper in Sinhala. He founded several voluntary associations in Colombo and was one of the pioneers in trade union activity; when he was first employed as a laborer, he founded a union in the Government Press, Colombo.

Batuvantudawe, Charles (1874–1940)
Son of Pundit Batuvantudawe, he was active in the temperance movement and the Buddhist schools movement. Educated at Royal College, Batuvantudawe proceeded to England where he became a barrister-at-law from Grey's Inn. He entered the State Council in 1936 to represent the Kalutara electorate and died in 1940. At the by-election that followed his son Upali was elected to the same seat.

Batuvantudawe, Don Andiris de Silva Sri Devaraksita (1819–92)
Born in Batuvantudawa near Galle, Batuvantudawe was ordained as a *bhikkhu* and studied under *bhikkhu* Walane. He disrobed in 1945 but remained a steadfast Buddhist. Equally proficient in Sinhala, Pali, and Sanskrit, he was one of the earliest scholars to edit classical literary works for printing. He was teacher to *bhikkhu* Hikkaduve, James D'Alwis, and many others. Batuvantudawe was the first Buddhist editor of a Sinhala periodical, *Yatalaba,* in the mid-1850s. He also took part in some early controversies between the Buddhists and the Christians by writing *Kristiani Prajnapti Khandanaya.* When, after years of Buddhist agitation, civil registration was established in 1888, Batuvantudawe was appointed a registrar.

Buddhaghosa,* bhikkhu *(A.D. 5th c.)
An Indian *brahaman* who became a Buddhist monk. He arrived in Sri Lanka in the early fifth century to translate into Pali the voluminous commentaries to the Buddhist canon compiled by the island *bhikkhus.* These commentaries remain to this day in the form he edited and translated. The Sinhala originals have disappeared. Although we hear of other commentators, Buddhaghosa is recognized as the greatest one.

Buddharakshita, Ven.* bhikkhu *Tibbotuvave (d. 1773)
He was the chief disciple of Saranankara and was recognized as being second only to the latter in erudition and piety. He was appointed deputy Sangha Raja by King Kirti Sri Rajasinghe. By this time he was also the head of the Malvatte Vihāraya, one of the two chief monasteries of the Siamese fraternity. Among

Tibbotuvave's literary contributions special mention should be made of the fourth part of the *Mahāvaṃśa,* which Tibbotuvave updated to the reign of Kirti Sri.

Canagaratnam, A. (d. 1929)
He was the elected representative of the Northern Province, southern division, in the Legislative Council from 1925 to 1929. He was a journalist and was the first chairman of the Jaffna Urban District Council.

Chelvanayagam, Samuel James Valupillai (1898–1977)
A lawyer by profession and, unlike most of the Tamil political leaders, a Christian by faith, he is best known as the founder of the Ilankai Tamil Arasu Kadchi (Ceylon Tamil State party), better known as the Federal party (1949). A teacher before entering politics as an associate of Ponnambalam, he later founded his own party in 1944 to work for a better deal for the Tamils. With the rise of Sinhala-Buddhist revivalism in the 1950s Chelvanayagam created a countermovement among the Tamils. One of his final political acts was the inauguration of the Tamil United Liberation Front, which had a secessionist aim. The two pacts he made with prime ministers Bandaranaike (1958) and Senanayake (1965) are considered now as the last attempts by the Tamil politicians to solve the ethnic problem within a unitary state.

Coomaraswamy, Ananda Kentish (1877–1947)
He was the son of Sir Muthu Coomaraswamy, a Sri Lankan Tamil, and Elizabeth Clay Beeby, an English lady. Having been formally educated in England and earning a doctorate in geology, Ananda arrived in Sri Lanka in 1903 to be appointed the director of the Geological Survey. He was a connoisseur of the traditional arts and crafts of Sri Lanka and India and used his tours of the island to get to know this declining aspect of the old culture. His monumental *Medieval Sinhalese Art* (1908) sums up almost all available knowledge on the subject. In order to encourage the Sri Lankans to preserve their traditional culture he founded the Ceylon Social Reform Society and inaugurated a journal, the *Ceylon National Review.* By 1917, having with him a large collection of ancient art treasures from India and Sri Lanka, he accepted the post of the curator of Oriental art in the Museum of Fine Arts at Boston and remained there until his death. He wrote voluminously on art, literature, and philosophy.

Coomaraswamy, Sir Muthu (1834–79)
Son of A. Coomaraswamy, the first representative of the Tamils in the Legislative Council (1835–36). Muthu, first educated in the Royal Academy, later proceeded to England where he became the first non-Christian South Asian to be admitted to the English Bar. He was appointed the Tamil Representative in the Legislative Council, in 1861, and held that post till his untimely death in 1879. He was a personal friend of Disraeli and was knighted in 1875. In the Legislative Council he advocated causes such as the promotion of Oriental Studies, the establishment of an Archeological Survey and the Colombo Museum. He translated into English the Pali *Sutta Nipata,* containing the Buddha's teachings,

the *Dathavamsa* (the story of the Tooth Relic) and *Arichchandra,* a Hindu story. He was married to an English lady and Ananda Coomaraswamy was their only child. Sir Muthu's nephews Ramanathan and Arunachalam were also prominent politicians.

Cumaratunga, Munidasa (1887–1944)
Cumaratunga was the most outstanding Sinhala language nationalist of the early twentieth century. He was a teacher and an inspector of Anglo-Vernacular schools before leaving government service to embark on a dynamic career "to uplift the *heḷa* (pure Sinhala) language." He edited with exegesis over thirty works of classical Sinhala literature and wrote over twenty-five school textbooks and several collections of poetry. He was the founding editor of two journals, *Subasa* (Sinhala) and *The Helio* (English), and was the founder of the group Heḷa Havula (Pure Sinhala Combine).

D'Alwis, James (1823–78)
The foremost bilingual (Sinhala-English) scholar in nineteenth-century Sri Lanka. He was a lawyer by profession but is best remembered as a scholar. Although he was a Christian, he kept close contact with *bhikkhus* and other Buddhist scholars. He was universally acknowledged as a leader of the Sinhala community and was appointed as the Sinhala representative in the Legislative Council in 1864 and 1875.

de Silva, John (1857–1922)
Having received an English education in the Colombo Academy and planning to be a teacher, de Silva studied Sinhala, Pali, and Sanskrit from Batuvantudawe. Drawn into the theater, de Silva wrote and produced the *Rāmāyaṇaya* in 1886 but, due to economic difficulties, suspended these activities to enter law college and became a solicitor. He returned to the theater but with a complete transformation in his outlook. Henceforth de Silva proceeded to utilize theater to inculcate nationalist sentiments, and he is remembered today as the producer of a large number of nationalistic plays using themes from Sinhalese history.

de Silva, Wilbert Arthur (1869–1942)
A veterinary surgeon by profession W. A. de Silva was a temperance worker, Buddhist educator, scholar, philanthropist, and politician. He was for some time president of the Buddhist Theosophical Society and the manager of its schools. He had considerable wealth, which he used to finance Buddhist causes; at the time of his death even his own house, the palatial "Sravasti," had been mortgaged. He entered the legislature in 1921 as an elected representative and after 1931 was the minister of health.

Dhammaloka, Ven.* bhikkhu *Ratmalane (1826–87)
Born in Ratmalana near Colombo, he was ordained at a young age. Later he studied under *bhikkhu* Walane Siddhartha. Ratmalane was an accomplished

painter and helped the restoration of many temples in the North Western Province. His greatest contribution was the founding of the Vidyalankara Pirivena in 1875 at Peliyagoda near Colombo. His pupil Dharmarama, who collaborated with him in many scholarly projects, was to continue the work Ratmalane started.

Dharmapala, Anagarika (1864–1933)
Son of a leading businessman in Colombo, he was inspired in his youth by the early Buddhist revivalists such as the *bhikkhus* Migettuwatte Gunananda and Hikkaduwe Sumangala. With the advent of Olcott and the founding of the BTS he became a full-time activist in Buddhist causes. Discarding the name David given to him by his parents, he adopted the name Dharmapala and became an *anagārika* (a new role of ascetic layman). As a devoted temperance worker, he toured the island denouncing the Westerners for corrupting the moral life of the Sinhalese people. Dharmapala is best remembered for the campaign he inaugurated for freeing Buddha Gayā, the birthplace of the Buddha, from the hands of a Hindu priestly landlord. He inaugurated an association called the Mahā Bōdhi Society, which, in addition to the above agitation, also ran some schools. He founded the paper *Sinhala Bauddhayā*. He also inaugurated a scheme to train Sinhalese youth in modern industries, sending some of them to Japan to be trained. Another of his modernistic schemes was to initiate Buddhist missionary activity abroad, sending *bhikkhus* to India and England for the purpose. During the last two years of his life he was ordained as a *bhikkhu*.

Dharmarama, Ven.* bhikkhu *Ratmalane (1853–1918)
The second and the most famous of the principals of Vidyālankāra Pirivena, which was founded by his teacher *bhikkhu* Dhammaloka. Dharmarama edited and printed a large number of Sinhala, Pāli, and Sanskrit works. One of his outstanding contributions was the clarification of orthographic conventions regarding the use of the letters cerebral *ṇ* and *ḷ* as against dental *n* and *l*. The journal *Satya Samuccaya* (1887), founded by him at the behest of his teacher Dhammaloka, was one of the earliest scholarly journals in Sinhala. The two collaborated in many projects such as the writing of the *Sanskruta Śabda Mālāva* and the editing of the twelfth-century Sinhala classic the *Dharmapradīpikāva*.

Dharmaratna, Pundit Matara (1844–1925)
He is better known as Pahan Katruu ("the editor of *Lak Miṇi Pahana*") because he edited this newspaper for several decades. He was born in Piladuwa near Matara in the southern littoral and was ordained as a *bhikkhu*. He went to Burma to study Pali and Buddhism. Soon after returning to the island in 1881 he disrobed but remained a steadfast Buddhist. He was considered an expert on Buddhist metaphysics (*abhidhamma*) and had many *bhikkhus* as his students. Having written and edited over fifty books, Dharmaratna is best known for his edition of the voluminous *Visuddhi Mārga Sannaya* (13th c.) with explicatory notes.

Elliot, Christopher (d. 1859)
A Baptist born in Ireland, he came to Sri Lanka in 1834 as a medical officer but was drawn into politics, and his was the first and most powerful demand for elective representation. The society he founded, called the Friends of Ceylon (1843), and the newspaper the *Colombo Observer,* which he edited, were the forums whereby he introduced to the colony some of the more advanced political views of the times: the separation of church and state, in which he campaigned against the Anglican establishment; and the adoption of the elective principle, whereby the native population would have the right to elect its representatives.

Epa Appuhamy, Don Philip de Silva (1810–91)
A pupil of *bhikkhu* Walane Siddhartha, Epa Appuhamy was a leading figure among the Buddhists of nineteenth-century Colombo. He was a pioneer in the revival of Āyurveda, a leading patron to the founding of Vidyōdaya Pirivena (1873), and in the establishment of Lankābhinava Viśruta Press (1863), one of the earliest printing presses of the Buddhists. He is best remembered today as the founder of the still continuing ephemeris *Āpā Panchānga Lita,* an authoritative reference work for astrologers.

Geiger, Wilhelm (1856–1943)
Born in Munich, Germany, Geiger became professor of Indo-Iranian languages at the University of Munich. Becoming interested in Pāli and Buddhist literature, he arrived in Sri Lanka in 1895 and wrote two books in German on the Sinhalese language. One of his greatest contributions to Sri Lankan studies was the editing and translation into English of the *Mahāvaṃśa,* the sixth-century historical chronicle and its additional sections, the so-called *Cūlavaṃśa* parts 1 and 2, compiled over time. The government invited him to advise on the compilation of the *Sinhalese Dictionary,* which was launched in 1927.

Goonesinghe, Alexander Ekanayaka (1891–1967)
Educated at Dharmaraja College, Kandy, he came to Colombo to study law and was drawn to politics. Organizing Colombo's working class in the 1920s, he became their undisputed leader until the emergence of the Marxists in the 1930s. The strikes he organized, such as the Colombo Harbour strike of 1927 and the Colombo tram-car strike of 1929, were the largest strikes to date. A devoted temperance worker, Goonesinghe founded several journals such as *The Searchlight* (in English) and *Vīrayā* (in Sinhala). He served as the chief government whip in the first parliament (1948).

Gunananda,* bhikkhu *Migettuwatte (1824–91)
Born in Migettuwatte, a village in the southern littoral, he was educated for some time in a mission school where he gathered a knowledge of English and an understanding of Christianity. Ordained at the age of twenty, he came to Colombo and stayed at the temple at Kotahena, whose chief incumbent was his uncle. Gunananda is best known as the foremost Buddhist orator in the Buddhist-Christian controversies in Baddegama (1865), Weragoda (1865),

Udanwita (1867), Gampola (1871), and Panadura (1873). Olcott's description "the terror of the missionaries" epitomizes his performance. Gunananda also organized voluntary associations, ran newspapers and periodicals, brought out pamphlets, and did itinerant preachings in the Buddhist cause. His diary records over four thousand such preachings.

Gunasekera, Abraham Mendis (1869–1931)

Educated in the Wesleyan Mission School of Amabalangoda, Gunasekera joined the government clerical service. While serving in Kalutara, he came under the influence of the reputed scholar *bhikkhu* Waskaduwe Subhuti from whom he learned Sinhala, Pāli, and Sanskrit. Because of his competence in languages, he was appointed a translator to the Registrar General's Office in Colombo. His *Comprehensive Grammar of the Sinhalese Language* (in English, 1891) was the most detailed grammar on the language yet available. He was also the editor of *Gñānāvabhāṣaya* (est. 1896), one of the earliest scholarly journals in Sinhala. Turning to lexicography, he produced an *English-Sinhalese Dictionary* (1905) and a *Sinhalese-English Dictionary* (1915).

Gunawardena, Don Philip Rupasinghe (1900–1972)

Son of a village headman and educated at Ananda College, he went to the University of Wisconsin in the United States to study agriculture. On his return to the island he joined hands with N. M. Perera, S. A. Wickramasinghe, and others to form the first Marxist political party in the island, the LSSP. Gunawardena entered the State Council as member for Avisawella in 1936. During the Second World War Gunawardena, N. M. Perera, and several other Marxist leaders were arrested by the colonial authorities, but they were able to escape from prison. Gunawardena was in the first parliament in 1948. In the 1956 general elections he formed a coalition with Bandaranaike and was appointed minister of agriculture. His greatest contribution was the Paddy Lands Act, which guaranteed the tenurial rights of tenant farmers. Gunawardena left government in 1958 and remained in the political wilderness until 1965, when he returned to parliament in a coalition with the UNP and became the minister of industries and fisheries. He lost his seat in 1970.

Gunawardene R. S. S. (Sir Senarath) (d. 1981)

Born in Matara, he was educated at St. Thomas' College, Matara, and St. Thomas' College, Colombo. He functioned for sometime as the principal of Sri Sumangala College, Panadura, a BTS school. In 1926 he qualified as an advocate and began to practice law as a member of the bar. As an active member of the Ceylon National Congress, he was also its secretary for nine years. In 1936 he entered the State Council to represent the Gampola seat. He was a close associate of S.W.R.D. Bandaranaike and was in the Sinhala Maha Sabha for some time. In the first parliament (1948–51) he was minister without portfolio. He was knighted and functioned as Sri Lanka's ambassador in the United Kingdom, United States, and Canada and as the country's permanent representative at the United Nations.

Gunawardhana, Mudaliyar William Frederick (1861–1935)
Equally proficient in Sinhala and English, Gunawardhana became the chief interpreter of the Department of Education, but he is remembered today as one of the foremost Sinhala scholars of the early twentieth century. His edition of and lengthy exegeses to the poem *Guttila Kāvyaya* (15th c.) and to the thirteenth-century grammar the *Sidat Saňgarāva* remain standard works today. In 1908 he inaugurated a journal named *Silumina,* which became a forum for the leading Sinhala scholars of the day. He also took part in several controversies of the time such as the Guttila Vādaya (1907) and Ārya-Draviḍa Vādaya (1918). The latter was initiated by Gunawardhana's pronouncement that the Sinhalese language had a Dravidian grammatical structure while having an Āryan (Indo-European) vocabulary. Gunawardhana's view was not supported by any other scholar.

Harischandra, Walisimha (1877–1913)
Born in Negombo, a coastal town north of Colombo, he first studied under *bhikkhus* and later attended Wesley College, Colombo, for an English education. Having come under the influence of Anagarika Dharmapala, he changed his name (from David de Silva), left law studies, in which he was engaged at the time, and took to full-time social and religious service. Following Dharmapala, he too became a *brahmācari* (lay celibate). As a devoted temperance worker, Harischandra toured the length and breadth of the island delivering lectures on Buddhist and nationalist themes. His greatest undertaking was the struggle to establish a sacred city in Anuradhapura, making the area occupied by the Buddhist ruins free of shops, government buildings, and lay dwellings. He was arrested on the charge of inciting a mob in the 1903 riots in Anuradhapura. He has written a number of guidebooks on Anuradhapura which contain glowing accounts of the ancient Sinhalese civilization.

Jayatilaka, Sir Baron (D. B.) (1868–1944)
He began his education at Vidyālankāra Pirivena under *bhikkhu* Dharmarama then joined the BTS schools and became the first principal of Dharmaraja College, Kandy, also serving for some time as principal of Ananda College, Colombo. He went to England and obtained a bachelor of arts, bachelor of laws, and master of arts degree from Oxford University. Upon his return to the island he entered politics and was elected to the Legislative Council in 1924 and later to the State Council. He functioned as minister of home affairs and the deputy chairman of the board of ministers (chairman being the governor) during the period 1931–42; he was knighted in 1932. Because of his erudition in Oriental languages, he was appointed editor-in-chief of the *Sinhala Dictionary* inaugurated in 1927. In 1942 he left politics to become Ceylon's ambassador in New Delhi. As an accomplished scholar, he edited a number of Sinhala classics for publication.

Jayewardene, Junius Richard (b. 1906)
Born into a family of lawyers and educated in Royal College, Colombo, he en-

tered the Law College and became a lawyer. He joined the Ceylon National Congress in the late 1930s. Jayewardene was fascinated by the Indian nationalist movement and attended the Ramgarh sessions of the Indian National Congress in 1940. He entered the State Council in 1942 as member for Kelaniya (which had been vacated by Sir Baron Jayatilaka). In the first parliament he was appointed minister of finance. Subsequently, he served in all UNP cabinets as minister of food and minister of state. In 1977, after being out of power for seven years, he led the UNP to a resounding victory. He is the architect of the 1978 constitution creating the post of executive president, which he himself filled until January 1989. One of his last political acts was the signing in 1987 of the Indo-Sri Lanka Agreement with Rajiv Gandhi, prime minister of India.

Lorenz, Charles Ambrose (1829–71)

A Burgher, educated at the Colombo Academy (the precursor of the Royal College), he studied law to become one of the most outstanding lawyers in nineteenth-century Sri Lanka. He was nominated by the government to represent the Burghers in the Legislative Council. Being an accomplished writer, he founded the journal *Young Lanka,* which became a forum for many English educated natives, such as James D'Alwis. Buying the *Examiner* from expatriate owners, he created the first native-owned English newspaper in the island. He is credited with coining the word *Ceylonese,* denoting an overarching national identity made up of individual ethnic identities.

Malalsekera, Gunapala Piyasena (1899–1973)

Son of an *āyurvedic* physician at Panadura, south of Colombo, he gave up plans to be a Western medical practitioner in order to study Oriental languages. He entered the Ceylon University College and obtained a bachelor of arts degree in Oriental languages. By this time he had come under the influence of Dharmapala and the revivalist movement and changed his original Western name, George Pieris. He taught at Ananda College for some time, where he, with his former teacher P. de S. Kularatna, introduced the Sinhala "national costume." He studied in England and obtained a master of arts degree and a doctorate. He returned to the island to be principal of Nalanda College and later joined the University College as a lecturer in Pāli. Earning the doctor of letters degree, he was appointed professor of Pāli, Sanskrit, and Sinhalese in 1939. When the University of Ceylon was established in 1942 he became Professor of Pāli and dean of the faculty of Oriental Studies. He was president of the All Ceylon Buddhist Congress from 1939 to 1957 and the founding president of the World Fellowship of Buddhists, serving from 1950 to 1958. Toward the end of his career he served as Sri Lanka's ambassador in the Soviet Union, United Kingdom, and Canada.

Müller, Friedrich Max (1823–1900)

Born in Dessan, central Germany, the son of a distinguished poet, Müller studied comparative philology and Sanskrit at the universities of Leipzig, Berlin, and Paris. In 1850 he accepted a professionship at the University of Oxford. In

1860 he was made professor of Comparative Philology there and held that post until his retirement in 1875. Perhaps his most ambitious project was the editing and translating of Indian religious works under the title *The Sacred Books of the East*. One of his most influential theories was that about the Aryans, promulgated sometime in the 1850s, whereby he identified the linguistic group with the ethnic group and implied that Aryans were superior to others (such as "the Semitic and Turanian races"). Although later, by about 1872, he qualified his earlier statements, it did not prevent some others from using those ideas for expressions of racial superiority.

Munidasa, Hemapala (1903–58)
He was a Sinhalese journalist and novelist, who in his early years came under the influence of Anagarika Dharmapala. Later Munidasa became the editor of *Sinhala Balaya* (Sinhala Power) and *Sinhalē* (Sinhala Land). Both these newspapers were sponsored by Bandaranaike, and Munidasa was his protégé during the 1940s and the 1950s. *Sinhalē* eventually became the organ of the SLFP. Munidasa is well known for his forceful writings in the causes of Sinhalese ethnicity and Buddhism.

Nalliah, Vallipuram (1909–76)
An educator before entering politics, he was a trained graduate and taught at Ramanatha Mission School of Batticaloa and was later a principal of the Government Men's Training School in Batticaloa. He was also a member of the Batticaloa Urban Council. He entered the State Council as member for Trincomalee-Batticaloa, having won a by-election in 1943. In the 1948 parliament he represented the Kalkudah seat and was appointed parliamentary secretary to the minister of health and local government. In the 1952 parliament he served as minister of posts and broadcasting.

Olcott, Colonel Henry Steel (1832–1907)
Olcott was a native of New Jersey, United States, and a veteran of the American Civil War. He was an agriculturist as well as a lawyer. His interest in philosophy led him to inaugurate the Theosophical Society in New York in 1875. Having learned of the Panadura controversy (1873) between Buddhists and Christians, he arrived in Sri Lanka in 1880. In Sri Lanka he is remembered today as a champion of Buddhism, and there is a statue of him in Colombo. He set up a Buddhist lay schools system and organized the Buddhist Defence Committee, the first attempt by Buddhists to fight for their rights. He was also associated with the designing of the Buddhist flag and the establishment of the Vesak holiday.

Pereira, John
Pereira was one of the few outstanding Sinhala scholars among the Christians in nineteenth-century Sri Lanka. In the 1850s he was the principal of the Colombo Teachers' Training College. As editor of *Śāstra Nidhānaya* (est. 1846),

he was the first Sinhalese to edit a Sinhala journal (the first Sinhala journals in the 1830s and 1840s were edited by European missonaries). Pereira edited two more Sinhala journals, *Śāstrālankāraya* (est. 1853) and *Siyabas Lakarī* (est. 1857). *Śāstrālankāraya* became famous for the Sav Sat Dam controversy carried out in its pages. Pereira was also the author of *Heladiv Rajaniya* (1853), a history of Sri Lanka. In the 1870s he was the principal of Borella English School in Colombo.

Perera, Edward Walter (1875–1953)
A lawyer by profession, Perera was one of the most prominent figures in the movement for constitutional reform in early twentieth-century Sri Lanka. He played a leading part in the post-riots campaign for justice in 1915, going to England with a petition and lobbying support for that cause. Perera had a flair for historical research. His *Ceylon Banners and Standards* (1916) was published as a memoir of the Colombo Museum and even today it remains an authoritative work. He was elected to the Legislative Council in 1921 to represent the Western Province. In the first State Council (1931) he represented the Horana seat. Disappointed with the Ceylon National Congress, he helped to form the Ceylon Liberal League in 1931. His attempts to enter the State Council again in 1936 and 1943 failed, and he retired from politics.

Perera, G. K. W. (d. 1956)
Perera was a lawyer by profession. He was educated at Ananda College and earned a much coveted university scholarship to study at Cambridge University, where he earned a degree. On his return he was principal of Nalanda College, and in 1931 he entered the State Council as elected member for Matara, where he served until 1936. After his defeat in the 1936 elections he was appointed Ceylon's trade commissioner in London.

Perera, Nanayakkarapathirage Martin (1905–79)
He was educated at Ananda College and later entered the London School of Economics, earning both the doctor of philosophy and doctor of science degrees. On his return he was a lecturer in the Ceylon University College. Perera was a leading figure in introducing Marxism in the island, founding, with several others, the LSSP in 1935. He entered the State Council as an elected member in 1936 and retained his seat in the legislature until 1977. He was the first leader of the opposition in independent Sri Lanka (1948). He held the post of finance minister (having joined a coalition government with the SLFP) in 1964–65 and 1970–75.

Pieris, Sir James (1856–1930)
He won a scholarship to Cambridge University, where he obtained a master of arts and a master of law degree. On his return to the island, he practiced as a lawyer before being appointed a district judge. He resigned that post to enter politics. He served as a member of the Colombo Municipal Council (1898–1908)

and in 1921 was elected to the Legislative Council as member for the Town of Colombo. In 1924 the council elected him the first Sri Lankan vice president of the council (the president being the governor). Pieris was a leading figure among the constitutionalist elite in the early twentieth century.

Piyaratana,* bhikkhu *Dodanduwe (1826–1937)
He was a well-known preacher and eventually became the chief high prelate of the Kalyani Chapter of the Amarapura Fraternity. He was a pioneer in the Buddhist schools movement, having started a school for boys at his native village Dodanduwa near Galle. He also prepared textbooks to be used in Buddhist schools since the only other available textbooks had been prepared by Christians.

Ponnambalam, G. G. (1902–77)
After receiving a preliminary education in Jaffna, he entered Cambridge University and became a barrister-at-law and one of the most sought-after criminal lawyers in Sri Lanka. He entered the State Council in 1934 as elected member for Jaffna. He is remembered as the founder of the Tamil Congress and for his "50-50 demand" for safeguarding minority interests. He joined the first cabinet of independent Sri Lanka (1948) as minister of industries, industrial research and fisheries.

Punchi Banda, Weragama (1856–92)
He was founding editor of the newspaper *Sarasavi Sañdaräsa,* which was the organ of the Buddhist Theosophical Society. Weragama was one of the first pupils of *bhikkhu* Hikkaduve in the Vidyodaya Pirivena. In addition to his contribution as a Sinhala scholar, Weragama, through his paper, campaigned for the declaration of the Vesak holiday and the establishment of Buddhist schools.

Saranankara, Ven.* bhikkhu *Weliwita (1698–1778)
He was one of the most revered of the *bhikkhus* of his day. His life spans the reigns of three kings, Narendrasinghe (1707–39), Sri Vijaya Rajasinghe (1739–47), and Kirti Sri Rajasinghe (1747–82). Saranankara initiated the literary and Buddhist revival movements in mid-eighteenth-century Kandy. The reestablishment of the *upasampadā* (higher ordination) in 1753, by his efforts and with the assistance of *bhikkhus* from Siam, was the beginning of the Siamese fraternity, which is the largest of the *bhikkhu* fraternities in Sri Lanka today. Saranankara was also one of the foremost scholars of the day, with equal command of Sinhala, Pāli, and Sanskrit. Kirti Sri bestowed on Saranankara the post of Sangha Raja (supreme head of the monkhood), but after his death the post was never filled again.

Senanayake, Don Stephen (1884–1951)
Educated at St. Thomas' College, Colombo, he was managing his father's properties when he became drawn into the temperance agitation at the behest of his elder brother F. R. He was arrested with several other Sinhalese leaders during

the riots of 1915. He entered the Legislative Council as an elected member in 1924 and held that seat in successive legislatures until his death in 1951. In 1931 he became the minister of agriculture, and he is best remembered for his services in reclaiming the jungles in the ancient sites of Sinhalese civilization in the North Central and Eastern provinces for irrigation and peasant settlement schemes. It was under his leadership that negotiations were conducted for the transfer of power from imperial hands, and he became the first prime minister of independent Sri Lanka in 1948.

Senanayke, Dudley Shelton (1911–73)
The elder son of D. S. Senanayake, he was educated at St. Thomas' College, Colombo, and proceeded to Cambridge University and obtained both a bachelor of science and bachelor of laws degree. On his return to the island, he entered politics and won the Dedigama seat in 1936, taking his place in the State Council. With J. R. Jayewardene he and some others formed a ginger group in the Ceylon National Congress. In the first parliament of independent Sri Lanka (1948), Dudley was appointed minister of agriculture. At his father's death in 1951 he was called upon to lead the government, thus becoming one of the youngest prime ministers in history. He resigned in 1953 when, at a general strike against food prices, law enforcement authorities shot and killed some agitators. Dudley became prime minister again twice, in 1961 and in 1965. His government, which lasted from 1965 to 1970, is remembered as possibly the most liberal administration since independence.

Senanayake, Fredrick Richard (1882–1926)
Educated at St. Thomas' College, Colombo, he attended Cambridge University, earning both a bachelor of arts and bachelor of laws degree. On his return to the island, he practiced as a barrister-at-law for a time but gave it up to manage his father's extensive properties and graphite industry. He became a devoted temperance worker, organizing the Hapitigam Korale Temperance Union, which was a formidable organization in the early twentieth century. He also founded an organization called Mahajana Sabhā (Peoples' Association) with local branches in many parts of the island. He was arrested during the 1915 Sinhala-Muslim riots on the charge of inciting a mob and is today well known for his generosity in funding Buddhist and nationalist causes.

Siddhartha, Rev. **bhikkhu** *Walane (1811–68)*
He was a pioneer in the revival of *pirivena* education. The Paramadhammacētiya Pirivena (1842), which he founded, was the precursor to the more dynamic Vidyōdaya (1873) and Vidyālankāra (1875) founded by his pupils. Walane was teacher to the famous scholars, *bhikkhus* Hikkaduwe Sumangala, Ratmalane Dhammaloka, and Pundit Batuvantudawe. Walane was also associated with the founding of the *Lak Miṇi Pahana* (1862), the first newspaper of the Buddhists. He was the leader of the breakaway group of *bhikkhus* of the Siamese fraternity who founded the Kalyāṇi Sāmagri Sangha Sabhāva in the 1860s and was elected its first Maha Nayaka (chief high prelate).

Sirisena, Piyadasa (1875–1946)
Born at Aturuwella in the southern littoral, he studied Sinhalese and English in local schools. At the age of twenty-one he came to Colombo to work at a furniture shop owned by the family of Anagarika Dharmapala. He came under the latter's influence and became an indefatigable critic of Westernization among the Sinhalese. In 1904 he launched the journal *Sinhala Jātiya* (Sinhalese Nation), which promoted Sinhalese-Buddhist causes. Sirisena was also a devoted temperance worker. He wrote more than ten novels and a large number of poems, and the outstanding feature of his numerous writings is the strong Sinhalese-Buddhist stance of the writer.

Siri Sivali,* bhikkhu *Bambarende (1908–85)
Born in Bambarenda in the southern littoral, he was ordained at a young age. He arrived in Vidyālankāra Pirivena for higher education and eventually went to Benares, India, to attend Kāśi Vidyapeeṭh, where he studied philosophy and several Indian languages. He was influenced by the Marxist movement at this time, and, although he did not claim to be a Marxist, he adopted a "progressive" attitude regarding social problems. On his return to the island he became a teacher at Vidyālankāra and a prodigious writer on Buddhist civilization, philosophy, and social issues. About language he advocated a simplified literary idiom that could reach the masses.

Sumana, Ven.* bhikkhu *Bulathgama (ca. 1795–ca. 1891)
Bulathgama Dhammalankara Siri Sumanatissa (his full name) was born in the Central Province and was ordained in the Siamese fraternity. But he migrated to Galle in the southern littoral and received higher ordination in the Amarapura fraternity. *Bhikkhu* Ambagahawatte, the founder of the Ramañña fraternity, was a pupil of *bhikkhu* Bulathgama. Thus, having close contacts with all three fraternities, Bulathgama used it to his advantage in organizing forces for revivalist activity. He was a key figure in the Baddegama controversy with the Christians (1865), in which *bhikkhus* from all the fraternities took part. He also helped to set up the first printing press of the Buddhists, the Lankōpakāra Press, in 1863, for which, in addition to receiving support from Sri Lanka, he was able to get a grant from the King of Siam. When Colonel Olcott and Madame Blavatsky arrived in the island in 1880 they were first received at *bhikkhu* Bulathgama's temple in Galle.

Sumangala,* bhikkhu *Hikkaduve (1826–1911)
Born in Hikkaduva, a village in the southern littoral, he was ordained at a young age and arrived in Ratmalana to study under *bhikkhu* Walane Siddhartha. In his early years Hikkaduve associated with *bhikkhu* Bulathgama and others, taking part in the Buddhist-Christian controversies. But his greatest contribution was as the founder of Vidyōdaya Pirivena (1873) at Maligakanda in Colombo. Being a highly competent scholar in Sinhala, Pāli, and Sanskrit as well as in English, he was considered with great respect even by the colonial authorities.

Tennakoon, Raipiel (1900–1965)
Born in Walallawita, a small village north of Colombo, and educated at local schools, he qualified as a trained Sinhala teacher in 1922. Cumaratunga, who was then the principal of the Balapitiya Sinhalese Training College, came to know Tennakoon and invited him to teach there. Having done so for ten years, he joined the schools again as a principal, serving in many parts of the island. Tennakoon was a key figure in the Heḷa Havula (founded by Cumaratunga). He also was a prodigious writer, producing over twenty-five long poems, a number of school textbooks, and several prose narratives. His forte was satire.

Vimalakitti,* bhikkhu *Medauyangoda (1903–68)
Born at Medauyangoda near Matara, he was ordained after receiving his primary education. He studied in several *pirivenas,* including Sunanda Pirivena at Beliatta and Vidyārāja Pirivena at Panadura. Having earned the degree of Prācina Pundit, he founded his own Siri Nanda Pirivena at Sarikkāmulla near Panadura. He was a competent historian and philologist and wrote many books on history, classical literature, and the history of the Sinhala language.

Weerasekera, Jayantha (1895–1949)
Having studied in the English medium at St. Joseph's College, Colombo, Weerasekera was inspired by Anagarika Dharmapala and attended classes at Vidyōdaya Pirivena to obtain a good command of classical Sinhala, Pāli, and Sanskrit. Soon he became a subeditor of *Sinhala Jātiya,* edited by Piyadasa Sirisena. At this time he made an acquaintance with Munidasa Cumaratunga, who was then a schoolteacher. This was to be the beginning of a lifelong association. Weerasekera was associated with all the nationalistic activities of Cumaratunga–in the journals *Subasa* and *The Helio* and the organization the Heḷa Havula. After Cumaratunga's death Weerasekera was considered the leader of the Heḷa Havula. Weerasekera was also an active member of the Ceylon National Congress. In 1948 he was elected one of its joint secretaries.

Wickremasinghe, Martin (1891–1976)
Born in Koggala near Galle, he was educated at Buona Vista College, Galle, and became a clerk at a business establishment in Colombo. He was interested in literary activity from his young days, writing his first novel, *Leela,* in 1914. He joined the Lake House group of newspapers in 1920 and became editor of *Silumiṇa* (weekly) and *Dinamiṇa* (daily). While working as a journalist, he continued with his own literary pursuits, producing over eighteen novels, several collections of short stories and a large number of books on literary history and literary appreciation, society, and culture of the Sinhalese. His works have been translated into English and Russian.

Abbreviations

B.E.	Buddhist Era
BTS	Buddhist Theosophical Society (Colombo)
CJHSS	*Ceylon Journal of Historical and Social Studies*
CP	Communist party
DP	*Dinakara Prakāśaya* (newspaper)
DMK	Dravida Munnethra Kazagam
DPI	Director of Public Instruction
EZ	Epigraphia Zeylanica
FP	Federal party
HCNC	*Handbook of the Ceylon National Congress*
IPKF	Indian Peace Keeping Force
JVP	Janata Vimukti Peramuna
LC	Legislative Council
LMK	*Lak Miṇi Kiruḷa* (newspaper)
LMP	*Lak Miṇi Pahana* (newspaper)
LSSP	Lanka Sama Samaja party
LTTE	Liberation Tigers of Tamil Eelam
Memoirs	*The Memoirs of James D'Alwis*
Sa.Sa.	*Sarasavi Sañdaräsa* (newspaper)
Sat. Sam.	*Satya Samuccaya* (newspaper)
SB	*Sinhala Bauddhayā* (newspaper)
SC	State Council
Si.Sa.	*Sihala Samaya* (newspaper)
SLFP	Sri Lanka Freedom party
SMS	Sinhala Maha Sabhā
SP	Sessional Paper
SS	James D'Alwis's introduction to the *Sidat Sañgarāva*
TULF	Tamil United Liberation Front
UCHC	*University of Ceylon History of Ceylon*
UF	United Front
UNP	United National party
YMBA	Young Men's Buddhist Association

Glossary

The meanings given here pertain only to the contexts in which the following words are found in this text, and therefore this glossary is a mere practical guide. There was no attempt made to give all meanings attached to each word.

abhidhamma—Buddhist metaphysics.
Amarapura Nikaya—The *bhikkhu* fraternity (with over twenty subdivisions) tracing its origin to *upasampadā* from Amarapura in Burma.
anagārika—Homeless. (Originally used with reference to a *bhikkhu,* but after Dharmapala it denotes a lay celibate.)
Āryavarta—The region in north India, between the Himalaya and Vindhya mountain ranges, where the original "Aryan" immigrants to the peninsula settled ca. second millennium B.C.
āyurvēda—Indigenous system of medicine.

bhikkhu—Buddhist monk.
bhūmiputra—A Sanskrit word meaning "sons of the land."
Bōdhi—Lit. "enlightenment," this is the *ficus religiosa* tree under which the Buddha attained enlightenment.
bōdhisattva—The Buddha-to-be.
brahmacāri—Celibate. (Originally used with reference to a *bhikkhu,* but after Harischandra, denotes a lay celibate.)
Burghers—Descendants of the Portuguese and the Dutch.

cētiya—Also referred to as *stūpa* or *säya.* The solid brick edifices, usually hemispherical, enshrining Buddha's relics.
cūla—Small or lesser.

dāgoba—See *cētiya.*
Daḷadā—The Tooth Relic. The Dalada Maligava is the Temple of the Tooth in Kandy.
Damiḷa—See *Demaḷa.*
Dāṭhā—Pali word for *Daḷada.*
däya—Nation (*jāti* in Sanskrit).
dāyaka sabhā—Association of temple patrons devoted to the welfare of a temple.
Demaḷa—Tamil.
Dhamma—The Buddhist doctrine (*dharma* in Sanskrit).
Dhammadvīpa—The island of the Buddhist doctrine.
dhātu—Relics (Buddhist objects of veneration). See *Śārīrika dhātu* and *Pāribhōgika dhātu.*

Durāva—Sinhalese caste. Traditionally toddy-tappers (palm trees are tapped to obtain a sap that is fermented to make an intoxicating drink or "toddy").

Eḷu (also *Heḷa*)—Pure Sinhalese, free of all extraneous linguistic borrowings.

goiya—Farmer.
govi—Sinhala caste. Considered the highest; traditionally farmers.

Heḷa—Same as Eḷu.

Kandy—The Anglicized name of the last Sinhala kingdom in the central hill country. (Adj. Kandyan.)
Karāva—Sinhala caste; traditionally fishermen.
kēśadhātu—Hair (relic).
kṣatriya—Royal caste.

ḷalāṭa—Forehead.
low country—The territories in the coastal plains which comprised the region under the colonial powers during Kandyan monarchy. (See *up-country*.)

mahajanaya—The people, the masses.
Mahā Nāyaka—Chief high prelate of a fraternity of *bhikkhus*.
Māra—The God of Death.
miccādiṭṭhi (*mityādṛsti*)—Heretical. Lit. "wrong vision."
Miśra Sinhala—The Sinhalese language form mixed with Pali and Sanskrit words.
mudaliyar—A native headman, usually in charge of a large provincial division. Sometimes this was an honorary title.
muhandiram—Originally meant a chief revenue officer under Kandyan kings. Under the British it was conferred on native officials in the administrative hierarchy, and it later became an honorary title below the rank of *mudaliyar*.

Nāyaka—Chief incumbent of a temple.
nikāya—Fraternity of monks. The Sinhalese *bhikkhus* are divided into three *nikāyas* (*Siyam, Amarapura, and Ramañña*).
Nirvāna—Final release from the cycle of birth and death.
nūrti—An operatic theatrical form (borrowed from nineteenth-century Bombay) which uses prose dialogue interspersed with songs.

pansala—Monastery.
para—Alien.
Pāribhōgika dhātu—The objects used by the Buddha, such as an alms bowl, which have become tokens of veneration.
perahära—A Buddhist procession with music and dancing.

pirivena—*Bhikkhu* institutions of learning usually attached to a temple.
pragatiśīli—Progressive.

Rajarata—Lit. "royal territory." One of the three traditional divisions of the island. This refers to the north central plains where the early Sinhalese kingdoms were located. Also see *Tri Siṃhala*.
Ramañña Nikāya—The fraternity of *bhikkhus* established in 1865 with the *upasampadā* obtained from Ramañña in lower Burma.
rajjuruvo—King.

Salāgama—Sinhala caste; traditionally cinnamon peelers.
samāgama—Voluntary association (pl. *samāgam*).
sammādiṭṭhi—Lit. "the correct vision" (meaning here Buddhism).
sandhi—Phonetic rules in word combinations.
sangha—Buddhist clergy; an order of *bhikkhus.*
Sangha Rāja—The supreme head of the Buddhist monkhood.
Śāririka dhātu—Corporeal relics of the Buddha or the *arahants* (Buddhist saints), which are considered objects of veneration.
Sāsana—Buddhist dispensation.
Sinhala—An adjective whose literal meaning is "descended from the lion." In the present study both *Sinhala* and its English derivation *Sinhalese* will be used. For clarity of expression *Sinhala* will generally refer to the language while *Sinhalese* will refer to the people and the culture.
Sinhaladvīpa—The island of the Sinhalese people.
sirita—Custom.
sivpasaya—The four requisites of the order of *bhikkhus:* robes, alms, medicine, and shelter.
Siyam Nikāya—The Siamese fraternity. The fraternity of *bhikkhus* established after the *upasampadā* was reestablished in 1853 with the help of *bhikkhus* brought from Siam (Thailand). This is the largest of the *nikāyas* in Sri Lanka.
stūpa—See *cētiya.*

Thēravadins—The orthodox adherents of the Buddhas teachings; also called Hinayanists as opposed to Mahayanists.
Thero—A senior *bhikkhu* status reached after ten years of *upasampadā.*
Tri Siṃhala—The Sinhala land consisting of the three divisions: Raja rata, Maya rata, and Ruhunu rata. Maya rata was the central highlands and Ruhunu rata the southern plains. (Also see *Rajarata.*) We hear of this appellation from about the twelfth century.

upāsaka—Lay devotee.
upasampadā—Higher ordination, which a *bhikkhu* has to undergo (after passing his twentieth birthday) by proving his suitablity to an assembly of over five *bhikkhus* having *upasampadā.*

up-country—The territories that were under Kandyan kings when the low country (see entry) was under the control of the Europeans.

vaḍiga—An ethnic appellation of the Nayakkars (the dynasty from south India which provided the four last kings of Kandy); the term later took a pejorative meaning.

vaṃśa—Lineage (as in *kṣatriyavaṃśa*); or chronicle (as in *Mahāvaṃśa*).

vargayā—Race.

vedavaru—Physicians.

Vesak Day—The full-moon day of May (in the second month of the Sinhalese calendar), marking the birth, enlightenment, and demise of the Buddha. This day is celebrated as the holiest day in the Buddhist calendar. The month also is called Vesak.

vihāraya—Temple (pl. *vihāra;* gen. *vihāre*).

vinaya—Code of Buddhist ecclesiastical discipline.

yakṣa (yakkha)—Malevolent supernatural being found in Buddhist mythology.

Bibliography

Official Documents

Addresses Delivered in the Legislative Council of Ceylon by the Governors of the Colony, vol. 2 (1860–77).
Administrative Reports of the Director of Education.
Debates of the Legislative Council of Ceylon.
Debates of the State Council of Ceylon.
Epigraphia Zeylanica, Colombo, Department of Archaeology, vols. I to VI.
Parliamentary Debates (Hansard), official report.
Reports on the Census of Ceylon.
Report on Education (sessional paper no. 7, 1867).
Report of the Commission on Constitutional Reform (Cmd. 7667), 1945.
Report of the Special Commission on the (Ceylon) Constitution (Cmd. 3131), 1928.
Report of the Select Committee on the Revision of the Constitution (Parliamentary ser., no. 14), 1978.

Newspapers and Periodicals in Sinhala

Bauddha Samaya Sangarava, 1887.
Dinakara Prakāśaya, 1891.
Dinamiṇa, 1940, 1944.
Dinapatā Pravurti, 1895.
Dinarada, 1924.
Gñānadarśaya, 1896.
Gñānāvabhāṣaya, 1896.
Govikam Saṅgarāva, 1896.
Guru Śiṣya Sangrahaya, 1901.
Guruvadana, 1929.
Guruvarayā, 1896.
Kamkaru Balaya, 1928.
Kamkaru Dhvajaya, 1930.
Kamkaru Haňḍa, 1928.
Kavaṭa Aňgana, 1902.
Kavaṭa Dūtayā, 1889.
Kav Kaḷaṁba, 1899.
Lak Miṇi Kiruḷa, 1881, 1890.
Lak Miṇi Pahana, 1862, 1889, 1901, 1903, 1934.
Lak Rivi Kiraṇa, 1895.
Lakväsiyā, 1928.
Lankā Kamkaru Prabōdhaya, 1922.

Lankā Taruṇayā, 1927.
Lankōpakāraya, 1881, 1882.
Loku Siñghō, 1926.
Mahā bōdhi Sañgarāva, 1902.
Mahajana Hañḍa, 1921.
Mahajana Mataya, 1921.
Mahajana Mitrayā, 1930.
Mahajana Sañgarāva, 1921.
Manōramā, 1926.
Mudalāli, 1927.
Pol Vävili Sañgarāva, 1887.
Rāma Säraya, 1926.
Rivikiraṇa, 1907.
Riviräsa, 1888.
Samagi Sañgarāva, 1931.
Samaya Sangrahaya, 1873.
Sañda Miṇa, 1926.
Sarasavi Sañdaräsa, 1882, 1884, 1885, 1890.
Sat Arunudāva, 1892.
Sat Siḷumiṇa, 1884.
Satyālankāraya, 1884.
Satya Mārgaya, 1867.
Satya Samuccaya, 1884, 1890, 1908.
Satyārtha Sangrahaya, 1920.
Sāhitya Tarangiṇi, 1929.
Sārārtha Pradīpikāva, 1863.
Sihala Samaya, 1903.
Sinhala Siri, 1924.
Siḷumiṇa, 1908.
Sinhala Avurudu Sañgarāva, 1915.
Sinhala Balaya, 1928, 1944, 1946.
Sinhala Bauddhayā, 1906, 1911, 1912, 1943.
Sinhala Jātiya, 1903.
Sinhala Mitrayā, 1913.
Sinhala Sēvakayā, 1930.
Sinhala Taruṇayā, 1908, 1909.
Siri Laka Situmiṇa, 1893.
Siri Sara Sañgarā, 1921.
Situmiṇa, 1929.
Siya Basa, 1925.
Śrī Dharma Srī, 1923.
Śrī Kavi Dhvajaya, 1921.
Śrī Lankā Guruvaraya, 1927.
Śrī Lankā Mahajana Hañḍa, 1923.
Śrī Lankōttanśaya, 1895.
Śrī Saddharma Śāstra Latā, 1924.

Subasa, 1939, 1940, 1941, 1942.
Swadēśa Prabōdhaya, 1921.
Swadēsha Mitraya, 1926.
Vaidya Śāstrālankāraya, 1894.
Vaidyādhāra Sangrahaya, 1896.
Velaňda Saňgarāva, 1895.
Vidyābharaṇaya, 1907
Vidyādarpaṇaya, 1893.
Vidyādīpikā, 1895.
Vidyōdaya, 1936.
Vīrayā, 1944.

Newspapers and Periodicals in English

Buddhist, 1892.
Ceylon Daily News, 1987.
The Ceylon National Review, 1906.
The Helio, 1941.
The Island, 1990.
The New Lanka, 1956.
The Sandaresa, 1905, 1906.
The Searchlight, 1928.
The Young Buddhist, 1921.
Young Lanka, 1921.

Books and Articles

Adikaram E. W. [1946] 1953. *Early History of Buddhism in Ceylon*. Colombo: Gunasena.

Ahubudu, Arisen. 1957. *Kumaratuňgu Äsura*, Colombo: Gunasena.

Alexandre, Pierre. 1972. *Languages and Language in Black Africa*, trans F. A. Leavy. Evanston: Northwestern University Press.

Amaramoli, Ven. *bhikkhu* Veragoda, ed. 1956. *Srī Saddharmāvavāda Sangrahaya of Tibbotuvawe Sri Siddhartha Buddharaksita*. Colombo: Ratnakara Press.

Ames, Michael M. 1967. "The Impact of Western Education on Religion and Society in Ceylon," *Pacific Affairs* 40, nos. 1–2:19–42.

——. 1973. "Westernization and Modernization: The Case of Sinhalese Buddhism." *Social Compass* 20, no. 2:139–70.

Amunugama, Sarath. 1975. "John De Silva and the Sinhala Nationalist Theatre." *Ceylon Historical Journal* 25, nos. 1–4:285–304.

——. 1979. "Ideology and Class Interest in One of Piyadasa Sirisena's Novels." In *Collective Identities*. *See* Roberts, ed., 1979, 314–36.

Arasaratnam, S. 1979. "Nationalism in Sri Lanka and the Tamils," In *Collective Identities*. *See* Roberts, ed., 1979, 500–519.

Ariyapala, M. B. 1968. *Society in Medieval Ceylon*. Colombo: Department of Cultural Affairs.

Arunachalam, Ponnambalam. 1906. "A Plea for a Ceylon University." *Journal of the Ceylon University Association* 1, no. 2:121–35.

Balakrishnan, N., and Gunasekera, H. M. 1977. "A Review of Demografic Trends." In *Sri Lanka. See* K. M. de Silva, ed., 1977, 109–30.

Balandier, Georges. 1970. *The Sociology of Black Africa.* New York: Praeger.

Balding, Rev. J. W. 1922. *One Hundred Years in Ceylon; or, the Centenary Volume of the Church Missionary Society in Ceylon.* Madras.

Bandaranaike, S. W. R. D., ed. 1928. *The Handbook of the Ceylon National Congress.* Colombo: Cave.

——. 1961. *Towards a New Era: Selected Speeches of S.W.R.D. Bandaranaike, 1931–1959.* Colombo: Department of Information.

Bandaranayake, Senake. 1978. "The External Factor in Sri Lanka's Historical Formation," *Ceylon Historical Journal* 25, nos. 1–4:74–94.

——. 1984. "The People of Sri Lanka: The National Question and Some Problems of History and Ethnicity," in *Ethnicity and Social Change in Sri Lanka,* ed. Social Scientists Association. A:i–xx, Colombo: Karunaratne.

Barclay, William, et al. 1976. Introduction to *Racial Conflict, Discrimination, and Power,* ed. William Barclay et al. New York.

Barnett, Steve. 1977. "Identity Choice and Caste Ideology in Contemporary South India," in *The New Wind: Changing Identities in South Asia,* ed. Kenneth David, 393–414. The Hague: Mouton.

Barth, Frederick. 1969. Introduction to *Ethnic Groups and Boundaries,* ed. Frederick Barth, 9–38. Boston: Little, Brown.

Bechert, Heinz. 1974. "The Beginnings of Buddhist Historiography in Ceylon: The Mahavamsa and Political Thinking." Paper presented to Ceylon Studies Seminar (Peradeniya) revised version in *Religion and the Legitimation of Power. See* Smith, ed., 1978, 48–72.

Bevan, Francis. 1907. "The Press," in *Twentieth Century Impressions. See* Wright, ed., 1907, 301–9.

Blackton, Charles S. 1970. "The Action Phase of the 1915 Riots," *Journal of Asian Studies* 39:235–54.

Brass, Paul R. 1974. *Language, Religion and Politics in North India.* Cambridge: Cambridge University Press.

Buddhadatta, Ven. *bhikkhu* Polwatte. [1964] 1950. *Samīpātītayehi Bauddhācāryayō* (Kotahena). Colombo: Gunasena.

Cady, John. 1958. *A History of Modern Burma.* Ithaca, N.Y: Cornell University Press.

Candidus, Henry. 1853. *A Desultory Conversation between Two Young Aristocratic Ceylonese.* Colombo: Examiner Press.

Chandraprema, C. A. 1990. "The JVP Insurrection of 1987–1989," serialized in *The Island,* 5 February 1979– .

Chater, Rev. James. 1815. *A Grammar of the Cingalese Language.* Colombo: Government Press.

Chaudhuri, Nirad C. [1951] 1976. *The Autobiography of an Unknown Indian.* Bombay: Oxford University Press.

Clerk, Robert P. 1974. *Development and Instability: Political Change in the Non-Western World*. Hinsdale, Ill.: Dryden.

Codrington, H. W., ed. 1920. *The Diary of Mr John D'Oyly*. Colombo: Government Press.

Coleman, James S. 1965. Introduction to pt. 3 of *Education and Political Development*, ed. James Coleman, Princeton, N.J.: Princeton University Press.

Coomaraswamy, Ananda. N.d. "Education in Ceylon," in *Art and Swadeshi*, ed. Ananda Coomaraswamy, 174–90. Madras: Ganesh.

——. 1946. *The Religious Forms of the Basis of Indian Society*. New York: Orientali.

——. 1947. *Am I My Brother's Keeper?* New York: John Day.

Committee for Rational Development. 1984. *Sri Lanka: The Ethnic Conflict*. New Delhi: Navrang.

Crouch, James. 1973. "Ananda Coomaraswamy in Ceylon," *Ceylon Journal of Historical and Social Studies*, n.s. 3, no. 2:54–66.

Culavamsa. 1953. Trans. Wilhelm Geiger. Colombo: Information Department.

Cumaratunga, Munidasa. 1961. *Heḷa Heliya I* (a collection of the writings of Cumaratunga). Colombo: Gunasena.

——. 1962. *Heḷa Heliya II* (a collection of the writings of Cumaratunga). Colombo: Gunasena.

——. 2483 B.E.: *Sasada Vivaranaya*. Colombo: Gunasena.

D'Alwis, James. 1852. *The Sidat Sangarawa: A Grammar of the Singhalese Language Translated into English with Introduction, Notes and Appendices*. Colombo: Government Press.

——. 1863. *Contributions to Oriental Literature; or, the Leisure Hours*, vols. 1 and 2. Colombo: Government Press.

——. 1870. *A Descriptive Catalogue of Sanskrit, Pali and Sinhalese Literary Works of Ceylon*, vol. 1. Colombo: Government Press.

——. 1878. *A Descriptive Catalogue of Sanskrit, Pali and Sinhalese Literary Works of Ceylon*, vol. 2. Colombo: Government Press.

——. 1939. *Memoirs and Desultory Writings of the Late Mr. James D'Alwis*, ed. C. A. Seneviratne. Colombo: Ceylon Observer Press.

Das Gupta, Jyotirindra. 1970. *Language Conflict and National Development*. Berkeley and Los Angeles: University of California Press.

——. 1975. "Ethnicity, Language Demands, and National Development in India," in *Ethnicity, Theory, and Experience*, ed. Nathan Glazer and Daniel P. Moynihan, 466–88. Cambridge, Mass.: Harvard University Press.

Davy, John. [1821] 1969. "An Account of the Interior of Ceylon and Its Inhabitants with Travels in that Island." *Ceylon Historical Journal* (Dehiwala) vol. 16.

Denham, E. B. 1912. *Ceylon at the Census of* 1911. Colombo: Government Press.

de Silva, Chandra Richard. 1980. "The Tamils and the Constitution of the Second Republic of Sri Lanka, 1978," *Sri Lanka Journal of the Social Sciences* 3, no. 1:33–41.

——. 1987. *Sri Lanka: A History*. New Delhi: Vikas.

de Silva, D. V. Richard. 1969. *Cumaratuṇgu Muni Dasna*. Colombo: Gunasena.

de Silva, K. M. 1965. *Social Policy and Missionary Organization in Ceylon, 1840–1855*. London: Longmans and Green.

——. 1967. "The Formation and Character of the Ceylon National Congress, 1917–1919," *Ceylon Journal of Social and Historical Studies* (*CJHSS*) 10:70–102.

——. 1972. "The Ceylon National Congress in Disarray, 1920–1921: Sir Ponnambalam Arunachalam Leaves the Congress," *CJHSS*, New Series 2:97–117.

——. 1973a. "The Ceylon National Congress in Disarray: The Triumph of Sir William Manning, 1921–24," *CJHSS*, New Series 3:16–38.

——. 1973b. "The Kandyan Kingdom and the British—The Last Phase, 1796 to 1818," *University of Ceylon, History of Ceylon* (*UCHC*) 3:12–33.

——. 1973c. "Religion and State in the Early Nineteenth Century," *UCHC* 3:187–212.

——. 1973d. "The Government and Religion: Problems and Policies, c. 1832 to 1910," *UCHC* 3:187–212.

——. 1973e. "The Legislative Council in the Nineteenth Century," *UCHC* 3:226–48.

——. 1973f. "Nineteenth Century Origins of Nationalism in Ceylon," *UCHC* 3:249–61.

——. 1973g. "The Reform and Nationalist Movement in the Early Twentieth Century," *UCHC*, 3:381–407.

——. 1973h. "The History and Politics of the Transfer of Power," *UCHC* 3:489–533.

——. 1977. "Historical Survey," in *Sri Lanka*. *See* K. M. de Silva, ed. 1977, 31–85.

——. 1981. *A History of Sri Lanka*. Delhi: Oxford University Press.

——. 1986. *Managing Ethnic Tensions in Multi-Ethnic Societies: Sri Lanka, 1880–1985*. Lanham, Md.: University Press of America.

——. 1987. *Separatist Ideology in Sri Lanka: A Historical Appraisal of the Claim for the "Traditional Homelands" of the Tamils of Sri Lanka*. Kandy: International Centre for Ethnic Studies.

——. 1991. "Indo-Sri Lanka Relations, 1975–89: A Study in the Internationalization of Ethnic Conflict" in *Internationalization of Ethnic Conflict*, ed. K. M. de Silva and J. H. May, 76–106. London: Pinter Publishers, 1991.

——, ed. 1977. *Sri Lanka: A Survey*. London: C. Hurst.

de Silva, K. M., et al., ed. 1988. *Ethnic Conflict in Buddhist Societies*. London: Pinter.

de Silva, M. W. Sugathapala. 1965. "Some Observations on the Scope of Sidat Sangarava," *Senarath Paranavitana Felicitation Volume*. Colombo: Gunasena: 67–88.

——. 1967. "The Effect of Purism on the Evolution of the Written Language," *Linguistics* 36:5–17.

——. 1970. "Some Linguistic Peculiarities of Sinhalese Poetry," *Linguistics* 60:5–26.

——. 1974. "Some Consequences of Diglossia," *York Papers in Linguistics* 1974: 71–90.

——. 1976. "Verbal Aspects of Politeness Expression in Sinhalese with Reference to Asking, Telling, Requesting and Ordering," *Anthropological Linguistics* 18, no. 8:360–70.

Deutsch, Karl W. 1975. "The Political Significances of Linguistic Conflicts," in *Multilingual Political Systems. See* Guy-Savard and Vigneault, eds., 1975, 7–28.

Devaraja, L. S. 1972. *The Kandyan Kingdom, 1707–1760*. Colombo: Lake House.

Devereaux, George, and Edwin M. Loeb. 1964. "Antagonistic Acculturation," *American Sociological Review* 8, no. 2:143–47.

de Vos, George, ed. 1976. *Responses to Change: Society, Culture, and Personality*. New York.

Dhammananda, Ven. *bhikkhu* Nawulle. 1969. *Madhyama Lankā Purāvṛutta*. Colombo: Gunasena.

Dhammananda, Ven. *bhikkhu* Walane, ed. 1916. *Pūjāvaliaya*. Colombo: Jinalankara Press.

Dhammawamsa, Ven. *bhikkhu* Kosgoda. 1971. "Välitoṭin Siduvū Sasanika Sēvaya," in *Välitoṭa*, ed. D. D. M. Seneviratne and P. D. P. Jayatilaka, 32–49. Colombo: Anula Press.

Dharmabandhu, T. S. 1973. *Sinhala Vīrayō*. Colombo: Gunasena.

Dharmadasa, K. N. O. 1967. *Spoken and Written Sinhalese: A Contrastive Study*. Master's thesis, University of York, Unpublished.

———. 1972. "Language and Sinhalese Nationalism: The Career of Munidasa Cumaratunga," *Modern Ceylon Studies* 3, no. 2:125–43.

———. 1974. "A Nativistic Reaction to Colonialism: The Sinhala-Buddhist Revival in Sri Lanka," *Asian Studies* 12, no. 1:159–79.

———. 1976. "Critical Theory and Sinhala Creative Writing in the Twentieth Century: An Attempt at Documentation." Paper presented to Ceylon Studies Seminar (Peradeniya). Reprinted in *Sri Lanka Journal of the Social Sciences* 3, no. 1 (1980): 67–88.

———. 1977. "Diglossia, Nativism and the Sinhalese Identity in the Language Problem in Sri Lanka," *International Journal of the Sociology of Language* 13:21–32.

———. 1979. "The Sinhalese-Buddhist Identity and the Nayakkar Dynasty in the Politics of the Kandyan Kingdom," in *Collective Identities. See* Roberts, ed., 1979, 99–129.

———. 1981. "Language Conflict in Sri Lanka," *Sri Lanka Journal of the Social Sciences* 4, no. 2:47–70.

———. 1988. "Buddhist Resurgence and Christian Privilege in Sri Lanka, c. 1940–1965," in *Ethnic Conflict in Buddhist Societies. See* K. M. de Silva et al., ed., 1988, 110–25.

———. 1989, "The People of the Lion: Ethnic Identity, Ideology and Historical Revisionism in Contemporary Sri Lanka," *Sri Lanka Journal of the Humanities* 15, nos. 1 and 2:1–35.

Dharmapala, Anagarika. 1965. *Return to Righteousness: A Collection of Speeches and Writings*, ed. Ananda Guruge. Colombo: Department of Cultural Affairs.

Dharmarama, Ven. *bhikkhu* Dodanduwe. 1965. "Doḍandūwé Piyaratana Tissa Mahā Swāmīhu," in *Apē Pan̆divaru*, ed. Gunnepana Gnana Seneviratne, 1–4. Colombo: Pracina Bhasopakara Samagama.

Dimont, Max I. 1973. *The Indestructible Jews*. New York and London.

Dominin, Leon. 1917. *The Frontiers of Language and Nationality in Europe*. New York: Geographical Society of New York.

Don Peter, Rev. Fr. W. L. A. 1963. "Pioneers of the Drama in Ceylon," in Don Peter, *Studies in Ceylon Church History*, 28–35. Colombo: Catholic Press.

Emeneau, Murray B. 1956. "India as a Linguistic Area," *Language* 32, no. 1:3–16.

Falnes, Oscar. [1933] 1968. *National Romanticism in Norway*. New York.

Farmer, B. H. 1965. "The Social Bases of Nationalism in Ceylon," *Journal of Asian Studies* 24, no. 3:421–39.

Ferguson, Charles A. 1959. "Diglossia," *Word* 15:325–40.

——. 1966. "National Sociolinguistic Profile Formulas," in *Sociolinguistics*, ed. William Bright, 309–15. The Hague: Mouton.

——. 1968. "Language Development," in *Language Problems*. *See* Fishman et al., ed., 1968:27–35.

Ferguson, John. 1887. *Ceylon in the Jubilee Year*. London and Colombo: John Haddon.

Fernando, M. E., ed. N.d. *Vaḍiga Haṭana Hevat Ähalēpola Varṇanāva* (Valigala Kavisundara Mudali). Colombo: Luxman.

Fernando, P. T. M. (Tissa). 1970a. "The Ceylon Civil Service: A Study of Recruitment Policies," *Modern Ceylon Studies* 1, no. 1:64–83.

——. 1970b. "The Post Riots Campaign of Justice," *Journal of Asian Studies* 29:255–66.

——. 1971. "Arrack, Toddy and Ceylonese Nationalism: Some Observations on the Temperance Movement," *Modern Ceylon Studies* 2:, no. 2:123–50.

——. 1972. "The Burghers of Ceylon," in *The Blending of Races*, ed. Noel P. Gist and A. G. Dwork, 61–78. New York: John Wiley and Sons.

——. 1973a. "The Western Educated Elite and Buddhism in British Ceylon: A Neglected Aspect of the Nationalist Movement," in *Contributions to Asian Studies*, ed. Bardwell L. Smith, 18–29. Leiden: Brill.

——. 1973b. "Buddhist Leadership in the Nationalist Movement in Ceylon: The Role of the Temperance Campaign," *Social Compass* 20, no. 3:333–46.

——. 1973c. "Elite Politics in the New States: The Case of Post-Independence Sri Lanka," *Pacific Affairs* 46, no. 3:361–83.

Fishman, Joshua A. 1965. "Varieties of Ethnicity and Varieties of Language Consciousness," *Monograph Series on Language and Linguistics* (Georgetown University), no. 18:69–79.

——. 1971a. "The Sociology of Language," in *Advances in the Sociology of Language*, ed. Joshua A. Fishman, 1:217–404. The Hague: Mouton.

——. 1971b. "The Impact of Nationalism on Language Planning: Some Comparisons between Early Twentieth Century Europe and More Recent Years in South and South East Asia," in *Can Language Be Planned*. *See* Rubin and Jernudd, eds. 1971, 3–20.

——. 1972a. *The Sociology of Language.* Rowley, Mass.: Newbury House.
——. 1972b. "Problems and Prospects of the Sociology of Language," in *Studies for Einar Haugen,* ed. Evelyn S. Firchow et al., 214–26. The Hague: Mouton.
——. 1972c. *Language and Nationalism: Two Integrative Essays.* Rowley, Mass.: Newbury House.
——. 1973. "Language Modernization and Planning in Comparison with Other Types of National Modernization and Planning," *Language and Society* 2, no. 1:23–43.
——. 1976a. "Foreword" to *Language and Politics. See* O'Barr and O'Barr, eds. 1976, v–vi.
——. 1976b. "The Future of Ethnicity in America," in *The Scandinavian Presence in North America,* ed. Erik Friis, 12–28. New York: Harpers.
——. 1977a. "The Sociology of Language: Yesterday, Today and Tomorrow," in *Current Issues in Linguistic Theory,* ed. Roger W. Cole, 51–75. Bloomington and London: Indiana University Press.
——. 1977b. "Language and Ethnicity," in *Language and Ethnicity. See* Giles, ed. 1977, 15–52.
——. 1977c. "Language, Ethnicity and Racism," *Monograph Series on Linguistics* (Georgetown University), 297–309.
——. 1977d. "The Phenomenological and Linguistic Pilgrimage of Yaddish: Some Examples of Functional and Structural Pidginization and Re Pidginization," in *Advances in the Creation and Revision of Writing Systems,* ed. Fishman, 293–306. The Hague: Mouton.
Fishman, Joshua A., and Vladimir C. Nahirny. 1966. "Organizational Leadership Interest in Language Maintenance," in *Language Loyalty in the United States,* ed. Fishman et al., 156–89. The Hague: Mouton.
Fishman, Joshua A., Charles Ferguson, and Jyotirindrs Das Gupta, eds. 1968. *Language Problems of Developing Nations.* New York: Wiley.
Flynn, Barbara W., and John M. Flynn. 1976. "The Evolution of Courts, Councils and Legislatures in India," in *Language and Politics. See* O'Barr and O'Barr, eds. 1976, 165–94.
Freeman, David. 1968. *Value Aggregates and the Ceylonese Language Dispute.* Ph.D. diss. University of Denver.
Garvin, Paul L. 1964. "The Standard Language Problem, Concepts and Methods," in *Language in Culture. See* Hymes, ed., 1964, 521–23.
Geertz, Clifford. 1963. "The Integrative Revolution," in *Old Societies and New States,* ed. Clifford Geertz, New York: Free Press.
Geiger, Wilhelm. 1938. *A Grammar of the Sinhalese Language.* Colombo: Royal Asiatic Society, Ceylon Branch.
——. 1950. Translation of *The Mahāvaṃśa.* Colombo: Information Department.
Gellner, Ernest. 1964. *Thought and Change.* London: Weidenfeld and Nicholson.
Ghose, Sanker. 1975. *Political Ideas and Movements in India.* Bombay: Allied Publishers.
Giles, Howard, ed. 1977. *Language and Ethnicity in Intergroup Relations.* New York: Academic Press.

Giles, Howard, R. Y, Bourhis, and D. M. Taylor. 1977. "Towards a Theory of Language in Ethnic Group Relations," in *Language and Ethnicity. See* Giles, ed., 1977, 307–48.

Godakumbura, C. E. 1955. *Sinhalese Literature.* Colombo: Colombo Apothecaries.

——. 1961. *Kiraḷa Sandēśaya.* Colombo: Gunasena.

——, ed. 1956. *Śāsanāvatīrṇa Varṇanāva.* Moratuva: D. P. Dodangoda.

Gooneratne, Yasmine. 1968. *English Literature in Ceylon, 1815–1878.* Dehiwala: Tisara.

Goonewardene, K. W. 1989, "Dutch Policy towards Buddhism in Sri Lanka and Some Aspects of Its Impact, c. 1640 to c. 1740." Mimeo, University of Peradeniya, Faculty of Arts Seminar.

Green, Arnold S. Review of S. Arasartnam's *Ceylon, Journal of Asian Studies* 24, no. 3:552–53.

Gunaratna, Rohan. 1987. *War and Peace in Sri Lanka.* Kandy: Institute of Fundamental Studies.

——. 1990. *Sri Lanka: A Lost Revolution.* Kandy: Institute of Fundamental Studies.

Gunasekera, Abraham Mendis. 1891. *A Comprehensive Grammar of the Sinhalese Language.* Colombo: Government Press.

Gunasinghe, Newṭon. 1972. *Buddhism and Economic Growth with Special Reference to Ceylon,* Master's thesis, Monash University.

Gunawadu, Amarasiri. 1957. *Maha Heḷa Vata.* Matara: Matara Merchants.

Gunawardana, R.A.L.H. 1979. "The People of the Lion: The Sinhala Ideology in History and Historiography," *Sri Lanka Journal of the Humanities* 5, nos. 1 and 2:1–36.

Gunawardhana, W. F. 1979. *Sinhala Vaag Vidyā Mūldharma.* Colombo: Godage.

Guruge, Ananda W. P. 1989. *Mahavamsa: The Great Chronicle of Sri Lanka.* Colombo: Associated Newspapers of Ceylon.

Guy-Savard, Jean, and Richard Vigneault, eds. 1975. *Multilingual Political Systems: Problems and Solutions.* Quebec: University of Laval Press.

Hapuarachchi, D. V. 1981. *Sinhala Nurti Yugayē Itihāsaya.* Colombo: Lake House.

Harischandra, Valisimha. 1912. *Puravidyāva.* Colombo: W. E. Bastain.

Haugen, Einar. 1950. "The Analysis of Linguistic Borrowing," *Language* 26: 210–31.

——. 1966a. "Dialect, Language, Nation," *American Anthropologist* 68:922–35.

——. 1966b. "Linguistics and Language Planning," in *Sociolinguistics,* ed. William Bright, 50–67. The Hague: Mouton.

——. 1971. "Instrumentalism in Language Planning," in *Can Language Be Planned. See* Rubin and Jernudd, eds., 1971, 281–89.

Hays, Carlton J. H. 1931. *The Historical Evolution of Modern Nationalism.* New York: Smith.

Heeger, Gerald A. 1974. *The Politics of Under-Development.* New York: St. Martin's.

Hesbacher, P., and Joshua A. Fishman. 1965. "Language Loyalty: Its Functions and Concomitants in Bilingual Communities," *Lingua* 13: 145–65.

Hettiaratchi, D. E., ed. 1974. *Dhampiā Atuvā Gäṭapadaya*. Colombo: University of Sri Lanka Press Board.

Hewawasam, P. B. J. 1968. *Mātara Yugayē Sāhityadharayan Hā Sāhitya Nibandhana*. Colombo: Department of Cultural Affairs.

Heyd, Uriel. 1954. *Language Reform in Modern Turkey*. Jerusalam: Israel Oriental Society.

Hodgkin, Thomas. 1956. *Nationalism in Colonial Africa*. London: Frederick Muller.

Horowitz, Donald L. 1980. *Coup Theories and Officer's Motives: Sri Lanka in Comparative Perspective*. Princeton, N.J.: Princeton University Press.

——. 1985. *Ethnic Groups in Conflict*. Berkeley: University of California Press.

Hulugalle, H. A. J. 1963. *The British Governors in Ceylon*. Colombo: Gunasena.

Hymes, Dell, ed. 1964. *Language in Culture and Society*. New York: Harper and Row.

Indrapala, K. 1966. *Dravidian Settlements in Ceylon and the Beginnings of the Kingdom of Jaffna*. Ph.D. diss., University of London.

——, ed. 1971. *The Collapse of the Rajarata Civilization*. Peradeniya: Ceylon Studies Seminar.

Inglehart, R. F., and M. Woodward. 1967. "Language Conflicts and Political Community," *Comparative Studies in Society and History* 10:27–45.

Jayakody, Dharmasiri. 1967. *Sinhala Peraḷiya*. Colombo: Gunaratne.

Jayasuriya, J. E. 1976. *Educational Policies and Progress during British Rule in Ceylon, 1796–1948*. Colombo: Associated Newspapers of Ceylon.

Jayatilake, D. B. (Sir Baron). 1933. Introduction to *A Dictionary of the Sinhalese Language*, vol. 1. Colombo: Government Press.

Jayawardene, V. K. (Kumari). 1971. "The Origins of the Left Movement in Sri Lanka," *Modern Ceylon Studies* 2, no. 2:195–221.

——. 1972. *The Rise of the Labor Movement in Ceylon*. Durham, N.C.: Duke University Press.

——. 1985. *Ethnic and Class Conflicts in Sri Lanka*. Colombo: Centre for Social Analysis.

Jayaweera, Swarna. 1969. "British Educational Policy in Ceylon in the Nineteenth Century," *Paedagogica Historica* 9, no. 1:68–90.

——. 1971. "Language and Colonial Educational Policy in Ceylon," *Modern Ceylon Studies* 2, no. 2:151–69.

——. 1973. "Education Policy in the Early Twentieth Century," *UCHC* 3:461–75.

Jayawickrama, N. A. 1962. *The Inception of the Discipline*, vol. 21 of Sacred Books of the Buddhists. London: Luzac.

Jennings, Sir Ivor. 1956. "Political Emotion," *New Lanka* 7, nos. 3 and 4:20–25.

Jennings, Sir Ivor, and H. W. Tambiah. 1952. *The Dominion of Ceylon*. London: Stevens.

Kanapathipillai K. 1948. "Ceylon and Its Contribution to Tamil," in *Souvenir of the Pageant of Lanka*, ed. S. Sanmuganathan, 39–51. Colombo: Associated Newspapers of Ceylon.

Kannangara, P. D. 1966. *The History of the Ceylon Civil Service, 1802–1833*. Dehiwala: Tisara.

Kautsky, John H. 1962. "An Essay on the Politics of Development," in *Political Change in Under-Developed Countries: Nationalism versus Communism*, ed. John H. Kautsky, 3–56. New York: Wiley.

Kearney, Robert N. 1967. *Communalism and Language in the Politics of Ceylon*. Durham, N.C.: Duke University Press.

Kedourie, Elie. 1971. Introduction to *Nationalism in Asia and Africa*, ed. Elie Kedourie. London: Weidenfeld and Nicholson.

Keeble, W. T., and Devar Suryasena. 1950. *Life of Sir James Pieris*. Colombo: Times of Ceylon Press.

Keller, Suzanne. 1963. *Beyond the Ruling Class: Strategic Elites in Modern Society*. New York: Random House.

Kidder, Robert L. 1976. "Language and Litigation in South India," in *Language and Politics. See* O'Barr and O'Barr, eds., 1976, 225–35.

Kiribamune, Sirima. 1978. "The Mahavamsa: A Study of the Ancient Historiography of Sri Lanka," in *Senarat Paranavitana Commemoration Volume*, ed. L. Prematilleke et al., 125–36. Leiden: E. J. Brill.

——. 1979. "The Dipavamsa in Ancient Sri Lankan Historiography," *Sri Lanka Journal of the Humanities* 5, nos. 1 and 2:89–100.

Kloss, Heinz. 1966. "Types of Multilingual Communities: A Discussion of Ten Variables," *Sociological Inquiry* 36:135–45.

——. 1967. "Abstand Languages and Ausbau Languages," *Anthropological Linguistics* 9, no. 7:29–41.

Knighton, William. 1845. *The History of Ceylon from the Earliest Times to the Present Time*. London: Longmans.

Knox, R. A. 1950. *Enthusiasm: A Chapter in the History of Religions*. Oxford and New York: Clarendon.

Kodikara, Shelton U., ed. 1989. *Indo–Sri Lanka Agreement of July 1987*. Colombo: The University of Colombo.

Kohn, Hans. 1929. *A History of Nationalism in the East*. London.

——. 1967. *Prelude to Nation-States: The French and German Experience*. Princeton, N.J.: Van Nostrand.

Laitin, David D. 1977. *Politics, Language, and Thought: The Somali Experience*. Chicago: University of Chicago Press.

Lambert, W. E. 1967. "A Social Psychology of Bilingualism," *Journal of Social Issues* 23, no. 2:91–109.

Lankachandra, Ariyaratna. 1958. *Srīmath Walisiṃha Harischandra Caritaya*. Colombo.

Lankananda, Ven. *bhikkhu* Labugama, ed. 1958. *Mandārampura Puvata*. Colombo.

Le Page, R. B. 1964. *The National Language Question*. London: Institute of Race Relations.

Lerner, Daniel. 1964. *The Passing of Traditional Society*. Glencoe, Ill.: Free Press.

Lerski, G. J. 1968. *Origins of Trotskysm in Ceylon*. Stanford, Calif.: Hoover Institution.

Leslie, Charles. 1973. "The Professionalizing Ideology of Medical Revivalism," in *Entrepreneurship and Modernization of Occupational Cultures in South Asia,* ed. Milton Singer, Durham, N.C.: Duke University Press.

Levenson, Jospeh R. 1959. *Liang Ch'i-Cha'o and the Mind of Modern China.* Cambridge, Mass.: Harvard University Press.

Linton, Ralph. 1943. "Nativistic Movements," *American Anthropologist,* n.s. 45, no. 2:230–40.

Lipsey, Roger William. 1974. *Signature and Significance: A Study of the Life and Times of Ananda Coomaraswamy.* Ph.D. diss., New York University.

Ludowyk, E.F.C. 1936. *English and English Education in Ceylon.* Ph.D. diss., Cambridge University.

——. 1966. *The Modern History of Ceylon.* London: Weidenfeld and Nicholson.

Lynch, Owen M. 1969. *The Politics of Untouchability: Social Mobility and Social Change in a City of India.* New York: Columbia University Press.

Mackinon, Kenneth. 1977. *Language, Education and Social Process in a Gaelic Community.* London: Routledge and Kegan Paul.

Majumdar, R. C., et al. 1965. "English Education," in R. C. Majumdar ed., *The History and Culture of the Indian People: British Paramountcy and Indian Renaissance.* pt. 2. Bombay: Bharatiya Vidya Bhavan.

Malalgoda, Kitsiri. 1970. "Millennialism in Relation to Buddhism," *Comparative Studies in Society and History* 12, no. 4:424–41.

——. 1972. "Sinhalese Buddhism: Orthodox and Syncretic, Traditional and Modern," *Ceylon Journal of Historical and Social Studies,* n.s. 2, no. 2:156–69.

——. 1973. "The Buddhist-Christian Confrontation in Ceylon, 1800–1800," *Social Compass* 20, no. 2:171–200.

——. 1976. *Buddhism in Sinhalese Society, 1750–1900: A Study of Religious Revival and Change.* Berkeley: University of California Press.

Marks, Thomas A. 1987. "India Acts in Its Own Interest," *Ceylon Daily News,* 6 July, 6.

Marshall, Henry. [1846] 1969. *Ceylon: A General Description of the Island and its Inhabitants.* Dehiwela: Tisara.

Martinus, O. E. 1941. *The Life of Col. T. G. Jayawardene.* Colombo: Cave.

Matthews, Bruce. 1985. "The Sri Lankan Buddhist Philosophy of History and Its Relationship to the National Question," *Ethnic Studies Report* 3 (2 July 1985): 81–87.

Mazrui, Ali A. 1967. *Towards A Pax Africana.* London: Weidenfeld and Nicholson.

McCully, B. T. 1940. *English Education and the Origins of Indian Nationalism.* New York: Columbia University Press.

Mendis, G. C., ed. 1956. *The Colebrooke Cameron Papers.* Oxford: Oxford University Press.

——. 1963. *Ceylon Today and Yesterday: Main Currents of Ceylon History.* (1957), 2d ed. Colombo: Associated Newspapers of Ceylon.

Mills, Lennox A. 1933. *Ceylon under British Rule, 1796–1932.* Oxford: Oxford University Press.

Monier-Williams, W. 1872. *A Sanskrit-English Dictionary*. Oxford: Oxford University Press.

Murdoch, Rev. John, and James Nicholson. 1868. *Classified Catalogue of Printed Tracts and Books in Singhalese*. Madras: Christian Vernacular Education Society.

Murphy, Rhoads. 1957. "The Ruin of Ancient Ceylon," *Journal of Asian Studies* 7, no. 2:181–200.

Myrdal, Gunnar. 1968. *Asian Drama: An Inquiry into the Poverty of Nations*. New York: Twentieth Century Fund.

Namasivayam, S. 1950. *The Legislatures of Ceylon, 1928–1948*. London: Faber and Faber.

Nanawimala, Rev. *bhikkhu* Kirielle. 1946. *Saparagamuvē Pärani Liyawili*. Ratnapura: Lawco Press.

Nandarama, ven. Kadawedduwe, and D. P. Samarasinghe. 1967. *Säňgavuṇu Utura*. Anuradhapura: Gunasekera and Co.

Nicholas, C. W., and S. Paranavitana. 1961. *A Concise History of Ceylon*. Colombo: Ceylon University Press.

Nissan, E., and R. L. Stirrat. 1987. "State, Nation and the Representation of Evil," *Sussex Papers in Social Anthropology*, no. 1. (pamphlet).

Norman K. R. 1978. "The Role of Pali in Early Sinhalese Buddhism," in *Buddhism in Ceylon and Studies on Religious Syncretism in Buddhist Countries*, ed. Heniz Bechert, 28–47. Gottingen: Vanderhock and Rupert.

O'Barr, William, and Jean F. O'Barr, eds. 1976. *Language and Politics*. The Hague: Mouton.

Obeysekere, Gananath. 1970. "Religious Symbolism and Political Change in Ceylon," *Modern Ceylon Studies* 1, no. 1: 43–63.

——. 1975. "Sinhalese Buddhist Identity in Ceylon," in *Ethnic Identity, Cultural Continuities, and Change*, ed. George de Vos and Lola Romanucci-Ross, 231–58. Palo Alto, Calif.: Mayfield.

Palita, Rev. Rekava, ed. 1955. *Kav Miṇi Kaňḍola Vādaya*. Ambalantota: Rohana Press.

Panditaratne, B. L., and S. Selvanayagam. 1973. "The Demography of Ceylon–An Introductory Survey," *UCHC* 3:285–302.

Pannakitti, Ven. *bhikkhu* Kotahene. 1965. "Ratmalane Dharmarama Maha Swamindrayo," in *Ape Paňdivaru*, ed. Gunnepana Gnana Seneviratne, 40–65. Colombo: Pracina Bhasopakara Samagama.

Pannasekera, Ven. *bhikkhu* Kalukndayawe. 1965. *Sinhala Puvatpat Saňgarā Itihāsaya*, vol. 1. Colombo: Gunasena.

——. 1966. *Sinhala Puvatpat Saňgarā Itihāsaya,*, vol. 2. Colombo: Gunasena.

——. 1967. *Sinhala Puvatpat Saňgarā Itihāsaya*, vol. 3. Colombo: Gunasena.

——. 1968a. *Sinhala Puvatpat Saňgarā Itihāsaya*, vol. 4. Colombo: Gunasena.

——. 1968b. *Sinhala Puvatpat Saňgarā Itihāsaya*, vol. 5. Colombo: Gunasena.

——. 1969. *Sinhala Puvatpat Saňgarā Itihāsaya*, vol. 6. Colombo: Gunasena.

——. 1970. *Svayaṃ Likhita Srī Prgnāsēkara Caritāpadānaya*. Colombo: Gunasena.

Paranavitana, Senerath. 1956. *Sigiri Graffitti, Being Sinhalese Verses of the Ninth and Tenth Centuries*. London: Oxford University Press.

———. 1959. "Aryan Settlements: The Sinhalese," *UCHC* 1:82–97.
———. 1970. *Inscriptions of Ceylon*, vol. 1, Colombo: Government Press.
———. 1971. *Art of the Ancient Sinhalese*. Colombo: Lake House Investments.
———. 1983. *Inscriptions of Ceylon*, vol. 2, pt. 1. Colombo: Department of Archaeology.
Park, Richard L. 1967. *India's Political System*. New York: Prentice-Hall.
Passin, Herbert. 1968. "Writer and Journalist in Transitional Society," in *Language Problems*. *See* Fishman et al., eds. 1968, 443–57.
Peiris, G. H. 1991. "An Appraisal of the Concept of a Traditional Tamil Homeland in Sri Lanka," *Ethnic Studies Report* 9, no. 1:13–39.
Percival, Robert. [1803] 1972. *An Account of the Island of Ceylon*. Farnborough: Gregg International.
Perera, E. W. 1907. "Ceylon under British Rule, 1796–1906," in *Twentieth Century Impressions*. *See* Wright, ed., 1907, 60–83.
Perera L. S. 1959. "The Sources of Ceylon History," in *UCHC* 1:46–73.
———. 1961. "The Pali Chronicles of Ceylon," in *Historians of India, Pakistan and Ceylon*, ed. C. H. Philips, 29–43. London: Oxford University Press.
Phadnis, Urmila. 1976. *Religion and Politics in Sri Lanka*. New Delhi: Manohar.
Pieris, Rev. Fr. Edmund. 1943. "Sinhalese Christian Literature of the XVIIth and XVIIIth Centuries," *Journal of the Royal Asiatic Society, Ceylon Branch* 35, no. 96:163–79.
Pieris, Paul E. 1950. *Sinhalē and the Patriots*. Colombo: Apothecaries.
Pieris, Ralph. 1949. "The Sociological Consequences of Imperialism with Special Reference to Ceylon." Ph.D. diss., University of London.
———. 1951–52. "Society and Ideology in Ceylon during a Time of Troubles," *University of Ceylon Review* 9, no. 3:171–85; 9, no. 4:266–79; 10, no. 1:79–102.
———. 1964. "Universities, Politics and Public Opinion in Ceylon," *Minerva* 2, no. 4:435–54.
Piyasena, L. 1972. "History at a Glance," *Buddhist*, 75th Anniversary Souvenir, Vap-Unduvap 2516, 2–3.
Poliakov, Leon. 1974. *The Aryan Myth: A History of Racist and Nationalist Ideas in Europe*, trans. Edmund Howard. Brighton: Sussex University Press.
Rabushka, Alwin, and Kenneth A. Shepsle. 1972. *Politics in Plural Societies: A Theory of Democratic Instability*. Columbus, Ohio: Charles A. Merrill.
Rahula, *Bhikkhu* Walpola. 1946. *Bhikṣuvagē Urumaya*. Colombo: Swastika.
———. 1966. *History of Buddhism in Ceylon*. Colombo: Gunasena.
Rajakaruna, Ariya. 1970. *Sāhitya Ruciyā Hā Navakathā Vicāraya*. Colombo: Ratna Prakasakayo.
———. 1972. *Sinhala Navakathāvē Ārambhaya*. Colombo: Gunasena.
Ratnasara, Ven. *bhikkhu* Hevanpola. 1970. *Britānya Pratpatti, Budusamaya Hā Piriven Adhyāpanaya*, 1815–1965. Colombo: Deepa.
Ratnatunga, Sinha. 1988. *Politics of Terrorism: The Sri Lankan Experience*. Canberra: International Fellowship for Social and Economic Development.
Ratnayaka, L. D. A. N.d. *Tower Hall Nāṭya Itihāsaya*. Colombo: Ratnayaka.
Ray, Punya Sloka. 1963. *Language Standardization*. The Hague: Mouton.

Report of the Commission on Constitutional Reform. 1945. (Soulbury Report), CMD 6677, London.

Report of the Select Committee on the Revision of the Constitution (Parliamentary Series, no. 14). 1978.

Report of the Special Commission on the Constitution. 1928. (Donoughmore Report), CMD 3131, London.

Rhys-Davids, T. W. 1890–94. *Questions of Milinda,* translation from Pali. London: Pali Text Society.

Rhys-Davids, T. W., and William Stede. 1972. *The Pali Text Society's Pali English Dictionary*. London: Pali Text Society.

Roberts, Michael. 1968. "The Rise of the Karavas." Paper presented to Ceylon Studies Seminar (Peradeniya).

——. 1969. "The Political Antecedents of the Revivalist Elite in the MEP Coalition of 1956." Paper presented to Ceylon Studies Seminar (Peradeniya).

——. 1973. "Elite Formation and the Elites, 1832–1931," *UCHC* 3:263–84.

——. 1974. "Problems of Social Stratification and the Demarcation of National and Local Elites in British Ceylon," *Journal of Asian Studies* 33, no. 4:549–77.

——. 1977. "Elites, Nationalisms and the Nationalist Movement in Ceylon," in Roberts, ed., 1977:xxix–cclxii.

——. 1978. "Ethnic Conflict in Sri Lanka and Sinhalese Perspectives: Barriers to Accommodation," *Modern Asian Studies* 12, no. 3:353–76.

——. 1979. "Meanderings in the Pathways of Collective Identity and Nationalism," in *Collective Identities. See* Roberts, ed., 1979, 2–39.

——. 1982. *Caste Conflict and Elite Formation: The Rise of a Karava Elite in Sri Lanka,* 1500–1931. Cambridge: Cambridge University Press.

——, ed. 1977. *Documents of the Ceylon National Congress and Nationalist Politics in Ceylon,* 1929–1950, Colombo: Department of National Archives.

——, ed. 1979. *Collective Identities, Nationalisms and Protest in Modern Sri Lanka.* Colombo: Marga.

Roberts, Michael, and Ananda Wickramaratne. 1973. "Export Agriculture in the Nineteenth Century," *UCHC* 3:89–118.

Robinson, W. 1971. "Restricted Codes and the Sociology of Language," in *Language Use and Social Change,* ed. W. H. Whiteley, 75–94. Nairobi: Oxford University Press.

Rocker, Rudolph. 1937. *Nationalism and Culture,* trans. Roy E. Chase. New York: Covici Friede.

Roff, W. P. 1967. *The Origins of Malay Nationalism.* Kuala Lumpur: University of Malaya Press.

Rogers, John D. 1987. *Crime, Justice and Society in Colonial Sri Lanka.* London: Curzon Press.

Roth, Guenther. 1968. "Personal Rulership, Patrimonialism and Empire-Building in the New States," *World Politics* 20, no. 2:194–203.

Rowland, Benjamin. [1938] 1985. *The Wall Paintings of India, Central Asia and Ceylon.* Delhi: Alfa Publishers.

Rubin, Joan, and Bjorn H. Jernudd, eds. 1971. *Can Language Be Planned? Sociolin-*

guistic Theory and Practice for Developing Nations. Honolulu: University of Hawaii Press.

Russel, Jane. 1976. *The Ceylon Tamils under the Donoughmore Constitution, 1931–1947*. Ph.D. diss., University of Sri Lanka, Peradeniya.

——. 1978. "Language, Education and Nationalism–The Language Debate of 1944," *The Ceylon Journal of Historical and Social Studies* n.s. 8, no. 2:38–64.

Ryan, Bryce. 1953. *Caste in Modern Ceylon*. New Brunswick, N.J.: Rutgers University Press.

——. 1961. "Status, Achievement and Education in Ceylon," *Journal of Asian Studies* 20, no. 4:463–76.

Samarasinghe, Vidyamali. 1988. "Ethno-Regionalism as a Basis for Geographical Separation in Sri Lanka," *Ethnic Studies Report* 2 (July): 21–51.

Samaraweera, Vijaya. 1977. "The Evolution of a Plural Society," in *Sri Lanka. See* K. M. de Silva, ed., 1977, 86–107.

Sangharakshita, Ven. *bhikkhu*. 1964. *Anagarika Dahrmapala: A Biographical Sketch*. Kandy: Buddhist Publication Society.

Sannasgala, P. B. 1961. *Sinhala Sāhitya Vaṃsaya*. Colombo: Lake House.

Sapir, Edward. [1921] 1949. *Language*. London: Harvest Books.

Saram, P. A. 1977. "Buddhism and Society in Modern Sri Lanka," *International Social Science Journal* 29:313–23.

Sarachhandra, E. R. (Ediriweera). 1950. *The Sinhalese Novel*. Colombo: Gunasena.

——. 1966. *The Folk Drama of Ceylon*. Colombo: Department of Cultural Affairs.

——. 1973. "Language and Literature in the Nineteenth and Twentieth Centuries," *UCHC* 3:342–55.

Sarkar, Sumit. 1973. *The Swadeshi Movement in Bengal, 1903–1908*. New Delhi: Peoples' Publishing House.

Sartori, Giovanni. 1966. "European Political Parties: The Case of Polarized Pluralism," in *Political Parties and Political Development*, ed. M. Joseph La Palombara and Myron Weiner, 137–76. Princeton, N.J.: Princeton University Press.

Schwartz, Theodore. 1973. "Cult and Context: The Paranoid Ethos in Melanesia," *Ethos* 1, no. 2:153–74.

Schwartz, Theodore. 1976. "The Cargo Cult: A Melanesian Response to Change," in *Responses to Change. See* de Vos, ed., 1976, 157–206.

Scott, Robert E. 1965. "Mexico: The Established Revolution," in *Political Culture and Political Development*, eds. Lucien W. Pye and Sidney Verba, 330–95. Princeton, N.J.: Princeton University Press.

Seelaratana, Ven. Hendiyagala. 1955. *Utura Diga Lankāva*. Colombo: Mahabodhi Press.

Sen, Ariya Kumar. 1952. "Tagore and Coomaraswamy," in *Homage to Ananda Coomaraswamy*, ed. C. Durai Raja Singham, 246–57. Singapore: Liang Brothers.

Shils, Edward. 1972a. *The Intellectuals and the Powers and Other Essays*. Chicago: University of Chicago Press.

——. 1972b. "Metropolis and Province in the Intellectual Community," in *Intellectuals. See* Shils, 1972a, 355–71.
——. 1972c. "Intellectuals in the Political Development of the New States," in *Intellectuals. See* Shils, 1972a, 386–423.
——. 1972d. "Asian Intellectuals," in *Intellectuals. See* Shils, 1972a, 372–85.
Siladhara, Rev. *bhikkhu* W. Sri. 1920. "Mohoṭṭiwattē Gunānanda Swāmin Wahansēgē Jīvana Caritaya," *Young Buddhist* 1, no. 1:20–23.
Silva, D. Peter. 1969. *Siyawasaka Adhyāpanaya Hā Guru Saṭana.* Colombo: Print Arts.
Silva, M. H. Peter. 1961. *The Influence of Dravida on Sinhalese.* Ph.D. diss., Oxford University.
——. 1966. *Sinhala Mahimaya.* Colombo: Gunasiri.
Singer, Milton. 1972. *When a Great Tradition Modernizes: An Anthropological Approach to Indian Civilization.* New York.
Siriweera, W. I. 1984. "The Dutthagamini-Elara Episode: A Reassessment," in *Ethnicity and Social Class in Sri Lanka,* ed. Social Scientists Association, 54–73. Colombo: Karunaratne.
Skinner, Thomas. [1891] 1974. *Fifty Years in Ceylon.* Dehiwala: Tisara.
Smith, Anthony D. 1986. *The Ethnic Origin of Nations.* Oxford: Basil Blackwell.
Smith, Bardwell L. 1978. "Kingship, the Sangha, and the Process of Legitimation in Anuradhapura, Ceylon: An Interpretive Essay," in *Religion and the Legitimation of Power in Sri Lanka,* ed. Bardwell L. Smith, 73–95. Chambersburg, Pa.: Prima Books.
Smith, Donald E. 1966a. "The Sinhalese Buddhist Revolution," in *South Asian Politics. See* Smith, ed., 1966, 453–88.
——. 1966b. "Political Monks and Monastic Reform," in *South Asian Politics. See* Smith, ed., 1966, 489–509.
——, ed. 1966. *South Asian Politics and Religion.* Princeton, N.J.: Princeton University Press.
Sorel, Georges. 1961. *Reflections on Violence.* New York: Collier.
Stevens, Alan M. 1973. "Bhasa Indonesia: Modernization and Nationalization," *Asia* 30 (Summer):70–84.
Sumangala, Ven. *bhikkhu* Hikkaduwe. 1907. "Buddhist Sects," In *Twentieth Century Impressions. See* Wright, ed., 1907, 290–92.
Sumatipala, K. H. M. 1968. *History of Education in Ceylon, 1796–1965.* Dehiwala: Tisara.
——. 1970. "Kotahena Riots and Their Repercussions," *Ceylon Historical Journal* 19, nos. 1–4:65–81.
——. N.d. *1960 Janatā Parājaya.* Kandy: Situmina.
Tambiah, S. J. 1986. *Sri Lanka: Ethnic Fratricide and the Dismantling of Democracy.* Delhi: Oxford University Press.
Tennent, Sir James Emerson. 1850. *Christianity in Ceylon.* London: John Murray.
Tiffen, Brian, and H. G. Widdowson. 1968. *Language in Education: The Problem of Commonwealth Africa and the Indo-Pakistan Sub-Continent.* Oxford: Oxford University Press.

Toussaint, J. R. 1935. *The Annals of the Ceylon Civil Service.* Colombo: Government Press.

Turnour, George. 1837. *The Mahavamso, in Roman Characters with Translation Subjoined: An Introductory Essay on Pali Buddhistical Literature.* Ceylon: Cotta Mission Press.

Vacissara, Ven. *bhikkhu* Kotagama. 1964. *Saranankara Sangharāja Samaya.* Colombo: Ratnakara.

van den Berghe, Pierre. 1968. "European Languages and Black Mandarins," *Transition* 7, no. 34:19–33.

von der Mehden, Fred R. 1963. *Religion and Nationalism in South East Asia.* Madison: University of Wisconsin Press.

——. 1974. "Secularization of Buddhist Politics: Burma and Thailand," in *Religion and Political Modernization: Comparative Perspectives,* ed. D. E. Smith, New Haven, Conn.: Yale University Press.

Wallace, Anthony F. C. 1956. "Revitalization Movements," *American Anthropologist* 58:264–81.

Warnapala, W. A. Wiswa. 1971. "Triumph of Competition in the Ceylon Civil Service," *Ceylon Journal of Historical and Social Studies* n.s. 1:62–77.

——. 1973. "Bureaucratic Transformation, c. 1910–1948," *UCHC* 3:408–27.

Weaver, Mary Ann. 1988. "A Reporter at Large: Sri Lanka," *New Yorker* (21 March): 39–84.

Weber, Max. 1968. *Economy and Society: An Outline of Interpretive Sociology,* ed. Guenther Roth and Claus Wittich. New York.

Weerawardene, I. D. S. 1951. *Government and Politics in Ceylon,* 1931–1946. Colombo: Ceylon Economic Research Association.

——. 1960. *The Ceylon General Election of* 1956. Colombo: Gunasena.

Weerasekera, Jayantha, ed. 1938. *Kukavi Vādaya.* Colombo: Gunasena.

Weiner, Myron. 1971. "Political Participation: Crisis of the Political Process," in *Crises and Development in Political Development,* ed. Leonard Binder et al., 166–75. Princeton, N.J.: Princeton University Press.

Weinreich, Uriel. [1953] 1964. *Languages in Contact: Findings and Problems.* The Hague: Mouton.

Whiteley, W. H. 1969. *Swahili: The Rise of a National Language.* London: Methuen.

Wickramaratne, L. Ananda. 1969. "Religion, Nationalism and Social Change in Ceylon, 1865–1885," *Journal of the Royal Asiatic Society, Great Britain* 56:123–50.

——. 1973. "Education and Social Change, 1932–1900," *UCHC* 3:168–86.

——. 1976. "Annie Besant, Theosophism and Buddhist Nationalism in Sri Lanka," *Ceylon Journal of Historical and Social Studies* n.s. 6, no. 1:62–79.

——. 1984. *The Genesis of an Orientalist: Thomas William Rhys Davids and Buddhism in Sri Lanka.* Delhi: Motilal Baranasidas.

Wickramasinghe, K. D. P. 1965. *Nūtana Sinhala Sāhityaya.* Colombo: Gunasena.

Wickramasinghe, Martin. 1949. *Sinhalese Literature.* Colombo: Gunasena.

Wickramasuriya, Sarathchandra. 1975. *A Linguistic Study of Early Sinhalese Prose Narrative.* Ph.D. diss., University of London.

——. 1976. "Strangers in Their Own Land: Ananda Coomaraswamy and Education in Colonial Sri Lanka," *Sri Lanka Journal of the Humanities* 1:1–26.

Wijayaratne, D. J. 1956. *History of the Sinhalese Noun.* Colombo: University of Ceylon Press.

Wijesekera, O. H. de A. 1955. "Pali and Sanskrit in the Polonnaruwa Period," *Ceylon Historical Journal* 4, nos. 1–4:91–97.

Wilson, A. J. 1966. "Buddhism in Ceylon Politics," in *South Asian Politics. See* D. E. Smith, ed., 1966, 510–30.

——. 1973. "The Development of the Constitution," *UCHC* 3:359–80.

——. 1988. *The Break-Up of Sri Lanka: The Sinhalese-Tamil Conflict.* London: C. Hurst.

Woolf, Leonard. 1961. *Growing: An Autobiography of the Years* 1904–1911. London: Hogarth Press.

Worseley, Peter. 1972. *The Third World,* 2d ed. Chicago: University of Chicago Press.

Wriggins, W. Howard. 1960. *Ceylon: The Dilemmas of a New Nation.* Princeton, N.J.: Princeton University Press.

Wright, Arnold, ed. 1907. *Twentieth Century Impressions of Ceylon.* London: Lloyd's Greater Britain Publishing.

Young, Crawford. 1976. *The Politics of Cultural Pluralism.* Madison: University of Wisconsin Press.

Youth Congress, Jaffna. 1939. *Communalism or Nationalism? A Reply to the Speech Delivered in the State Council on the Reform Dispatch by G. G. Ponnambalam Esq.* Chunnakam: Tirumakal Press.

Zimmer, Heinrich. 1961. *The Art of Indian Asia.* Princeton, N.J.: Princeton University Press.

Zolberg, Aristide. 1968. "The Structure of Political Conflict in the New States of Tropical Africa," *American Political Science Review* 62, no. 1:70–87.

Zvelebil, Kamil V. 1974. *Tamil Literature.* Weisbaden: Otto Harrassowitz.

Index